Microsoft

MW00906198

Troubleshooting
Microsoft

Excel 2002

Microsoft Office XP Application

Laurie Ann Ulrich

PUBLISHED BY
Microsoft Press
A Division of Microsoft Corporation
One Microsoft Way
Redmond, Washington 98052-6399

Copyright © 2002 by Laurie Ann Ulrich

All rights reserved. No part of the contents of this book may be reproduced or transmitted in any form or by any means without the written permission of the publisher.

Library of Congress Cataloging-in-Publication Data
Ulrich, Laurie Ann.
    Troubleshooting Microsoft Excel 2002 / Laurie Ann Ulrich.
        p. cm.
    Includes index.
    ISBN 0-7356-1493-8
    1. Microsoft Excel for Windows.   2. Electronic spreadsheets.   3. Business--Computer
programs.   I. Title.

    HF5548.4.M523 U433   2002
    005.369--dc21   2001059083

Printed and bound in the United States of America.

1 2 3 4 5 6 7 8 9   QWT   7 6 5 4 3 2

Distributed in Canada by Penguin Books Canada Limited.

A CIP catalogue record for this book is available from the British Library.

Microsoft Press books are available through booksellers and distributors worldwide. For further informa-tion about international editions, contact your local Microsoft Corporation office or contact Microsoft Press International directly at fax (425) 936-7329. Visit our Web site at www.microsoft.com/mspress. Send comments to *mspinput@microsoft.com*.

FrontPage, Microsoft, Microsoft Press, MS-DOS, the Office logo, PivotChart, PivotTable, PowerPoint, Visual Basic, Windows, and Windows NT are either registered trademarks or trademarks of Microsoft Corporation in the United States and/or other countries. Other product and company names mentioned herein may be the trademarks of their respective owners.

The example companies, organizations, products, domain names, e-mail addresses, logos, people, places, and events depicted herein are fictitious. No association with any real company, organization, product, domain name, e-mail address, logo, person, place, or event is intended or should be inferred.

Acquisitions Editor: Alex Blanton
Project Editor: Judith Bloch

Body Part No. X08-41926

Acknowledgments

I must thank Alex Blanton for the opportunity to work on the Troubleshooting series for Microsoft Press. It's been a great experience—both the first edition and this revision for Excel 2002.

I absolutely have to thank Judith Bloch of Microsoft Press for her organizational and editorial efforts. While revising an existing book isn't as difficult as writing one from scratch, it can be difficult to keep track of what's new, what's changed, and what's finished. She made it all happen easily (for me, anyway!) and quickly. Thanks also to Wendy Zucker at Microsoft Press. I'm grateful to the crew from nSight, Inc., who helped polish and produce this edition, especially Tempe Goodhue, project manager; Chris Russo, technical editor; Joe Gustaitis, copy editor; Rebecca Merz, senior editorial assistant; and Patty Fagan, desktop specialist. A good book requires more than a good author—it requires a great team, and I sure had one on this book. My heartfelt thanks go to each and every one of them.

I'd also like to thank my students—the thousands of people I've trained to use Office in general and Excel in particular since the early 1990s. No single user can ferret out all of the problems that can arise in an application—it's just not possible to use all the features often enough and in enough different ways to run into everything that can go wrong. Without my students, who put Excel through its paces both in class and on the job, any list of troubleshooting items I'd have compiled wouldn't have been nearly as comprehensive as I hope this one is.

Thanks also go, yet again, to my friend and fellow trainer, Jim Moore. His input on the first edition, much of which remains in this edition, was invaluable.

Quick contents

Contents

Contents

Contents

Contents

About this book

Troubleshooting Microsoft Excel 2002 is designed to help you avoid spending lots of time sifting through information to find the answer to a problem. Instead, the design of the book helps you quickly cut to the chase and find the answer to the problem you're experiencing.

How to use this book

The book covers the major and minor features of Excel 2002, Microsoft Office XP's spreadsheet application. While we assume you'll be consulting this book on an as-needed basis, it can be read cover to cover or in an exploratory way. When you do consult it to solve a specific problem, however, you'll find that the solutions are worded without any technical jargon—other than naming Excel features with which you might be experiencing difficulty. You'll recognize your own descriptions of problems because the problems solved in this book come directly from the author's decade of teaching people

to use Excel. Her students have furnished most of the problems in the book, and the readers of her other books on Office in general and Excel in particular have provided the rest. In short, this book is for users, written from users' perspectives to reflect the needs of users of all levels.

Flowcharts

At the beginning of each chapter, you'll find a flowchart that helps you diagnose your problem and takes you to the correct topic. On the flowchart, you'll see questions with yes or no answers. As you follow the arrows on the chart, you'll find yourself directed to the topic that covers your problem. Also on the flowchart, you'll find "quick fixes"—problems that require only a few steps to solve. Instead of directing you to another page in the book, you'll find the description of the problem as well as its solution in the "Quick fix" box right there on the flowchart. Each flowchart also contains a list of chapters with related information that can be of further help.

Solutions spreads

After the flowchart helps you find the right page, you'll turn to a solution topic. For each problem listed, you'll find a complete discussion of the problem—how it might have occurred, why you might be concerned, and examples of how the given feature or command can and should be used. This section is called the "Source of the problem." It is followed by a "How to fix it" section, which describes, in detail, how to solve the problem. Chapters also contain tips and sidebars with additional information, cautionary tales, and real-world examples of how to use features related to the problem at hand.

Find the right solution to your problem quickly and efficiently.

Avoid unnecessary down-time using **Quick Fixes** to get you back to work.

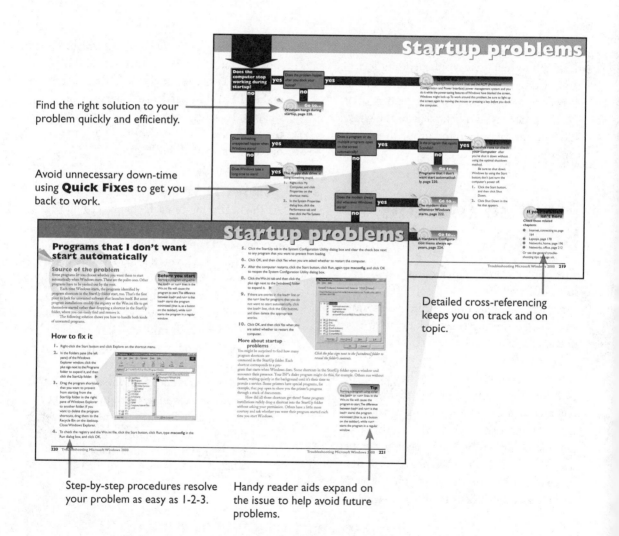

Detailed cross-referencing keeps you on track and on topic.

Step-by-step procedures resolve your problem as easy as 1-2-3.

Handy reader aids expand on the issue to help avoid future problems.

Troubleshooting tips

To troubleshoot, as defined by the *Microsoft Computer Dictionary*, is to "isolate the source of a problem in a program, computer system, or network and remedy it." But how do you go about isolating the source of the problem in the first place? Generally, if you know the source of a problem, you're more than half way to solving it—or at least you know who you need to call to fix it. In reality, however, the source of a problem might not be obvious, might be a symptom masquerading as the source, or might reveal itself to be something other than you initially thought. Does this sound like the very act of troubleshooting is a problem unto itself? Perhaps, but don't let that idea take root. Microsoft Excel provides some significant tools for you to employ as you troubleshoot problems with your workbooks and their content.

How to troubleshoot

The easiest way to isolate a problem is to start broad (Are you having trouble printing your worksheet?) and then narrow down the scope (Are you having trouble printing your entire worksheet on one page?) until you've reached a specific question you're not sure

how to answer (Have you used the Page Setup dialog box?). The questions help you view the problem objectively while they narrow down the solution.

As you take a fresh look at each problem, guided by the ever-narrowing questions, take note—literally—of the problem and its symptoms. When does it occur? What's happening at that time? Does it happen consistently or only when a specific set of circumstances exist? Effective troubleshooting is a skill, and one that takes some time to acquire. Hey, if everyone were good at it, who'd need a Troubleshooting book? Seriously, though, you can hone your troubleshooting skills by unleashing your powers of observation and as much objectivity as you can muster. The more you know about when a problem occurs, the surrounding circumstances, and how it affects your use of Excel, the closer you are to solving the problem.

Furthermore, the process of observing the problem in action and identifying its source makes it much easier to take advantage of the solutions in this book. Take the time to go through the flowcharts. You'll not only find the solution to your current problem, you'll find a lot of related information that can help you resolve problems you've had in the past as well as prevent problems in the future.

Help!

"Help!" need not be a plea for assistance, screamed into the void with no hope of response. Excel's Help files, accessed directly or with the help of any one of the Office Assistant characters, can be a great tool in your troubleshooting arsenal. Between the Index, Contents list, Answer Wizard, and Office Assistant there are so many ways to pose your question or search for the cause of your problem. Usually, help that can refine your sense of the problem is close at hand.

Simply click the Microsoft Excel Help button, click Microsoft Excel Help on the Help menu, or click the Office Assistant and then type a question in the What Would You Like To Do box. The Office Assistant will then suggest that you click a topic, such as Troubleshoot Printing, to view the related Help topics; yours will most likely be among them. Not too shabby, huh?

If you're not sure how to word a question to the Office Assistant, or if you just don't want to deal with the Office Assistant at all, try typing the single word "Troubleshoot" in the Type Keywords box in the Help window. "Wait a minute," you say. "What Help window?" If all you can see is the Office Assistant, right-click him (or her, or it) and then click Options on the shortcut menu. In the Office Assistant dialog box, clear the Use The Office Assistant check box and click OK. To access the Help window thereafter, click Microsoft Excel Help on the Help menu. If you click the Index tab, you can type keywords to search by to find the solution to your problem. Using either the Office Assistant or the Help window's Index results in the same choices for Help topics, so feel free to use whatever method works best for you. There are many roads to the same destination!

If you're still stuck

I've endeavored to anticipate the most common problems Excel users run into, but I can't possibly cover them all. I've taught Excel for ten years, and that decade of experience was helpful in determining which problems were the most common. But I'm sure you'll have at least one problem that I haven't solved in this book.

If you run into a dead end, you can turn to Microsoft product support or to other resources, such as the following:

- *http://support.microsoft.com/support/excel/content/faq/default.asp*, a Microsoft Product Support page with a link to frequently asked questions about Excel 2002

- *http://www.microsoft.com/office/excel*, the Microsoft Excel product Web site

- *http://www.microsoft.com/office*, the Microsoft Office product Web site

- *http://search.support.microsoft.com/kb*, the Microsoft searchable Knowledge Base

- *http://www.zdnet.com/zdhelp/*, a popular technology Web site with helpful tips.

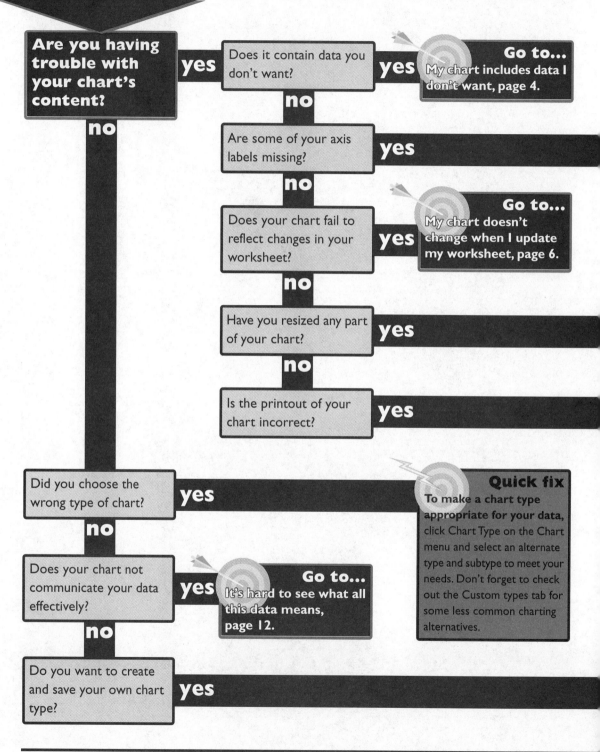

Are you having trouble with your chart's content?

yes → Does it contain data you don't want?

- **yes** → **Go to...** My chart includes data I don't want, page 4.
- **no** → Are some of your axis labels missing? **yes**
- **no** → Does your chart fail to reflect changes in your worksheet?
  - **yes** → **Go to...** My chart doesn't change when I update my worksheet, page 6.
- **no** → Have you resized any part of your chart? **yes**
- **no** → Is the printout of your chart incorrect? **yes**

no → Did you choose the wrong type of chart?

- **yes** → **Quick fix**

  To make a chart type appropriate for your data, click Chart Type on the Chart menu and select an alternate type and subtype to meet your needs. Don't forget to check out the Custom types tab for some less common charting alternatives.

- **no** → Does your chart not communicate your data effectively?
  - **yes** → **Go to...** It's hard to see what all this data means, page 12.
- **no** → Do you want to create and save your own chart type? **yes**

Charts

Quick fix

If your axis labels are missing or illegible, this is probably due to a reduction in the chart's overall size or a reduction of the plot area. Try reducing the font size for the axis labels by clicking on the axis (or any one of the visible labels) and use the Size button on the Formatting toolbar to reduce the font until all of the labels appear.

Go to...

I've resized my plot area, and now all the chart elements don't fit, page 8.

Go to...

My chart doesn't look the way I expect when I print my worksheet, page 10.

If your solution isn't here, check these related chapters:

- Exporting and importing, page 120
- PivotTables, page 254

Or see the general troubleshooting tips on page xv.

Quick fix

To create and save your own chart type for future use:

1. Right-click the chart and choose Chart Type from the shortcut menu.
2. On the Custom Types tab, click the User-Defined option, and click the Add button to create a new chart type.
3. Give the chart type a name and click OK.

My chart includes data I don't want

Source of the problem

You know the saying, "It's all in the wrist"? Well, your unwanted data could simply be the result of selecting an extra row or column—a slip of the mouse that grabbed too much stuff, resulting in unwanted plotted points or pie slices.

If your mousing skills are beyond reproach, it could just be that you made an error when selecting the cell range you wanted to chart. Did you include the totals at the foot of a series of rows or in the last column in the range? Normally, you don't want to plot the totals because they make it hard to visually interpret the numbers that contributed to them. Did you simply select the wrong range of cells from the wrong part of the worksheet? You're not alone—it's easy to do, and we've all done it. The good news is that fixing the problem is nearly as easy as causing it was.

The following steps will show you how to get rid of that unwanted data.

How to fix it

1. Right-click the chart in your worksheet and then click Source Data on the shortcut menu that appears.

2. On the Data Range tab of the Source Data dialog box, look in the Data Range box. It contains a range statement, which includes the name of the sheet from which you selected the chart's data and the range of cells you selected within that sheet, such as =Evaluations!$B$5:$F$9, where "Evaluations" is the name of the sheet and the cells included in the chart data are in cells B5 through F9. ▶

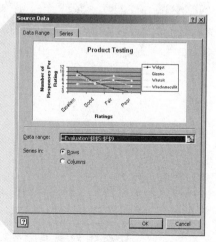

3. If the data you need to plot is on a different sheet, click that sheet's tab in the open workbook. If the desired data is within the active sheet, stay right where you are.

4. When you're on the sheet that contains the data to be plotted, click the first cell in the range you want to plot, and drag through the adjoining cells until only those that you want to plot in the chart are selected. As soon as you begin to drag, the previously listed range disappears from the Data Range text box; a new range is built as you drag your mouse.

5. Click OK to redraw the chart using your revised range of cells.

Make the bad charts stop!

The secret to including only the data you want in your chart is obviously to select only the desired data in the first place. No surprise there. But what if you're not sure which data is the right data? Here are some pointers:

- Excel uses shorthand for referencing cell ranges. For example, A4:C10 indicates that all cells from the fourth row in column A to the tenth row in column C are included in the range. Some cell ranges include dollar signs before the column letters and row numbers in the cell references (for example, $A$4:$C$10). The dollar signs indicate absolute, or fixed, cell references that won't change if your worksheet changes. An exclamation point next to a sheet name in a cell reference means that the referenced cells are located in a worksheet other than the one in which you are working.

- Think about what you're charting. If you're charting sales, leave out the columns pertaining to expenses. If you're charting this year's productivity figures, omit the column that includes projections for the part of this year that hasn't happened yet. You'd be surprised how much time you save by stopping and taking a look at your data and imagining the resulting chart before you start selecting cells to chart.

- When charting a series of totaled columns and/or rows, include the column headings and row labels (which become your axis labels and legend text), but leave out the totals.

- Just because data appears in contiguous sections on your worksheet doesn't mean you have to include all of those sections on your chart. To select noncontiguous sections of a worksheet, use the Ctrl key when selecting the sections. For example, if you want to chart columns B, C, D, and F (not E), drag through the data in columns B, C, and D, and then release the mouse button. Press and hold down the Ctrl key, drag through the cells you want in column F, release the Ctrl key, and then release the mouse button. Your data range will include two sheet name references and two sets of cell ranges, but that's no problem—the second set of references and ranges resulted from your using the Ctrl key to add to an existing selection.

Tip

If your chart is on its own sheet and you want to delete it, delete the entire sheet. If the chart is an object within a sheet, click the chart's boundary to select the entire chart and press the Delete key.

When all else fails

The Chart Wizard is such a simple tool to use that if your chart is totally wrong, you can just delete it and start over. For most charts it takes only a couple of minutes to complete the process. Yeah, we're usually taught not to take the easy way out. Well, in this case, it's okay.

My chart doesn't change when I update my worksheet

Source of the problem

You've got a chart, you've got a worksheet, and when you change the worksheet data, you expect the chart to change with it—bars to get taller or shorter, pie slices to get thinner or fatter, lines to move up or down on the chart. Why don't they change? There are a couple of potential causes.

First, you could be editing part of your worksheet that isn't linked to the chart. When you select worksheet data and then create a chart based on it, a link between the cells and the chart is created. If you then forget which part of your worksheet was plotted in the chart and edit the wrong part of the worksheet, the chart won't change. The fix for this is obvious—edit the right part of your worksheet, and the chart will be updated. Not sure which part is the right part? See "My chart includes data I don't want" on page 4. You need to check the Data Range for the chart by right-clicking the chart and clicking Source Data on the shortcut menu. You'll see that the current range in the Data Range box is selected, allowing you to simply type a new range to replace the highlighted selection. Once you know the range of cells that was included in your chart, you know which cells to edit if you want the chart to change.

If you've established that you are working with the correct data, you have to consider the second possibility: You might have inadvertently severed the link between the data and the chart. Is your chart based on data in your open worksheet (the one that contains the chart)? If not, perhaps the worksheet that contains the data was moved, renamed, or deleted. If the source data was removed, either from your computer or from the chart by severing the link, the chart will be blank. If the chart has data in it, the first problem is your most likely cause.

How to fix it

1. Confirm that the correct cells are linked to the chart by right-clicking the chart, clicking Source Data on the shortcut menu, and examining the selected range in the Data Range box on the Data Range tab. (The corresponding cell range is also indicated by a dashed rectangle on the source worksheet.)

2. If the correct cells are linked to the chart but the chart is blank, your source data is completely gone—it might have been inadvertently deleted by you or someone else who works with your data. Regardless of the cause, you have to reenter it from whatever manual source (say, a written list of sales totals) or electronic source (such as another worksheet or a Microsoft Word table) that you used when you originally built your worksheet.

3. If the data is correct but not linked properly, you'll have to reestablish the link. If necessary, switch to the worksheet containing the chart. (If the worksheet is in a different workbook, navigate to

where the workbook is stored, open it, and then click the tab of the worksheet that contains the cells with which you want to establish a link.) Right-click the chart and click Source Data on the shortcut menu that appears. Drag through the cells to be charted and release the mouse button. ▶

4. Click OK to close the Source Data dialog box and redraw the chart with the reestablished data.

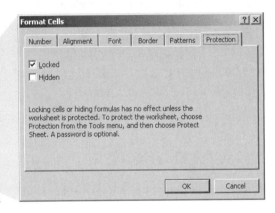

	A	B	C	D	E	F	G	H	I
1									
2				Source Data - Data range:				?×	
3		Product Testing		=Evaluation!$B$5:$F$9					
4					Ratings:				
5		Name of Product	Excellent	Good	Fair	Poor	TOTALS		
6		Widget	10	5	2	0	17		
7		Gizzmo	8	4	6	3	21		
8		Whatsit	4	5	8	6	23		
9		Whachamacallit	9	4	1	0	14		
10		TOTALS	31	18	17	9	5R x 5C		
11									
12									

Fool me once...

If other people have access to your worksheets, it's possible that they could make changes to the data that prevent your charts from being updated. It's essential to treat your workbooks and work-sheets carefully, protecting their contents from being accidentally deleted by you or by others who work with the same files. To keep your chart data from being deleted, protect it. Select the cells that contain the data that is linked to your chart (be they in the same or a different workbook) and click Cells on the Format menu. In the Format Cells dialog box, click the Protection tab and make sure the Locked check box is selected. ▶

For this lock to take effect, you must then protect the entire sheet that contains the data. On the Tools menu, point to Protection and then click Protect Sheet. In the Protect Sheet dialog box, type a password (if you want to be able to edit or delete the data yourself, but prevent others from doing so), and use the checklist to select the type or types of user actions you'll allow in the pro-tected areas—the defaults are Select Locked Cells and Select Unlocked Cells. You might be able to safely add actions like Insert Hyper-links or Sort, as they won't change the data. After setting up your protection, click OK. ▶

The worksheet is now protected, preventing changes to the locked range of cells and thus protecting the chart you have based on them. (Note that if you want to edit data on a sheet and you didn't allow any editing when you set up your protec-tion in the Protect Sheet dialog box, you will have to unprotect the sheet using your password, make your changes, and then protect the sheet again—choose Tools, Protection, Unprotect Sheet to turn off the protection (be prepared to enter your password).

I've resized my plot area, and now all the chart elements don't fit

Source of the problem

Your chart looked great, but you thought that if you increased the size of the plot area—the actual chart where the data is plotted—the chart would be more legible and attract more attention. You were probably right about that, but now that you've resized the plot area, your legend is overlapping the chart or your axis titles are so big that they're too cumbersome for the chart. ▶

What to do? If you're married to the new size of the plot area, you can resize the entire chart object to make more room for the items that don't fit. An alternative is to resize or relocate only those items that don't fit so that they work within the chart object as it is.

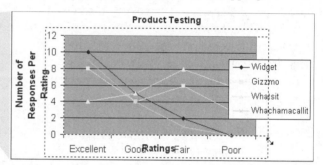

How to fix it

To resize your chart object, follow these steps:

1. Click outside your chart to deselect it. This makes certain that no individual element within your chart, such as the legend or chart area, is selected.

2. Click once in the background of the chart object. (The easiest way to select this background correctly is to click the chart object's boundary.) Handles will appear on the four corners and in the middle of the top, bottom, left, and right sides of the chart object.

3. Point to a corner handle until the mouse pointer changes to a two-headed arrow.

4. Drag diagonally away from the chart's center to adjust both your chart's width and height. (You can resize the chart proportionally by holding down the Shift key as you drag.) A dashed box appears and resizes to match your mouse movement. ▶

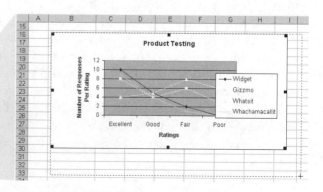

5. When the chart is the size you want it to be, release the mouse button.

6. Now that your chart object is resized, the titles that looked too big might look more proportionate and your legend might fit without overlapping the chart. If not, consider reducing the size of the plot area; this will automatically reduce the titles as well.

If the plot area must remain the size you have it and resizing the chart object was either impossible or didn't help, follow these steps to resize or reposition the legend and to resize the axis titles:

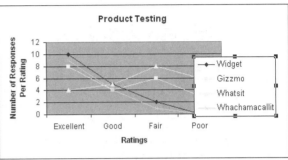

1. Click once on the legend to select it. Handles appear on the corners and in the middle of each side. ▶

2. Reduce the legend font size by choosing a smaller number than the Size button on the Formatting toolbar. Or you can choose Format, Selected Legend, and in the resulting Format Legend dialog box, click the Font tab and adjust the font size there. ▶

3. After reducing the font size of the legend text, resize the legend object—you can drag any of the handles to adjust its width and height so that it will economically encompass the smaller text.

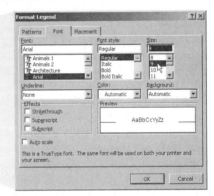

4. Sometimes a legend that spans the bottom of the chart in a long strip rather than residing on the left or right in a box is more space-saving. In the Format Legend dialog box (to open it, choose Format, Selected Legend), click the Placement tab and choose Bottom. ▶

5. Click OK to close the dialog box.

6. To resize the axis titles, click each one and then use the Formatting toolbar's Font Size button to choose a smaller font size.

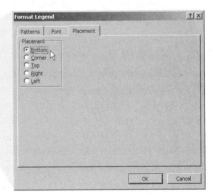

My chart doesn't look the way I expect when I print my worksheet

Source of the problem

Problems printing a chart are generally caused by one of two things: the position of the chart on the worksheet or the size of the chart itself. In the case of the chart's position, if the chart falls over the edge of a worksheet print area—either one you have set manually or one imposed by the size of the page and its margins—part of the chart will be cut off when you print the worksheet. If the chart is too big to fit on a page or so small that it's illegible when you print it, how the chart was resized after it was created is the culprit.

How to fix it

If your chart is being partially cut off when you print it, follow these steps:

1. On the sheet containing the chart, click Page Break Preview on the View menu. (Make sure the chart isn't selected, or else the Page Break Preview command won't be on the menu.) In Page Break preview, solid blue lines enclose the entire print area of the worksheet; any worksheet element that falls outside these lines and into the solid gray area will not be printed. Horizontal and vertical dashed blue lines indicate breaks between pages within the print area; any worksheet element that falls outside these lines will be broken across printed pages. ▶

2. To make sure your chart is printed completely on one page, drag the chart so that it appears completely within both the solid and dashed blue lines of the page on which you want it to be printed.

3. On the Standard toolbar, click the Print Preview button and confirm that your entire chart will now fit on a page. If it still doesn't fit, repeat the previous steps, moving the chart until it fits within the page.

4. When the chart fits properly, switch back to Normal view.

If your chart is too big to fit on a page or is too small to read, follow these steps:

1. If necessary, switch to Normal view by clicking Normal on the View menu.

2. Click the chart to select it. Make sure the chart itself, and not one of its internal elements, is selected by clicking just within the chart's boundary.

3. Resize the chart by dragging the chart's corner handles. Make it larger (drag outward) if it's too small to read; make it smaller (drag toward the chart's center) if it's too large to fit on the page when you print it.

4. Make sure your chart will fit on the page by clicking the Print Preview button on the Standard toolbar. ▶

5. If your chart still overflows the page, continue to resize it until it fits.

Other chart printing problems and solutions

It's rare that you won't be able to print your chart or that you'll be able to print it only partially. This is usually the result of problems with your printer—your printer does not have enough memory to handle the amount of information being sent to it, or the driver (the file that tells your printer and computer how to communicate) has gone bad or was never right from the start.

A good procedure for any printing problem is to cancel the print job and turn off the printer. Wait a few seconds, turn the printer back on, and then try to print your chart again. If you still can't print the chart, try quitting Excel and restarting Windows. Reopen Excel and the worksheet containing your chart and attempt the print job again.

If you still can't print the chart, try reinstalling your printer. Click the Start button, point to Settings, and then click Printers. In the Printers window, double-click the Add Printer icon. A series of dialog boxes will walk you through the process of selecting your printer from a list of manufacturers and models. (You might need to insert the original CD-ROM from which you installed the software.) If this also fails to solve the problem, you might need to install a new printer driver. You can probably download one from your printer manufacturer's Web site.

> **Tip**
>
> For more information on printing your worksheets and controlling their size and layout when you print them, see "Printing" on page 268.

It's hard to see what all this data means

Source of the problem

Charts are created to convey a graphical message about numeric data. That message generally tells one of two stories: a trend (usually told with line charts) or a comparison (shown by bar, column, and pie charts). Bar and column charts can also show a trend, assuming the bars or columns represent, for example, sales over a series of months, quarters, or years. The trend is evident, but may not be obvious. The goal of any chart is to convey the numeric message quickly, and if someone has to ponder the chart and refer to the data in order to get the message, the chart has failed.

If the chart type you've selected doesn't tell the whole story, you can try switching to a different chart type. (See the "Quick fix" on page 2.) But for complex data or a story that includes, for example, both a trend and comparisons, this might not solve the problem. You'll want to combine both bars and columns that show comparisons and a line that shows a trend over time. To better illustrate the story you want to convey, add a trendline to your chart.

How to fix it

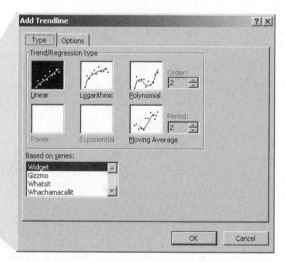

1. Click your chart's boundary to select the entire chart.

2. On the Chart menu, click Add Trendline.

3. In the Add Trendline dialog box, click the Type tab (or the Trend tab, depending on the chart type you started with), and select the type of line you want to add—there are a total of six possible types and Linear is the most popular and applicable. ▶

4. Choose which series you want the trendline to follow from the Based On Series list.

5. If you want to give the trendline a new name, click the Options tab and type the name in the Custom box.

6. If you want your trendline also to serve as a forecast for future data, enter the number of periods (months, years, days, whatever you're plotting) in the Forecast section of the dialog box.

7. Click OK to apply the line to your chart.

But what about pie charts?

A pie chart can show only one data series, whereas bar, line, and column charts can show several series in the same chart. Because pies show only comparisons, they are rarely used to show trends.

Other ways to add to the chart's message

To control the message conveyed by a trendline, you can use the Drawing toolbar's Line or Arrow tools to manually draw a line that skims the tops of your bars or just tracks the columns in one data series rather than in the entire chart. If the plotted data series follow a span of time, they're already showing a trend by themselves. Adding the line emphasizes the trend so that no one misses the point.

You can draw two kinds of lines: straight and "multi-jointed." To add a straight line, click the Drawing button on the Standard toolbar (if the toolbar isn't already visible). Then click the Line or Arrow button on the Drawing toolbar, move the mouse pointer to the worksheet, and hover over the part of your chart where you want the trendline to begin. Your mouse pointer will appear as a crosshair. Drag the mouse, following the tops of the bars to create a single straight line. ▶

Sometimes your trend doesn't convey a simple "Sales are on the decline" message. If your numbers (and therefore the heights of the bars) go up and down across the width of the chart, your trendline should do the same. Use the AutoShapes Freeform line tool to draw a segmented line that changes its direction. Click the AutoShapes button, point to Lines, and then click the Freeform tool. Drag to draw the first segment of the line (the portion of the line before the trend changes). Then click and drag in a different direction to continue drawing at a new angle. ▶

Tip

You might notice the Set Intercept = check box on the Options tab of the Add Trendline dialog box. The intercept is where the trendline you want to add should cross the value (or *y*) axis. By default, the trendline crosses at the zero point, which is normally the bottom of the axis. To start the trendline at any other point on the value axis, enter that value in the Set Intercept = box.

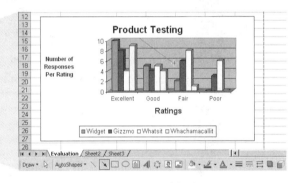

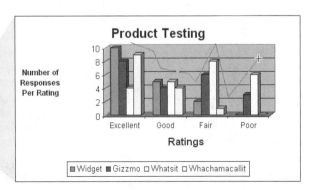

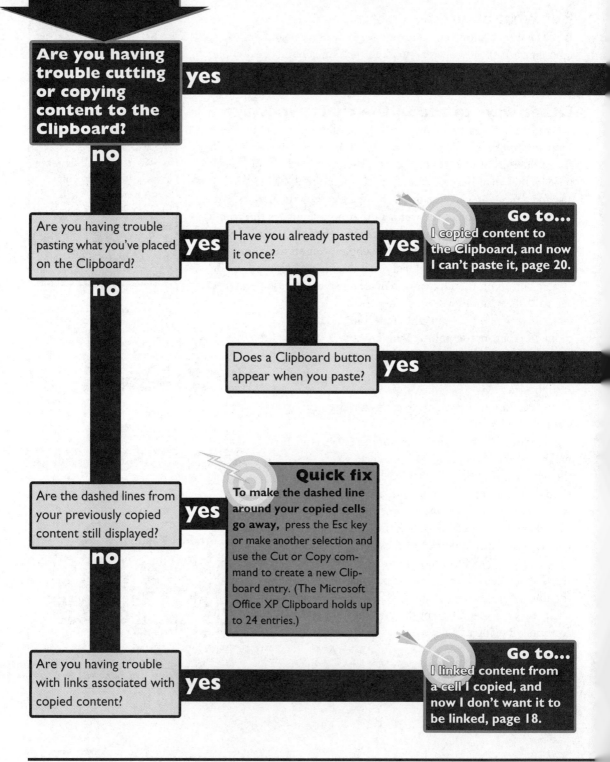

Are you having trouble cutting or copying content to the Clipboard?

yes →

no ↓

Are you having trouble pasting what you've placed on the Clipboard?

yes → **Have you already pasted it once?**

yes → **Go to...**
I copied content to the Clipboard, and now I can't paste it, page 20.

no ↓

Does a Clipboard button appear when you paste?

yes →

no ↓

Are the dashed lines from your previously copied content still displayed?

yes → **Quick fix**
To make the dashed line around your copied cells go away, press the Esc key or make another selection and use the Cut or Copy command to create a new Clipboard entry. (The Microsoft Office XP Clipboard holds up to 24 entries.)

no ↓

Are you having trouble with links associated with copied content?

yes → **Go to...**
I linked content from a cell I copied, and now I don't want it to be linked, page 18.

Clipboard

Are you trying to cut or copy more than one thing to the Clipboard? **yes** Are you attempting to cut or copy more than 24 items to the Clipboard? **yes**

no

Quick fix

To cut or copy more than 24 items to the **Office XP Clipboard,** you can delete individual entries or clear the entire clipboard using the Clipboard pane. Choose View, Task Pane, and choose Clipboard from the list of available panes.

Go to...

I can't cut or copy the content from one of my cells, page 22.

Go to...

When I paste into a cell, I get a Clipboard button and I'm not sure why, page 16.

If your solution isn't here, check these related chapters:

● Entering data, page 108

● Hyperlinks, page 214

Or see the general troubleshooting tips on page xv.

When I paste into a cell, I get a Clipboard button and I'm not sure why

Source of the problem

Microsoft Office XP and the 2002 suite of applications are much more interactive than previous versions of the software. This level of interactivity is demonstrated by the appearance of new buttons when certain actions take place. When you type text in Microsoft Word, for example, and AutoCorrect kicks in to make a correction or change to what you've typed, a button appears, offering options on whether to keep the correction or change. When it comes to Microsoft Excel, the interactivity largely pertains to pasted content—if you copy text from Word and paste it into your worksheet, a Clipboard button appears. This button asks if you want to maintain the formatting that the text had back when it was in Word or if you want the pasted content to follow Excel's formatting within the target worksheet. ▶

The Clipboard button also appears when you paste Excel content from one workbook or another worksheet onto the active sheet. In this case, the button looks the same as it does when it appears after Word content is pasted, but the options for dealing with the pasted content are different, and you have more options for controlling how the formatting and content are pasted. ▶

If the pasted content looks fine as is, you can ignore these buttons, or you can use them to customize your pasted text and numbers. If you really hate that these buttons appear and never find yourself taking advantage of the options they offer, you can turn them off—from within Excel and across the suite as well.

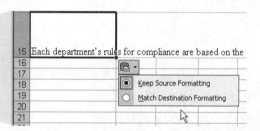

Tip

When you paste content from one spot in the worksheet to another, if you copy the original content, a flashing border surrounds that content. As soon as you paste and then press the Escape key, however, that flashing border goes away. Something else goes away, too—the Paste Options button on the pasted content.

How to fix it

1. To turn the Clipboard button off, choose Tools, Options, and click the Edit tab.

2. In the second column of Edit options, click the check box next to Show Paste Options Buttons to remove the checkmark—this option is on by default. ▶

3. Click OK to close the dialog box and put your changes into effect.

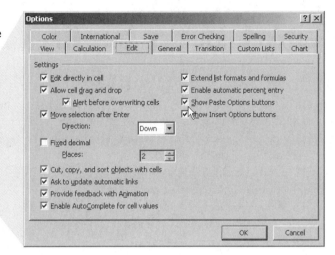

Another action that may result in the display of an option button is an insertion. When you choose Columns (or Rows) from the Insert menu, an Insert Options button may appear, offering choices for how the new row or column should be formatted. ▶

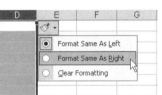

When you insert a row or rows, the options include following the formatting of the row above or the row below the new row or ignoring all surrounding formats and inserting a generic row with no special formatting at all. When columns are inserted, you can choose to apply the formatting of the column to the left or right of the new column or to insert a column that adheres to the default settings for the workbook and nothing more.

If you don't want these options buttons to appear, you can follow virtually the same procedure used to turn off the Paste Option buttons—choose Tools, Options, and then, on the Edit tab, remove the checkmark next to Show Insert Options Buttons.

Tip

If the worksheet into which you're inserting new rows or columns has no special formatting applied—nothing changed or reformatted since the workbook was created—the Insert Options button won't appear when you insert new columns or rows, because there won't be any formatting to apply or not apply to the new columns or rows.

I linked content from a cell I copied, and now I don't want it to be linked

Source of the problem

It's very handy to be able to copy content from one place in the workbook or worksheet and paste it to another spot and link the source to the target. It's a powerful tool because if you change the original entry (the source), the pasted version (the target) changes as well. This makes it possible to repeat content from one worksheet in another and know that you only have to update the original content in the source worksheet to update the pasted content as well. The result? In one round of editing, you can update an entire workbook if key areas are linked to one another. ▶

Of course, into each handy and powerful feature a little rain must fall. What if you don't want the two parts of the worksheet linked anymore? Or what if someone else sets up a link in a worksheet you use, and you want to update the source and not have the target reflect the change? Linked cells within the same workbook are very convenient things until the link outlives its usefulness, which can happen quite often during the life of a workbook.

	A	B	C	D	E	F
3		1st Q.	2nd Q.	3rd Q.	4th Q.	Average
4	Operations	25%	30%	35%	40%	33%
5	Support	22%	25%	28%	31%	27%
6	Information Technology	13%	30%	47%	64%	39%
7	Accounting	14%	16%	22%	20%	18%
8	Administrative Services	34%	26%	18%	10%	22%
9	Sales	45%	43%	43%	42%	43%
10	Marketing	22%	50%	78%	80%	58%
11	Warehousing	60%	45%	29%	15%	37%
12						
13	**Summary**	Average				
14	Operations	33%				
15	Support	27%				
16	Information Technology	39%				
17	Accounting	18%				
18	Administrative Services	22%				
19	Sales	43%				
20	Marketing	58%				
21	Warehousing	37%				

These cells are linked to their duplicates above, so that the summary is always updated when the source data is changed.

The solution to this problem lies in severing the link—essentially divorcing the two parts of the worksheet. They continue to live in the same workbook, but what happens to one no longer affects the other.

The following steps show you how to create a link as well as how to sever it.

How to fix it

Before we sever a link between two areas of a worksheet, let's make sure you know how to create the link in the first place. To link one cell's content to another cell where the original (source) cell's content will be pasted, follow these steps:

1. Click in the cell containing the content you wish to paste and link to another location in the workbook.

2. Choose Edit, Copy, or press Ctrl+C.

3. Move to the cell where the copied content will be pasted and click in that cell to activate it.

4. Choose Edit, Paste Special. The Paste Special dialog box opens. ▶

5. Click the Paste Link button. The paste operation is performed, and the connection to the source cell is established at the same time.

6. Press Escape to remove the flashing border around the source cell and continue working.

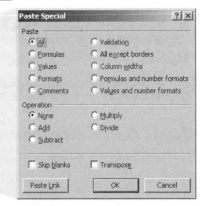

Once two cells are linked, if you edit the source cell, the target cell changes to reflect the edit—this applies only to content changes, however, not to formatting. You can change the font, size, even cell formatting (changing it from Currency to Percentage, for example), and the target cell will be unaffected. The target changes only if you change the number or text in the source cell.

Now, if you no longer want that connection between source and target to exist, follow these very simple steps to sever the link:

1. Click in the target cell.

2. Edit the cell content in some way—delete it, change the number, edit the text. Make a change to something other than formatting. This will break the link.

3. Test the disconnection—go back to the source cell and make a content change—and note that the target cell no longer changes to match the source.

If you want to reestablish the link, you must repeat the Paste Special process, copying source cell content to another cell, using the Edit, Paste Special command, and the Paste Link option.

Linking blocks

You can link a block of cells to another block of cells by selecting a range before issuing the Copy command. When you go to Paste and set up the link, just right-click the cell that will serve as the first cell in the target range, and choose Paste Special from the shortcut menu. Of course, you'll use the Paste Link button in this case, too.

Once linked, any changes to any of the cells in the target (including currently blank cells) will affect the same cells (in terms of their position in the range) in the target block.

Tip

First it was here... then it was there. If you cut a cell containing data linked to another cell, the link between the cells remains. This applies whether you cut the source or the target.

I copied content to the Clipboard, and now I can't paste it

Source of the problem

Unlike a Word document, in which you can copy text to the Clipboard and then paste it as many times as you like into as many documents as you'd like, Excel allows only one paste per copy—or so it seems, anyway. Imagine you've just selected a cell on Sheet 2, and you want to copy and paste it to a cell on Sheet 3. You issue the Edit, Copy command and then hop to Sheet 3, where you click in the target cell and click the Paste button or choose Edit, Paste. The content you copied from Sheet 2 appears, and all is well.

But then, as your imaginings continue, you realize you want to paste the same thing onto Sheet 4, where a summary of the other sheets' activity is stored. You look up at the toolbar and see that the Paste button is dimmed. You right-click the target cell on Sheet 1 and see that the Paste and Paste Special commands are dimmed. The Edit menu's Paste commands are dimmed as well. What is this, a conspiracy? You can paste only once? That seems rather severe, doesn't it? ▶

Okay, that's enough questions—here are the answers:

- Yes, it's true that you can paste only once. This is because the ability to paste many times increases the margin for error through repeating unwanted content in unwanted places. Most worksheet content is unique, so this control has been placed on the use of the Paste command to prevent unintentional repetitions.

- Although it appears that you can paste only once, you can, in fact, paste as many times as you'd like in the current Excel session. The trick is to use the Clipboard task pane rather than relying on the Edit menu, toolbar, or keyboard shortcuts. Those commands give you access only to the last item placed on the Clipboard. The Clipboard task pane gives you access to up to 24 cut and copied items from as many Office XP applications as you want.

The goal, then, if you want to paste something repeatedly, is to display the Clipboard task pane and make efficient use of it.

How to fix it

The Clipboard task pane should appear as soon as you add more than one thing to the Clipboard. This includes entries added to the Clipboard in Word, Microsoft PowerPoint, Microsoft Access, or Microsoft Outlook in the current Windows session—as long as a single Office XP application is open, the Office Clipboard will save previous entries (made by using the Cut or Copy commands). If you only have one thing on the Clipboard, or if for any reason the Clipboard task pane isn't showing, follow these steps to display it:

1. From the View menu, choose Task Pane. It will most probably appear in its New Document form, the default view of the task pane, should no other version of it have been displayed in the current Excel session.

2. Click the triangle on the task pane's title bar and choose Clipboard. The Clipboard task pane is displayed. ▶

3. Be careful not to click any of the listed Clipboard entries until and unless you're ready to insert them.

Once the Clipboard task pane is displayed, you can paste any cut or copied entry as many times as you like. You can paste the entries into an Excel worksheet, Word document, PowerPoint presentation, or even into Microsoft FrontPage or Access documents.

The Clipboard in Office XP supports up to 24 entries, but you may find that you need more—not that you'd be juggling 24 different entries and actively pasting all of them—but you may want to add something to the Clipboard when all 24 of the entries have been filled. If you use the Cut or Copy command when there are already 24 entries on the Clipboard, the oldest entry (the first one you made during the current session with Office XP) will be removed in favor of the newest.

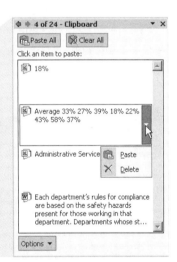

But what if you want to keep the oldest entry? You can pick which entry to get rid of, making room for a new entry without forsaking an existing entry you intend to use again or haven't yet used. To remove an individual entry on the Clipboard, point to the entry without clicking on it. When a box forms around it and you see a drop triangle at the far right end of that box, click the triangle and choose Delete. ▶

You can also right-click any entry and choose Delete from the shortcut menu.

XP stands for extra pasting?

Office 97 supported one Clipboard entry at a time—and as soon as a second item was cut or copied to the Clipboard, the previous entry was replaced. Office 2000 allowed up to 12 entries, and a Clipboard toolbar to view and control them. Office XP allows up to 24 Clipboard items and a very intuitive task pane through which to manage them.

I can't cut or copy the content from one of my cells

Source of the problem

You want to take the content in one of your worksheet cells and move (cut) or copy it to another cell, and when you attempt to do so (with the Paste command), the new entry fails to appear on the Clipboard task pane. This can be for one of two reasons:

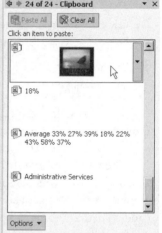

- The item you're trying to cut or copy is already on the Clipboard, exactly as it exists in the active cell.

- There are more than 4 megabytes (MB) of content on the Clipboard of a computer with less than 64 MB of RAM or 8 MB of content on the Clipboard of a computer with 64 MB of RAM or more. ▶

If either of these scenarios exists, the solution is the same—get rid of the item or items that are preventing your latest cut or copied entry to the Clipboard and then attempt the cut or copy procedure again.

How to fix it

To remove an individual item from the Clipboard, follow these steps:

1. Display the Clipboard task pane if it isn't already displayed. Choose View, Task Pane, and then click the task pane title bar and choose Clipboard from the resulting menu.

Don't cut yourself!

A reason that you may not be able to cut something from a worksheet is that the worksheet (or a portion thereof) may be protected, preventing any removal of content. Of course, if this is the cause, a prompt will appear when you attempt to cut the content, informing you that the worksheet is protected and telling you to go to the Tools menu to choose Unprotect Sheet. You'll probably need a password.

2. Locate the Clipboard entry that you want to delete and right-click it.

3. Choose Delete from the resulting shortcut menu.

4. Try your Cut or Copy command again. If it still doesn't work, try clearing the Clipboard entirely by clicking the Clear All button at the top of the Clipboard task pane. ▶

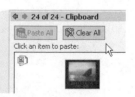

It's important to realize that you can cut or copy content to the Clipboard from virtually any Windows-based application. While a recognizable icon will accompany the entries that came from Office XP suite applications, this may not be the case when it comes to entries that came from applications outside of the suite. ▶

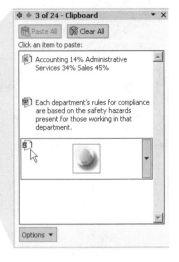

When you go to clear the Clipboard or to remove an individual entry, pay attention to the icon that indicates the source of the entry—and think about whether or not the source content is available for cutting or copying the content again should it be needed. When in doubt, wait to clear the item or the entire Clipboard until you've determined the status of the source content.

You may also notice that content on the Clipboard looks different from the way it did in the native application—this is especially true when it comes to text that came from Word, PowerPoint, or FrontPage, where special fonts and other text styles may have been applied. This difference between the way text looked when it was cut or copied as opposed to how it looks on the Clipboard task pane is due to the fact that all text is displayed in the Tahoma font on the Clipboard pane—even if it was in Times New Roman or some other font when it was cut or copied. ▶

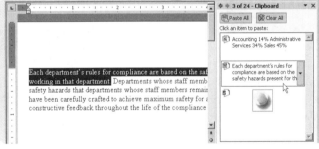

Don't worry, though—when the content is pasted, the original formatting will accompany it, although you can choose not to keep the formatting from the source and make the pasted content match the formats in place in the target cell(s) instead. To access your pasted content's formatting options, use the Paste Option button that appears when you paste the content and choose whether or not to retain the source formatting. ▼

Tip

You can't cut or copy groups of noncontiguous cells—if you attempt it, Excel prompts you that it's not possible to continue and suggests that you select a single cell or range and try again. Why would such a limitation exist? Because it's assumed that you will follow your Cut or Copy command at some point with a Paste command —at which point Excel would have to figure out where to put the cut or copied content and place it in the same configuration in the target cells. Rather than deal with all the possible conflicts that could arise from that, Excel restricts you to cutting and copying single or contiguous cells only.

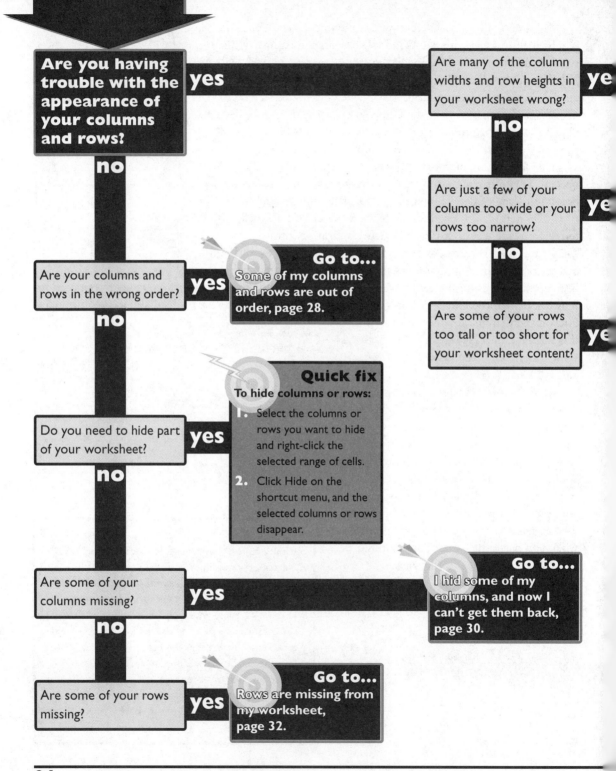

Are you having trouble with the appearance of your columns and rows?

yes →

Are many of the column widths and row heights in your worksheet wrong?

ye →

no ↓

Are just a few of your columns too wide or your rows too narrow?

ye →

no ↓

Are some of your rows too tall or too short for your worksheet content?

ye →

no ↓

Are your columns and rows in the wrong order?

yes →

Go to...
Some of my columns and rows are out of order, page 28.

no ↓

Quick fix
To hide columns or rows:

1. Select the columns or rows you want to hide and right-click the selected range of cells.

2. Click Hide on the shortcut menu, and the selected columns or rows disappear.

Do you need to hide part of your worksheet?

yes →

no ↓

Are some of your columns missing?

yes →

Go to...
I hid some of my columns, and now I can't get them back, page 30.

no ↓

Are some of your rows missing?

yes →

Go to...
Rows are missing from my worksheet, page 32.

Columns and rows

Go to...

I adjusted my row heights, and now my new entries don't fit, page 26.

Quick fix

To adjust the width of a single column or row, follow these steps:

1. Point to the seam to the right of the column's letter.

2. Drag to the left to make the column narrower or drag to the right to make it wider.

Quick fix

To make all of your columns the same width or your rows the same height:

1. Select your entire worksheet by pressing Ctrl + A.

2. Point to the seam between any pair of column letters or between any pair of row numbers.

3. Drag to the left or right to adjust all the columns' width, or drag up or down to adjust the height of all the rows.

If your solution isn't here, check these related chapters:

- Exporting and importing, page 120
- PivotTables, page 254

Or see the general troubleshooting tips on page xv.

I adjusted my row heights, and now my new entries don't fit

Source of the problem

By default, Microsoft Excel adjusts the height of rows for you if you increase the font size of your entries or make your content bold and therefore need the rows to be taller. Sounds like you'd never need to play with row heights on your own, right? Wrong. There are plenty of reasons to adjust row heights manually. One of the most common is to achieve a spread-out look with white space between rows' content. On the other hand, you might want to make your rows narrower to adjust to very small text, because Excel doesn't shrink rows below the default height of 12.75, even if you choose a tiny font size. Or, you might want to turn a blank row into a border by shading it and making it very thin, thereby creating an obvious separation between sections of a worksheet. ▶

These manual adjustments can cause problems, however. Suppose you made a row taller to accommodate big text, and now you need to reduce the size of that text. When you choose a smaller font size, the row will remain tall, leaving a lot of white space—a problem if you weren't looking for white space. Now imagine that you reduced a row's height and later increased the content's size. Excel won't resize the row automatically once you've tinkered with the height manually, so you end up with a short row with tall text, with the tops of the letters cut off. ▶

Resolving these problems is easy, requiring only that you restore the row or rows in question to a size that meets the needs of the text in the row.

	A	B	C	D	E	F
1						
2			INVOICE			
3						
4						
5				Date:	6/5/2002	
6						
7	To:					
8	Kline Trucking					
9	123 Gravel Boulevard					
10	Philadelphia PA 19117					
11						
12	Service Rendered	Date	Hours	Rate	Total Due	
13						
14						
15						
16						
17						
18						

	A	B	C	D	E	F
1						
2						
3	Invoicing Summary					
4						
5		Week 1	Week 2	Week 3	Week 4	Week 5
6	January					
7	February					
8	March					
9	April					
10	May					
11	June					
12	July					
13	August					
14	September					
15	October					
16	November					
17	December					
18						

Columns and rows

How to fix it

1. Select the rows that are no longer sized appropriately. If you want to fix only one row, click a cell in the row you want to resize. To select a series of contiguous rows, drag through their row numbers. If the rows are noncontiguous, hold down the Ctrl key, click the row numbers for the rows you want, and then release the key when you've selected them all. ▶

2. Point to the bottom seam of any of the row headings (the buttons with the row numbers on them) of the row or rows you want to fix and then double-click. The rows are automatically resized to fit the tallest entry in each row. ▶

More woes with rows

Rows start out just big enough to display 10-point or 12-point text, with a little room above and below the text. This can look a bit cramped, and if you have many rows of similar content, it can be hard to read. In addition, if you're printing your worksheet without the gridlines when your data is housed in that tight an arrangement, your eye might accidentally stray up or down a row as you read across the page.

To make more visual room on your worksheet, you can make some or all of your rows taller, as shown in the example, even if you don't increase your fonts beyond the default 10-point size. ▶

Simply select the entire worksheet by pressing Ctrl+A or select a specific range by dragging through the row numbers for the range of rows you want to resize. Using any seam between the row headings, drag down to make the rows taller. As you're dragging, a ScreenTip appears to show the adjusted row height.

Tip

You can set a specific row height for one or more rows by selecting the rows you want to adjust and then right-clicking. When the shortcut menu appears, click Row Height, type a measurement in the Row Height dialog box, and then click OK. All your selected rows will be resized to the height you specified.

Tip

Once you've reset the row heights to automatically accommodate the tallest entry, Excel will return to resizing those rows if you increase the font size again.

Some of my columns and rows are out of order

Source of the problem

First let's make it clear what "my columns are out of order" really means. It doesn't mean that Excel suddenly forgot the alphabet and row M is appearing before row G. Rather, "columns out of order" refers to column headings and content that are not in a logical order in relation to other headings and content in the worksheet. For example, if you're setting up a database, it's easy to forget a column (like Date Hired in a database that stores employee information) and then throw it in at the end, only to wish later that it were in a different place—perhaps earlier in the list of columns or between two related pieces of data. Having the columns in your worksheet in the same order as a manual source of data or in the order that you think about the content can save a lot of time and help you avoid errors as you enter data. ▶

	Last Name	First Name	Department	Current Salary	Bonus %	Date Hired	Insurance Y/N	Insurance Carrier
	Chambers	Rosemary	Accounting	$ 65,500.00	5.7%	11/15/1996	Y	HMO
	Patrick	Kaitlin	Accounting	$ 62,500.00	5.8%	9/23/1995	N	None
	Freifeld	Iris	Accounting	$ 78,500.00	6.2%	8/3/1993	Y	HMO

Employee Data

Now, hang on a minute. Does this mean *you're* the source of the problem? Well, yes. But don't feel bad; we've all done it, and we'll all do it again. The goal is to know how to fix the problem when it inevitably arises, and the solution is easy—you just have to move the columns around until they're in the order you want them.

How to fix it

1. Select the column that you want to move by clicking its column heading (the button at the top of the column with the column letter on it).

2. From anywhere in the range of selected cells, point to the left or right edge of the selected column (the selected column will have two thick side borders). Your mouse pointer turns into a four-headed black arrow. (If you point to the left or right seam of the column heading, the pointer becomes a black double arrow.) ▶

3. Using the *right* mouse button, drag the column to the desired location among the other columns. Release the mouse button.

> ### Tip
> If the column you want to move contains a merged cell (perhaps you've applied the Merge And Center command to the title of the worksheet), you cannot drag the column to a new location. First remove the Merge formatting. To do this, select the merged cell and click Cells on the Format menu. On the Alignment tab, clear the Merge Cells check box and click OK. Now you can move your column and, when it's properly placed, remerge the cell as desired.

Current Salary	Bonus %	Date Hired	Insurance Y/N
$ 65,500.00	5.7%	11/15/1996	Y
$ 62,500.00	5.8%	9/23/1995	N
$ 78,500.00	6.2%	8/3/1993	Y

Columns and rows

4. On the shortcut menu, click Shift Right And Move. ▶

5. Check your column's new position. If you dropped it in the wrong spot, repeat steps 2 through 4 until the column is where you need it to be.

Move it *and* lose it?

Be careful when you move worksheet content, be it entire columns or a block of cells. If you simply drag the text from place to place, you run the risk of replacing the content where you drop the text (and deleting the existing content in the process). Of course, a dialog box appears with a message asking if you want to replace the content at your destination. Be sure to read this message (and others like it) thoroughly and click Cancel if you had intended to do something else. Be careful not to get into the habit of clicking OK without reading messages first!

If you copy or cut content from one location and then paste it in another location using the Copy, Cut, and Paste commands or the corresponding toolbar buttons, no such prompt appears—the paste operation replaces anything that was already in place, no questions asked. A way around this? Always drag with your right mouse button. You'll then be able to choose the Shift And Move command from the shortcut menu, protecting existing content at the new location.

Rearranging rows

If your rows are out of order, meaning that you want the content in one row to be above another row rather than below it, you can drag that row's content into a new position in the same way you drag a column. Click the row heading to select the row and then point to the bottom edge of the selected cells, not the seam of the row heading. Hold down the right mouse button and drag the row up or down, releasing the mouse button when you reach the appropriate spot. On the shortcut menu that appears, click Shift Down And Move.

Tip

If you need to move more than one consecutive column, select them by dragging through their column letters and then point to an outer edge of the selected cells. When your mouse pointer becomes a left-pointing arrow, drag the columns with the right mouse button and put them where you want them. When you release the mouse button, the shortcut menu will appear; click Shift Right And Move.

All in one fell swoop

You can move more than one column at a time—simply select a series of contiguous columns by dragging through their control buttons, and then grab the edge of the group of selected columns and drag them with your right mouse button. You can't move noncontiguous columns, however, so if you need to move B, D, and F two columns to the right, you'll have to do each column individually.

I hid some of my columns, and now I can't get them back

Source of the problem

At some point, you might decide to hide some columns in your worksheet—perhaps to conserve space or to protect confidential data from being viewed by others. Later, you might want to bring the columns back so that you can work on them or use their cells in formulas—but you can't seem to make the columns reveal themselves. Being unable to bring the hidden columns back would certainly be a problem!

If you're thinking, "Then I won't ever hide my columns," imagine this: You have a worksheet for tracking employee information. It includes salary data in columns E and F, which you wisely chose to hide so that anyone viewing or printing the worksheet wouldn't get an eyeful of information that should remain confidential. ▶

Good choice. But now you need to update the salary columns to reflect recent raises, so you need to bring the hidden columns back into view. Wait a minute; they won't come back!

When you attempt to drag a column back into view using the column headings (the buttons with the column letters on them), you end up only widening the adjoining columns. If you've hidden multiple columns, you might have trouble bringing one or all of them back. What to do? Well, you can drag column headings to reveal the hidden column or columns, or you can use the Unhide command. Essentially, you reverse the steps you took to hide the columns in the first place.

	A	B	C	D	E	G	H
1							
2		Employee Data					
4		Last Name	First Name	Department	Date Hired	Bonus %	Insurance Y/N
5		Chambers	Rosemary	Accounting	11/15/1996	5.7%	Y
6		Patrick	Kaitlin	Accounting	9/23/1995	5.8%	N
7		Freifeld	Iris	Accounting	8/3/1993	6.2%	Y
8		Lambert	Harry	Administration	2/15/1998	7.0%	Y

Tip

Dragging to widen the columns isn't always easy. Because you did such a good job hiding the columns, it's hard to tell whether you're dragging the seam to widen the column that's hidden or the column next to it! The trick is to select the columns both before and after the hidden column or columns. Point to the seam between the two columns, and then drag the double-headed arrow to widen the columns and expose the hidden ones. The width of the formerly hidden columns is equal to that of the two adjusted visible columns. After you do this, you might have to readjust column widths to your liking.

How to fix it

To reveal a hidden column by widening it, follow these steps:

1. Point to the seam between column headings and be on the lookout for a special mouse pointer—a variation of a two-headed arrow. When a column is hidden, the two-headed arrow appears to be split down the middle. ▶

E	G	H
Date Hired	Bonus %	Insurance Y/N
11/15/1996	5.7%	Y
9/23/1995	5.8%	N

2. When the split two-headed arrow appears, drag it to the right to widen the hidden column. Once the hidden column is visible again, it appears in place in the worksheet, and you can adjust its width as needed to view the column's content.

To reveal a hidden column by using a menu command, follow these steps:

1. Select the columns on either side of the hidden column.

2. Right-click anywhere in the selected columns' cells.

3. Click Unhide on the shortcut menu.

Come out, come out, wherever you are

If you have more than one hidden column, you can reveal all hidden columns in one fell swoop. (See the tip in "Rows are missing from my worksheet" on page 33.) Press Ctrl+A to select the entire worksheet and then right-click any of the column headings. On the shortcut menu, click Unhide. Voilà! All your hidden columns are revealed. (If you want to unhide only specific columns using the shortcut menu, you need to select the column to the right of the hidden column or columns and click Unhide for each of the hidden columns.)

> **Tip**
>
> In case you're wondering how to hide multiple columns in the first place, it's easy. Select the columns you want to hide by dragging through their headings. (To select nonadjacent columns, hold down the Ctrl key while you click the headings for the columns you want to select.) Right-click anywhere on the selected cells and click Hide on the shortcut menu.

Outsmarting smart people

Won't other Excel users who open your worksheet also know how to unhide information? They might, and that may be an unacceptable risk if the data you're hiding is sensitive or secret. To prevent anyone unhiding your hidden data, protect your worksheet by following these steps:

1. Select the column to be hidden and the columns on both sides of it.

2. Choose Format, Cells, and on the Protection tab, be sure Locked is selected.

3. Click OK.

4. Now apply protection to the entire worksheet, enabling the protection you just applied. Choose Tools, Protect Sheet. You'll be asked to provide a password.

You can reverse this procedure when you want to redisplay the hidden columns by choosing Tools, Unprotect Sheet and supplying the password. After that, you can use any of the techniques described here to unhide your columns.

Rows are missing from my worksheet

Source of the problem

At some point, you might be working in a worksheet and notice a gap in row numbers. Or you might look for data that you know exists, but you can't see it. Maybe you know the data still exists because there's a formula that refers to a cell in that row and the formula still works. That data has got to be there! So what's going on? Just as you can hide columns (see "I hid some of my columns, and now I can't get them back" on page 30), you can hide rows on a worksheet. You can hide them by selecting the row or rows, right-clicking any of the selected cells, and clicking Hide on the shortcut menu.

You can also hide them by reducing their height to zero, a technique that is often applied inadvertently. For example, you might attempt to select a series of rows to format them but instead of just clicking the row headings (the buttons with the row numbers on them) to select the rows, you click the seam between the rows and drag, thereby resizing the rows. Or you might attempt to resize a row and accidentally hide the row altogether. In this example, rows 5 and 6 are hidden. ▶

Because it happens accidentally, you might not notice the problem right away. What to do? You can employ one of two methods: dragging to reveal the hidden rows or utilizing the Hide command's companion, Unhide.

	B	C
1		
2	Employee Data	
3		
4	**Last Name**	**First Name**
7	Balinski	Joseph
8	Balsamo	Anthony
9	Elmaleh	Miriam
10	Fox	Seymour
11	Frankenfield	Daniel

How to fix it

To reveal one or more hidden rows, follow these steps:

1. When you locate the missing row number(s) (indicating a hidden row or rows), select the rows above and below them.

2. Point to the seam between any two of the selected rows' headings. Your mouse pointer turns into a split two-headed arrow.

3. Double-click. All of the rows are set to an equal size, and that includes the hidden row or rows. By making all of the selected rows the same size, the hidden rows are unhidden by default.

Columns and rows

To reveal a hidden row using a menu command, follow these steps:

1. Select the row above and below the hidden row or rows.

2. Right-click any of the cells in the selected rows.

3. Click Unhide on the shortcut menu. ▶

To reveal all hidden rows at once, press Ctrl+A to select the entire worksheet, right-click anywhere on the worksheet, and click Unhide on the shortcut menu.

Revealing rows reverses risks

If you're keeping a list of records in your worksheet, be careful when hiding rows within the list. If you hide rows, sorting those rows might not appear to work, and if you filter for data that's contained in the hidden row(s), you won't be able to see the data. Before doing any sorting or filtering of your data, reveal all your hidden rows by pressing Ctrl+A, right-clicking a row heading, and clicking Unhide on the shortcut menu. With all your rows visible, use the Data menu's Sort and Filter commands as needed.

Tip

Another quick way to reveal all your hidden rows—or columns, for that matter—is to select your entire worksheet (press Ctrl+A), point to any seam between row or column headings (your mouse pointer will appear as a two-headed arrow), and double-click. This technique is normally used for resizing rows or columns to fit their largest entry. In so doing, you return any zero-height rows or zero-width columns to the default size, which is 12.75 for rows, and 8.43 for columns.

Comments

Do you want to control the appearance of your comments?

yes

no

Are you having trouble hiding your comments?

yes

Go to...
Comments and track-change comments pop up on the screen, and I don't want them to, page 36.

no

Are your comments missing from your worksheet printout?

yes

no

Are some of your comments no longer needed?

yes

no

Are you having trouble keeping track of the changes made to your worksheet?

yes

Go to...
Other people make changes to my worksheet, and I want to keep track of those changes, page 40.

no

Do you want to veto some of the changes others have made to your worksheet?

yes

Go to...
I don't want to keep some of the changes made since Track Changes was turned on, page 42.

Go to...

I don't want my name to appear in the comment box, page 38.

Quick fix

To include comments in your printout, follow these steps.

1. On the File menu, click Page Setup.

2. On the Sheet tab of the Page Setup dialog box, click the Comments drop-down arrow, and click At End Of Sheet or As Displayed On Sheet to indicate where in your printout you want your comments to appear.

Quick fix

Get rid of a comment quickly by right-clicking the cell with the comment (look for the red triangle in the cell's upper-right corner) and clicking Delete Comment on the shortcut menu.

If your solution isn't here, check these related chapters:

- Drawing shapes and lines, page 96
- Hyperlinks, page 214
- Printing, page 268

Or see the general troubleshooting tips on page xv.

Comments and track-change comments pop up on the screen, and I don't want them to

Source of the problem

If the worksheet you're working in includes comments and information about editing done to it, you might find that boxes pop up right when you're trying to get work done. To solve this problem, you need to understand what these boxes are and where they come from.

Microsoft Excel is designed to support teamwork—two or more people working on a single worksheet—and their need to communicate easily about the worksheet without phone calls or e-mail messages. To facilitate this (or your own multilevel editing process), you can add comments to a worksheet to annotate its content. For example, you can remind yourself or others to do something or explain where to find supporting information. You can also use Track Changes to have Excel insert track-change comments whenever someone edits a cell in the worksheet. The history of the edit—who made it, what the edit was, and when it was made—is stored as a comment in the cell.

Comments are indicated by red triangles in a cell's upper-right corner. Track-change comments are indicated by blue triangles in a cell's upper-left corner. (Cells can have both comments and track-change comments.) The triangles indicate that a cell has a comment and/or has been edited, so you don't have to check the actual comments all the time. ▶

	A	B
1		
2	Department Compliance	
3		1st Q.
4	Operations	25%
5	Support	22%
6	Information Technology	13%
7	Accounting	14%
8	Administrative Services	34%
9	Sales	45%
10	Marketing	22%
11	Warehousing	60%
12		

Many users become aggravated when comment boxes pop up all over the place as they edit their worksheets. It can seem as though every time you move your mouse pointer, a little box pops up to distract you! What's actually happening is that when your mouse passes over a cell with a comment or track-changes information attached to it, Excel thinks you want to see the comment or information associated with that cell. ▶

The solution lies in telling Excel what you want to see on the screen. You can tell Excel to not display red triangles and comments or, if you are working with Track Changes turned on, you can turn off on-screen highlighting of edited cells. This will prevent Excel from displaying blue triangles and comments that describe the edits that have been made.

	A	B	C	D	E
1					
2	Department Compliance				
3		1st Q.	2nd Q.	3rd Q.	4th Q.
4	Operations	25%	30%	35%	40%
5	Support	22%	25%	28%	31%
6	Information Technology			47%	64%
7	Accounting			18%	20%
8	Administrative Services			18%	10%
9	Sales			43%	42%
10	Marketing			78%	80%
11	Warehousing			30%	15%
12					
13					

Laurie Ulrich:
This dept's VP has been on leave, and his stand-in is not fully aware of all the compliance issues. I think this explains their performance.

and Track Changes

How to fix it

To keep comments from popping up on your worksheet, follow these steps:

1. On the Tools menu, click Options and in the Options dialog box, click the View tab.

2. In the Comments section, click None. This won't delete your comments, but it will prevent the red triangles from being displayed while you're working, and the comment boxes won't appear as your mouse pointer moves over commented cells. ▶

3. After you've finished working in a worksheet, you can turn the display of comment triangles back on by clicking Options on the Tools menu and then resetting the Comments option to Comment Indicator Only on the View tab.

Tip

Inserting a comment is easy—simply right-click the cell where you want to insert the comment and click Insert Comment on the shortcut menu. A text box appears, into which you can type your comment. After you enter the comment, click outside the box to complete the process. A small red triangle appears in the cell's upper-right corner.

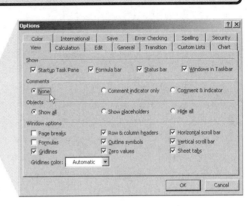

To prevent blue triangles and comments from appearing when Track Changes is turned on, follow these steps:

1. On the Tools menu, point to Track Changes and then click Highlight Changes.

2. In the lower left corner of the Highlight Changes dialog box, clear the Highlight Changes On Screen check box. ▶

3. Click OK to close the dialog box and continue working in your worksheet. Track Changes will still be turned on, but you won't see the track-changes comments, and blue triangles will not appear in the upper-left corner of any edited cells.

Tip

If Track Changes is turned on but the on-screen display of changes is turned off, remember to turn the display back on before anyone else edits or views your worksheet. Without the blue triangles displayed on the screen, other users won't know that Track Changes is on, and they might not realize that their edits will be tracked. On the Tools menu, point to Track Changes, click Highlight Changes, and select the Highlight Changes On Screen check box to redisplay blue triangles and comments.

Comments

I don't want my name to appear in the comment box

Source of the problem

When you insert a comment in your worksheet or edit something while working with Track Changes turned on, your name is included in the comment box. Comments, indicated by a red triangle in the upper-right corner of a cell, are a tool that you can use to insert notes to yourself or others who use a worksheet. Track Changes is a tool that monitors changes to a particular worksheet, including who has made those changes and when they were made. Cells edited while Track Changes is turned on are indicated by a small blue triangle in the upper-left corner of a cell. It makes sense to have the name of a comment's author in the comment box so that if others are viewing comments and perhaps even adding their own comments to the worksheet, it's clear who said what.

You might, however, prefer to keep your name out of it—perhaps you're editing a worksheet on behalf of someone else, or you want your comments to be anonymous so that any suggestions or questions posed are not given more or less credence because of their author. You can remove names from existing comments by editing comments manually. You can also remove a name association from a workbook and see to it that names are not included in a particular workbook in the future.

To remove names from existing comments, follow these steps.

How to fix it

1. Point to a cell that contains a comment (any cell with a red triangle in the upper-right corner), and when the comment is displayed, right-click the cell.

2. Click Edit Comment on the shortcut menu. The comment box remains on the screen with the insertion point active within the box.

3. Select the displayed name in the comment box and press Delete. You can press Delete again to pull the comment text up one line, as needed. ▶

Tip

If you're working with a group of people who are editing the same workbook, you can have all users change their User Name setting to a different made-up name: User1, User2, and so on. You can also ask each person to come up with a unique name or nickname and enter that in the User Name box.

and Track Changes

To eliminate names from future comments in the active workbook, follow these steps:

1. On the Tools menu, click Options.

2. In the Options dialog box, click the General tab and look at the User Name box. The name in this box will appear on all comments. ▶

3. You can delete the content of the User Name box, or you can replace it with something anonymous, such as *User 1* or *Editor*. If you leave the field blank, the word *Default* will appear in the comment boxes you create from then on. As *Default* might be confusing to other users, it's probably best to type something to replace your actual name, even if you only type a dash or an x, so that Excel doesn't insert *Default* for you.

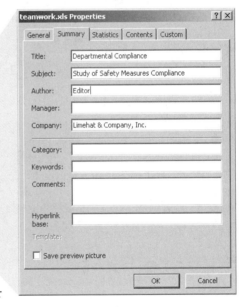

My identity? No comment

Excel derives the name that appears in the comment box from the user information entered when the software was installed. If you don't want any of your work—workbooks, comments, edits done while Track Changes is turned on—to bear your name, you have to edit this user information. On the File menu, click Properties and then click the Summary tab. (The name in the Author box is the name Excel will associate with any workbook created on your computer.) ▶

You can edit or delete the author name. If you completely remove the author name from your current workbook and any workbooks you later create, an ellipsis (…) will appear in the Author box because the box requires an entry. Unless you are working on an administrator's computer (such as a Windows 2000 Advanced Server computer), the user name assigned to a particular workbook will override the name that appears in the Properties dialog box.

Note that your old workbooks will still show your name in their Properties dialog boxes, so if you want to change them, you'll have to open them individually and edit the dialog box for each one. The Properties dialog box can be viewed by anyone who opens your workbook—whether they open it from an e-mail message, over your network, or from a floppy disk—so bear that in mind as you make your changes to the Author box and other boxes, such as Company and Manager.

Other people make changes to my worksheet, and I want to keep track of those changes

Source of the problem

So, you've set up a worksheet, and you've entered the data. Someone else comes along and makes changes to the layout (for example, column headings and row labels) or the data. You open the worksheet the next day, and you have no idea who made the changes or why. This can be disconcerting, especially if you didn't know other people would be editing your worksheet. Even if you were aware that others would be making changes, you probably want to know exactly which cells were changed and who made the changes.

That's where Excel's Track Changes feature comes in. By turning Track Changes on, you can keep track of which cells have been changed, what they used to contain, what they contain now, who made the change, and when the change was made. ▶

Despite the Big Brother sound of all that, you'll find that Track Changes can be a significant tool for any worksheet edited by more than one person, or even a worksheet that only you use. No one can remember everything, and you might need a reminder as to which cells you've edited.

When Track Changes is turned on, by default the entire worksheet is tracked for any changes or additions by any user. You can edit the track-changes settings, however, by using the When, Who, and Where boxes in the Highlight Changes dialog box.

	A	B	C	D	E
1					
2	Department Compliance				
3		1st Q.	2nd Q.	3rd Q.	4th Q.
4	Operations	25%	30%	35%	40%
5	Support	22%	25%	28%	31%
6	Information Technology	13%	30%	47%	64%
7	Accounting				
8	Administrative Services				
9	Sales				
10	Marketing				
11	Warehousing				
12					

Laurie Ulrich, 7/13/2001 11:07 PM:
Changed cell A8 from 'Administration' to 'Administrative Services'.

How to fix it

1. On the Tools menu, point to Track Changes and then click Highlight Changes.

2. Click the Track Changes While Editing check box.

3. To limit tracking to a specific time frame or specific people, select the check box next to When or Who, and then click the down arrow and select your preference.

4. To limit tracking to a specific cell or range, select the check box next to Where. Then click the cell or drag through the range of cells in which you want to use Track Changes. When you've made your range selection, you'll see the range selection displayed in the Where box. (If you want Track Changes to apply to the entire worksheet, leave the Where box blank.) ▶

5. Choose whether or not you want to see the edits on-screen all the time. If you don't want to see them, clear the Highlight Changes On Screen check box.

6. Click OK to turn Track Changes on with the settings you specified.

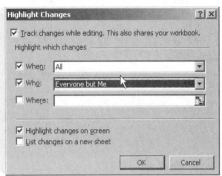

I know what you did last edit

When Track Changes is turned on, the cells that have been edited have a blue triangle in the upper-left corner of the cell. When you move the pointer over a cell bearing that triangle or click it, a comment box appears showing the name of the person who made the change or addition, the time and date that the cell was last edited, what the cell originally contained, and what the change was. (Comment boxes might also pop up when you move your mouse pointer over cells with a red triangle in the upper-right corner. If any of these boxes get in your way, see "Comments and track-change comments pop up on the screen, and I don't want them to" on page 36.)

Track Changes can be turned off at any time, and, at some point, you need to turn it off and accept or reject each of the changes made to the worksheet. The process for doing this is covered in "I don't want to keep some of the changes made since Track Changes was turned on" on page 42. If people have made changes you don't want to keep, you can throw them out and revert to the original worksheet content.

Covering one's tracks

Track Changes isn't foolproof. Other users can turn Track Changes off while they're working, thus hiding the fact that they've made changes. If you don't want to alert people to the fact that Track Changes is on, point to Track Changes on the Tools menu, click Highlight Changes, and clear the Highlight Changes On Screen check box in the Highlight Changes dialog box. There will be no visible sign that Track Changes is turned on, and you can turn the screen highlighting back on when you're ready to inspect the worksheet. Of course if people need to know what others have done in order to make their own changes, you'll have to leave highlighting turned on and trust that, in the spirit of teamwork, no one will turn Track Changes off.

I don't want to keep some of the changes made since Track Changes was turned on

Source of the problem

Actually, this is a good problem to have. The beauty of using Track Changes, in addition to being able to see who made the changes and when, is that you can go through the worksheet and choose which changes stay and which changes go.

When Track Changes is turned on, any edits you or others make to a worksheet are, well, tracked. You see the history of the changes in a comment box, and any cell that has been changed is indicated by a small blue triangle in its upper-left corner. The very fact that you're working with Track Changes turned on means that you can easily find each change that has been made to your worksheet and choose whether or not to keep it. This includes actual changes, new information added to your worksheet, and any deletions. You can choose which person's edits to review (and to accept or reject), which ranges of the worksheet to review, and which changes within those ranges to review. As long as Track Changes is on, you can turn back the clock and make it as though no one ever touched your worksheet.

How to fix it

1. On the Tools menu, point to Track Changes and then click Accept Or Reject Changes to display the Select Changes To Accept Or Reject dialog box. ▶

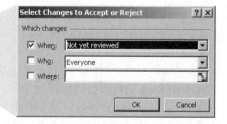

2. To review changes made since a particular date, click the When down arrow and click Since Date in the list. Today's date will appear in the box, and you can edit it by typing a past date.

3. To review only those changes that were made by a particular person, click the Who down arrow and make a selection from the list. The list offers Everyone and Everyone But Me.

4. If you want to review only part of your worksheet, click in a cell and drag through a range of cells to specify a portion of your worksheet to review. The dialog box will shrink to expose the whole worksheet, and you can drag through the range of cells you want to review. ▶

5. Once your review settings are in place, click OK to begin reviewing the changes that have been made. Each one will appear in the Accept Or Reject Changes dialog box, showing the name of the person who made the change, when it was made (date and time), and what the change was. ▶

6. Click Reject to get rid of whatever change was made. The cell's entry reverts to what it was before Track Changes was turned on. Assuming you turned Track Changes on just before you made the worksheet available for use by others, and assuming none of them turned Track Changes off, you'll be able to return the worksheet to the way you left it before others got their hands on it!

7. As you click Reject (or Accept, if you run into any changes you want to keep), the dialog box shows you each change, one by one. When you have reviewed all of the changes, the dialog box closes, and you are returned to your worksheet.

Tip

You can click the Reject All button in the Accept Or Reject Changes dialog box if you want to get rid of all changes without having to review each one. On the Tools menu, point to Track Changes and then click Accept Or Reject Changes. If necessary, save the workbook when prompted. When the Select Changes To Accept Or Reject dialog box appears, make sure the Where check box and text box are clear and then click OK. In the Accept Or Reject Changes dialog box, click Reject All. When you're prompted to confirm your intention to reject all changes without reviewing them, click OK to proceed. (Likewise, you can click Accept All to accept all changes without reviewing them.)

Tip

Once you've rejected (or accepted) changes and the reviewing process is over, you cannot undo your rejection or acceptance of the edits. Other than saving the file with a different name before beginning the reviewing process and then going back to the original file, you cannot get the changes back once you've rejected them and the rejection/acceptance process is complete.

Do you need help setting up your conditional formats?

yes

no

Do you need to turn off conditional formatting?

yes

no

Do you need to set up multiple conditions?

yes

Go to...
I don't know how to set up multiple conditions, page 48.

no

Are you having trouble getting conditional formatting to work?

yes

Go to...
I applied conditional formatting, but it didn't work, page 50.

no

Is the Conditional Formatting command dimmed on the menu?

yes

no

Do your conditional formats fail to change when you update your data?

yes

Go to...
The conditional formats I set up aren't updated when I edit my worksheet, page 52.

no

Are you having trouble changing your conditional formats?

yes

Go to...
I'm not sure how to change my conditional formats, page 54.

Go to...
I'm not sure how to set up conditional formatting, page 46.

Quick fix

Turn off conditional formatting by following these steps.

1. Click Conditional Formatting on the Format menu and click the delete button.

2. When the Delete Conditional Formatting dialog box appears, select the check box for each condition you want to delete.

3. Click OK twice to close the dialog boxes.

Quick fix

The Conditional Formatting command is unavailable if Excel is in Edit mode, if your worksheet is currently set to be shared, or if Track Changes is turned on.

If your solution isn't here, check these related chapters:

- Formatting numbers, page 146
- Formatting text, page 156
- Formatting worksheets, page 168

Or see the general troubleshooting tips on page xv.

I'm not sure how to set up conditional formatting

Source of the problem

The Conditional Formatting dialog box isn't terribly self-explanatory, so don't feel bad that you didn't yell, "Of course! I understand!" the first time you tried to use this feature. The conditional formatting concept is simple, though: show the cells whose values are in a range that is greater than some specified number or that contain some certain value or formula. Setting up the criteria so that the conditional formatting is applied to the right cells, however, is not always a snap.

When you set up conditional formatting, it's important to know what you want the formatting to tell you. What is it you're looking for? Do you want to be alerted if any employee's "Remaining Sick Days" hits zero? Do you want to see all the sales figures that exceed $150,000? If you know what it is you want flagged, you're more than halfway there.

The second part of the process involves expressing a "say when" aspect to Microsoft Excel, which means choosing an operator (*Greater Than, Less Than, Equal To*, and so on) and entering or selecting a value that Excel should compare with the cells in your selected range. After that, you just need to tell Excel what formatting it should use to flag the cells that meet the criteria you've established.

Another thing to keep in mind: It's important to set up formats that will stand out. Many people think their conditional formats aren't working, when in reality, they chose a subtle change—such as changing the color of the text from black to navy blue—that's easy to miss, especially when the worksheet is printed.

So, the problems you might run into with conditional formatting can usually be fixed by thinking things through before you start setting up your criteria. With some prep work under your belt, you'll master conditional formatting in no time.

The following steps will help, too.

How to fix it

1. Select the range of cells you want to apply conditional formatting to. To select noncontiguous ranges, hold down the Ctrl key, click and/ or drag through the noncontiguous cells and ranges you want to include, release the mouse button, and then release the Ctrl key. ▶

	A	B	C	D	E	F	G	H	I	J	K
1											
2											
3											
4			DIVISION GOALS								
5			SALES IN MILLIONS (US $)								
6			2001				2002				
7			Q1	Q2	Q3	Q4	Q1	Q2	Q3	Q4	
8		Northeast	5.24	5.5	5.76	6.02	6.28	6.54	6.8	7.06	
9		Midwest	6.35	6.45	6.55	6.65	6.75	6.85	6.95	7.05	
10		South	2.54	2.5	2.46	2.42	2.38	2.34	2.3	2.26	
11		Southwest	7.2	7.5	7.8	8.1	8.4	8.7	9	9.3	
12		West	4.23	4.5	4.77	5.04	5.31	5.58	5.85	6.12	
13		TOTALS	25.6	26.5	27.3	28.2	29.1	30.0	30.9	31.8	
14											
15											

2. On the Format menu, click Conditional Formatting to display the Conditional Formatting dialog box. ▶

3. In the Condition I section of the dialog box, leave the first box set to Cell Value Is if you want to apply conditional formatting to specific values. (If you want to apply conditional formatting to a specific formula, click Formula Is in the list and then type the formula you want to format.)

> **Tip**
>
> If you want to format a formula in your worksheet, click Formula Is in the first box of the Condition I section of the dialog box. Then you can either enter the exact formula you want to highlight through formatting or click a cell within your worksheet that contains the formula.

4. Choose an operator from the box next to Cell Value Is. (If you've selected Formula Is instead of Cell Value Is, you won't need to choose an operator.)

5. In the next box or boxes (depending on which operator you chose), type a value or values or select a cell in the worksheet that contains the value you want. ▶

6. Click the Format button. The Format Cells dialog box appears. You can choose font formatting and border and pattern settings to apply to the cells that meet your conditions. Click OK when you have finished setting the formats you want. ▶

7. In the Conditional Formatting dialog box, click OK to apply your formatting.

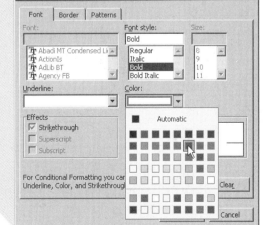

> **Tip**
>
> Be sure to choose formats that will stand out against whatever formatting is already in place in your worksheet. If, for example, your text is already bold or in a different color, the conditional formatting should not include a change to bold or that color.

I don't know how to set up multiple conditions

Source of the problem

Sometimes a simple "If any cell in this range is less than 1, change the background to blue" condition isn't enough. What if you also want to know if any cells contain a value greater than 5? If you want to know which employees have no sick days left *and* which employees haven't used any sick days at all, for example, you need a second set of conditions to format cells that meet this second criteria. There is no single operator within the Conditional Formatting dialog box that will cover cells that are both less than 1 and more than 5.

To apply formatting to more than one set of conditions, you need to set up a second (and perhaps third) set of conditions to compare to your selected range of cells.

How to fix it

1. Select the range of cells to which you've already applied conditional formatting and to which you now want to add a second set of conditions. You can also select a range to which you have not applied any conditional formatting and apply a brand new set of conditions to it.

2. On the Format menu, click Conditional Formatting.

3. If conditions for Condition 1 are not already set, use the Condition 1 section of the Conditional Formatting dialog box and click either Cell Value Is if you want to apply conditional formatting to specific values, or Formula Is if you want to apply conditional formatting to a specific formula.

4. Choose an operator from the box next to Cell Value Is (if you've selected Formula Is instead of Cell Value Is, you won't need to choose an operator).

5. In the next box or boxes (depending on which operator you chose), type a value or values or select a cell in the worksheet that contains the value you want. ▶

6. Click the Format button. The Format Cells dialog box appears. Choose font formatting and border and pattern settings to apply to the cells that meet your conditions. Click OK when you have finished setting the formats you want.

7. Click the Add button. The dialog box expands to display a Condition 2 section. This isn't an *And* or an *Or* addendum to the first condition, but a completely separate set of conditions.

8. Set up the Condition 2 criteria the same way you did the Condition 1 criteria. Then click the Format button and specify the formatting. You can apply the same formats used for Condition 1 or apply a new set of formats, bearing in mind that the conditional formatting will be applied in the order that the conditions were created—items meeting Condition 1 will be formatted first, and so on. Click OK to return to the Conditional Formatting dialog box. ▶

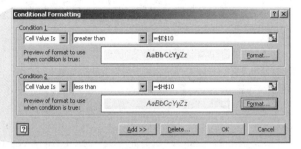

9. If you need a third set of conditions, click Add again, specify an operator and a value, or a formula, and then specify your formatting options. ▶

10. When you've established all the conditions, click OK to apply the conditional formatting to your worksheet.

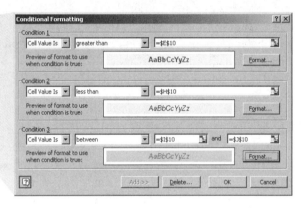

What did blue mean again?

It's a good idea to apply different formatting to each set of conditions so that you can tell one from another. Obviously, the cells themselves will tell the story, but if your criteria for Condition 1 isn't glaringly different from Condition 2—for example, Condition 1 makes all cells over 50,000 blue, and Condition 2 makes all cells between 40,000 and 50,000 blue—you might not remember later if you had one condition for "anything over 40,000" or if you set two sets of criteria. Having all cells between 40,000 and 50,000 turn green instead of blue will show that two sets of conditions are at work.

If you're sure you'll forget which formats indicate which criteria, you can add a comment (Insert, Comment) to a blank cell somewhere on the worksheet and type a small legend to your formatting in it—"blue means…, and green means…".

Tip

You can set multiple conditions to work like *And* or *Or* criteria. Say you want to isolate people aged 20 through 25 from a long list. If you use the *Between* operator to set a single condition for the values between 20 and 25, the formatting will be applied only to 21, 22, 23, and 24. Instead, set Condition 1 to Greater Than Or Equal To 20 and Condition 2 to Less Than Or Equal To 25. If you apply the same formatting to both conditions, it appears as if only one condition is set, but you've included the comparison values of 20 and 25.

I applied conditional formatting, but it didn't work

Source of the problem

As the name implies, conditional formatting is formatting that is applied only if certain conditions, or criteria, are met. How conditional formatting will work is determined by the range of cells that you select before clicking the Conditional Formatting command on the Format menu, the conditions you specify, and the formatting you choose to apply to content meeting those conditions. If any one of these elements is out of whack, the formats won't be applied or they'll be applied to cells other than those you want to format. In short, the cause of the problem is a conflict in the way conditional formatting was set up.

Solving the problem requires you to retrace your steps—figure out which cells you specified for conditional formatting, what conditions you set, and what formatting you chose to apply. Also, be sure some of the selected data actually meets those conditions—this is a common source of the problem we're discussing here.

This might sound like an instance where "Just forget it, do it again," is appropriate, but that's not the plan. What you need to do when conditional formatting appears to fail is to make sure you haven't applied it to the wrong cells, given it criteria that can't be met by the selected cells (such as numerical values when the cells contain text), or assigned formatting that doesn't make any visual difference in the worksheet appearance (maybe the numbers were *already* bold). If, after exploring all these possible holes in the setup, you still can't make it work, then go to the next plan: "Just forget it, do it again!"

How to fix it

1. To determine which cells have been selected for conditional formatting, click Go To on the Edit menu.

2. In the Go To dialog box, click the Special button and then click Conditional Formats in the Go To Special dialog box. ▶

3. Check that All is selected as the Data Validation option.

4. Click OK. The range of cells that was selected for conditional formatting is highlighted. If you have set up multiple conditions, select a cell in the range you want to format, and repeat steps 1 through 3, selecting Same instead of All in the Go To dialog box.

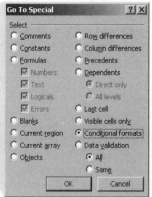

5. To determine what criteria were applied to your range of cells, click Conditional Formatting on the Format menu to display the Conditional Formatting dialog box. ▶

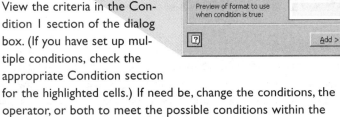

6. View the criteria in the Condition 1 section of the dialog box. (If you have set up multiple conditions, check the appropriate Condition section for the highlighted cells.) If need be, change the conditions, the operator, or both to meet the possible conditions within the selected range on the worksheet.

7. Click the Format button to check your formatting in the Format Cells dialog box. If you only made text bold or changed the text color, the format might already be in use in the selected range or be too subtle to notice. Make whatever formatting changes you want and then click OK to close this dialog box.

8. In the Conditional Formatting dialog box, click OK to apply any changes you made to the selected range.

You can always start over

Conditional formatting is a very simple feature, but you have to really think about what data is within the range to which the formatting is applied. For example, suppose you use the *Greater Than* operator and type *5000000.00* in the value box (as opposed to clicking a cell that contains a value that you want to compare to all the other cells in the selected range). If there are no numbers over 5,000,000 in the worksheet, none of your cells will be formatted. A simple extra zero or two can be the culprit.

If after checking everything you've done, the conditional formatting still doesn't work, click Conditional Formatting on the Format menu, and in the Conditional Formatting dialog box, click the Delete button. Select the check boxes for each of the conditions you want to delete (all of them, if you want) and then click OK. You can then start over, being careful to establish criteria that will apply to at least one of the cells in the range you specify for conditional formatting.

Tip

One of the most common errors in setting up conditional formatting is failing to select the entire range of cells that should be checked for values meeting the conditional criteria. Many people forget to select a range before setting up their conditional formats and then wonder why they don't work. If you click Conditional Formatting on the Format menu with a single active cell selected, that's the one and only cell to which conditional formatting will be applied.

The conditional formats I set up aren't updated when I edit my worksheet

Source of the problem

Excel's Conditional Formatting feature doesn't tell you when you've set conditions that don't work or if the multiple conditions you set contradict one another. Nor does it tell you if your new entries don't meet the conditions that you previously set. It also doesn't tell you that if you edited a portion of your worksheet that wasn't included in your conditional format settings, those edits don't have any impact on your conditional formatting. It doesn't tell you much, does it?

This all sounds like more than one source of the problem, but it isn't. When your conditional formatting doesn't change even though you've edited the worksheet such that the cell values should either return to an unformatted state (because they no longer meet your conditions) or change to a different format (because they meet a different set of conditions now that they've been edited), you've probably edited a section of the worksheet that either has no conditional formatting set or that has a set of conditions applied that you've forgotten about.

In either case, the solution lies in reviewing your conditions for the edited cells and determining if what you expect to happen is possible given the conditions you've set for the cells in question.

> **Tip**
>
> If you selected or entered a particular cell's address as your value setting for one or more of your conditions, make sure that cell's contents haven't changed. If they have, your edited cells might not meet the condition's criteria because the new value isn't the same as it was when you originally established the conditional formatting.

How to fix it

1. First determine which cells have conditional formatting applied. On the Edit menu, click Go To and then click the Special button in the Go To dialog box.

2. Click Conditional Formats in the list of options and then click All under Data Validation. This will highlight any cells in your worksheet to which conditional formatting has been applied.

3. Click OK to see which cells are highlighted. ▶

4. If there are multiple conditional formats set throughout your worksheet, select a cell or range of cells to which conditional formatting has been applied. Then repeat steps 1 and 2, but choose Same from the Data Validation options in the Go To Special dialog box. This will show only the cells with the same conditional formatting as the cells currently selected in the worksheet.

		DIVISION GOALS							
		SALES IN MILLIONS (US $)							
		2001				2002			
	Q1	Q2	Q3	Q4	Q1	Q2	Q3	Q4
Northeast	5.24	5.5	5.76	6.02	6.28	6.54	6.8	7.06
Midwest	6.35	6.45	6.55	6.65	6.75	6.85	6.95	7.05
South	2.54	2.5	2.46	2.42	2.38	2.34	2.3	2.26
Southwest	7.2	7.5	7.8	8.1	8.4	8.7	9	9.3
West	4.23	4.5	4.77	5.04	5.31	5.58	5.85	6.12
TOTALS	25.6	26.5	27.3	28.2	29.1	30.0	30.9	31.8

5. If it turns out that you are editing cells to which conditional formatting is applied, you must find out if the new content in the cells conflicts with the conditions set or if two or more conditions apply to the same cells. On the Format menu, click Conditional Formatting and review the conditions you've set in the Conditional Formatting dialog box.

Tip

If you set two conditions for one section of the worksheet, and both of them could apply to the same cells, only the first condition's formatting will be applied.

6. Perhaps the new cell values are still within the conditions; in this case no formatting change is warranted. However, if the new cell values now meet the criteria for Condition 2 as well as the criteria for Condition 1, only Condition 1's formats will be applied. To solve the problem of two or more conditions applying to the same cells, click Delete, select the check box for Condition 1, and then click OK twice.

I'm not sure how to change my conditional formats

Source of the problem

Change is a good thing, but only if you know how to make the change! If you're using someone else's workbook or you have no memory of how the conditional formatting that's in place was established, you might encounter a problem when you want to adjust the conditions or remove them altogether.

Changing or deleting conditional formats is easy, assuming you know to which cells conditional formats were applied, and how those conditions were set in the first place. This is really a two-phase solution: You start by revealing the cells to which conditions are applied, and then you go to the source of the conditional formats—the Conditional Formatting dialog box.

How to fix it

1. Unless you already know the full range of cells to which conditional formatting was applied, you must first identify the range. On the Edit menu, click Go To and then click the Special button in the Go To dialog box.

2. Select Conditional Formats from the list of options and then select All from the options under Data Validation. This will highlight any cells in your worksheet to which conditional formatting has been applied.

3. Click OK to view the worksheet and see which cells are highlighted. The cells might be in one contiguous range or scattered over much of the worksheet.

	A	B	C	D	E	F	G	H	I	J	K
1											
2											
3											
4			DIVISION GOALS								
5			SALES IN MILLIONS (US $)								
6			2001				2002				
7			Q1	Q2	Q3	Q4	Q1	Q2	Q3	Q4	
8		Northeast	5.24	5.5	5.76	6.02	6.28	6.54	6.8	7.06	
9		Midwest	6.35	6.45	6.55	6.65	6.75	6.85	6.95	7.05	
10		South	2.54	2.5	2.46	2.42	2.38	2.34	2.3	2.26	
11		Southwest	7.2	7.5	7.8	8.1	8.4	8.7	9	9.3	
12		West	4.23	4.5	4.77	5.04	5.31	5.58	5.85	6.12	
13		TOTALS	25.6	26.5	27.3	28.2	29.1	30.0	30.9	31.8	
14											

4. If there are multiple conditional formats set throughout your worksheet, select a cell or range of cells to which conditional formatting has been applied, and then repeat steps 1 and 2, but choose Same from the Data Validation options. This will show only the cells with the same conditional formatting set as the cells currently selected in the worksheet.

5. With the cells highlighted, click Conditional Formatting on the Format menu.

6. In the resulting Conditional Formatting dialog box, look at the conditions set in Condition 1 (and perhaps Condition 2 and 3 if the range of selected cells includes second and third conditions).

7. Make whatever changes you want to the operator (Greater Than, Less Than, and so on), the value (either a cell address containing a comparison value or a value typed manually into the dialog box), the formula, the formats, or all these criteria. ▶

8. If you want to remove one or more of the conditions, click the Delete button, and in the Delete Conditional Formatting dialog box, select the check boxes for any or all of the conditions you want to remove. ▶

9. Click OK to return to the Conditional Formatting dialog box and click OK again to put your changes into effect.

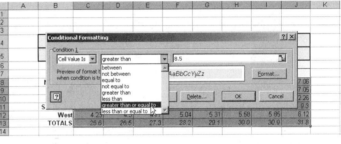

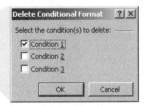

> **Tip**
>
> If more than one condition can apply to the same cell or cells, only the first condition will be applied. If you remove Condition 1 but leave Condition 2, Condition 2's formats will take the place of the previous conditional formatting applied to the cells.

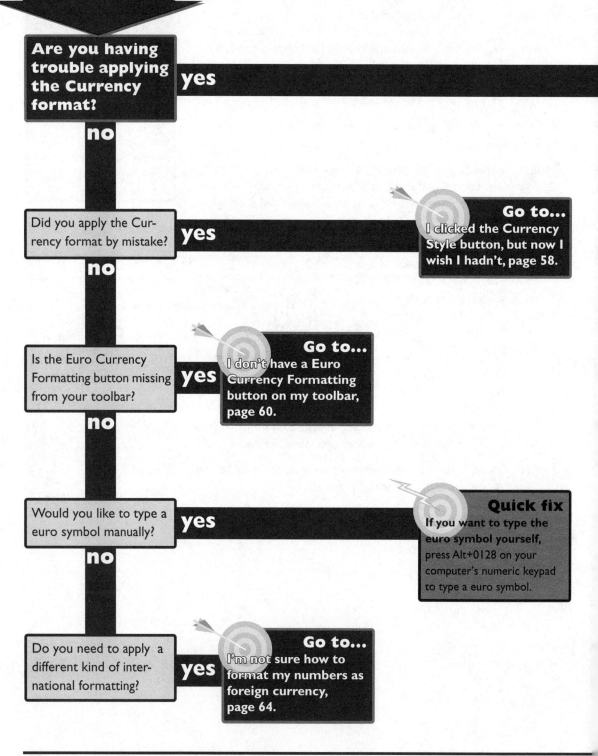

Are you having trouble applying the Currency format?

yes

no

Did you apply the Currency format by mistake?

yes

no

Go to...
I clicked the Currency Style button, but now I wish I hadn't, page 58.

Is the Euro Currency Formatting button missing from your toolbar?

yes

no

Go to...
I don't have a Euro Currency Formatting button on my toolbar, page 60.

Would you like to type a euro symbol manually?

yes

no

Quick fix
If you want to type the euro symbol yourself, press Alt+0128 on your computer's numeric keypad to type a euro symbol.

Do you need to apply a different kind of international formatting?

yes

Go to...
I'm not sure how to format my numbers as foreign currency, page 64.

Currency

Have your numbers turned into pound signs?

yes

no

Quick fix

If your numbers now appear as pound signs, it's because your numbers are too wide for the column. Double-click the seam to the right of the column heading (the letter at the top of the column), and the column will size to meet the needs of your numbers.

Do your numbers have decimal places that you don't want?

yes

no

Quick fix

To reduce the number of displayed decimal places, follow these steps.

1. Select the cells containing numbers with unwanted decimal places.

2. Click the Decrease Decimal button on the formatting toolbar until the decimal places are reduced as needed.

Has the number you entered changed since you applied the Currency format?

yes

Go to...

When I press Enter, the number I typed changes, page 62.

If your solution isn't here, check these related chapters:

- Formatting numbers, page 146
- Formulas, page 178
- Functions, page 192

Or see the general troubleshooting tips on page xv.

I clicked the Currency Style button, but now I wish I hadn't

Source of the problem

It's easy to accidentally click the wrong button on a toolbar—there's not a lot of wiggle room between the buttons, and even though Microsoft Office XP's buttons are highlighted as you point to them, you can still misfire and click the wrong one. Say you wanted to see the zeroes after the decimal point in a cell or range, and instead of clicking the Increase Decimal button, you clicked the Currency Style button. Or maybe you didn't click the wrong button at all—you might have *thought* you wanted to format the numbers as currency, and now you wish you hadn't. Whether the click was accidental or the result of a moment of impetuous formatting, it's often easy to resolve—simply click the Undo button.

But what if the click wasn't the last thing you did, and you don't want to undo the other stuff you've done to your worksheet since then? If that's the case, the resolution gets slightly more involved. Slightly. We're talking about opening a dialog box and making a selection, so don't worry—your numbers will be back to non-currency status in no time at all!

How to fix it

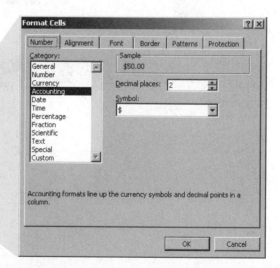

1. If necessary, reselect the cells that were incorrectly formatted as currency.

2. Right-click the selection and then click **Format Cells** on the shortcut menu. The **Format Cells** dialog box appears.

3. Click the Number tab, if necessary, to display numeric formatting options. ▶

4. To set the cells back to the default format, click General in the Category list.

5. Click OK to close the dialog box and change the formatting of the selected cells.

If you meant to click the Percentage Style button when you accidentally clicked Currency Style, there's no need to go back to General format—just choose Percentage from the Category list.

Who said Accounting?

When you go to the Format Cells dialog box to change the formatting back to General, you'll notice that Accounting is the format that's in force. You'd think it would be Currency, but that's not the case. You have to apply that format directly from the Format Cells dialog box—clicking the Currency Style button on the Formatting toolbar does not apply the Currency format.

Funny money

If you don't find a currency format that you like, you can create your own. Click Custom in the Category list of the Format Cells dialog box to see the Type section, which displays options for creating formats for currency, dates, times, and so forth. ▶

To create your custom format, use any of the following symbols or abbreviations to designate the parts of a number and how you want them displayed in your worksheet.

Your two cents

If you want to include decimal places for selected cells, click Number instead of General in the Category list of the Format Cells dialog box. In the Decimal Places box, specify the number of decimal places you want to display. If you like, choose a comma separator or negative number format in the section below the Decimal Places box, and then click OK.

For example, if you select #,##0.00 from the Type list and change it in the Type box to #,###.00, your customized format will apply commas for numbers in the thousands, display two decimal places, and won't insert a zero if the number has no digits to the right of the decimal.

Symbol	Stands for
#	A number
?.?	Decimal numbers with the decimals aligned
?/?	Fractions with the division symbols aligned
$	A dollar sign to be added to the number
h:	Hours
mm:	Minutes
ss	Seconds
d	Days
m	Month
y	Year
@	Text after the number (for example, " units"@)

Tip

If you find yourself hitting the Currency Style button a lot by accident, try dragging it to a new location on the toolbar—somewhere farther away from frequently used buttons. Hold down the Alt key, drag the toolbar button to a new location on either the Standard or Formatting toolbar, and then release the Alt key.

I don't have a Euro Currency Formatting button on my toolbar

Source of the problem

If your version of Office isn't specifically for the European Union, you won't find the Euro button on the Formatting toolbar by default. The default installation of Microsoft Excel 2002 does offer euro currency formatting on the Number tab of the Format Cells dialog box, but you need to select the Euro button from a list of add-ins before it will appear on the Formatting toolbar for use in quick euro-formatting.

How to fix it

1. On the Tools menu, click Add-Ins to display the Add-Ins dialog box.

2. View the list of available add-ins, and select the Euro Currency Tools check box. ▶

3. Click OK. You might be prompted to insert the Office XP installation disk to make the Euro button available if you didn't install euro support when you originally installed Office.

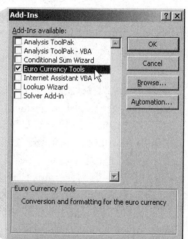

No Euro Currency Tools add-in?

If Euro Currency Tools is not on the Add-Ins Available list, you'll need to install it by using Add/Remove Programs in the Control Panel. You'll be prompted to insert the Office installation CD-ROM, and a series of dialog boxes will take you through the process of installing the tools. Once the tools are installed, you'll see the Euro button on the Formatting toolbar. ▶

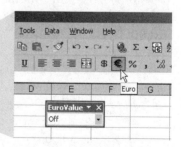

When the euro tool is added to your Formatting toolbar, you also acquire a floating Euro toolbar. If you click the drop arrow, you can choose from a variety of exchange rates by country. ▶

Tip

If your printer cannot print the euro symbol, a box rather than the symbol will appear in your printout. If this happens, contact your printer manufacturer. You might be able to get the required fonts for your printer by downloading them from the printer company's Web site, and then you'll be able to print the euro symbol.

Some fonts snub the euro

The euro symbol can be printed only in certain fonts, so beware when changing the fonts for sections of your worksheet that are formatted with the Euro button. The following commonly used fonts are euro-friendly:

- Arial
- Arial Black
- Comic Sans
- Courier New
- Impact
- MS Sans Serif
- Tahoma
- Times New Roman
- Verdana

This doesn't mean that no other fonts are friendly to the euro—many of the fonts you have on your computer will be perfectly happy to display and print the euro symbol. Just don't be shocked if some of them won't!

When I press Enter, the number I typed changes

Source of the problem

You type a number in your worksheet, and when you press Enter or Tab to confirm your cell entry, the number changes! Is it magic? A trick to mess with your mind? Nope, it's actually supposed to happen, but if you aren't expecting it or don't want it to happen, it can be an unpleasant surprise.

This phenomenon most often occurs in worksheets that someone other than you developed, or worksheets that you created and formatted some time ago. Why? Because when a number changes from what you typed to some other number, it's the result of formatting, and you might not know (or remember) what formatting was applied to the cells you're working with. Specifically, cells formatted with the Currency, Number, or Accounting formats available in the Format Cells dialog box get rounded according to the dialog box's Decimal Places setting. For example, say you type *567.85* and as soon as you press Enter, the number changes to *568*. In this case, the cell is most likely formatted to display no decimal places. Consequently, the decimal number you typed is rounded to the nearest whole number. ▶

	A	B	C	D	E	F	G	H
		Q1	Q2	Q3	Q4	Q1	Q2	Q3
Northeast		5.2	5.5	5.8	6.0	6.3	6.5	6.8
Midwest		6.4	6.5	6.6	6.7	6.8	6.9	7.0
South		2.5	2.5	2.5	2.4	2.4	2.3	2.3
Southwest		7.2	7.5	7.8	8.1	8.4	8.7	9.0
West		4.2	4.5	4.8	5.0	5.3	5.6	5.9
TOTALS		25.6	26.5	27.3	28.2	29.1	30.0	30.9

fx 5.76

The solution is simple—to have numbers appear the way you type them, you have to make sure the cells are formatted to accommodate the number of decimal places you are using. If you don't want to display decimal places but you don't want your entries to be rounded, remove the numbers to the right of the decimal (delete them from your entries) so that the number cannot be rounded.

Even when Excel doesn't *display* decimals in your worksheet, it does *store* decimal numbers in your worksheet. To make sure that a cell or cells are indeed being rounded and to see what formatting is in place, click the affected cell, and take a look at the Formula bar. If the Formula bar displays the number you typed, decimals and all, your cells are formatted to display no decimals. As a result, the numbers you typed are being rounded.

> ### Tip
> You can use the Increase Decimal button on the Formatting toolbar to add decimal places to selected cells. However, if you use it on a large range of cells (an entire column, for example), be sure that the top cells of the range contain numbers, and not blank space or letters. Otherwise, the button won't work. This applies to the Decrease Decimal button as well.

How to fix it

1. Select the cell or cells in which your numbers are being rounded.

2. Right-click the selection and click Format Cells on the shortcut menu.

3. On the Number tab, increase the decimal places to 2. ▶

4. Click OK.

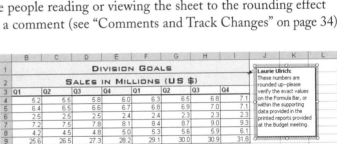

Well-rounded worksheets

When working with large currency amounts, it can be distracting to have cents (or their equivalents in other currencies) displayed, not to mention that columns have to be much wider to accommodate the additional numbers. For these reasons, people often don't want decimal places to appear. If you also don't want rounding to occur, you can refrain from entering any decimal places, as previously suggested. If you want to enter them but don't want them to be displayed, you must use the rounding option. You can, however, alert the people reading or viewing the sheet to the rounding effect with a prominently placed text box or a comment (see "Comments and Track Changes" on page 34) inserted into the worksheet title indicating that the worksheet contains rounded numbers. ▶

Tip

To insert a text box, click the Drawing button on the Standard toolbar and then click the Text Box button on the Drawing toolbar that appears. Use the crosshair pointer to draw a text box and then start typing.

I'm not sure how to format my numbers as foreign currency

Source of the problem

When you click the Currency Style button or apply the Currency formatting, the currency formatting that is applied by default is based on the regional settings for your installation of Microsoft Windows. If you live in the United States, your currency format is likely dollars and cents. If you often work with a different currency, this default won't be appropriate some or all of the time.

For example, currency in the United Kingdom uses periods where commas are used in U.S. currency (£1.000 is one thousand British pounds). With Excel, you can change the symbol in front of your currency amounts, but that's about it. So you can change a dollar sign to a pound sign, but that won't make Excel give up the commas for periods. To be able to apply foreign currency formats with the appropriate monetary symbols and use of commas and decimals for various national denominations, you need to change the Windows Regional Settings.

How to fix it

To change the currency symbol in Excel, follow these steps:

1. Select the cells that you want to format with a different national currency symbol.

2. Right-click the selection and then click Format Cells on the shortcut menu.

3. In the Format Cells dialog box, click the Number tab if necessary.

4. In the Category list, click Currency if you don't need the currency symbols and decimal points to align, or click Accounting if you do.

5. Click the Symbol drop-down list.

6. Scroll through the list and select a currency symbol. (The country's name appears next to the currency symbol.) ▶

7. In the Decimal Places box, type or scroll to the number of decimal places you want to display.

8. If appropriate, click a format in the Negative Numbers list and then click OK.

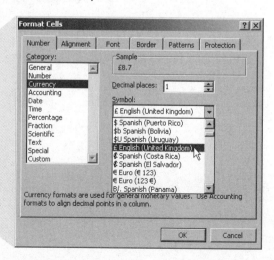

Currency

To change the Windows Regional Settings so that your currency is in a different format by default, follow these steps, as seen in a Windows 2000 environment. (Your commands and dialog box names will differ slightly if you're working in Windows 98.)

1. Click the Start button, point to Settings, click Control Panel, and then double-click Regional Options.

2. On the General tab of the Regional Options Properties dialog box, select a country from the drop-down list. (Keep in mind that the country you choose will affect the way the time and date appear on the Windows taskbar; how dates, times, and currency symbols appear in other Office applications; and how the default dictionary checks spelling.) ▶

3. Click the Currency tab and view the options in the Currency Symbol, Decimal Symbol, and Digit Grouping Symbol drop-down lists. If more than one is available for the selected country, the alternative(s) will appear when you click the drop-down arrows. ▶

4. When your default settings are the way you want them to be, click OK. You'll be alerted that the changes won't take place until you restart your computer.

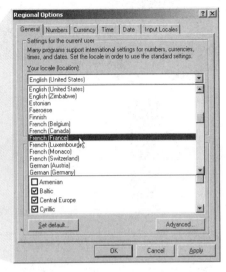

Tip

You can change your regional settings temporarily so that your worksheet formatting is appropriate for a particular currency. You might change them before creating a worksheet, save or print the worksheet so that you can distribute it to interested parties, and then restore the default regional settings for your version of Windows.

Tip

Be careful when changing your regional settings. Your outgoing e-mail messages will appear in the time format of the country you select, and this might be confusing to some of your e-mail recipients. If it's possible to get by with just changing the currency symbol and not adjusting your regional settings, you should consider taking this "path of least resistance."

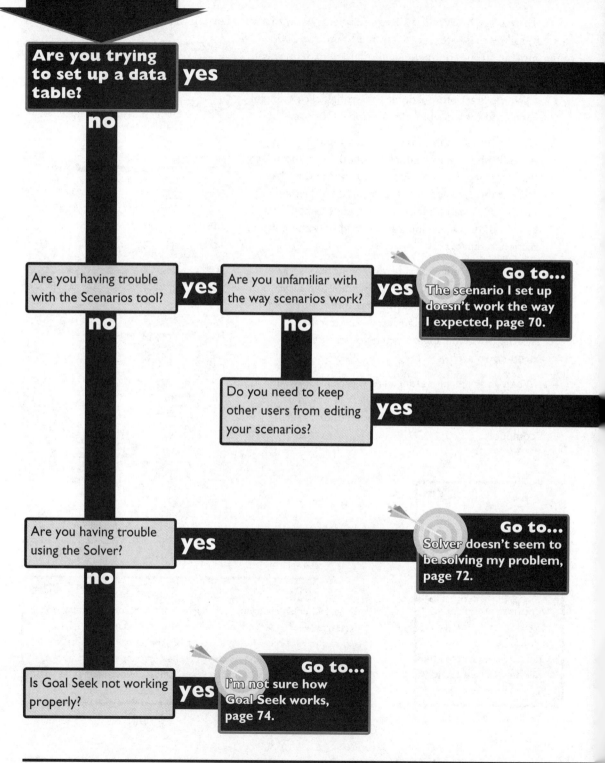

Are you trying to set up a data table?

yes

no

Are you having trouble with the Scenarios tool?

yes

Are you unfamiliar with the way scenarios work?

yes

Go to...
The scenario I set up doesn't work the way I expected, page 70.

no

no

Do you need to keep other users from editing your scenarios?

yes

Are you having trouble using the Solver?

yes

Go to...
Solver doesn't seem to be solving my problem, page 72.

no

Is Goal Seek not working properly?

yes

Go to...
I'm not sure how Goal Seek works, page 74.

Data analysis

Do you get an error message when you try to set up the table?

yes → **Go to...** I get an error message when I try to set up a data table, page 68.

no

Do you want to prevent your data table from recalculating when your worksheet opens?

yes → **Quick fix**
Change the Calculation options for your worksheet by choosing Tools, Options. Click the Calculation tab and choose the Automatic Except Tables option, and then click OK.

Quick fix
To protect your scenarios from unwanted edits, choose Tools, Scenarios and check the Prevent Changes option in the Scenarios dialog box. You can also Hide a scenario by selecting it and clicking the Hide checkbox.

If your solution isn't here, check these related chapters:

- Entering data, page 108
- Filtering records, page 136
- Sorting data, page 310

Or see the general trouble-shooting tips on page xv.

I get an error message when I try to set up a data table

Source of the problem

Data tables are a valuable tool—if you can structure your worksheet properly and provide the right information in the Table dialog box. If your structure or information, or both, are incorrect, an error message will result—telling you that your instructions for building the table are incorrect. To avoid getting this error message, it's important to have a clear understanding of what data tables are and what they do. From the examples here, you should be able to build your own or fix the ones you might have tried to build—you know, the one that gave you the error message that sent you to this book! ▶

First, what is a data table? It's a range of cells that take a formula and one or more of its contributing cells and sets up a series of alternate results to that formula based on alternate entries into the cells used in that formula. For example, if you have a product for which you're considering raising the price, you might want to set up a worksheet that shows you the new price at a variety of increase percentages—if you increase the price by 20 percent, the new price will be this, and if you increase the price by 25 percent, the new price will be that. Rather than set up a series of formulas and variables for them (in this case, the multiplier is the variable, as the current price is a fixed amount), you can set up a data table that tells Microsoft Excel where the alternate multipliers are, and it performs a copy of the sample formula on each of the variable amounts, also using the contents of the fixed cell. ▶

In the sample on this page, the data table includes a series of multipliers (the amounts by which cell F8 is multiplied to get the New Price) in cell H8, H9, and so

	D	E	F	G	H
6		Price Increase			
7		Product Name	Current Price	Increase	New Price
8		Gizzmo	$ 5.00	1.5	$ 7.50
9				1.75	$ 8.75
10				2	$ 10.00
11				2.25	$ 11.25
12				2.5	$ 12.50
13				2.75	$ 13.75
14				3	$ 15.00
15					

on down column H for every alternate multiplier. The data table is the range of cells from G8 through H14.

Microsoft Excel dialog: Input cell reference is not valid. OK

How to fix it

If your data table is already set up, fixing it requires making sure that the variables are in the right place and that you specify them properly when asked to identify the location of the variables. If you haven't built your data table yet, the key to building it successfully is to make sure the worksheet is structured correctly. To build a table properly, follow these steps:

Data analysis

1. Type your column headings that identify the parts of your worksheet.

2. Type the fixed amount into the worksheet. This might be the amount of a loan, the current price of a product, the current number of sales you're generating, or the number of employees you have.

3. In another cell (the specific cell you choose is dictated by your worksheet layout), enter a starting variable—something by which the fixed amount is calculated to achieve some result. In the case of a price change, it's the percentage by which the current price will be multiplied to come up with a new price.

4. In another cell, again dictated by your worksheet layout, create the formula that will use the fixed amount and the variable. This cell will contain the result of the calculation that uses your fixed amount and the variable.

5. Enter the variables that will be used in the data table's copies of the formula. These numbers should be placed in a column or row beneath the fixed amount, starting variable, and formula.

With your worksheet set up, you can proceed to turn it into an actual data table:

1. Select the range of cells containing your fixed amount, starting variable, and formula, plus the cells containing your additional variables. Select the range as a block rather than gather cells with the Ctrl key. It's okay if you have blank cells in the range.

2. Choose Table from the Data menu. The Table dialog box opens. ▶

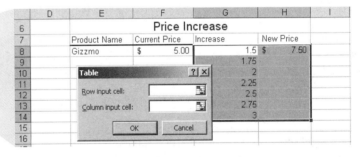

3. If your variables are in a row, click in the Row Input Cell box. If they're in a column, click in the Column Input Cell box.

4. Click in your worksheet, indicating the input cell you want to use for the variables. This is normally the first cell in the series of variables in the row or column.

5. Click OK.

After you click OK, the calculations are performed and the results are inserted into the worksheet based on the variables you entered. If you enter new variables in place of the old ones, the calculations will update, showing you new results. To get rid of the table and start over—maybe you set it up wrong or just want to redesign the worksheet—just select the range of cells that includes the variables and their results and press the Delete key.

The scenario I set up doesn't work the way I expected

Source of the problem

The Scenarios tool is very handy if you need to play "what if?" games with your data. The feature is fairly foolproof, but inadequate planning and simple mistakes in selecting cells and ranges can result in a scenario that either gives incorrect results or doesn't work at all. It's one of those annoying "garbage in, garbage out" situations where Excel is just doing what you ask it to. If you ask it to do something wrong, you get the wrong results.

If you've already experienced a problem with a scenario, the best and quickest way to fix it is to delete the existing scenario and start over. To delete a scenario, choose Tools, Scenarios and, in the dialog box, click once on the scenario by name and then click the Delete button. With the bad scenario gone, you can focus on not creating a bad one again, and that involves a thorough understanding of scenarios—what they do and how they do it. ▶

Scenarios are situations you set up by saying, "If I change this cell to contain this number, what happens to my worksheet formula?" For example, if you're tracking performance for a group of employees and you know they have a goal of producing a certain level of sales or a certain number of products, you can set up scenarios that change the conditions that contribute to achieving the goal. What if you assign more employees to the task? What if you have them work more hours? You can set up a *More Employees* scenario that will insert a new number of workers into the worksheet, enabling you to see production results for 20 people as opposed to 15. If you want to see what happens if they work more hours, set up a *Work More* scenario that increases their *Hours Worked* field to 45 rather than 40 hours per week.

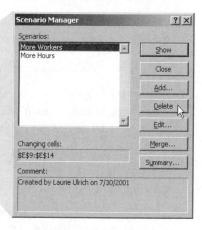

You can create as many scenarios as you want, changing virtually any data in your worksheet—as long as the data is used in a formula—so that changing it will have some impact. Changing employee names, for example, won't be of much use, but changing product numbers (for the products they have to produce) might, if the formula that calculates projected productivity uses the product number in some way.

How to fix it

To set up a scenario properly from the start, follow these steps:

1. In the worksheet containing the data to which the scenario should apply, choose Tools, Scenarios.

2. In the Scenarios dialog box, click the Add button to create a new scenario.

3. In the Add Scenario dialog box, type a name for your new scenario and then either type the cell or range of cells that you want to change into the Changing Cells field or click the Shrink button at the end of that field to select the cells on the worksheet. ▶

4. As needed, augment the existing Comment to describe the purpose or goal of the scenario.

5. If you don't want anyone to be able to change your scenario, leave the Prevent Changes check box checked. If you want to hide the scenarios (to prevent anyone seeing the scenarios at all), click the Hide option. For either or both of these options to take effect, the worksheet must be protected (choose Tools, Protection, Protect Sheet).

6. Click OK to move to the next step and view the Scenario Values dialog box. ▶

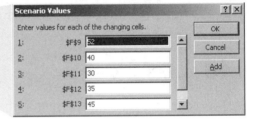

7. Enter the values that this scenario should insert for each of the cells you selected in the Changing Cells field. You can use the Tab key to move through the fields quickly.

8. Click OK to complete the scenario or Add to complete this scenario and go back to the Scenarios dialog box to add another scenario.

Imagine...

So you've added the scenario, and now you want to use it. To play your "what if?" game, simply choose Tools, Scenarios and choose the one you want to use. Click that scenario by name and then click the Show button. Your data changes, now including the data you entered into the Scenario Values dialog box, and any formulas based on those cells update as well.

To restore your data to its pre-scenario state, you can click the Undo button (or press Ctrl+Z) to undo the application of the scenario to your data. If that's not possible, you can create a scenario that puts your original data back—something you might want to do before creating the scenarios that change the data in the first place. If you didn't do this ahead of time, simply create a new scenario after the fact, called *Original Data*—and enter your original data into the Scenario Values dialog box. You can save the scenario for use in restoring your worksheet to its original values.

Solver doesn't seem to be solving my problem

Source of the problem

"Solver" is quite a name to live up to. You'd think you could type in "I can't get my spouse to take out the garbage" and it would respond with a list of foolproof suggestions. Well, it's not quite that wonderful, but it is pretty useful when it comes to setting up a worksheet that shows you how to achieve a desired result. This should not cause you to confuse Solver's purpose with that of Goal Seek, yet another of Excel's data analysis tools. Solver works by showing how different data will affect your bottom line. If you want to increase profits and your profit numbers are based on sales less expenses, Solver will insert alternate sales and expense numbers (based on any constraints you choose to impose to assure a realistic solution) and a higher profit is the result.

If you've attempted to use Solver and haven't seen the results you expected, the problem probably lies with the information you provided when asking Solver for a solution. It's easy to select the wrong cells and to enter inaccurate constraints, so don't feel bad.

How to fix it

To use Solver, first take a look at your worksheet and make sure you're clear in your own mind about the formula(s) in it and which data contributes to the results of those formulas. Only those cells can be altered with Solver, and you need to tell Solver what limits are appropriate. For example, if you want higher profits but know that expenses can't be reduced by more than 30 percent, include that in your Solver setup by setting up a constraint on your expense numbers. No sense hearing that if you reduce expenses by 50 percent that profits will rise if it's impossible to cut expenses that much. After this small amount of planning and preparatory analysis, you're ready to set up a solution with Solver:

1. In the worksheet that requires a solution, choose Tools, Solver.

2. In the Solver Parameters dialog box, tell Solver which cell's contents should change—this represents the solution you're looking for. Click in the Target Cell field and then click a cell on the worksheet to indicate where the solution should appear. ▶

3. In the Equal To options, choose the Max, Min, or specific Value Of for the Target cell.

Data analysis

4. Type a range of cells into the By Changing Cells box. You can also click the Shrink button to reduce the size of the dialog box temporarily or drag the dialog box aside so you can drag through the cells that should be changed in order to provide the desired solution.

5. If there are Constraints, such as the fact that the Sales Salaries can't be increased or there's a budget cap on advertising, click the Add button and use the resulting Add Constraint dialog box to tell Solver which cells can't exceed a given amount. ▶

6. After setting up any Constraints, click OK in the Add Constraints dialog box and return to the Solver Parameters dialog box.

7. Click Solve to close the dialog box and see what solution Solver has in mind for your particular "problem."

8. Once the solution is inserted into the By Changing Cells range and the Target Cell is altered accordingly, Excel prompts you, asking if you want to keep the results of the Solver "solution." You can choose Keep Solver Solution or Restore Original Values. If you'd prefer, you can save the data inserted by the Solver as a Scenario (click the Save Scenario button and then give the new scenario a name), which restores the worksheet to original status. You can do this as well as keeping the Solver results or restoring your worksheet to its original content. ▶

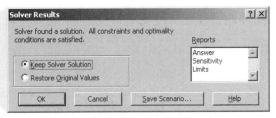

> **Tip**
>
> Notice the Guess button in the Solver Parameters dialog box? If you click it without entering anything into the By Changing Cells dialog box, Solver will guess which cells should be changed in order to alter the content of the target cell appropriately.

> **Tip**
>
> Before you do any data analysis or use any Excel feature that will alter your data in any way, save the workbook you're in. That way, if you accept the results of the Solver (or the calculations of a data table or the meddling of a scenario), you can close the file without saving rather than having to reconstruct the worksheet to its preanalysis state.

I'm not sure how Goal Seek works

Source of the problem

Excel's Goal Seek feature can be as problematic as the things you try when pursing a real-life goal. You think you know the way, but when you perform a specific task or try something, it doesn't get you closer to your goal. Sometimes the goal simply isn't attainable and you blame the process. With Excel, you can run into problems using Goal Seek if you (a) aren't sure of your goal, (b) have set the wrong goal, so when you achieve it you think, "That's not what I wanted!", or (c) give Goal Seek the wrong instructions. ▶

The solution to using Goal Seek, therefore, is to understand how it works and to make sure you know what your goal actually is.

	A	B	C	D	E	F	G	H	I
4		Sales Analysis							
5		Second Quarter							
6			Sales Revenue	Cost of Sales					
7			Gross Sales	Sales Payroll	Advertising	Marketing	Gross Profit		
8		New York	52975438	549350	35000	1450	52389638		
9		Philadelphia	43892359	450670	25450	25650	43390589		
10		Boston	33489123	325650	45670	2350	33115453		And this
11		Chicago	25763092	375470	238946	13457	25135219		number is the
12		Houston	15789234	430570	36550	2750	15319364		one that's most
13		Phoenix	24567812	250750	25975	14750	24276337		likely to change
14		San Francisco	12349865	275450	350750	27650	11696015		
15		TOTALS	208826923	2657910	758341	88057	205322615		
16									
17		Changing the cost of			This number				
18		sales numbers for the			needs to be				
19		New York office will help			higher				
20		achieve our goal.							

Sheet1 / Sheet2 / Sheet3

How to fix it

To fix your misunderstanding about Goal Seek, let's go through the Goal Seek process, step by step:

1. In the worksheet for which you need help attaining a goal, choose Tools, Goal Seek.

2. Using the Goal Seek dialog box, enter the address of the cell that needs to change in the Set Cell field. This is the cell that, if your goal were reached, would contain a specific number—say, $1,000,000 in sales, a total expense percentage of just 35 percent, and a total payroll of $25,000,000. ▶

   Goal Seek
   - Set cell: G8
   - To value: 60000000
   - By changing cell: $D$8

   OK   Cancel

3. In the To Value field, enter the goal—the number you want to see in the Set Cell field.

4. In the By Changing Cell field, enter the address of the cell that needs to change in order for your goal to be achieved. If, for example, your total gross profit needs to be $60,000,000 and you know that your advertising expense needs to come down in order for that to happen, enter the cell address of the cell containing your total advertising expense.

5. Click OK. Goal Seek goes to work and instantly changes the content of both the By Changing Cell field and the Set Cell field. A dialog box appears, informing you of your success. If you click OK, the changes are applied. If you click Cancel, the worksheet is unaffected. ▶

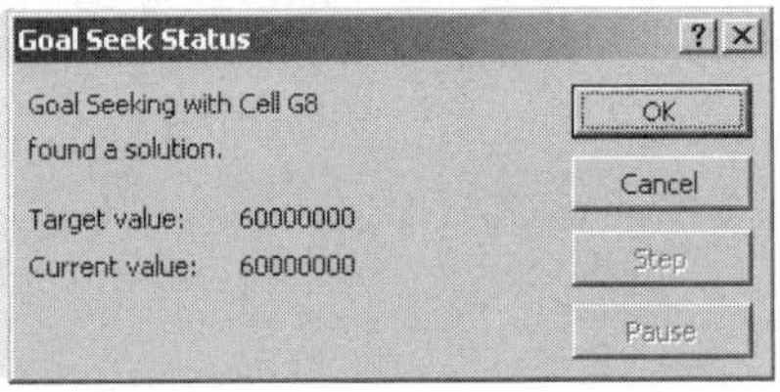

Goal Seek Status ? X

Goal Seeking with Cell G8 found a solution.

Target value: 60000000
Current value: 60000000

OK
Cancel
Step
Pause

If you don't like the change in your data that makes the goal possible— unlike Solver, you can't tell Goal Seek that the By Changing Cell field can only go as high as X or as low as Y—you can simply click the Undo button to remove the change and return your Set Cell field to its pre-Goal Seek content. If the Goal Seek Status dialog box is still open, you can click the Cancel button to prevent the solution from being applied.

If you want to try again, just repeat the steps and try a different goal or a different By Changing Cell field, or both. Sometimes changing your goal to a more attainable one makes the changes you need to make more realistic.

Tip

You can move the dialog box out of the way to click in the Set Cell and By Changing Cell fields if you don't know the address off the top of your head. You can also use the Shrink button at the end of each of those fields, but it's kind of unnecessary—the Goal Seek dialog box is rather small and simply dragging it aside (drag it by its title bar) should be sufficient.

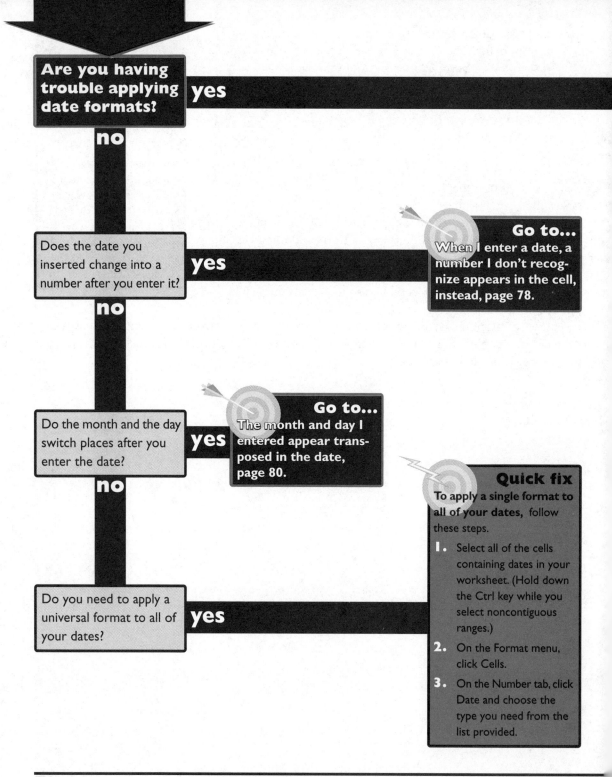

Are you having trouble applying date formats?

yes

no

Does the date you inserted change into a number after you enter it?

yes

no

Go to...
When I enter a date, a number I don't recognize appears in the cell, instead, page 78.

Do the month and the day switch places after you enter the date?

yes

no

Go to...
The month and day I entered appear transposed in the date, page 80.

Do you need to apply a universal format to all of your dates?

yes

Quick fix
To apply a single format to all of your dates, follow these steps.

1. Select all of the cells containing dates in your worksheet. (Hold down the Ctrl key while you select noncontiguous ranges.)

2. On the Format menu, click Cells.

3. On the Number tab, click Date and choose the type you need from the list provided.

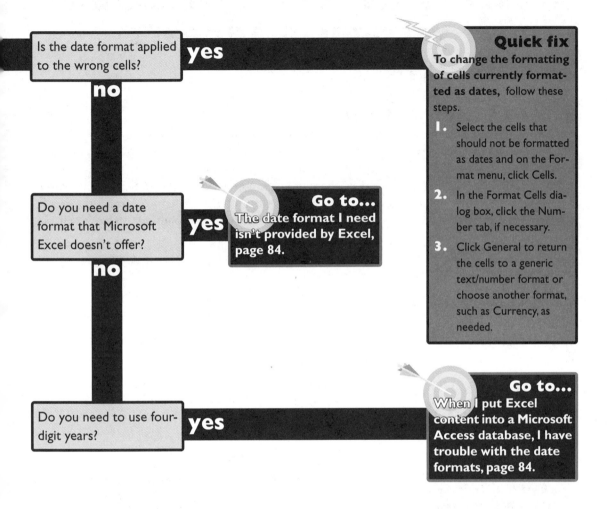

Is the date format applied to the wrong cells?

yes

no

Do you need a date format that Microsoft Excel doesn't offer?

yes

no

Do you need to use four-digit years?

yes

Go to...
The date format I need isn't provided by Excel, page 84.

Quick fix
To change the formatting of cells currently formatted as dates, follow these steps.

1. Select the cells that should not be formatted as dates and on the Format menu, click Cells.

2. In the Format Cells dialog box, click the Number tab, if necessary.

3. Click General to return the cells to a generic text/number format or choose another format, such as Currency, as needed.

Go to...
When I put Excel content into a Microsoft Access database, I have trouble with the date formats, page 84.

If your solution isn't here, check these related chapters:

- Entering data, page 108
- Formatting numbers, page 146
- Formatting worksheets, page 168

Or see the general troubleshooting tips on page xv.

When I enter a date, a number I don't recognize appears in the cell

Source of the problem

You enter *4/27* into a cell but instead of *27-April* or *4/27* (or whatever date format you expect to see), you get *37373*. What's going on? If you type an accepted date format, such as *3/15*, *3-15*, or *3/15/00* into a cell that has been formatted with another numeric format, you won't see a date—you'll see a number that fits Microsoft Excel's interpretation of what you typed, based on the formatting in force in that cell. For example, if the cell has the General or Number format, the date will be translated into an ordinary number. If it has the Currency or Accounting format, it will have a dollar sign. Other formats, such as Percentage or Scientific, will also result in glaringly obvious non-date numbers. ▶

Cell formatting is very easy to apply, so applying the wrong format can happen frequently. To solve the problem, there is no need to reenter the dates—just change the format of the cells to the Date format that meets your needs.

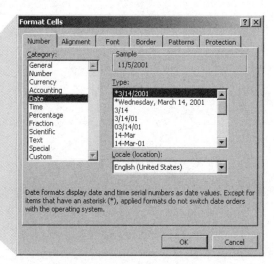

How to fix it

1. Select the cells that aren't showing up as dates.

2. Right-click the selection and then click Format Cells on the shortcut menu.

3. In the Format Cells dialog box, click the Number tab, if necessary. Click Date in the Category list, and then in the Type list, click the appropriate format for how you want the date to be stored and displayed. ▶

4. Click OK to apply the format you chose to the selected cells. (If Excel still doesn't recognize the numbers as dates, you might have to retype the dates to make them appear in the format you want.)

Dates

Keep it to yourself

Suppose all the dates you want to enter are in the current year, and displaying the year would be redundant. You can choose to enter the entire date (month, day, and year) but to display only the month and day. Select the cells in which you want to apply the format, right-click the selection, and click Format Cells on the shortcut menu. Click Date in the Category list, and in the Type list, click one of the formats that display only the month and day (such as 3/14 or 14-Mar). Then click OK. Even if the dates you enter contain the year, they will appear in the cells as only the month and day. However, they will appear as you typed them (with years) in the Formula bar. ▶

If necessary, you can always display the full date later by repeating the steps for displaying the Number tab of the Format Cells dialog box and then choosing a date format that includes the year before clicking OK.

	A	B	C
		A6	▼	fx 11/5/2001
1			
2		Travel Expenses
3			
4		Sales	Marketing
5	Week Starting:		
6	5-Nov	$ 2,573.29	$ 2,135.00
7	12-Nov	$ 2,560.50	$ 2,400.50
8	19-Nov	$ 4,576.51	$ 2,986.00
9	26-Nov	$ 3,574.90	$ 3,411.50
10	Month Total:	$ 13,285.20	$ 10,933.00
11			

Tip

If you open a blank, new workbook (based on the blank workbook template), the entry *5/10* will display as 10-May. This isn't because the cells are formatted for dates, but because the General format that's in place is fairly intuitive in dealing with your entries and made a good guess based on what you typed. If you had typed *5-10*, 10-May would also result.

Tip

If you don't see the AutoFill handle in the bottom right corner of the selected cell(s), you need to turn on drag-and-drop editing. On the Tools menu, click Options and display the Edit tab. Select the Allow Cell Drag And Drop option and click OK.

Follow that format

Need to quickly include a list of dates in your worksheet, such as all the dates in a given month? Type the first two dates, such as *3/1* and *3/2*, and format those cells as you want all dates in the list to appear. Next select both cells, and using the AutoFill handle (the cross-shaped pointer that appears in the bottom right corner of the selected cells), drag downward through the adjoining cells in the column to fill in the remaining dates. Excel knows how many days are in each month, so when, for example, you drag past the cell containing 3/31, the next cell will contain 4/1. You can also set up a series of dates based on a weekly or biweekly pattern, such as every Monday (for a meeting schedule or weekly expense report), and let AutoFill complete the series based on just two weeks' dates as example. ▶

	A	B
4		Sales
5	Week Starting:	
6	5-Nov	$ 2,573.29
7	12-Nov	$ 2,560.50
8	19-Nov	$ 4,576.51
9	26-Nov	$ 3,574.90
10	3-Dec	
11	10-Dec	
12	17-Dec	
13	24-Dec	
14	31-Dec	
15	7-Jan	
16	14-Jan	21-Jan
17	21-Jan	
18		
19		

The month and day I entered appear transposed in the date

Source of the problem

Even if you format cells to store and display dates, there can still be some surprises. By default, when you type a date such as *December 10*, Excel displays it as *10-Dec*, with the day first, followed by the month. This differs from some preferred date formats, especially in the United States, where dates are commonly written or typed with the month first, followed by the day. ▶

Can you change this default? Well, no, you can't change the list of date formats Excel offers by default, but you can create a format that meets your needs for a month-day display and make that format available for current and future cell formatting. Creating a new Number format requires specifying

the structure for a cell entry, such as *mmm-dd* for a date that should appear as *Mar-15*. The *mmm* represents the first three letters of the month's name, and the *-dd* indicates that a dash and the day should follow the month.

	A	B	C	D	E
A11		fx 12/10/2002			
1					
2		Travel Expenses by Department			
3					
4		Sales	Marketing	Info. Tech	Operations
5	Week Starting:				
6	5-Nov	$ 2,573.29	$ 2,135.00	$ 58.65	$ 298.75
7	12-Nov	$ 2,560.50	$ 2,400.50	$ 204.38	$ 302.50
8	19-Nov	$ 4,576.51	$ 2,986.00	$ 350.11	$ 306.25
9	26-Nov	$ 3,574.90	$ 3,411.50	$ 495.84	$ 310.00
10	3-Dec				
11	10-Dec				
12	17-Dec				

How to fix it

1. Select the cells where the new date format should apply.

2. Right-click the selection and then click **Format Cells** on the shortcut menu.

3. In the Format Cells dialog box, click the Number tab if necessary and then click Custom in the Category list.

4. Type the format you want to create in the Type box. For example, if you want dates to be displayed as Dec-10 when you enter 12/10, 12-10, or December 10, create the custom format mmm-dd. ▶

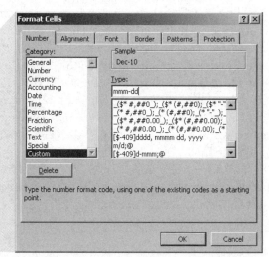

5. Click OK to apply the new date format to the selected cells.

As you like it

You can create date formats to suit any desired date display—*mmm-dd-yyyy, yyyy-mmm-dd*—any combination of month, day, and year will work. If you use two *m*'s, the month is displayed as a number, and if you use three, it is displayed as text. The format *mm-dd-yyyy* will turn an entry of *12/10/2002* into *12-10-2002* whereas *mmm-dd-yyyy* will turn *12/10/2002* into *Dec-10-2002*. If you type slashes instead of dashes in your custom format, you change the character that divides the sections of the date. If you don't want any divisional characters to appear, you can type the format as *mmm dd yyyy* with a single space between the date sections, and the entered date will appear as *Dec 10 2002*. ▶

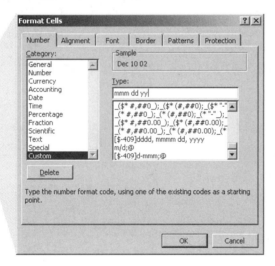

Tip

To apply the custom format to other cells after you've created it, select the cells that you want to format, right-click the selection, and then click Format Cells on the shortcut menu. In the Format Cells dialog box, make sure the Number tab is selected and then click Custom in the Category list. In the Type list of custom formats, find the format you created, click the format to select it, and then click OK to apply it.

Tip

If you want the entire name of the month to appear, such as *December* instead of *Dec*, type *m* four times in the Type box when you create a custom date format. Excel recognizes the four *m*'s as the month's full name, no matter how long or short the name actually is. For example, the format *mmmm dd yyyy* will result in a date such as *December 15 2002*, or even *May 03 2002*.

Tip

Want to see the day of the week as well? Create a formula that begins with four *d*'s, as in *dddd, mmmm dd, yyyy* to see *Wednesday, August 23, 2002* displayed in your worksheet.

The date format I need isn't provided by Excel

Source of the problem

Excel offers the most frequently used date formats, and for most users and their worksheets these formats are more than adequate. However, some people work with date formats from various countries or need to accommodate some other set of circumstances. If you fall in this special needs group, Excel's default offerings might not be sufficient.

A common problem is an inconsistency between the date that's entered and the date that Excel perceives based on that entry. This is especially apparent if you cite the day before the month. For example, if you enter dates with single-digit days—such as *2/3* for *2 March*, *7/3* for *7 March*, and *9/3* for *9 March*—Excel will interpret the entries as dates, but not those you intend—instead, Excel will interpret those entries as *February 3*, *July 3*, and *September 3*, respectively. If you enter *15 January, 2002* as *15/1/2002*, Excel will enter *15/1/2002* in left-aligned General format instead of right-aligned Date format. ▶

If this or similar situations occur when you use Excel, don't worry—you aren't stuck with forcing your data into an inappropriate format. You can create your own date formats and apply them to existing and future worksheets.

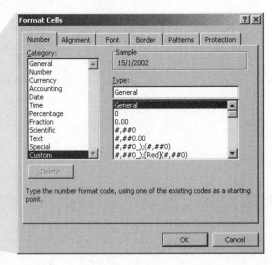

How to fix it

1. To create your own date format, select the cells to which the new format should apply, right-click the selection, and click Format Cells on the shortcut menu.

2. In the Format Cells dialog box, click the Number tab, if necessary.

3. In the Category list, click Custom. A list of existing custom formats appears in the Type list on the right side of the dialog box, along with a box into which you can type a new format. ▶

4. If necessary, select and delete the contents of the Type box, and type your own new format. Note that the dialog box suggests starting with one of the existing custom formats and then modifying it.

5. For a European date format, type a format such as dd/mm/yyyy. This format tells Excel that the first two digits entered represent the day, the second two digits represent the month, and the last four represent the year. If you prefer the month to be spelled out, increase the number of month characters to four.

6. Click OK to apply the new format. The format is saved for future use and can be found in the Type list (in the Custom Category) the next time you need to apply it.

If you have dates already entered in the cells you selected, you might have to retype the dates in the standard month-day-year format recognized by Excel so that the dates will appear with the new custom format in the worksheet.

> **Tip**
>
> If you've applied a custom format to any cells in a worksheet that others will use, it's a good idea to add a comment to one of the cells describing the format and how it displays and stores entries. (See "Comments and Track Changes" on page 34.)

> **Tip**
>
> Using four *m*'s in your date format will tell Excel to display the entire name of the month, even if there are more than four letters in the month.

Does anybody know what time it is?

If you want to enter the time along with the date, Excel offers a variety of date and time combinations in the Format Cells dialog box. You can customize these formats as needed by clicking Custom in the Category list and then typing a custom date and time format in the Type box. (You can also modify an existing format by scrolling through the Type list, clicking the closest match, and then adding or changing elements as needed in the Type box.) Click OK to implement your new format.

When devising a date and time format, remember that an *m* represents the month as long as it accompanies a *d* (for day) or a *y* (for year). If the *m* is accompanied by an *h* (for hours) or an *s* (for seconds), Excel recognizes the *m* as minutes. The format *mmmm dd, yyyy / hh:mm:ss*, for example, will display an entry typed as *3/15/2000 08:25:50* as March 15, 2000 / 08:25:50.

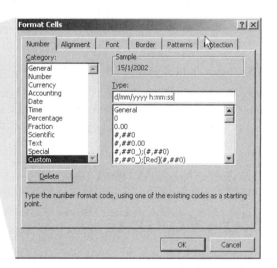

When I put Excel content into a Microsoft Access database, I have trouble with the date formats

Source of the problem

Now that we're well into the new millennium, it no longer strikes us as unusual to see years noted with four digits rather than the once familiar two (the cause of so many dire predictions as 1999 clicked into 2000). Although it's become standard operating procedure to store years as four digits, you may still find yourself working with workbooks created before the turn of the century. If you're importing or pasting your Excel worksheet's data into a Microsoft Access database that stores all four digits of the year, it's essential that your worksheet follow suit.

By default, Excel turns a two-digit year entry into a four-digit entry, even if you're working in Excel 97 or Excel 2000. For example, if you type *3/15/00* into a cell, it is stored as 3/15/2000. If you check the Formula bar (where the entry is displayed), the full four-digit year appears there, too. ▶

So what's the problem? If a format that displays only two digits for the year has been applied to cells that will contain dates, you might find that the data imported or

	A	B	C	D	E	F
	A6	▼	*fx* 11/5/2001			
1						
2		Travel Expenses by Department				
3						
4		Sales	Marketing	Info. Tech	Operations	Accounting
5	Week Starting:					
6	11/5/2001	$ 2,573.29	$ 2,135.00	$ 58.65	$ 298.75	$ 125.00
7	11/12/2001	$ 2,560.50	$ 2,400.50	$ 204.38	$ 302.50	$ 54.00
8	11/19/2001	$ 4,576.51	$ 2,986.00	$ 350.11	$ 306.25	$ 320.00
9	11/26/2001	$ 3,574.90	$ 3,411.50	$ 495.84	$ 310.00	$ 88.00
10	12/3/2001					
11	12/10/2001					

pasted into your Access database has two-digit years instead of the four digits required. The solution is simple—make sure your dates are set to store and display four-digit years if you will use the worksheet information to fill in a database outside of your current worksheet or beyond the Excel application itself.

How to fix it

1. To format all the dates in your worksheet so that the year is stored and displayed with four digits, select all of the

> **Tip**
>
> To check quickly on the format applied to any cell, right-click the cell and then click Format Cells on the shortcut menu. The Format Cells dialog box appears with the currently applied format selected. If you are truly just checking, press Esc to exit the dialog box without making any changes.

date-bearing cells. You can select nonsequential ranges by holding down the Ctrl key as you drag through blocks of cells or click individual cells.

2. Right-click the selection and then click Format Cells on the shortcut menu.

3. If necessary, click the Number tab and then click Date in the Category list.

4. Scroll through the date formats in the Type list and click a format with a four-digit year, such as 3/14/2001. ▶

5. Click OK to apply the selected format and close the dialog box.

Don't touch my yyyyears, please

If other people use your worksheet, and you don't want to risk two-digit years being entered or displayed, protect the cells that contain dates.

To apply protection and to control which cells are protected (rather than protecting the whole sheet), select cells that *can* be edited (the cells that *don't* contain dates). Right-click the selection and then click Format Cells on the shortcut menu. On the Protection tab, turn off the Locked option and click OK. On the Tools menu, point to Protection and then click Protect Sheet. In the resulting dialog box, be sure to check the Format options to prevent people from changing your date formats. You can apply a password from within the dialog box (make sure it's something you'd never forget!) and then distribute that password to people you want to be able to edit the protected cells. ▶

Once the protection is turned on, the date cells in the active worksheet will be protected from any changes. Attempts to change, delete, or add content to the protected date cells will result in an error message indicating that the cells are read-only.

Tip

If the people you're trying to keep from tinkering with your date display formats know Excel, they'll know how to turn off protection, freeing themselves to make any kind of changes they want. If protecting a worksheet is essential, always use a password—this prevents Excel-savvy users from circumventing your security.

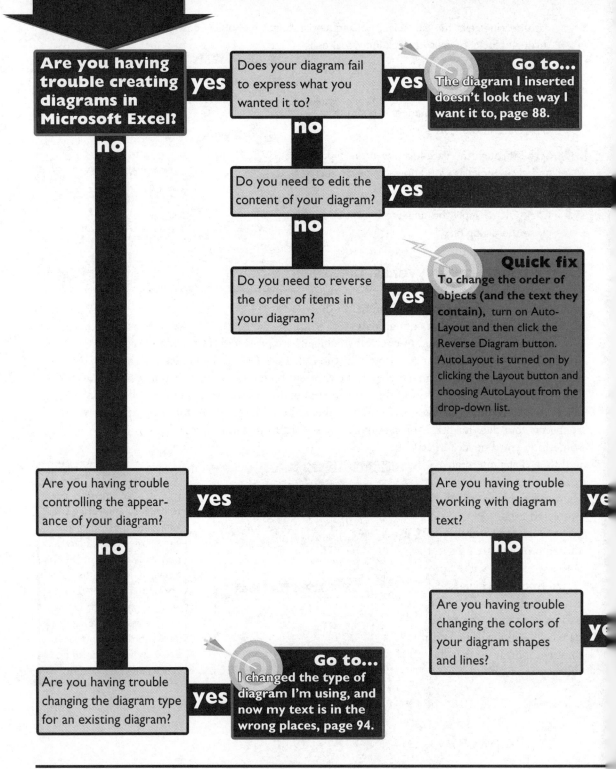

Are you having trouble creating diagrams in Microsoft Excel?

yes → Does your diagram fail to express what you wanted it to?

yes →

Go to...
The diagram I inserted doesn't look the way I want it to, page 88.

no ↓

Do you need to edit the content of your diagram?

yes →

no ↓

Do you need to reverse the order of items in your diagram?

yes →

Quick fix
To change the order of objects (and the text they contain), turn on Auto-Layout and then click the Reverse Diagram button. AutoLayout is turned on by clicking the Layout button and choosing AutoLayout from the drop-down list.

no ↓ (from first question)

Are you having trouble controlling the appearance of your diagram?

yes →

Are you having trouble working with diagram text?

ye

no ↓

Are you having trouble changing the colors of your diagram shapes and lines?

ye

Are you having trouble changing the diagram type for an existing diagram?

yes →

Go to...
I changed the type of diagram I'm using, and now my text is in the wrong places, page 94.

Diagrams

Quick fix

To edit your diagram text, simply click on the diagram shapes and begin typing new content. You can use your mouse to select existing text, use the delete and backspace keys to edit existing content, and then type replacement text as needed.

Go to...

When I add text to my diagram, it doesn't fit in the allocated space, page 90.

Go to...

I don't like the color of my diagram shapes and lines, page 92.

If your solution isn't here, check these related chapters:

- Drawing shapes and lines, page 96
- Graphics, page 204

Or see the general troubleshooting tips on page xv.

The diagram I inserted doesn't look the way I want it to

Source of the problem

Diagrams are a handy new feature in the Microsoft Office XP suite of programs. You can add them to Microsoft Word documents, Microsoft PowerPoint presentations, and Microsoft Excel worksheets. A worksheet is a great place to use a diagram, because the diagram simply and quickly conveys information that is not so easily conveyed in your worksheet cells.

For people new to creating diagrams using preset designs, the feature may take some getting used to. It may seem inflexible compared to either Excel's AutoShapes tools or some elaborate diagramming software external to the Office XP suite.

Excel offers five different diagram types, and perhaps your impression that the diagram doesn't look as you expected or wanted is because the available diagram types don't meet your needs. If this is the case, it's important to note that the diagrams can all be highly customized, and you can always add your own shapes to the basic diagram. ▶

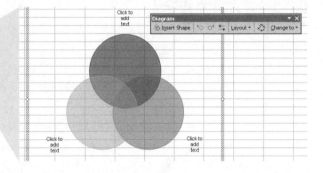

If the problem is that you feel the diagram you created doesn't tell the story or convey the message you wanted it to, it might be that you selected the wrong diagram type (easily solved, just pick a different type), you included the wrong information in the diagram (easily solved, just type new information to replace the old), or you included the right information, but in the wrong order (this is especially likely if you're using a diagram type that conveys an order of operations, such as a cycle diagram). This, too, is easily solved by editing the text and numbers you've added to your diagram.

Picking the right diagram type is one of the first and most effective ways to solve a diagram problem—whether you're encountering that problem after creating a diagram or whether you're about to create one and have no idea which kind to use. If you're using the right kind, the solution normally lies in changing the diagram's content or format.

How to fix it

To change diagram types, follow these steps:

1. Click once on your diagram to select it. The Diagram toolbar should appear. If it doesn't, right-click the diagram and choose Show Diagram Toolbar from the shortcut menu.

2. Click the Change To drop-down list. ▶

3. Pick a different diagram type. The one you're currently using is dimmed so that you don't pick it again.

4. You may be prompted to turn AutoFormat on so that the change in diagram types can proceed. Click Yes to turn it on, and the change in type you selected is applied to the diagram.

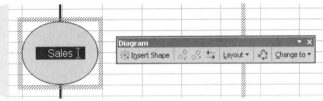

To change the content of your diagram, follow these steps:

1. Click on the diagram to select it.

2. Go to the diagram shape that contains unwanted content and, if it's a single word or number, double-click it. If it's a phrase or sentence, drag through the text. ▶

3. Type the replacement content.

4. Repeat steps 1 through 3 for each segment of the diagram until the content makes sense.

If your content is fine but the diagram needs an added shape—perhaps a text box or callout or a shape that's not part of the diagram type with which you're working—follow these steps:

1. Make sure your diagram isn't selected—click in a cell outside the diagram and make certain its handles and the border around it aren't displayed.

2. Click the AutoShapes tool, select a category, and from that category select a shape from the palette. ▶

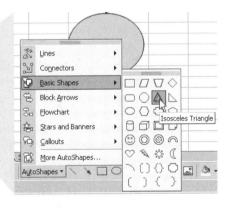

3. Draw the shape near the diagram.

4. With the shape selected, begin typing. The text you type becomes part of the shape. If the shape is a callout with a line pointing from the shape to something else, click the line and redirect it, as needed.

> **Tip**
> Once you've created a diagram and added shapes to it, you can group them by clicking once on the diagram to select it and then, with the Shift key pressed, clicking on the added shapes to select them, too. Then choose Draw, Group to make the diagram and the shapes a single unit.

When I add text to my diagram, it doesn't fit in the allocated space

Source of the problem

This problem rears its ugly head when you type text in text boxes and into AutoShapes. However, even though a diagram appears to simply be a preset arrangement of AutoShapes and text boxes and you can encounter the same problems as you do with those items, the solutions to the problems aren't the same. Moreover, a diagram may consist of AutoShapes, but unlike regular AutoShapes, you can't type directly into the shapes in a diagram—even where it appears that that's what you're doing, you're really typing into a text box placed on top of an AutoShape, and that box can't be resized.

When you type more than will fit or wrap properly in a diagram text box, because you can't resize the text box, you have to resize the entire diagram. If you can make the entire diagram bigger (if there's room for that on your worksheet), more of your text will fit because the text boxes will resize in proportion to the change in diagram size. ▶

How to fix it

To resize your diagram, follow these steps:

1. Click once on the diagram to select it. The Diagram toolbar appears. (Or, you can open it by right-clicking the diagram and choosing Show Diagram Toolbar from the shortcut menu.)

2. Click the Layout drop-down list and select Scale Diagram.

3. Using the small white circle-shaped handles that appear on the diagram corners and in the middle of each side, drag outward to make the diagram larger. If you use a corner handle, the diagram will maintain its current width-to-height proportions.

With the diagram resized, more of the existing text in any of the diagram text boxes should be visible. If there's room to do so without obscuring worksheet content, continue to resize the diagram until the text boxes are large enough to house and display all of your text.

To reformat your text so that it fits without resizing your diagram (or if you can't resize it any more than you have, yet the text boxes still aren't big enough), follow these steps:

1. Right-click the text box in question.

2. Choose Format, AutoShape from the shortcut menu.

3. In the resulting Format AutoShape dialog box, click the Font tab and adjust the font or size of the text, or both. ▶

4. As needed, click the Margins tab and reduce the internal margins on the left, right, top, or bottom of the box, or all four. In so doing, you allow more room for text.

5. Click OK to apply your changes.

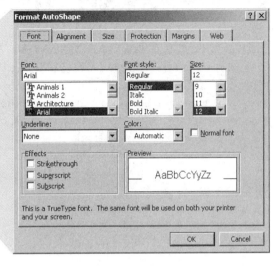

If these changes don't work, you can try a more drastic approach—leave the diagram text box blank and create your own new text box on top of the diagram box. You'll be able to size your text box because it won't be locked into the diagram's overall design. Downside? The text box might overlap the shapes and lines that make up the graphic portion of the diagram (the exact reason the diagram's text boxes aren't resizable), and you have to format the text box so that it doesn't follow the default—white interior, black border—unless that works with your diagram. If you do go with this approach, be sure to group the diagram and the added text boxes—if you don't, when you move one, the other won't follow.

More, more, more

You can always add more shapes to your diagram, providing more places to type the text that doesn't currently fit (assuming the font/size reduction and diagram scaling don't do the trick).

To add another shape to your diagram—another step in a cycle diagram, another level to a pyramid, another circle to a Venn diagram—right-click the diagram and choose Insert Shape from the shortcut menu. You can repeat this as many times as you like. You can also add shapes to a diagram through the Diagram toolbar—just click the Add Shape button and a shape will be added to the diagram, relative to the portion of the diagram that's selected at the time.

If you don't like the current stacking order of your pyramid or the order of the elements in any other kind of diagram, click the Reverse Diagram button, also found on the Diagram toolbar. This can be a very handy command if you find that you've approached your diagram content in the wrong order—placing top-priority items at the bottom of a stack or some other inadvertent reversal.

Tip

When you're reformatting your diagram text, you can use the Formatting toolbar and skip opening the Format AutoShape dialog box if you don't intend to adjust the text box's margins.

I don't like the color of my diagram shapes and lines

Source of the problem

Diagrams you create with the Office XP Insert Diagram or the Organization Chart tool adhere to some defaults in terms of appearance—the color of the shapes, the thickness of the lines, the format of the text you type into the diagram text boxes. Any or all of these defaults may not work for you—you might want a different color scheme, or you might want a whole new look for the diagram. A diagram filled with a single color can be boring and less informative than one with multiple colors— don't you agree? ►

The solution isn't to take the diagram apart and reformat all the parts individually (although this is possible). It's much easier to choose a new look from the Diagram Style Gallery. Each diagram has alternate "looks," one of which will surely go better with your worksheet's existing format. ►

Once you've applied a new format to your diagram, you can tweak individual elements, the simplest being the font applied to text in the diagram. To really take advantage of the diagram features in Office XP, it's best to work with what's there—if you spend more time customizing the preset charts, you might as well have built it from scratch by yourself!

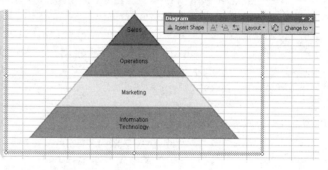

How to fix it

To change the layout of a diagram, follow these steps:

1. Click once on the diagram you have.

2. With the diagram selected (handles and a border appear on its perimeter), click the AutoFormat button on the Diagram toolbar. ►

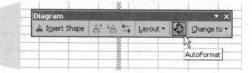

3. In the resulting Diagram Style Gallery, view the various format alternatives—simply click once on each one (the names will vary slightly depending on the diagram type you have in place) and check the sample that displays on the right side of the dialog box. ▶

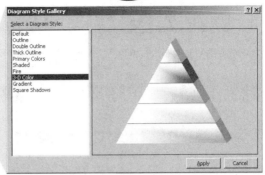

4. To select a format for your diagram, double-click it or click it once and then click the Apply button in the dialog box.

To return to the default diagram format at any time, reopen the Diagram Style Gallery and choose Default from the list of styles.

I did it my way

You can, if you feel you must, build your own diagrams from scratch. This takes much more time than using the preset diagrams through the Diagram tool, but if you really need total flexibility in terms of shapes, colors, sizes, text, and lines, or perhaps an entirely different type of diagram than those offered, you probably need to design your own.

To design your own diagram, you'll need to use the AutoShapes button on the Drawing toolbar and draw your own shapes. You can create visual connections between the shapes with lines (use the Line or Arrow tool) or by drawing arrow shapes (found in the Block Arrows category in the AutoShapes menu). ▶

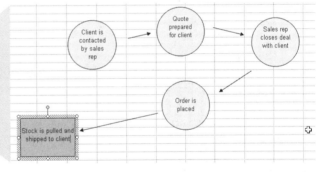

Full coverage of some of the problems you might encounter in your use of the AutoShapes tool and related features is found in the chapter entitled "Drawing shapes and lines," on page 96, but suffice it to say that all you need to do is pick your shapes, one at a time, from the AutoShapes menu categories (they're named in such a way that it's easy to figure out which category contains which types of shapes) and then draw connecting lines or arrows as needed.

You can type on any AutoShape and make the text part of the AutoShape by selecting the shape and then simply typing whatever should appear inside the shape. To control how the text wraps within the shape and how the shape relates to the text, right-click the shape and open the Format AutoShape dialog box. From within that dialog box, click the Alignment tab and turn on Automatic Size to make the shape grow to fit the text typed inside it.

> **Tip**
>
> If the toolbar didn't appear as soon as you selected the diagram, right-click the diagram and choose Show Diagram Toolbar from the resulting shortcut menu.

I changed the type of diagram I'm using, and now my text is in the wrong places

Source of the problem

The Diagram feature is pretty intuitive when it comes to positioning your text when you change from one type of diagram to another. For example, if you currently have a pyramid diagram with six levels on it and you change to a cycle diagram, there will be six segments in the diagram, each accompanied by a text box with the text from your pyramid. This indicates some level of intuition, because by default, a cycle diagram has only three segments and three accompanying text boxes. Of course, by intuition, I don't mean that the diagram will also include the seventh segment you were about to add, but it will accommodate all of the parts of your current diagram when you switch types—it builds the new chart so that it supports what's going on in the current one. ▶

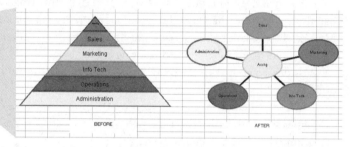

So where could this go wrong? Well, when you change diagram types, you also change the meaning of your text. For example, if you started out in a pyramid diagram, which shows priority, levels of importance, and/or relationships between things that rely on other things as their foundation, and you switch to a cycle diagram, your text will now appear in text boxes along a circle and it may appear that a process or flow of activity is implied. If your text or numerical content was in stacked order on the pyramid, you may have to rearrange it and perhaps edit it in the cycle (or other) diagram so that it's in the right order and it's telling the right story.

One obvious solution to this problem is to avoid having the problem in the first place—choosing the right diagram type up front and not building any content into it until you're sure it's right for what you want to do. If that's already a moot point because you're looking at a Venn diagram and you want it to be a target diagram or if you need to take your pyramid and turn it into an organization chart, you'll have to rearrange and edit your text to meet the needs of the new diagram type.

How to fix it

To rearrange text in your new diagram, you have two choices. You can cut and paste text from one box to another, or you can just retype the text. You can't cut and paste the text boxes themselves, only the text within them, so you'll probably end up doing a combination of these two things.

To cut text from one diagram text box to another, follow these steps:

1. Display the clipboard task pane, so you have ready access to the multiple selections you're going to cut and paste.

2. Select the text inside the first text box you want to move to another spot in the diagram. You can double-click to select a single word, but you'll have to select any phrases, sentences, or paragraphs by dragging your mouse or using the Shift and arrow keys.

3. Choose Edit, Cut or press Ctrl+X. This places the text on the Clipboard (you see it on the clipboard task pane). ▶

4. Go to each of the boxes containing text that needs to be in another box and repeat steps 2 and 3.

5. With the text from all of your boxes on the clipboard task pane, start depositing the text in the right places. Click on a now-empty text box and then click the desired text from the task pane—it appears in the box.

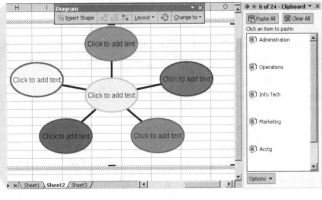

6. Repeat step 5 for all the boxes in your diagram until you've repositioned all of the text.

If you need to edit individual text boxes, either before or after rearranging their content, simply click in the text to activate your cursor, use the Delete and Backspace keys to get rid of unwanted text and type new text as needed.

You're not the boss of me

Because an organization chart is technically not a diagram, it's not available from within the Diagram toolbar's Change To list. If you built a pyramid or cycle diagram (typical alternatives for certain organization charts), you'll have to rebuild it entirely from scratch and delete the existing diagram. You can use the previous procedure to capture your text box content on the Clipboard (so you can paste it all into the appropriate blocks on your organization chart), but other than that, you have to begin from square one. After deleting your diagram, click the Diagram button and choose the Organization Chart type from the Diagram Gallery. The resulting chart looks a lot like a diagram (it actually is a diagram, but people have always called them organization charts rather than organization diagrams), and you can paste your content into the blocks and use the Organization Chart toolbar to add shapes and change your chart's layout. ▶

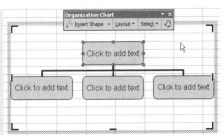

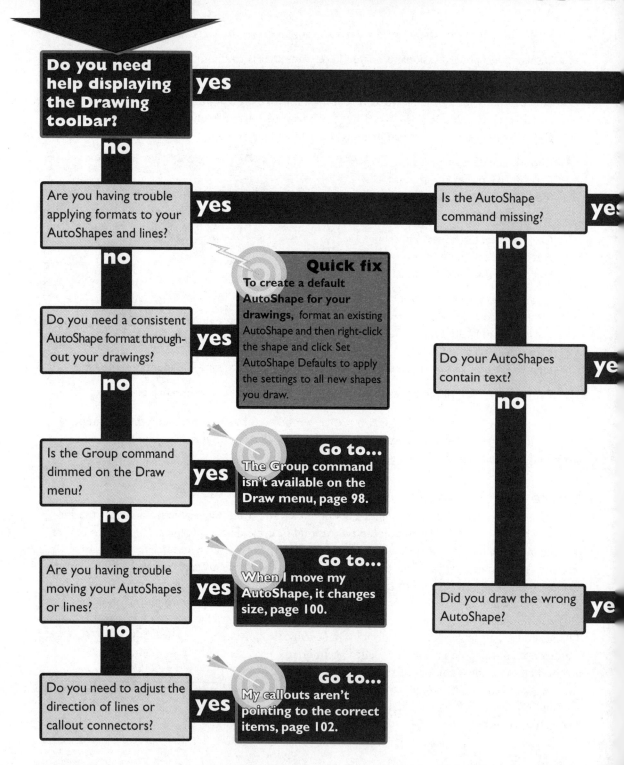

Do you need help displaying the Drawing toolbar?

yes

no

Are you having trouble applying formats to your AutoShapes and lines?

yes

no

Is the AutoShape command missing?

yes

no

Quick fix

To create a default AutoShape for your drawings, format an existing AutoShape and then right-click the shape and click Set AutoShape Defaults to apply the settings to all new shapes you draw.

Do you need a consistent AutoShape format through-out your drawings?

yes

no

Do your AutoShapes contain text?

ye

no

Is the Group command dimmed on the Draw menu?

yes

no

Go to...
The Group command isn't available on the Draw menu, page 98.

Are you having trouble moving your AutoShapes or lines?

yes

no

Go to...
When I move my AutoShape, it changes size, page 100.

Did you draw the wrong AutoShape?

ye

Do you need to adjust the direction of lines or callout connectors?

yes

Go to...
My callouts aren't pointing to the correct items, page 102.

g shapes and lines

Quick fix

To display the Drawing toolbar, follow these steps.

1. Right-click any visble toolbar or menu.

2. Click Drawing on the shortcut menu.

Quick fix

If the AutoShape command is missing from the Format menu, you don't have an AutoShape or line selected. Click once on any AutoShape or line and click the Format menu again—the AutoShape command will be available.

Is some of your AutoShape text missing?

yes

Go to...

I typed text into an AutoShape, and some of it is hidden, page 104.

no

Do you need to change the angle of your AutoShape text?

yes

Go to...

I rotated my shape, but its text didn't rotate with it, page 106.

Quick fix

To change an existing AutoShape to a new shape, follow these steps.

1. Select the AutoShape and click the Draw button on the Drawing toolbar.

2. On the Draw menu, click Change AutoShape and select a new shape from the submenu. The new shape will retain all of the current shape's formatting and content.

If your solution isn't here, check these related chapters:

- Diagrams, page 86
- Formatting text, page 156
- Hyperlinks, page 214

Or see the general troubleshooting tips on page xv.

The Group command isn't available on the Draw menu

Source of the problem

If you've spent several minutes aligning or positioning two or more objects on your worksheet and you don't want to accidentally move one or both of them out of that alignment, you can group the objects to protect their relative positions. Grouping drawn objects—AutoShapes, WordArt objects, lines, arrows, text boxes—is a great way to maintain their current positions, at least relative to one another. Grouping objects is easy—simply click the Draw button on the Drawing toolbar and then click Group on the menu that appears. But wait! The Group command is dimmed on the Draw menu! What can you do? ▶

The answer is simple. By definition a group is two or more objects, so you need to have two or more objects selected when you click the Draw menu.

The following steps show you how to group objects successfully every time.

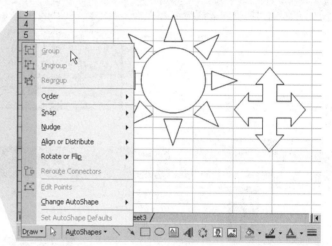

How to fix it

1. To select multiple objects on your worksheet, click the Select Objects button (the arrow next to the Draw button) on the Drawing toolbar and then click and drag to draw a dotted-line rectangle that completely encompasses the objects you want to group. ▶

2. Release the mouse button when you have surrounded the objects you want; you'll see handles around each one of the objects, indicating that the objects are selected.

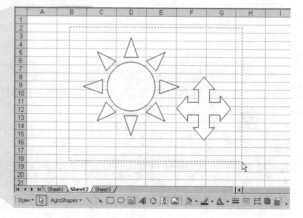

3. Click the Draw button and then click Group to group the individual objects. ▶

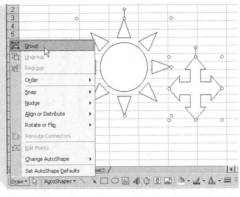

Tip

If the objects you want to group aren't close to one another or there are objects between them, hold down the Shift key as you click each of the objects you want to select. You can also use the Shift key to augment a multiple selection made with the mouse. If you see handles around all but one or two of the items you intend to group, hold down the Shift key and click on each of the items missing from the current group. When all the items you want to formally group are selected, release the Shift key and proceed to issue the Draw, Group command.

Tip

If you want to sever the relationship between members of a group of objects, select the group, click the Draw button, and then click Ungroup on the Draw menu.

Groups of groups of groups

You can group groups of objects as well as individual objects. Suppose you've already created a group of objects and now you want to add another object or another group to that group. Click the Select Objects button on the Drawing toolbar and then drag to surround both the existing group and the new group or object with a dotted-line rectangle. In this example, the existing group is selected, and a new object is being added to the selection. ▶

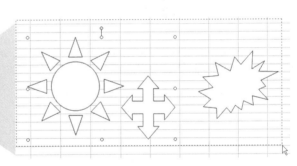

Once the existing group and the new group or object are all selected, click the Draw button and then click Group.

Safety in numbers

Grouping objects doesn't just protect related graphics from being accidentally repositioned; it allows you to do things to the entire group rather than having to operate on each member of the group individually. For example, if you want to make all the objects in the group a little larger or smaller, simply select the group and then drag one of the handles (a corner handle if you want the objects to retain their horizontal and vertical proportions). Drag outward to make all the objects larger, or drag toward the group's center to make the objects smaller. ▶

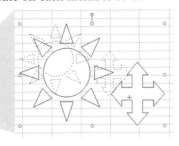

When I move my AutoShape, it changes size

Source of the problem

Oops! You wanted to move that AutoShape from the left side of your worksheet to the right, but when you did, all of a sudden the shape got much bigger. What happened? The answer lies with your mouse pointer. Of all the programs in the Microsoft Office suite, Microsoft Excel has the greatest variety of mouse pointers. It has pointers for entering content into cells, editing cell content, pasting cells from one place to another, copying cells, drawing objects, selecting objects, resizing objects—the list can seem endless. So the reason your AutoShape got bigger rather than moving is that you probably didn't notice that the mouse pointer had changed form. You simply missed the fact that when you wanted to move your AutoShape, your mouse pointer was in resize mode and not in move mode. ▶

How to fix it

1. If necessary, click Undo to reverse the erroneous resizing of your AutoShape.

2. Select the object that you want to move and then point to the center of the object, staying clear of the object's handles. Your mouse pointer will turn into a four-headed arrow. ▶

3. Hold down the mouse button, drag the object to the desired location, and then release the mouse button.

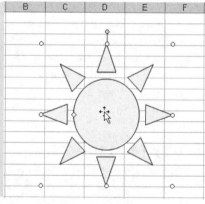

Nudge, nudge

As an alternative to dragging your objects to move them, try using the arrow keys on your keyboard. Click once on the object (or group), and when its handles appear, press the arrow keys to move it up, down, left, or right. Each press of the key nudges the object one pixel at a time.

This nudging technique does more than eliminate your need to identify a move vs. a resize mouse pointer; it also allows you to move an object in one direction at a time. If you use the mouse pointer to move an object, you might end up moving it in more than one direction, simply because you're a human and not a robot. For example, if you try to drag your object down, you'll probably end up moving it a little to the right or left as well, whether or not you realize it when you're dragging. ▶

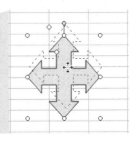

Another benefit is that you can nudge two ungrouped objects exactly the same distance. For example, if you have two circles and they both need to be moved up a hair, select one of them and then press the Up arrow key, counting the number of times you press it to get it to the desired location. Then select the second circle and press the Up arrow key the same number of times. Voilà! You've nudged both objects the same amount.

To base nudging increments on the grid rather than on pixels, turn on Snap To Grid. Click the Draw button, point to Snap on the Draw menu, and then click To Grid. Each press of the arrow keys will then nudge your selected object one grid point.

If you want to leave your object where it is and create a duplicate in a new location on your worksheet, drag the object while holding down the right mouse button. The original object remains in place, and a "ghost" of the object follows your mouse pointer. When you release the mouse button at the desired location for the new object, a shortcut menu automatically appears—click Copy Here in that menu.

Tip

You can nudge your selected object or group by pointing to Nudge on the Draw menu and then clicking Up, Down, Left, or Right in the resulting submenu.

My callouts aren't pointing to the correct items

Source of the problem

You can annotate parts of your worksheet, charts, or even drawn objects by using callouts with descriptive information. Callouts—boxes, circles, or cartoon bubble-like shapes that contain text—are visually linked to data or graphical content by a connecting line that stretches from the callout box. The line will point to the subject of the callout. However, if you move the subject of a callout by cutting or moving content or repositioning a chart or graphic, the callout will not move with it and will no longer point to that subject.

Another possible reason for a misdirected callout is that the callout itself was repositioned or resized. Often in an attempt to move a callout box or to make a callout box bigger, the connecting line is redirected.

Solving these problems requires understanding the parts of a callout and knowing how to redirect its connecting line so that it points to the desired content or object.

> ### Tip
>
> Don't confuse callouts with comments. *Callouts* are drawn on top of the worksheet and aren't attached to the worksheet's data. *Comments* are visible only if you point to the cell the comment is attached to. See "Comments and Track Changes" on page 34 for information about comments.

How to fix it

1. Click once on the edge of the callout box to select the box, its content, and the line pointing from the callout to the callout's subject. ▶

2. Point to the diamond at the end of the callout line and wait for the mouse pointer to change to a small white arrowhead.

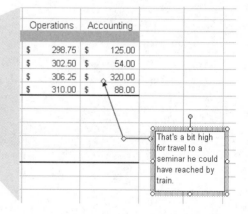

Operations	Accounting
$ 298.75	$ 125.00
$ 302.50	$ 54.00
$ 306.25	$ 320.00
$ 310.00	$ 88.00

That's a bit high for travel to a seminar he could have reached by train.

3. Drag the handle until the line is pointing to the intended subject of the callout. ▶

4. If necessary, reposition the callout box so that it is a reasonable distance from the subject. To do this, click away from the callout and then reselect it by clicking the callout box. When the mouse pointer turns into a four-headed arrow, move the box (not the line) so that the line stays where you just put it.

They went that-a-way...

If you want your callout line to have an arrowhead at the end of it, click the callout line to select it. When yellow diamonds appear on the line (indicating that the line and callout are selected), click the Arrow Style button on the Drawing toolbar and then click a style on the menu. For example, to get a single arrowhead pointing away from the callout and toward the callout's subject, click the left-pointing arrow in the list of arrow styles. ▶

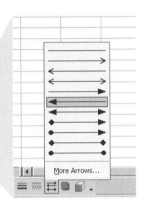

Tip

You can change the color of the callout border and connecting line by using the Line Color button on the Drawing toolbar. Select the callout, click the drop-down arrow to the right of the button, and then click a color on the palette.

I typed text into an AutoShape, and some of it is hidden

Source of the problem

A lot of people think that to have text appear in an AutoShape, you must place a text box on top of the shape and type the text into that box. But it's really much simpler to add text to an AutoShape itself. With your AutoShape selected, simply begin typing. The text you type appears within the shape, and in the case of paragraph text (more than a word or two), the text wraps within the confines of the shape.

Sounds good, eh? Well, normally it is, but you can run into a problem if you type more text into the shape than can appear within the shape's current size. The text that goes beyond the "window" within the shape's borders becomes hidden from view. ▶

The solution to this problem requires you to make a change. You can resize the shape, reduce the font size, edit the text to convey the basic information in fewer words, or—perhaps more attractive than the other options—ask Excel to size the shape for you, making it fit the amount of text you've typed.

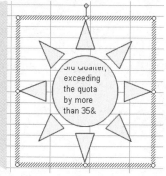

How to fix it

To increase the size of the AutoShape so that all of your text fits within it, follow these steps:

1. Click the edge of the shape to select it and display its handles.

2. Right-click the shape and choose Format AutoShape from the shortcut menu.

3. In the resulting dialog box, click the Alignment tab and turn on the Automatic Size option. This will cause the shape to grow (or shrink) to fit the text you've typed. If you edit the text in the future, increasing or decreasing its quantity or size, the shape will again accommodate it automatically. ▶

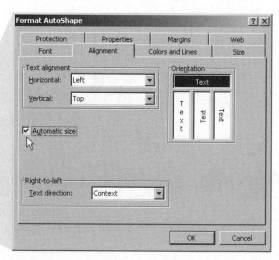

If you can't allow the shape to get bigger (which it will if you use the Automatic Size option and you currently have more text than shape), you have to make the text smaller so that more of it appears in the shape. To do that, follow these steps:

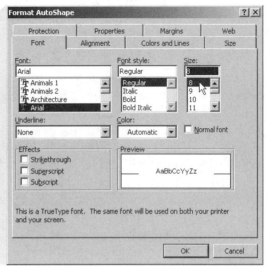

1. Click the AutoShape's border to select both the shape and its text.

2. Right-click the selected shape and then click Format AutoShape on the shortcut menu.

3. Click the Font tab if necessary and then make changes to the font, size, and style of the text so that all the text can fit in the shape. ▶

4. When you are finished making adjustments, click OK to view the results.

And if your text still doesn't fit...

Sometimes your text won't fit within the AutoShape even after you resize the shape or reformat the text. And sometimes you won't be able to resize the shape, but you still need all of the text to fit. At these times, you can reformat the margins of the shape so that it can hold more text.

> **Tip**
>
> You can also use the Formatting toolbar's Font and Font Size buttons to adjust the appearance of your AutoShape text.

Use the Margins tab of the Format AutoShape dialog box to adjust the margins within a selected AutoShape. Select the AutoShape, right-click it, and click Format AutoShape on the shortcut menu. Click the Margins tab if necessary, adjust the margins in the Left, Right, Top, and Bottom boxes as needed, and then click OK.

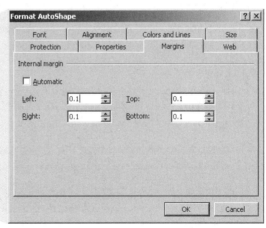

Remember that these margins are much smaller than page margins, so to allow the most amount of room inside the shape without the text touching the borders of the shape, set the margins to .1" or .2"—a tenth or a fifth of an inch. ▶

I rotated my shape, but its text didn't rotate with it

Source of the problem

By default, when you rotate your AutoShape, Excel leaves the text in the AutoShape at a 0° angle, running at the same angle as the text and numbers typed into your worksheet cells. This default is problematic for just about anyone rotating a text-bearing AutoShape because most people want the text to rotate with the object. Here, the star has been rotated, but the text stayed in place. ▶

Depending on your text rotation goals, you have two possible solutions. The first solution offers you the most flexibility in rotating your text and objects, but it involves placing a WordArt object on top of the AutoShape and rotating the WordArt to the same degree as the shape. The second solution is less flexible in that it offers limited text rotation capabilities, but with this solution, you don't have to insert an additional object into your worksheet— you simply change the alignment applied to the AutoShape text.

Sales in 3rd Quarter are up by 35% !

How to fix it

To place WordArt on top of your AutoShape and rotate it to the same degree as that of the shape, follow these steps:

1. Leave your rotated AutoShape empty or delete any existing text by right-clicking the shape, clicking Edit Text on the shortcut menu, and pressing the Delete key.

2. Click any worksheet cell to deselect the AutoShape. (Don't worry about choosing a spot for your WordArt right away; you can move the object where you want it later.)

3. Click the WordArt button on the Drawing toolbar to display the WordArt Gallery dialog box, select the WordArt style that you want to use by clicking the sample, and then click OK.

4. In the Edit WordArt Text dialog box, replace the instructional text with the text you want to rotate on top of your AutoShape. If you want, change the font, font size, and formatting and then click OK.

> **Tip**
>
> Why can't you just put a simple text box on top of the AutoShape, rotate the shape, and then rotate the text box to match? Because text boxes can't be rotated! If you select a text box and then go to the Draw menu, the Rotate or Flip command will be available, but its submenu items will be dimmed. Sorry...

5. Move the mouse pointer over the center of the WordArt object. When the pointer changes to a four-headed arrow, move the WordArt object until it is positioned on top of the AutoShape. (With the WordArt object selected, you can resize and adjust its shape as needed by dragging the object's handles.)

6. Click and drag the green rotate handle on the WordArt object. When the mouse pointer changes to a circular arrow, click and drag to spin the WordArt text to match the rotation angle of your AutoShape. ▶

7. Click any cell in the worksheet to deselect the WordArt object and hide the WordArt toolbar.

To prevent accidental rotation of either the WordArt or the AutoShape, group your WordArt and AutoShape objects. First select them both by clicking one object and then holding down the Shift key as you click the second object. Then with both objects selected, click the Draw button on the Drawing toolbar, and click Group on the menu.

To change the alignment of your AutoShape text without adding a WordArt object, follow these steps:

1. Select the AutoShape containing text, right-click it, and then click Format AutoShape on the shortcut menu.

2. On the Alignment tab, click the desired text alignment settings in the Horizontal or Vertical Text drop-down lists—or both if you want. As needed, select a 90-degree text setting in the Orientation section.

3. Click OK to apply the new alignment and orientation to your AutoShape's text.

Rotating in tandem

When you rotate objects with the Free Rotate tool (found in the Draw, Rotate or Flip submenu), you're using your eye to achieve what *looks* like matching angles. To make sure your AutoShape and WordArt objects are rotated to the exact same angle, first ungroup the objects by clicking on them, clicking the Draw button on the Drawing toolbar, and then clicking Upgroup. Then right-click the AutoShape and click Format AutoShape on the shortcut menu. On the Size tab, note the measurement in the Rotation box. Next right-click the WordArt object, and click Format WordArt on the shortcut menu. Click the Size tab, and in the WordArt object's Rotation box, enter the same measurement you noted for the rotation of the AutoShape. You can then group the two objects again.

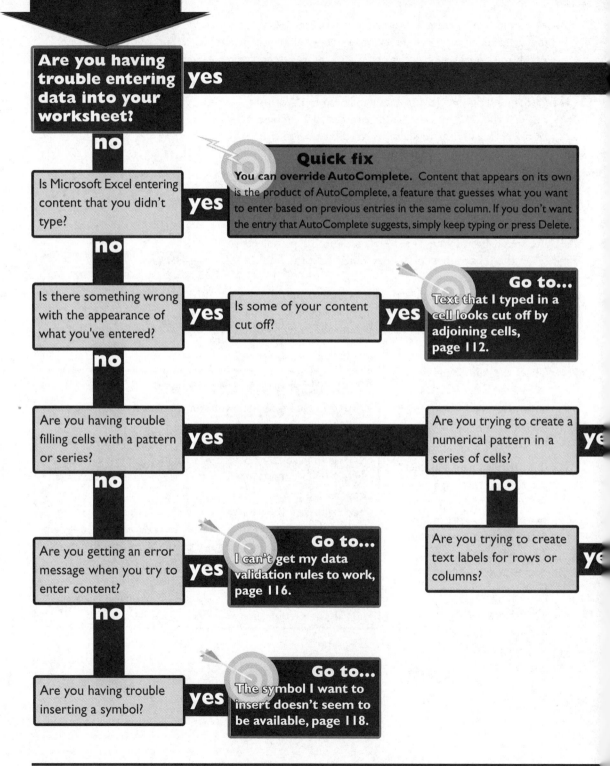

Are you having trouble entering data into your worksheet?

yes

no

Is Microsoft Excel entering content that you didn't type?

yes

Quick fix
You can override AutoComplete. Content that appears on its own is the product of AutoComplete, a feature that guesses what you want to enter based on previous entries in the same column. If you don't want the entry that AutoComplete suggests, simply keep typing or press Delete.

no

Is there something wrong with the appearance of what you've entered?

yes

Is some of your content cut off?

yes

Go to...
Text that I typed in a cell looks cut off by adjoining cells, page 112.

no

Are you having trouble filling cells with a pattern or series?

yes

Are you trying to create a numerical pattern in a series of cells?

ye

no

Are you getting an error message when you try to enter content?

yes

Go to...
I can't get my data validation rules to work, page 116.

Are you trying to create text labels for rows or columns?

ye

no

Are you having trouble inserting a symbol?

yes

Go to...
The symbol I want to insert doesn't seem to be available, page 118.

Entering data

Do you need to enter content into a specific range of cells?

yes

Quick fix

To enter content into a range of cells, follow these steps.

1. Select the range of cells and then begin typing in the first cell.

2. Press Enter to move from cell to cell within the selected range.

3. When you've finished entering content within that range, click outside of it to deselect it.

no

Does the active cell reject your entry?

yes

Go to...

When I type in the active cell, nothing happens, page 110.

Quick fix

To establish and fill in a numerical pattern, follow these steps.

1. Type the first two numbers of the pattern into adjoining cells and then select those two cells.

2. Using the fill handle in the second cell, drag through the remaining cells in the range to complete the pattern.

Go to...

I'm tired of entering the same series of labels in my worksheets, page 114.

If your solution isn't here, check these related chapters:

- Columns and rows, page 24
- Formatting text, page 156
- Formulas, page 178
- Graphics, page 204

Or see the general troubleshooting tips on page xv.

When I type in the active cell, nothing happens

Source of the problem

The operative word in this situation is "active." Even people with a reasonable amount of Microsoft Excel experience will make the mistake of attempting to enter data into a cell other than the active cell. The active cell is the cell that has a thick, black border around it, and its address appears in the Name box to the left of the Formula bar. It's very easy to start typing and wonder why the cell you think should change doesn't. Then you discover that another cell was active when you started to type and that content is being added to a cell other than the one you wanted to edit.

Why might you become confused as to which cell is active? If you've applied thick, black borders to any cells, if you've changed your cell shading to black (in which case the active cell will have a thick, white border), or if you're concentrating on the particular cell where you intend to make an entry and forget to click it (leaving a previously clicked cell as the active cell), you might have trouble determining which cell is active. The latter situation, forgetting to click the right cell, results in an additional problem—whatever you type ends up in the wrong cell, and if the active cell contains content when you started to type, you overwrite it when you type the new content! To determine which cell is active, you need to take only a few steps.

How to fix it

1. Look in the Name Box and note the address of the active cell. ▶

2. If the address appearing in the Name Box does not represent the cell in which you want to work, press Esc to undo any changes you might have accidentally made to existing material in that cell.

3. Click the cell in which you want to work and then do what you need to do.

Microsoft Excel - weekly expenses.xls					
File Edit View Insert Format Tools Data Window Help					
A4					
	A	B	C	D	E	F
1						
2		Travel Expenses by Department				
3						
4		Sales	Marketing	Info. Tech	Operations	Accounting
5	Week Starting:					
6	11/5/2001	$ 2,573.29	$ 2,135.00	$ 58.65	$ 298.75	$ 125.00
7	11/12/2001	$ 2,560.50	$ 2,400.50	$ 204.38	$ 302.50	$ 54.00
8	11/19/2001	$ 4,576.51	$ 2,986.00	$ 350.11	$ 306.25	$ 320.00
9	11/26/2001	$ 3,574.90	$ 3,411.50	$ 495.84	$ 310.00	$ 88.00
10	12/3/2001					

Tip

When you press Esc, you lose whatever's just been entered into the active cell, leaving the cell with the content that existed before the last attempt to edit it or returning the cell to a blank state if no material previously existed in that cell.

Watch that mouse

Pressing Enter or Tab after working in a cell is a good habit to get into. Using the mouse button to click another cell after making or modifying an entry confirms cell entries in a manner similar to pressing Enter or Tab, but be aware that you run the risk of leaving a cell active when you're really finished working with it, thereby making it vulnerable to unintended edits when you're trying to work in another cell. If you use the mouse to scroll to another part of your worksheet and then forget to click another cell to make it active, you might overwrite material in the cell in which you were just working without knowing it!

If you get into the habit of clicking another cell—or, better yet, pressing Enter or Tab—immediately after you add or modify a cell entry, you'll be more confident that your entries will stay intact—in the cells where you want them to be!

> **Tip**
>
> Need to get back to the beginning of the worksheet quickly? Press Ctrl+Home. You'll exit the cell you're in (confirming your most recent edit) and go back to cell A1 in one fell swoop.

> **Tip**
>
> If your insertion point is blinking in any cell, you must press either Enter or Tab to confirm the cell's entry, or Esc to abandon any changes just made to the entry in the active cell. When a cell contains a blinking insertion point, any formatting you apply using menus, toolbar buttons, or keyboard shortcuts will affect any content you enter after the insertion point, but not until you press Enter or Esc. If you apply formatting with cells or content selected, the formatting will apply to the selected text.

Text that I typed in a cell looks cut off by adjoining cells

Source of the problem

You've typed your text in a cell, and you've pressed Enter or Tab. You look at the cell you just finished editing, and the end of the word or phrase is missing—cut off at the right end of the cell. What's going on? If the cell to the right of the one you just typed in has content, there's your culprit—but this only applies when there is text in the active cell. If the active cell contains only numeric content, the content of the cell to the right is immaterial. If you type text into a cell and that text overruns that cell's column width, the text that doesn't fit will be obscured, or *truncated*, by the cell to the right if (and only if) that cell has content. ▶

If you type purely numeric content into a cell and type more than will fit into the cell's current width, Excel either expands the column to accommodate the numeric entry or turns the numbers you typed into pound signs (########) to signify that there isn't room for the entire entry. This will happen whether or not there is content in the cell to the right. This prevents your thinking that the number in a cell is only 10000 when it's really 10000000. It could be very confusing if too many numbers in a cell were handled the way too much text is handled. Missing letters in a word draw immediate attention, and you notice what's missing. Cutting off a number could cause major confusion, because you wouldn't necessarily spot the omitted content.

When it comes to text, though, if the cell to the right is empty, a portion of the overflow text will appear to spill into that cell's space, though it won't actually fill the cell itself. (This is good for worksheet titles that normally appear in cell A1. Cell B1 is usually empty, so long titles just flow over any adjoining cells as needed.) Generally, however, you want cell content to fit in the cell it was intended for, and so you need to make your columns wide enough to accommodate a worksheet's content. If you have already entered content and it's been truncated, you need to widen the column that contains the cell with the overrun text.

How to fix it

To widen a column to accommodate a particular entry, follow these steps:

1. Hold the mouse pointer over the right seam of the heading of the column you want to widen. (Note that you don't have to actually select the column to widen it.) Here, Column D is being widened to reveal the entire entry in cell D4. ▶

2. When the pointer changes to a double-headed arrow, hold down the mouse button and drag the seam to the right.

3. Release the mouse button when the column is wide enough to fit the entry.

To widen a column so that none of its entries is truncated by entries in an adjacent column, first point to the column heading's right seam. (You don't have to select a column to widen it.) When the pointer changes to a double-headed arrow, double-click the right seam of the column's heading to widen the column to fit its widest entry.

Don't widen, be happy

Just as it saves time and effort to format a word processing document after the entire document's typed (rather than stopping to format as you type), you can adopt a similarly relaxed attitude about your worksheet's appearance while you're in the process of building the worksheet's content. Wait until all of your content is entered, ignoring any text that doesn't quite fit in the cells, and then select the column or columns you want to adjust. Hold your mouse pointer on the seam between two of the selected columns, and when the pointer changes to a double-headed arrow, drag the seam to adjust the selected columns so that all of the selected columns are widened to a universal size. It's a good idea to use the widest entry in the selected columns as your guide, as shown in the sample. ▶

Alternatively, you can select the entire worksheet, right-click any column's heading, and then click Column Width on the shortcut menu. In the Column Width dialog box, type a numeric column width that should apply to all of your worksheet's columns and then click OK. The number you type should equal the maximum number of characters you want to appear across the column width; for example, if you type 20, then the column width will be adjusted to accommodate 20 characters, including spaces. After you adjust the columns in the entire worksheet, you might need to adjust individual columns with entries that are larger or smaller than the global column width you set.

Tip

If you have a large worksheet with many cells that fall outside the visible portion of your worksheet, double-clicking the seam of a column heading to widen the column might have unexpected results. The widest entry might not be the truncated entry you can see and were trying to fix—another cell above or below the visible portion of the worksheet might contain entries that are even longer, and the column could become much wider than you intend. It's safest to scroll through the worksheet to find such entries, and if they're longer than the column width you had in mind, either shorten them or use the Wrap Text feature to make the text wrap onto multiple lines. Select the cells in which you want to wrap text (or press Ctrl+A to select the entire worksheet) and then press Ctrl+1 to display the Format Cells dialog box. Click the Alignment tab, select the Wrap Text check box, and then click OK.

I'm tired of entering the same series of labels in my worksheets

Source of the problem

It can be a real pain in the neck to build worksheets that have content similar to other worksheets—especially if you find yourself building these similar worksheets frequently. You know you've typed these exact words before—a list of locations, names, or products—and it aggravates you to know you're repeating your efforts and leaving yourself vulnerable to typos and other errors. Well, repeat yourself no more!

You might be aware that Excel completes lists automatically. For example, if you enter the heading Quarter 1 in a cell and then use the fill handle to drag that entry through the adjoining cells, Excel fills those cells with Quarter 2, Quarter 3, and Quarter 4. If you keep going, Excel starts all over again with Quarter 1. You can also complete lists of months or days of the week this way.

But what if you need a list of items that Excel doesn't know the order of, such as the list of your company's remote offices (Philadelphia, New York, Atlanta, Phoenix, San Francisco, and so on) or a list of products you track every month in a sales worksheet (A578-3B, A578-4B, A578-7C, B345-4E)? Excel lets you create a custom list that you can flesh out simply by typing any item in the list in an individual cell. You can base a custom list on existing content (in a worksheet where you've already typed a whole series of entries) or build a custom list from scratch.

How to fix it

To create a custom list from existing content, follow these steps:

1. Select the cells in your worksheet that contain the row or column labels that you want to turn into a custom list.

Tip

You can create as many custom lists as you need, and you can edit any list you've created. (Be aware that you can't edit the lists that are installed with Excel, such as months of the year or days of the week.) To edit one of your lists, click Options on the Tools menu, click the Custom Lists tab, and select the custom list you want to edit in the Custom Lists box. Click in the List Entries box, make edits as you need to, and then click OK. To remove a list completely, select the list in the Custom Lists box, click Delete, click OK to confirm the deletion, and then click OK a second time to close the Options dialog box.

2. On the Tools menu, click Options.

3. In the Options dialog box, click the Custom Lists tab.

4. Click the Import button to bring in the content of the cell range listed in the Import List From Cells box. (This is the range you selected in step 1.) ▶

5. If you need to change a list entry, click next to the entry in the List Entries box and then edit the entry's text as needed. You can also add items to the list this way or rearrange the order of the list.

6. Click OK to close the dialog box.

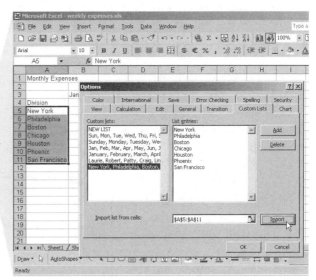

To create a custom list from scratch, follow these steps:

1. With any worksheet open, click Options on the Tools menu.

2. In the Options dialog box, click the Custom Lists tab.

3. With NEW LIST selected in the Custom Lists box, click in the List Entries box.

4. Type the list, pressing Enter after each item.

5. When your list is complete, click the Add button. Your list will appear in the box on the left side of the dialog box, with each item in the list separated by a comma.

6. Click OK to close the dialog box.

Once you've created your custom list, you can use it in any new or existing worksheet. Enter any item from the list in a cell, use that cell's fill handle to drag through the adjoining cells (in either the row or column), and release the mouse button to enter the remaining list items. The items will appear in the adjoining cells in the order you entered them in the list. If you drag through more cells than there are items in the custom list, the series will begin again with the first of the list items.

It's also important to note that the series will always fill in in the order in which the items appeared when you imported or typed the list from scratch. For example, if your list contains five cities—New York, Philadelphia, Detroit, Milwaukee, and Seattle—and if you start typing with Detroit and use the fill handle, the next item in the list will be Milwaukee. You won't get to New York until the list begins again or you restart the list manually with that city.

I can't get my data validation rules to work

Source of the problem

Suppose your Excel database requires specific entries in some of the fields, such as complete department names in an employee list (to prevent the use of both "Mktg." and "Marketing" or "Acctg." and "Accounting," which can make filtering and sorting difficult) or only numeric content in an employee number field.

To restrict the data that can be entered, you have set up rules, called *data validation* rules, but they aren't working! Now your database is at risk for inaccurate or inappropriate entries, especially if you're not the only one making entries in the worksheet. What happened?

> ### Tip
> Why can't you just put a comment or text box on the worksheet to advise users what kind of data you want them to enter? Sometimes people ignore such advisories, and without data validation rules in place, Excel can't prevent entries that could result from ignored advisories. Excel will accept anything you type—text, numbers, symbols inserted with keyboard shortcuts—and doesn't make so much as a peep if you type something that doesn't make sense or that isn't appropriate for the cell where you've entered it.

Two possible scenarios that can prevent data validation rules from working are:

- The cell material wasn't typed directly into the cells, but was copied or cut and then pasted in them.
- You've made an entry in a cell for which no rules were established.

The solution to the first possibility is simple—don't allow anyone to paste content into cells in which data validation rules apply. For the latter possibility, you need to figure out which cells have rules applied to them and then check and correct the rules that are in place, if any corrections are needed.

How to fix it

To check for data validation rules, follow these steps:

1. On the Edit menu, click Go To.

2. In the Go To dialog box, click Special.

3. In the Go To Special dialog box, click the Data Validation option and leave the All default setting in place. ▶

4. Click OK to have Excel select all cells with data validation rules applied to them.

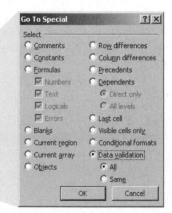

Entering data

Once you've determined which cells have rules applied to them, check the rules for omissions or errors by following these steps:

1. With the cells with data validation rules still selected, click one of these cells and then click Go To on the Edit menu.

2. Click Special, click the Data Validation option, and then click Same below it. Click OK to select the cells where the active cell's data validation rules are also applied.

3. On the Data menu, click Validation.

4. In the Data Validation dialog box, examine the Allow box and all other applicable settings in the Validation Criteria section to make sure the settings are correct. ▶

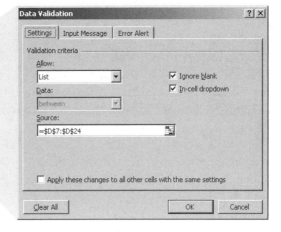

Rules are meant to be broken...sort of

Data Validation rules control what you can enter into selected cells, and that's a great thing when you're trying to keep people from entering erroneous or inappropriate data in a worksheet. You might encounter a problem with creating lists of acceptable entries, however. When you select the Source cell range in the Data Validation dialog box, the cells you designate as containing the acceptable entries are not protected by the rule, even if they're within the range of cells to which the rule applies.

For example, if you're applying a rule to cells B1 through B25 and cells B1 through B6 are the Source range—meaning they contain the handful of entries that are acceptable for use in cells B1 through B25—the entries you make in cells B1 through B6 will (a) be allowed to violate the rule, and (b) become part of the list of acceptable entries for the range to which the rule is applied, no matter what you enter in those cells. Why is this? Search me. I don't imagine it was an intended part of the feature, because it can certainly blow holes in your validation rules. To eliminate this problem, make your Source range a block of cells that are away from the working part of your worksheet—squirrel them away in some obscure place in the workbook, where no one will possibly make any entries after the rule is created.

> **Tip**
>
> In the Data Validation dialog box, examine the Error Alert tab and make sure the Show Error Alert After Invalid Data Is Entered check box is selected. If this check box is clear, Excel won't display a prompt indicating that the validation rules have been violated, and that alone could lead you to believe that the rules aren't working properly. If you need to, select this check box, click a type of error message symbol in the Style list, type appropriate messages in the Title and Error Message boxes, and then click OK.

The symbol I want to insert doesn't seem to be available

Source of the problem

Symbols can be a very cool thing to add to your worksheets, and before Excel 2002 you couldn't add them to worksheets without pasting them from another application, such as Microsoft Word or Microsoft PowerPoint. How can symbols be useful in a worksheet environment? You can use them for decoration, information, or both.

For decorative purposes, imagine you're tracking your stocks. Some are doing well, others aren't. You decide to keep the moneymakers and the losers in two separate columns or worksheets, just to keep them apart. To help you instantly differentiate the two groups, you can insert a picture of a bull or a bear (from the Animals font) into the worksheet. In a cell above the stocks that are

doing well, insert the bull and above those that aren't doing so well, insert the bear. You can also access a variety of fun shapes and pictures, such as phones, geometric shapes, bombs (great for using with data that's surprising or potentially earth-shattering), and people. ▶

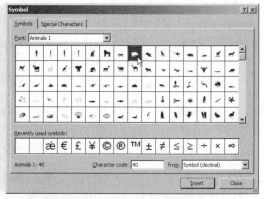

For informative purposes, you can access foreign currency and mathematical symbols. Of course, once inserted, the symbols appear in a cell just like text or numbers—they're actually just the characters within a font other than one that typically offers letters of the alphabet or the Arabic numbers from 0 to 9. Mathematical symbols can't be used in formulas, as only the standard characters +, -, /, and * (addition, subtraction, division, and multiplication, respectively) will work in a formula or function. ▶

So with symbols serving an essentially graphical role, what could go wrong? Well, if you try to use the Insert, Symbol command to access a list of symbols and special characters, but the one you want to use isn't there (or you can't find it), you're probably a little annoyed. Where did it go? Was it never there in the first place?

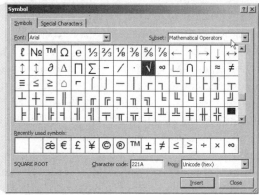

The key to finding the right symbol is knowing what kind of symbol it is (which font contains it) and making sure that the right subset (category, if you will) for the font in question is displayed. Your choices are Unicode and ASCII, and it's worth checking both subsets for any font you choose.

Entering data

How to fix it

To make sure that you're looking in the right place, follow these steps to peruse the symbol libraries and check the subsets (categories) to make sure you're not limiting the listing and thus making it *seem* as though the symbol you want is unavailable:

1. Choose Symbol from the Insert menu. The Symbol dialog box opens.

2. Scroll through the Font list and look for the one that contains the symbol you wanted. If you have no idea which font it's in, poke around through the likely candidates. For example, if you're looking for an arrow, try Arrows1 or Arrows 2 (if you have that font) or Wingdings. ▶

3. To make sure you're seeing the entire group of symbols within a particular font library, check the Subset field—by default, it should be on Basic Latin, if this is the first time you've used the Insert Symbol command. Scroll through the list of subsets and see if you can find the symbol you need when you choose an alternative.

4. When you've found the symbol you need, click once on it and click the Insert button.

5. Click Close to close the dialog box and return to your worksheet. The symbol you inserted appears in the active cell.

Symbolically speaking

You can insert some symbols with keyboard shortcuts—for example, pressing Alt+168 on the numeric keypad will give you an upside-down question mark, useful if you're typing a question in Spanish (you'll use a "regular" question mark at the end of the question as well), or if you want to create a unique emoticon using the upside-down question mark as a nose. To see which keyboard shortcut to use for a symbol you want to insert quickly in the future, refer to the Symbol dialog box—at the bottom of the dialog box a Character Code designation appears for any symbol you select. To insert that symbol with the keyboard later, press the Alt key, and with that key held down, type the numeric keys, one at a time. The symbol will appear after you type the last number in the shortcut, and then you can release the Alt key.

Tip

The name of the symbol you click in the dialog box appears in the lower-left corner of the dialog box. This is very handy if you know which symbol you want by looking at it but never knew what it was called. I've run into that a lot with math and engineering symbols that clients use in their worksheets—they're still "Greek" to me, but at least now I know what to call them!

Are you having trouble exporting Microsoft Excel content to other applications?

yes

no

Are you having trouble importing content from your Microsoft Word document into Excel?

yes

no

Go to...
When I paste a Word table into my worksheet, the table's content appears in the wrong cells, page 124.

Do you receive an error message when you try to edit an object that you imported into Excel?

yes

no

Quick fix
If an error message appears when you try to edit imported objects, a lack of memory is the most likely culprit. Close other applications that are open or save your work and restart your computer to free up system resources.

Are you unable to insert an object into your worksheet?

yes

no

Go to...
The object type I want isn't listed in the Object dialog box, page 122.

Quick fix
You can make Excel 2002 workbooks accessible for earlier versions. When saving your Excel 2002 workbooks for people using Excel 2000 or 97, use the Save As Type list in the Save As dialog box to select the version of Excel that they use.

Are people who use older versions of Excel unable to open the workbooks that you send them?

yes

Are you having trouble exporting worksheet cells to Word?

yes →

Go to...
When I paste Excel cells into a Word table, the content appears in the wrong cells, page 126.

no

Are you having trouble exporting an Excel chart to a Word document?

yes →

Go to...
The chart I pasted into a Word document doesn't change when I update the Excel data, page 130.

no

Is your Excel chart changing unexpectedly after you paste it into a PowerPoint slide?

yes →

Quick fix
If the Excel chart you pasted into your PowerPoint presentation changes whenever you edit your Excel data (the data on which the chart was based), there's a link between the chart and the slide. Simply delete the chart and repaste it, being certain to click the Paste command (*not* Paste Link) on the Edit menu—no link will be established, and the chart will not change.

no

Is your Excel data appearing in the wrong place when you export it to Microsoft Access?

yes →

Go to...
When I paste Excel data into an Access table, column headings appear as the first record, page 134.

If your solution isn't here, check these related chapters:

- Charts, page 2
- Hyperlinks, page 214
- Saving, page 278

Or see the general troubleshooting tips on page xv.

The object type I want isn't listed in the Object dialog box

Source of the problem

Your worksheet needs something—an editable graphic, a document, a movie, a sound—and you click Object on the Insert menu in the hope of selecting one of these items. To your surprise, however, the object you want to insert isn't in the Object Type list in the Object dialog box. How can that be?

The list of objects in the Object dialog box is based on the software installed on your computer. Any Microsoft Office-compatible software that's properly installed will appear in the list. If the object you want isn't in the list, either the software that produces such an object isn't installed on your computer or the software isn't compatible with Microsoft Windows, or Office, or both.

To solve the problem, first make sure the software you need (such as sound-recording or editing software if you want to insert a .wav file object) is actually installed on your computer. If it's not, install it. If the software is installed and you believe it is compatible with Windows and Office, try uninstalling and then reinstalling the software, so that if it is compatible, you'll be confident that the installation was complete. Plus, you'll have given Office a chance to recognize the software and offer the software's objects as insertable object types in Microsoft Excel's Object Type list.

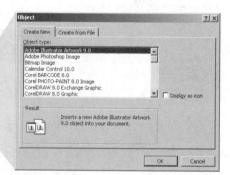

How to fix it

To verify that your computer contains the software that supports the object type you want, try one of these methods:

- Check the Programs list on the Start menu. Look for the software you believe supports the object type you want to insert. If you find the software listed on the Programs menu, click the item on the menu to see if the software runs properly. A menu item for deleted software often remains on the Start menu, unless a thorough uninstall operation was performed, usually with the Add/Remove Programs feature in Control Panel.

- Open Windows Explorer or My Computer and then examine the Program Files folder. When software is installed, Windows normally creates a folder for the software as a subfolder of the Program Files folder. If you find a folder for the software, examine the folder and its own subfolders for an executable file (normally ending in an .exe extension) that starts the program. When you find the executable file, try double-clicking it to see if the program runs.

● If you know the name of the program, click Start, point to Search (if you're using Windows 2000, Find if you're using Windows 98 or Millennium), and then click Files Or Folders. In the resulting

dialog box, enter search criteria, such as the program name or a portion of it, as needed in the Find: All Files dialog box. (The command names might vary slightly in Windows 98 or Windows Me, but the process is basically the same as the one described here.) ▶

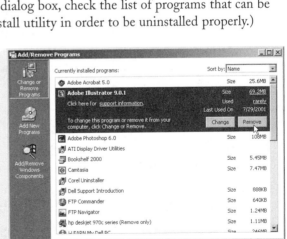

Pleased to meetcha

If you find the software through one of these methods, but the type of object is definitely not in the list of those that you can insert in your Excel worksheet (double-check the Object dialog box list, just to be sure), uninstall the software and reinstall it. Doing so should make Office "see" that the software is there and available.

To uninstall the software, don't just select its folder in the Windows Explorer or My Computer window and press Delete. No! This will remove the core programs, but won't thoroughly remove all the files that were planted throughout other folders in your system when the software was installed. Open Control Panel by clicking Start, pointing to Settings, and clicking Control Panel, and then double-click the Add/Remove Programs icon.

In the Add/Remove Programs Properties dialog box, check the list of programs that can be uninstalled. (Software must come with an uninstall utility in order to be uninstalled properly.) When you find the software you want to uninstall, select it, and click the Remove button. Windows will prompt you to confirm your intention to uninstall the selected software. (Again, the command names might vary slightly if you're using Windows 98 or Windows Me.) ▶

Once you've uninstalled the software, install the software again from the original CD-ROM or floppy disks. Office should be able to recognize the software and include its objects in the list of those that you can insert in all Office applications.

When I paste a Word table into my worksheet, the table's content appears in the wrong cells

Source of the problem

You might think a Microsoft Word table and an Excel worksheet would be so similar that they'd work together seamlessly. In most cases, you'd be correct. However, sometimes you'll find that when you paste a Word table into your Excel worksheet, the columns and rows you neatly arranged and filled in Word look like a big mess in the worksheet. ▶

When your Word table becomes an Excel puzzle, it's generally the result of cells that were either split in the Word table, or drawn with the Draw Table feature (used to create cells with random widths and heights) in conjunction with the Insert Table tool or on its own. Often, the appearance of a mess in Excel is just the result of changes in row heights and column widths that occur when you force the table material into the structure of an Excel worksheet. With a little tidying up, you can make the worksheet table a near twin of the Word table. If the table's material is in the wrong place, you might need to move some of the text around by dragging it from one cell to another until all of the table's material is where you want it.

	A	B	C	D	E	F	G
1							
2							
3		Weekly Time Sheets					
4		Last Name	Week Starting	Hours Worked	Rate per Hour		
5		Fitzsimmons	15-May	42	$16.50		TOTAL PAY
6		Mattaliano	15-May	45	$17.25		$693.00
7		Krauss	15-May	38	$15.50		$776.25
8		Kelley	15-May	40	$16.25		$589.00
9							$650.00
10							

How to fix it

Operating on the table you've pasted into Excel, follow these steps to clean things up a bit, working toward making the range of cells in Excel look like the table you had in Word:

1. To resize a column, point to the right seam of the column's heading, and when your pointer turns to a horizontal two-headed arrow, drag the seam to resize the column as you want.

2. To resize a row, point to the bottom seam of the row's heading and then drag the seam to resize the row as needed. (Generally, row heights need to be adjusted only if the Word table was drawn by hand or if more than one line of text is typed into a cell in Word, causing the row to become taller as the text wraps in the cell.)

3. Using drag-and-drop editing, move misplaced content from one cell to another by selecting the cell or cells containing the misplaced content, pointing to the edge of the cell or cells, and—when your mouse pointer turns to a four-headed arrow—dragging the content to the cell or cells in which you want it to appear. ▶

4. Repeat these steps until all of your content is where you want it.

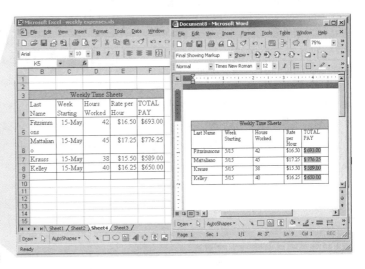

Weekly Time Sheets					
Last Name	Week Starting	Hours Worked	Rate per Hour		
Fitzsimmons	15-May	42	$16.50	TOTAL PAY	
Mattaliano	15-May	45	$17.25	$693.00	
Krauss	15-May	38	$15.50	$776.25	
Kelley	15-May	40	$16.25	$589.00	
				$650.00	

Imitation is the sincerest form of worksheet formatting

Excel looks at the formatting applied to the Word table and applies its closest match. For example, if you split a cell in one row but didn't split the cell directly below it in the next row, Excel will apply the Merge And Center command to the cell that wasn't split, allowing it to span two worksheet cells. If you typed a paragraph of text into your table cell and the text wrapped, Excel will turn on the Wrap Text setting for that cell in the worksheet. Border and cell shading applied in Word will be applied in Excel as well; as a result, you'll notice that cells with borders that are cut or copied from Word have a printable hairline border on them in Excel. ▶

If you want to remove or edit any of the formats Excel applies based on how you've formatted the Word table, select the cells involved, right-click the selection, and then click Format Cells on the shortcut menu. In the Format Cells dialog box, adjust the formatting as needed and then click OK.

Tip

When measuring the space that the text takes up, try to remember that 72-point text takes up roughly 1 square inch per character. Therefore, 10-point text (the Excel default point size) is roughly $1/7^{th}$ of an inch per character. So, for example, if the column in your Excel table has to be 1 inch wide to match the size you set in Word, you can fit seven 10-point characters across it. This basic equation should help you "do the math" to match Excel column widths to the equivalent Word settings.

When I paste Excel cells into a Word table, the content appears in the wrong cells

Source of the problem

Word and Excel are both part of the Microsoft Office XP suite of applications, so one assumes, and justifiably so, that the two applications and their files can play well together. Most of the time, you can paste Word content into an Excel worksheet and, conversely, Excel worksheet content into a Word document.

However, sometimes the worksheet cells that contain the material you need to transfer to a Word table do not weather the trip to Word intact. If you cut or copy worksheet cells to the Clipboard and then paste the material into a Word table, you might find that the pasted cells erroneously move or reorder the existing table cells in a way that you don't want. The cause? Not providing the appropriate landing strip—in other words, a clean, empty part of the Word document—on which the Excel content can land. The cells you pasted into the table shove Word's table cells over, and the table structure you took the time to set up to house your Excel content is completely messed up.

You can generally paste a Word table into an Excel worksheet with little hassle. (See "When I paste a Word table into my worksheet, the table's content appears in the wrong cells" on page 124.) So you might assume that, when pasting Excel worksheet content into a Word document, you'd have to paste the worksheet cells into an existing table. After all, because Excel's worksheet structure follows the pattern of a table, Excel provides a compatible environment for Word tables. It makes sense that you'd want Word to return the favor. The problem is that when you paste Excel content into Word, Word creates a separate table for the Excel material. Therefore, if you paste the Excel cells into an existing table, the cells form a table nested within the Word table, and the columns and rows you set up become extra baggage.

You can take one of three different approaches to solving the problem of Excel content messing up your existing Word table.

ting and importing

How to fix it

If pasting the Excel material into a Word document was the last action you did, you can undo the action and paste the material in a more appropriate place by following these steps:

Tip

By default, cut or copied Excel worksheet content usually appears in your Word document as a table with no borders, unless borders were applied to the original cells in Excel. If you want to apply borders to the new table in Word, you can either use the Tables And Borders toolbar buttons, or click Borders And Shading on the Format menu to access the Borders And Shading dialog box.

1. Press Ctrl+Z to undo the paste.
2. Click an insertion point outside the table, on a blank line.
3. Press Ctrl+V to paste the table outside the existing Word table.

If it has been a while since the Excel material was pasted in the Word document, you can cut the Excel material and then paste it in a more appropriate place by following these steps:

1. In Word, select the nested table that contains the Excel content and then press Ctrl+X to cut the table to the Clipboard.
2. Delete the Word table or if you want to keep it for another purpose, press Enter before or after the table to insert a few blank lines.
3. Paste the previously nested Excel table onto a blank line as a separate entity.

If you want to leave the pasted Excel content where it is and just get rid of the extra columns and rows in the Word table, follow these steps:

1. Using the mouse pointer, select the rows of the table you created before pasting. (Be sure not to select the row containing the nested table.)
2. Delete the rows by pointing to Delete on the Table menu and then clicking Rows.
3. Repeat steps 1 and 2, selecting the extraneous table columns and clicking Delete and then Columns on the Table menu to get rid of the extra columns.

Travel Expenses by Department					
Week Starting:	Sales	Marketing	Info Tech	Operations	Accounting
11/5/2001	$2,573.29	$2,135.00	58.65	298.75	125.00
11/12/2001	$2,560.50	$2,400.50	204.38	302.50	54.00
11/19/2001	$4,576.51	$2,986.00	350.11	306.25	320.00
11/26/2001	$3,574.90	$3,411.50	495.84	310.00	88.00

Troubleshooting Microsoft Excel 2002 127

When I paste Excel cells into a Word table, the content appears in the wrong cells

(continued from page 127)

Just the words, ma'am

What if you want just the content inside the cells of an Excel worksheet, but not the cells themselves, to appear in a Word table? Imagine you have a cell in an Excel worksheet that contains a sentence, paragraph, or large number that you'd rather not retype—all you want to do is grab the text from the cells and paste it into your Word document without worrying about the Excel cells coming along for the ride. Can it be done? Yep. Just double-click the Excel cell that contains the text and then select the text you want to copy. ▶

After you've made your selection, press Ctrl+C to copy the material to the Clipboard. Then, in your Word document, position the insertion point where you want the copied material to appear and press Ctrl+V to paste the copied text.

	A	B	C
1			
2		Travel Expenses	
3			
4		Sales	Marketing
5	Week Starting:		
6	11/5/2001	2573.29	$ 2,135.00
7	11/12/2001	$ 2,560.50	$ 2,400.50
8	11/19/2001	$ 4,576.51	$ 2,986.00
9	11/26/2001	$ 3,574.90	$ 3,411.50
10	12/3/2001		

Thou shalt be converted

When you paste cells from an Excel worksheet into a Word document, the worksheet cells are quickly converted into Word table elements. If you want, you can just as quickly convert the Word table into non-table text. To select the table, click it, point to Select on the Table menu, and then click Table. On the Table menu again, point to Convert and then click Table To Text. In the Convert Table To Text dialog box, click the Tabs option in the Separate Text With section and then click OK to convert the table into a tabular list.

> **Tip**
>
> If you convert a table to text and choose tabs, commas, or some other character as the separator between the cells' content, you can use Word's Find And Replace feature to seek out the characters and replace each of them with a space. Click Replace on the Edit menu to access the Find And Replace dialog box.

The chart I pasted into a Word document doesn't change when I update the Excel data

Source of the problem

It's great that you can paste content, such as a chart, from an Excel worksheet into a Word document (or into a PowerPoint presentation slide, for that matter), and whenever you edit the worksheet, the chart you pasted into the Word file updates to reflect those changes. Wait—you mean that's not happening? Oops.

Automatic updates, such as the one that's supposed to be happening in your chart, occur through a link between the *target* (the Word document in which you pasted the chart) and the *source* (the Excel worksheet from which you copied the chart in the first place). Normally, your Excel chart is updated in the Word document whenever you edit the Excel material used to build the chart because the pasted content is linked to the source. If the source and target aren't connected, the pasted content exists in isolation—no updates will occur, and the most you can do is edit the pasted chart by double-clicking it in the Word document. Excel's menus and toolbars will appear on the screen, and you can edit the chart as you normally would in Excel. However, the edits you make to the chart in the Word document will not affect the original chart in the source worksheet.

What can you do? Well, if you've already pasted the chart using only the Paste command on the Word Edit menu (or its equivalent toolbar button or keyboard shortcut), delete the chart and paste it again, this time using the Paste Special command. With the Paste Special feature, you can establish the links you need to update the chart in the target Word document whenever you make changes to the chart in the source Excel workbook.

How to fix it

1. In the Excel worksheet, select the chart you want to paste into Word.

2. On the Edit menu, click Copy to move a copy of the chart to the Clipboard.

3. Switch to or open the target Word document and position your insertion point where you want the chart to appear.

4. On the Edit menu in Word, click Paste Special. (Be sure to click Paste Special, not Paste.)

5. In the Paste Special dialog box, make sure that Microsoft Excel Chart Object is selected in the As list, and then click the Paste Link option to create a connection between the source and target files. ▶

6. Click OK to complete pasting the chart into the Word document.

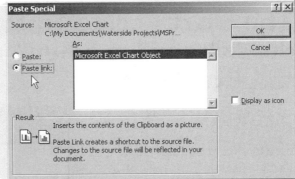

You can test your link by editing the source file, and then checking the chart in the target file. Within a few seconds, depending on your computer's memory and processor speed, the changes will appear in the linked chart. ▶

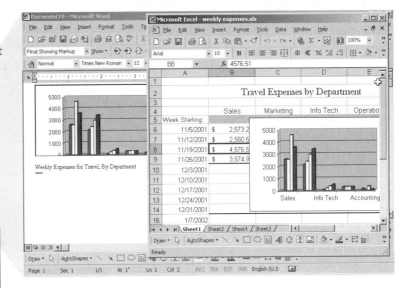

Tip

If you cut an Excel chart from its original worksheet—or if you rename, move, or delete the workbook file entirely—the chart you pasted into the Word document won't get updated when you change your source data. For the connection between the source and the target to be established and maintained, both files have to remain intact, with their original file locations and original names as they existed at the time you pasted the Excel chart into the Word document.

The chart I pasted into a Word document doesn't change when I update the Excel data

(continued from page 131)

Links like the Sphinx?

The link between your Excel chart and Word document will remain in place forever. Well, almost. The link will survive until and unless you sever it by clicking Links on the Edit menu in the Word document and then clicking the Break Link button. (Click Yes when you are prompted to confirm the break.) ▶

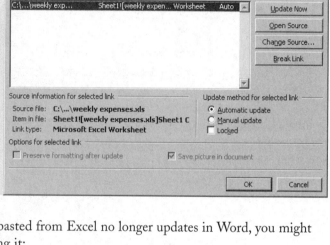

However, you might discover that you've also broken this link by accident. If you find that the chart you pasted from Excel no longer updates in Word, you might have done the following without realizing it:

- You might have accidentally deleted the source file.

- You might have moved either the source file or the target file to another directory or disk.

- You might have renamed either the source or target file.

If you've deleted the source file containing the Excel chart, you can delete the linked chart in Word, re-create the chart in a new Excel workbook, and use the Paste Special feature in Word to link the new chart to the Word document.

If you've moved or renamed the Excel workbook that contains the linked chart, don't worry; you can edit the link in Word. In the Word document containing the Excel chart, click Links on the Edit menu, and then click Change Source in the Links dialog box to display the Change Source dialog box. ▶

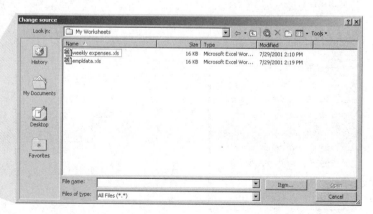

In the Change Source dialog box, locate the moved or renamed source file, select it, and then click Item. Excel displays the Set Item dialog box. ▶

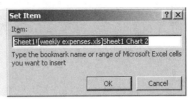

In the Set Item dialog box, select the old source file name in brackets, type over the selection, and make sure the sheet and chart numbers are correct. Click OK, click Open to confirm the new link, and then click OK to close the Links dialog box.

In the Links dialog box, you can choose how the link will update—automatically (the default), manually, or never (by choosing the Locked option). If you want to control when the target is updated, choose Manually. This will require you to click Links on the Edit menu when you open the target file, and then click the Update Now button to update the file with any changes made back at the source.

When I paste Excel data into an Access table, column headings appear as the first record

Source of the problem

A lot of Excel users are also Microsoft Access users, maintaining the same or similar data in both applications. Often, Excel houses simple list-type databases that users maintain daily; users import the worksheets into Access to flesh out a larger database on a weekly or monthly basis. However, you might encounter a problem when you're importing your Excel worksheet into Access for the

first time or if someone else converted an Excel worksheet to Access and missed the step in the Link Spreadsheet Wizard that converts Excel column headings to Access field names. Your column labels from the Excel worksheet appear as the first record in the converted Access table. ▶

    This problem is the result of a misstep while working in the Link Spreadsheet Wizard that appears whenever you open an Excel workbook in Access. If the First Row Contains Column Head-

	Field1	Field2	Field3	Field4	Field5	Field6	
▶	Last Name	First Name	Department	Date Hired	Bonus %	Insurance Y/N	Insur:
	Balinski	Joseph	Sales	9/2/1989	6.8%	Y	HMO
	Balsamo	Anthony	Administration	2/27/1997	6.7%	N	None
	Elmaleh	Miriam	Human Resourc	8/24/1995	5.0%	N	None
	Fox	Seymour	Marketing	7/15/1993	6.0%	Y	BCB!
	Frankenfield	Daniel	Sales	5/25/1992	6.8%	Y	HMO
	Freifeld	Iris	Accounting	8/3/1993	6.2%	Y	HMO
	Fuller	Robert	Sales	11/18/1995	6.0%	Y	HMO
	Geiger	Mary	Administration	4/30/1992	6.5%	Y	HMO
	Kline	Desiree	Marketing	3/15/1997	7.2%	Y	BCB!
	Lambert	Harry	Administration	2/15/1998	7.0%	Y	BCB!
	Maurone	Richard	Sales	6/13/1999	6.5%	Y	BCB!
	Mermelstein	David	Sales	10/4/1993	6.2%	Y	BCB!
	Miller	David	Marketing	9/24/1995	5.0%	N	None
	Pederzani	Bruce	Sales	1/3/1995	6.2%	Y	BCB!
	Shuster	Merrick	Sales	4/30/1995	6.5%	N	None
	Talbot	Ann	Marketing	6/7/1997	5.0%	Y	BCB!

ings check box in the first step of this wizard is not selected, Access treats every row in your Excel worksheet equally, and consequently doesn't recognize that the first row in the original Excel worksheet really represents the field names and not the data. It's easy to fix, requiring some minor table editing in Access or repeating the Link Spreadsheet Wizard process and checking the First Row Contains Column Headings checkbox, and then you're on your way.

    Of course, one way to fix this problem is not to cause it in the first place. You can set up an Access table to house your Excel content and have the field names already set up in the Access table. The Access field names don't have to match your Excel column labels exactly, but for clarity's sake, they should be similar.

How to fix it

To add Excel records to an existing Access table (with appropriate field names in place), follow these steps:

1. If you've already created your Access table, enter field names that match the names you're using in your Excel worksheet, open that table, and leave it open awaiting the Excel content.

2. Switch to or open your Excel worksheet and select the cells containing the data you want to add to the Access table. Do *not* include the row of the worksheet that contains your column labels.

3. On the Edit menu, click Copy to place the Excel data on the Clipboard.

4. Switch back to the Access table and click the first cell of the first row of the table.

5. On the Edit menu, click Paste Append. The Excel data appears in the table. Click Yes to confirm pasting the records.

Your Excel data will fill the rows of the Access table and fill the same number of columns in the table as you pasted from Excel. This might or might not populate all of the columns (fields) in the Access table, as some of them might not have been mirrored in the structure of your Excel worksheet. ▶

Last Name	First Name	Department	Date Hired	Bonus%	Insurance Y-N	Carrie
Balinski	Joseph	Sales	9/2/1989	6.8%	Y	HMO
Balsamo	Anthony	Administration	2/27/1997	6.7%	N	None
Elmaleh	Miriam	Human Resourc	8/24/1995	5.0%	N	None
Fox	Seymour	Marketing	7/15/1993	6.0%	Y	BCBS
Frankenfield	Daniel	Sales	5/25/1992	6.8%	Y	HMO
Freifeld	Iris	Accounting	8/3/1993	6.2%	Y	HMO
Fuller	Robert	Sales	11/18/1995	6.0%	Y	HMO
Geiger	Mary	Administration	4/30/1992	6.5%	Y	HMO
Kline	Desiree	Marketing	3/15/1997	7.2%	Y	BCBS
Lambert	Harry	Administration	2/15/1998	7.0%	Y	BCBS
Maurone	Richard	Sales	6/13/1999	6.5%	Y	BCBS
Mermelstein	David	Sales	10/4/1993	6.2%	Y	BCBS
Miller	David	Marketing	9/24/1995	5.0%	N	None
Pederzani	Bruce	Sales	1/3/1995	6.2%	Y	BCBS
Shuster	Merrick	Sales	4/30/1995	6.5%	N	None
Talbot	Ann	Marketing	6/7/1997	5.0%	Y	BCBS
Ulrich	Lillie	Human Resourc	12/15/1992	5.5%	Y	HMO

Record: ◄◄ ◄ 1 ► ►I ►*

Recycle your Excel column labels

If your Access table was new and had no field names yet, you can use the Excel column labels to create them. Instead of selecting all of your Excel data except the row containing column labels, include that row in your selection. On the Edit menu, click Copy, and then switch to your new Access table. Click the first cell of the first row (under Field1). On the Edit menu, click Paste Append, and then click Yes to confirm pasting the records.

Your first record in the table will now be the field names from your Excel worksheet—and these names must be transferred to the field names at the top of each column in the Access table. To do this, double-click the first Access field name, and while the Field1 text is highlighted, type the field name you see in the first record. Move on to Field2 and repeat the process, continuing until all of the field names have been replaced by the column labels from your Excel data.

The last step of recycling column labels is to delete the first record—simply click the record number to the left of the row, and press Delete. The row will disappear, and you'll be prompted to confirm your intention to delete the record by clicking Yes.

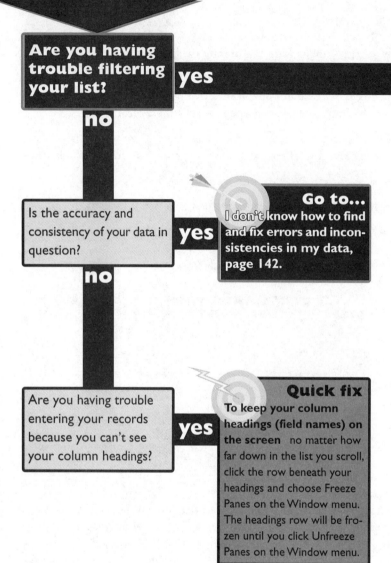

Are you having trouble filtering your list?

yes

no

Is the accuracy and consistency of your data in question?

yes

Go to...
I don't know how to find and fix errors and inconsistencies in my data, page 142.

no

Are you having trouble entering your records because you can't see your column headings?

yes

Quick fix
To keep your column headings (field names) on the screen no matter how far down in the list you scroll, click the row beneath your headings and choose Freeze Panes on the Window menu. The headings row will be frozen until you click Unfreeze Panes on the Window menu.

Filtering records

Does your AutoFilter not work as you expect it to?

yes →

Go to...
When I filter my list, all of my records disappear, page 138.

no ↓

Are you having trouble with the Advanced Filter command?

yes →

Go to...
The advanced filter I applied didn't work, page 144.

no ↓

Are you unable to apply the filter criteria you want?

yes →

Go to...
I don't see my filter criteria in the Auto-Filter list, page 140.

no ↓

Do you need to find all the blank fields in your worksheet?

yes →

Quick fix
To find all your blank fields, use AutoFilter. With AutoFilter on, (on the Data menu, point to Filter and then click AutoFilter in the sub-menu), click the drop-down arrow on the right side of the column you think contains the blank fields, and then click Blanks. Repeat these steps for as many columns as you believe have blank entries.

If your solution isn't here, check these related chapters:
- Outlining, page 244
- Searching for data, page 290
- Sorting data, page 310
Or see the general trouble-shooting tips on page xv.

When I filter my list, all of my records disappear

Source of the problem

Well, that's not what you expected to happen, eh? But don't worry—it's actually a common problem, especially if you are working with a large data list—also called a *database*—that contains hundreds of rows of information—also known as records. It's easy to establish AutoFilter (automatic filtering) criteria that either exclude all records in a database or refine the list to include no records. You'll normally see these effects when you filter the list and subsequently apply criteria that none of the records that are currently displayed can meet. In this example, none of the records in this list meet the specified criteria. ▶

What normally causes this problem is using the Custom AutoFilter feature. With the Custom option in any field's AutoFilter list, you can set a filter criterion such as Is Greater Than, Is Less Than, or Contains and compare this criterion to an entry you type in the Custom AutoFilter dialog box. For example, you can set up a custom filter that looks for all employees earning a bonus of 7 percent or greater or for all HMO subscribers whose bonus is less than 6 percent.

If the database contains no employees who subscribe to an HMO and receive a bonus of less than 6 percent, or if you've already filtered the list down to people who subscribe to a private insurance carrier, applying the custom filter you set will result in all the currently displayed records disappearing. They're not deleted, but they're hidden because they don't meet the criterion. It's easy to set the criterion to a value that doesn't exist in the database, by either entering a typo or not being fully aware of all the data stored in the database when setting up the filter. If you're working with someone else's list, the latter cause is probably the culprit. Regardless of why no records are displayed, solving the problem involves resetting one or more filter criteria to display the records you need to see.

How to fix it

1. Check your database for drop-down arrows that are blue. Blue drop-down arrows in a filtered database indicate columns—also called fields—to which filters have been applied.

2. In any field with a blue drop-down arrow, click the arrow and then click All in the drop-down list. This will remove the filter applied only to this field and bring back any records that the filter caused to be hidden. ▶

3. Repeat step 2 for as many fields as needed, until you have displayed all the records you want.

	B	C	D	E	G	H	I
1							
2	Employee Data						
3							
4	Last Name	First Name	Department	Date Hired	Bonus %	Insurance Y/N	Insurance Carrier
25			(All)				
26			(Top 10…)				
27			(Custom…)				
28			Human Resources				
29			Marketing				

Start big, end small

When applying filters to your database, the process can be easy. For example, imagine that you want to refine the list by a single field—saying, in effect, "Show me all the employees who work in Accounting." This requires that only the Department field be filtered. On the other hand, if you need to see all the employees in Accounting who are using the company's HMO for health insurance and who were hired prior to 1998, you'll need to filter three fields: Department, Insurance Carrier, and Date Hired.

When filtering a list, it's a good rule of thumb to start with the field that has the most duplicate entries and end with a field that has few or no duplicates. For example, in an employee list, you might want to filter for all the employees in a specific department who earn more than a certain salary per year and who were hired before a certain date. If the Department field has a lot of duplicates, you'll probably end up with more possible entries on which to use filters for the Bonus % and Date Hired fields, which would most likely have fewer duplicates in their columns.

When filtering more than one field, you should filter the fields in the appropriate sequence. Be sure not to eliminate some of the records you want to end up with by filtering an out-of-sequence field first. Using the Uses The HMO, Works In Accounting, and Hired Before 1998 criteria in the previous example, you would want to filter the Department field, then the Insurance Carrier field, and then the Date Hired field. Filtering in any other order could remove employees who are Accounting, who subscribe to the private carrier or don't use insurance, or who were hired after 1998. If you aren't familiar with the database (or the data stored in it), you might not realize that products in the database that meet your criteria are presented in an order that you don't intend.

> **Tip**
>
> You can redisplay all the records in one fell swoop and still keep the AutoFilter feature active by removing all filters. Click any field in your database. On the Data menu, point to Filter and then click Show All.

I don't see my filter criteria in the AutoFilter list

Source of the problem

The AutoFilter list for any column, or *field*, shows all of the entries for that field, whether you are working with a list of information, or *database*, that contains 10 rows or 1000. If you choose an entry from a field's AutoFilter list, the only rows, or *records*, that will be displayed are those that match that specific entry in that specific field. So if you go to make a selection in the AutoFilter list and you don't see the entry that you want to filter on, you will know that the entry was not designated properly in the selected field in any of the records.

What could be the cause of this? There are several possible explanations for a missing AutoFilter entry:

- **A skipped row.** A row might have accidentally been inserted or skipped in the database you want to filter. Because AutoFilter recognizes only continuous and contiguous entries in a database, all you have to do in this case is delete the empty row. After you delete the empty row, the missing entry will appear in the AutoFilter drop-down list. ▶

- **Typos.** If you're looking for the name Smythe and if someone typed Smithe or Smyth instead when entering data in the database, you won't see Smythe in the AutoFilter list. If you suspect a typo is at the root of your missing entry problem, look for spellings that are similar to the entry you're looking for. (Don't forget misspellings!)

- **Other fields have already been filtered.** If other fields have been filtered, thus reducing the displayed records, any new filter will apply to only those reduced number of records. For example, if your database contains 1000 records but has been filtered down to 20 records, and if you then filter another field, 20 or fewer entries will be available in the AutoFilter list. The one record you are looking for might be hidden by the previously applied filters. If previous filters are the suspected cause, you have to remove them and then search for your record from the complete list of records in the database.

- **Entries in the wrong field.** Be sure to carefully examine the columns on either side of the field that you're filtering to make sure the entry you're looking for wasn't typed by accident into either column. For example, a zip code entry might have been typed into the phone number field, or a city entry could have been typed into the street address field. ▶

Date Hire	Bonus %	Insurance Y/N	Insurance Carrier	
	E	G	H	I	J
11/15/1996	5.7%	Y	HMO	
9/23/1995	5.8%	N	None	
8/3/1993	6.2%	Y	HMO	
2/27/1997	6.7%	N	None	
4/30/1992	6.5%	Y	HMO	
2/15/1998	7.0%	Y	BCBS	
8/24/1995	5.0%	N	None	
12/15/1992	5.5%	Y	HMO	
11/27/1993	6.3%	Y	BCBS	
7/15/1993	6.0%	Y	BCBS	
3/15/1997	7.2%	BCBS	Y	
9/24/1995	5.0%	N	None	
6/7/1997	5.0%	Y	BCBS	
9/2/1989	6.8%	Y	HMO	
5/25/1992	6.8%	Y	HMO	

How to fix it

1. Click any cell other than one containing a heading.

2. On the Data menu, point to AutoFilter and then click Show All. All filters will be removed, although AutoFilter will remain in effect.

3. Click the drop-down arrow for the field containing the entry you need. Assuming none of the other potential causes of hard-to-find records are at work, the entry you're looking for should appear in the AutoFilter list.

Seek and ye shall find

If you have used AutoFilter to look for a record and been unsuccessful, another way to look is to use Microsoft Excel's Find command.

Using Find, you can search the entire worksheet for a specific word, number, or even a single character. You can search all contents, formulas, or comments that have been added to annotate your worksheet.

To search the entire worksheet, press Ctrl+A to select the entire worksheet and then press Ctrl+F to display the Find dialog box. To display a full set of search options, click the Options button to expand the dialog box. ▶

In the Find What box, type what you want to find and then click the Find Next button. Excel will locate and display any instances of your Find What entry, and you can continue to click Find Next until the one you want to change is found.

Tip

If you're searching for a single letter or number (such as *A* or *3*), make sure the Find Entire Cells Only check box is selected. Otherwise, Excel will find every instance of that letter or number, even when it is part of words or larger numbers.

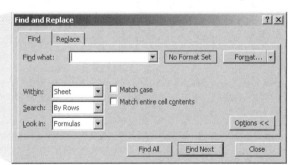

I don't know how to find and fix errors and inconsistencies in my data

Source of the problem

From a filtering standpoint, consistency is probably the second most important feature of the records in any database—second after accuracy, that is. If, for example, you have a Department field in an employee database, it won't do to enter "Accounting" for one record and "Acctg." for another. Why would variations on the spelling or abbreviation of a word be a problem? Because if you later want to filter for all people in the Accounting department, none of the people in the Acctg. department will meet the filter criterion, despite the fact that they, too, are in the Accounting department. You would have to filter twice to find all the people in this one department. ▶

Finding these inconsistencies is simple; fixing them is just a matter of entering the correct data after you've found the inconsistencies you want to eliminate.

	B	C	D	E
1				
2	Employee Data			
3				
4	Last Name	First Name	Department	Date Hire
5	Chambers	Rosemary	(All)	11/15/1996
6	Patrick	Kaitlin	(Top 10...)	9/23/1995
7	Freifeld	Iris	(Custom...) / Accounting	8/3/1993
8	Balsamo	Anthony	Acctg.	2/27/1997
9	Geiger	Mary	Administration	4/30/1992
10	Lambert	Harry	Human Resources / Marketing	2/15/1998
11	Elmaleh	Miriam	Mktg.	8/24/1995
12	Ulrich	Lillie	Sales	12/15/1992
13	Zerbe	Robert	Human Resources	11/27/1993

How to fix it

1. To make sure you can see all entries, including ones that are inconsistently spelled, abbreviated, or numbered, point to Filter on the Data menu, and then click Show All. (If this command is unavailable on the Filter submenu, you are already seeing all entries.)

2. Click the drop-down arrow on the right side of the column that has inconsistent entries. Examine the drop-down AutoFilter lists to find both the correct entry you want to retain and the alternate entry causing the inconsistency. Make a note of both entries' exact spellings.

3. Press Ctrl+H to display the Find And Replace dialog box (the Replace tab will be selected).

Tip

Don't forget to save your database after each round of edits and be sure to save more frequently if the edits are numerous. Especially if you do have to make a lot of edits, you wouldn't want to repeat them! Commit the keyboard shortcut for saving (Ctrl+S) to memory —you're much more likely to save if you don't first have to stop typing.

4. In the Find What box, type the entry that causes the inconsistency. In the Replace With box, type the entry you want to retain. ▶

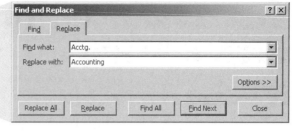

5. Click Find Next to locate the first instance of the erroneous entry and then click Replace to replace the entry with the spelling or numbering you prefer.

Continue clicking Find Next and then Replace to correct each instance individually, and then click OK when a message box notifying you that no more matches are found appears. (You can also simply keep clicking Replace, which will take you to the next instance of the Find text and replace it. If you are sure that replacing all specified entries at once will not cause conflicts with similar data, click Replace All to replace every instance of the offending entry with one fell swoop.)

6. Repeat steps 2 through 5 for additional inconsistent entries, as needed.

An ounce of prevention is worth hours of editing

Unless you like to search for errors and edit them—perhaps hundreds of them, considering that each worksheet can contain as many as 65,000 records—you'd be wise to set up your database worksheet so that only certain entries will be accepted. Wouldn't it be great if users attempting to enter "Acctg." for the Department field received an error message that informed them that only certain department names are accepted in the field?

You can create such error messages through Excel's Data Validation feature.

To apply data validation, select the column that you want to control. On the Data menu, click Validation. In the Data Validation dialog box, make sure the Settings tab appears and then click List in the Allow drop-down list. In the Source text box, type the acceptable entries, separating each with a comma. ▶

On the Input Message tab, you can create your own input messages to advise users which entries are acceptable for the cells in which they are working. On the Error Alert tab, you can create your own error messages to inform users that they've typed entries that don't meet the data validation rules you've applied. These alerts will appear as needed, when the user works in the selected column's cells.

(If you have any trouble with this feature, see "I can't get my data validation rules to work" on page 116.)

The advanced filter I applied didn't work

Source of the problem

Excel's Advanced Filter feature might not seem like the most intuitive tool on the planet, so don't feel bad if you get an error message or if the filter just plain doesn't work. Once you understand exactly how this particular filter operates, however, you'll find it helpful as an alternative to the more limited capabilities of the AutoFilter command.

Using the Advanced Filter feature, you can set one or more criteria for filtering your data list, or *database*, and then either reduce the database to the rows (also known as records) that meet the criteria or copy the records that meet the criteria to a separate place in the workbook—on the same sheet or on a different sheet.

So the problem is that you applied a filter and nothing happened, or you got the wrong records, or Excel threw an error message up on the screen to taunt you.

What could have gone wrong? Any of the following could be the culprit:

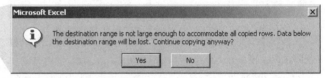

- The range you selected in the Copy To box in the Advanced Filter dialog box does not contain enough room for the filtered records to be copied.

- You could have accidentally made an error selecting the criteria range.

- None of your records match the criteria you've set.

With these potential causes for problems, it's understandable that your first (or second, or third) attempt to use Advanced Filter has run aground. The solution is usually simple, albeit enigmatic. Repeating the Advanced Filter command with a greater understanding of what the feature can do is usually the best approach.

How to fix it

1. Set up a range for the criteria you want in the rows above the database you want to filter. (You might have to insert several blank rows above your column headings to prepare for the actual Advanced Filter process.)

2. Select the column headings, or *field names*, for the columns, or *fields*, you want to filter and copy them to the first row of the criteria range.

Filtering records

3. Type the entries you want to filter for under the copied column headings. ▶

4. With your criteria range set up and your criteria entered, click inside the database list, point to Filter on the Data menu, and then click Advanced Filter.

5. In the Advanced Filter dialog box, choose how Excel will display the results of the filter. Click either Filter The List In-Place (which reduces the displayed list to the records that meet the criteria) or Copy To Another Location (which displays the records that meet the criteria in another place on the same worksheet or in another worksheet in the open workbook).

6. Verify the cells that appear in the List Range box. Excel should select all of the rows and columns included in the range to be filtered. However, you can select the cells you want to filter by clicking outside the Advanced Filter dialog box and then selecting the range you want. The Advanced Filter dialog box temporarily shrinks so that you can see the range you're selecting. When you release the mouse button, the dialog box displays the range you've selected.

7. In the Criteria Range box, select the field headings and entries you set up earlier.

8. If you click the Copy To Another Location option, specify a range of cells into which Excel should copy the records that meet your filter criteria in the Copy To box.

9. Click OK to apply the filter. ▶

	Last Name	First Name	Department	Date Hired	Bonus %	Insurance Y/N	Insurance Carrier
1	Last Name	First Name	Department	Date Hired	Bonus %	Insurance Y/N	Insurance Carrier
2			Accounting			Y	HMO
3							
4							
5							
6	**Employee Data**						
7							
8	Last Name	First Name	Department	Date Hired	Bonus %	Insurance Y/N	Insurance Carrier
9	Chambers	Rosemary	Accounting	11/15/1996	5.7%	Y	HMO
10	Patrick	Kaitlin	Accounting	9/23/1995	5.8%	N	None
11	Freifeld	Iris	Accounting	8/3/1993	6.2%	Y	HMO
12	Balsamo	Anthony	Administration	2/27/1997	6.7%	N	None
13	Geiger	Mary	Administration	4/30/1992	6.5%	Y	HMO
14	Lambert	Harry	Administration	2/15/1998	7.0%	Y	BCBS
15	Elmaleh	Miriam	Human Resources	8/24/1995	5.0%	N	None

Tip

If you want to create a report based on the records that meet your criteria, it's a good idea to click the Copy To Another Location option in the Advanced Filter dialog box. This approach also keeps your advanced filter list intact in case you want to use the AutoFilter or Sort features on the original list.

	Last Name	First Name	Department	Date Hired	Bonus %	Insurance Y/N	Insurance Carrier
1	Last Name	First Name	Department	Date Hired	Bonus %	Insurance Y/N	Insurance Carrier
2			Accounting			Y	HMO
3							
4	Last Name	First Name	Department	Date Hired	%	Y/N	Carrier
5	Chambers	Rosemary	Accounting	11/15/1996	5.7%	Y	HMO
6	Freifeld	Iris	Accounting	8/3/1993	6.2%	Y	HMO
7							
8							
9	**Employee Data**						
10							
11	Last Name	First Name	Department	Date Hired	Bonus %	Insurance Y/N	Insurance Carrier
12	Chambers	Rosemary	Accounting	11/15/1996	5.7%	Y	HMO
13	Patrick	Kaitlin	Accounting	9/23/1995	5.8%	N	None
14	Freifeld	Iris	Accounting	8/3/1993	6.2%	Y	HMO
15	Balsamo	Anthony	Administration	2/27/1997	6.7%	N	None

Is Microsoft Excel displaying a number different than you expected?

yes

no

Are you having trouble formatting numbers as percentages?

yes

no

Quick fix

To turn a number into a percentage, select it and click the Percentage Style button. This feature works best with numbers that are actually the result of a formula that calculates a percentage—such as 10 divided by 50, which equals .2 or 20 percent.

Are you having trouble displaying decimals as fractions?

yes

Go to...

The fractions I entered aren't displayed correctly, page 152.

no

Quick fix

If you can't tell your negative and postive numbers apart, right-click any cell and click Format Cells. In either the Numbers or Currency category, click a format in the Negative Numbers list.

Are you having trouble displaying negative numbers?

yes

no

Do you need a number format that Excel doesn't offer?

yes

Go to...

None of the available number formats meets my needs, page 154.

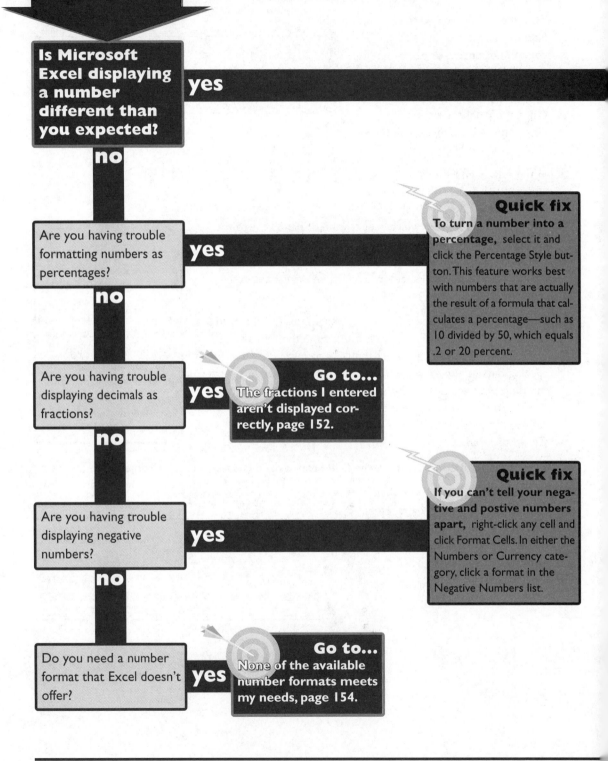

Are you having trouble entering numbers that end in zero?

yes → **Go to...** When I type a decimal ending in zero, the zero disappears, page 148.

no

Is the number you entered aligned incorrectly?

yes → **Go to...** I typed a number, but it's not right-aligned, page 150.

If your solution isn't here, check these related chapters:

- Currency, page 56
- Formatting text, page 156
- Formatting worksheets, page 168

Or see the general troubleshooting tips on page xv.

When I type a decimal ending in zero, the zero disappears

Source of the problem

As you're zipping along entering your data, you enter a number, say 3.50, and as soon as you press Enter, the zero disappears, leaving you with 3.5 in the cell. Not really a major disappointment, but if the cell is in the Price column for a list of products, a price of 3.5 doesn't make sense. "Format it as currency!" you say. Well, maybe not. Not all numbers that represent money have to be formatted as currency—a simple two-decimal number format will do just fine, especially if you don't want to see dollar signs on each number.

So what's the problem? Why is Microsoft Excel dropping your zero? Because by default all cells are formatted as General content, and that particular format drops the zero for decimals ending in zero. When the General format sees numbers, it right aligns them, drops the zero, and that's it. Yes, its handling of decimals can be a pain, but no, you aren't stuck with it.

Solving the problem requires either a proactive plan or a reactive one. You can either format the Price column (or your version thereof) for two decimal places before you enter any content, or you can format it after you've entered your content, restoring all those zeroes to visibility in the worksheet. Either way, the steps are the same.

Tip

Should you be proactive or reactive? It's really a matter of preference—neither approach is better than the other or more labor-intensive. If you never want to see your zeroes disappear, format the columns that will contain price-like numbers ahead of time; if you don't mind seeing them disappear for a while (until you've finished making your entries), bring them back later by formatting after the fact.

How to fix it

1. As you build the headings and layout of your worksheet, select the column(s) or range(s) that you want to be formatted as numbers with two decimal places displayed.

2. On the Format menu, click Cells.

3. In the Format Cells dialog box, make sure the Number tab is visible. The General format is selected by default unless you are working with a blank worksheet or have applied another format to cells within your worksheet.

Tip

You can't use the Increase Decimal or Decrease Decimal buttons on blank cells, so this approach is a reactive one. If you think the toolbar buttons are the way to go, wait until all of your entries are made before you use them.

4. Click the Number category and view the options on the right side of the dialog box. Using the Decimal Places box, you can specify how many decimal places you want to display. If 2, the default setting, does not appear in the Decimal Places box, return the setting to 2 by clicking the up or down arrows. ▶

5. Click OK to apply the format and close the dialog box.

All at the click of a button

Instead of opening the Format Cells dialog box, you can also adjust the decimal settings for any selected cell or range by using the Increase Decimal button on the Formatting toolbar. Of course, you can also use the Decrease Decimal button if more than two decimal places are displayed.

Select the cell or range (including whole columns and rows) to be reformatted and be sure that only numerical content appears in the selected range. If the column heading is already typed, drag through the cells that contain numbers—the decimal formatting buttons don't work if the selected range contains anything other than numbers—rather than clicking the column letter to select the entire column. Click the Increase Decimal button once to increase the setting from one decimal place to two places and then click a cell outside the range to deselect the cells you just formatted. ▶

Do as I do, not as I say

If you don't want to wait until all of your numerical entries are made to use the Increase Decimal button, enter one of your numbers, select the cell containing it, and then click the Increase Decimal button until the desired number of decimals are displayed.

With that cell still selected, click the Format Painter button, which copies the formatting of the selected cell, and then drag through the remaining empty cells in the range. They'll then be ready to accept your entries, including those with decimals ending in zero, and the zeroes will be displayed. ▶

I typed a number, but it's not right-aligned

Source of the problem

By default, numerical content is right-aligned. As you type a number in a cell, the number builds from the left side of the cell. When you press Enter, however, the number moves to the right side of the cell. This is the case whether the cells where you're typing are formatted as General, Number, Currency, or Accounting (the category list options in the Format Cells dialog box). Dates and times are also right-aligned, even though they contain text.

So what's going on when you type a number in a cell, press Enter, and the number remains on the left side of the cell? One of two things can be causing this phenomenon: how the cell is formatted or a typo. How can this be?

Imagine these scenarios:

- The Align Left button (found on the Formatting toolbar) was accidentally clicked while the cell (or a range containing the cell) was selected.

- Left alignment was similarly applied through the Format Cells dialog box.

- You typed some nonnumerical character when entering the number in the cell—a period instead of a comma (to separate thousands), a space, the letter O instead of zero (0), a lower-case L instead of a 1, or additional symbols that would normally be accepted as numerical content—an extra decimal point, two slashes, two dashes, or two commas typed together.

Should any of these situations occur, your numeric entry will be left-aligned. In the case of the accidental use of the Align Left button, Excel still thinks the entry is numerical, but thinks you want it left-aligned. In the case of typos, the addition of nonnumerical content convinces Excel that you're entering the equivalent of text.

The solution to this problem is to determine the cause (formatting or typo) and either reformat or edit the cell.

> **Tip**
> Don't forget the Center button—this can be accidentally applied just as easily as the Align Left button. If your number moves to dead center in the cell after you press Enter, formatting is your culprit—no typo will result in a centered number.

> **Tip**
> Your cell could be set to left alignment as the result of formatting applied to previous content. If you've done some renovations in your worksheet, taking stuff from here and putting it there, you might be entering numbers into what was a column or row formatted for text, with left alignment previously applied.

> **Tip**
> You can quickly change the alignment of any cell or selected range by pressing easily remembered keyboard shortcuts: Ctrl+R for right alignment, Ctrl+L for left alignment, and Ctrl+E for center alignment. Why E and not C? Because C was taken by Copy (Ctrl+C).

How to fix it

To change formatting from left to right alignment using the Formatting toolbar's alignment buttons, follow these steps:

1. Select the cell or range for which you want to change the alignment formatting.

2. Click the Align Right button. The numerical content will move to the right side of the selected cells.

To change formatting from left to right alignment by editing text, follow these steps:

1. Select the cell that contains a typo or a nonnumerical character.

2. Make whatever changes are necessary to the entry in the Formula bar to edit the cell, moving or removing whatever's wrong with the entry. ▶

With only the best indentions

Another cause of seemingly odd alignments is the use of Excel's Indent feature, which can be applied (accidentally or on purpose) from the toolbar or in the Format Cells dialog box.

Why would someone indent in a worksheet? To create a simple visual distinction between content in vertically adjoining cells, or to show hierarchy between entries, such as a total at the top level and the numbers that created it beneath. ▶

To apply or remove an indent, click a cell or select a range of cells and click the Increase Indent or Decrease Indent button on the Formatting toolbar. You can also click Cells on the Format menu, and on the Alignment tab of the Format Cells dialog box, use the up and down arrows of the Indent spin box to increase or decrease the indent currently set. (The default is zero.)

Tip

If your entry is numerical, clicking the Increase Indent button when the entry is selected left-aligns the number no matter how it was previously aligned. Be careful when you use the Increase Indent button, or you might have to reapply right alignment or centering to numerical content that you want to keep that way!

The fractions I entered aren't displayed correctly

Source of the problem

Although the stock market might be abandoning fractions for decimals, many people still like fractions. They don't want to hear that four out of five dentists surveyed recommend something; they want to see that $4/5$ (four-fifths) of all dentists agree.

Of course, Excel's default treatment of a typed fraction is to turn it into a date. If you type $4/5$ into a cell to which no special formatting has been applied, it becomes 5-Apr as soon as you press Enter (if you're working in a U.S. date format). If you typed your number as a decimal such as .80, you can turn that into a fraction ($4/5$) by applying any one of several Fraction formats to the cell in question. ▶

Whether you typed your fractions and they turned into dates, or you typed your entries as decimals and now you want to see them as fractions, the same solution is called for—apply Fraction formatting to the cell or range.

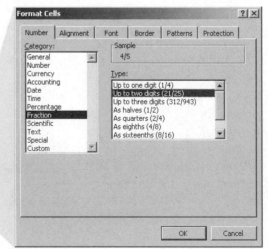

How to fix it

1. Select the cell or range that contains or will contain numbers that should be displayed as fractions.

2. Click Cells on the Format menu.

3. In the Format Cells dialog box, click the Number tab.

4. Click the Fraction category and select the fraction format you want to apply from the Type list. You can control the number of digits in the fraction or designate whether the fraction is expressed in halves, quarters, eighths, sixteenths, tenths, or hundredths. (You might have to retype the fractions after you've formatted the cells to get the results you want.) ▶

5. Click OK to apply the format and close the dialog box.

That's either a fraction or very high blood pressure

It's a good idea to annotate your worksheet with a comment or callout to indicate to other users that a given range of cells is for-matted for fractions. This will

Tip

When you make your fraction format selection from the Type list, choose carefully. Say, for example, your cell contains 3.5 now. If you apply the Fraction format and choose As Tenths (3/10) from the Types list, 3.5 becomes 3 5/10 (three and five-tenths). This might be confus-ing to people who expect 3.5 to turn into 3 1/2.

prevent confusion when someone enters a number such as .786, and it turns into $393/500$. To insert a comment, right-click the cell and click Insert Comment on the shortcut menu. In the text box that appears, type *This cell is formatted to store all entries as fractions* or something to that effect. To confirm your new comment, click any cell.

If you prefer to annotate a range of cells, use callouts. Click the AutoShapes button on the Drawing toolbar, point to Callouts, click one of the callout options, and drag to draw a callout with a line pointing to the cell where you started to drag. Then type the callout's text. (The callout can contain the same text you might enter in a comment.) You can also use the drawing tools on the Drawing toolbar to add an extra arrow pointing from the callout to the cells so that it's clear that the callout refers to a range of cells. ▶

	D4	▼		f_x	0.8			
	A	B	C	D	E	F	G	H
1								
2			**Chemical Analysis**					
3								
4			Nitrogen	4/5				
5			Lead	3/4				
6			Chlorine	1/10				
7					Data is stored as			
8					decimals, but			
9					displays as fractions.			

Tip

The use of comments is covered in greater detail in "Comments and Track Changes" on page 34. You can find out more about using AutoShapes and callouts in "Drawing shapes and lines" on page 96.

None of the available number formats meets my needs

Source of the problem

Excel has nine different types of number formats that you can apply, and most of them have several variations—different ways to express negative numbers, different currency symbols, and choices about how many decimals are displayed or how thousands are separated. There is also the Special format category, which offers formatting for Social Security numbers, phone numbers, and zip codes.

So how can the number format you need be missing? Easy. If your worksheet contains serial, credit card, bank routing, product, or identification numbers, or if it contains any number format that includes dashes, slashes, dots, or fixed-position letters or symbols, you'll need to create your own number format.

Why not just enter the number with all the extra trimmings? Because it wastes time. If you knew you could enter 34-A5-7891 and skip the dashes and the A, wouldn't you want to? Aside from saving time, entering just the numbers can help reduce the margin for typing errors.

So how do you tell Excel where to insert dashes, letters, and other symbols in your entry so that all you have to type is the numbers? You build a custom number format, that's how.

How to fix it

1. Select the range of cells that needs the custom format.

2. Click Cells on the Format menu.

3. In the Format Cells dialog box, make sure the Number tab is visible.

4. Select the Custom category, scroll through the list of existing custom formats, and look at how they're expressed. (Note that the existing custom formats use pound signs to indicate numbers entered by the user and intervening characters, such as hyphens, to separate the numbers into segments.) Look for a format that closely matches the way in which you want to display numbers in the selected range and then select it so that you can use it as a basis for the custom format you want to design. If you can't find one that even comes close, pick one that has some of the elements you need—*d*'s, *y*'s, and *m*'s for dates, #'s for numbers, decimals, and so on. Then at least you'll have some of the features you'll need.

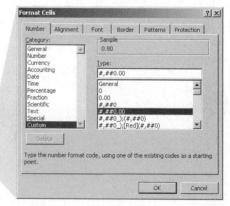

5. Delete any of the selected format's characters that you don't want by highlighting them with your mouse pointer in the Type box and pressing the Backspace key. Alternatively, you can simply highlight the entire string of characters in the Type box and enter your format—the characters you type will override the existing ones. Remember, too, that you can break your number into only four or fewer sections through the use of intervening symbols.

6. Click OK to apply the format and close the dialog box.

The sky's the limit, unfortunately...

Why "unfortunately"? A lack of limitations is usually a good thing. In this case it's unfortunate because although the custom format you create will control the placement of numbers that you type within the format, it won't control how many numbers you type. For example, if your worksheet contains product numbers such as 15379-A5-62, the creation of a format #####-A#-## will allow you to type *15379562*, and have it all fall into place. There's nothing stopping you, however, from entering *153795625897126*, which would result in 15379562587-A1-26. You could also enter too few numbers, such as *153795*, and 153-A7-95 would result. Although the format inserts the symbols for you, it doesn't require that a certain number of numbers be entered.

How can you prevent people from entering too many or too few numbers? Set up validation rules for the range of cells in your worksheet that will be formatted with the custom number format. Select the range that will use the custom format you created, and click Validation on the Data menu. On the Settings tab of the Data Validation dialog box, select Text Length in the Allow box, select Equal To in the Data box, and type the number of digits you want people to type in the Length box. ▶

Click OK to set the validation rule and close the dialog box. If you want, you can also create custom input and error messages by clicking the Input Message and Error Alert tabs and following the instructions on each tab. Even if you don't create a custom error message, if anyone tries to enter more or fewer numbers than the validation rule specifies, a default error message appears, notifying users that the correct number of digits must be entered before the cell can be filled.

> **Tip**
>
> Your custom number format can have only four sections—for example, you can set up a format to build 123-45-67-89, but not 123-45-67-89-0. Your entry can have an unlimited number of numbers in it, but the groups created by the intervening symbols or letters are limited to four.

> **Tip**
>
> When entering the number of digits in the Length box, don't count the symbols or letters that the custom format will be inserting for you—just count the number of digits that the user will type.

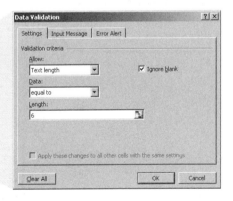

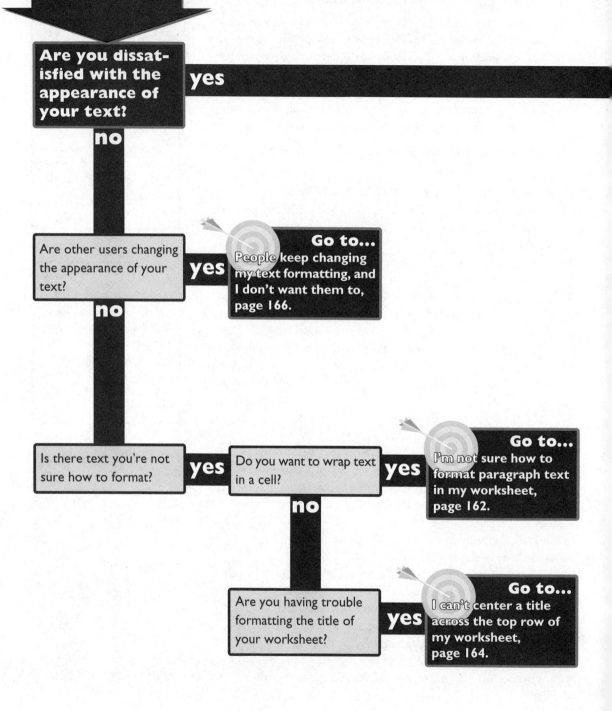

Are you dissatisfied with the appearance of your text?

yes

no

Are other users changing the appearance of your text?

yes

Go to...
People keep changing my text formatting, and I don't want them to, page 166.

no

Is there text you're not sure how to format?

yes

Do you want to wrap text in a cell?

yes

Go to...
I'm not sure how to format paragraph text in my worksheet, page 162.

no

Are you having trouble formatting the title of your worksheet?

yes

Go to...
I can't center a title across the top row of my worksheet, page 164.

Formatting text

Are you having trouble with the size of your text?

yes → **Go to...** My worksheet text is too small to read, page 158.

no

Does some of your text disappear after you press the Enter key?

yes → **Quick fix** **Make missing text reappear.** Text that's too wide for a column will overflow on top of (not into) the cell to its right. If the cell on the right contains text or numbers, however, your overflow text from the cell on the right will be chopped off at the edge of its cell. You can reduce the font size or widen the column by right-clicking the column heading and choosing Column Width. Enter a larger number for the column width and click OK.

no

Are you having trouble making your worksheet look uniform?

yes → **Go to...** The format of my text isn't consistent throughout my worksheet, page 160.

no

Are you unsure which fonts to use to give your worksheet a professional look?

yes → **Quick fix** **Avoid using very ornate or artistic fonts** except for occasional use in titles. Fonts such as Arial (the default) and Times New Roman are the conventional fonts in business environments.

If your solution isn't here, check these related chapters:

- Formatting numbers, page 146
- Formatting worksheets, page 168

Or see the general troubleshooting tips on page xv.

My worksheet text is too small to read

Source of the problem

By default, Microsoft Excel applies the 10-point Arial font to all text and numeric content. For some people, that's just too small. A worksheet in 10-point Arial can seem rather cramped and difficult to read, especially if the content is crowded into narrow columns and rows.

The solution to this problem depends on whether you want to change only the view on your screen or actually resize fonts in both displayed and printed worksheets. If you find it difficult to read your menus and toolbar buttons as well as your worksheet content, consider lowering your monitor resolution to 800 x 600 or 640 x 480. If you want larger text to appear in both displayed and printed worksheets, use a larger font size for some or all of your worksheet content.

Tip

Most monitors can display an 800 x 600 screen, but some older monitors cannot handle higher resolutions, such as 1024 x 768. To avoid problems, don't increase your screen resolution without checking the monitor's user guide to see what resolution it is capable of supporting.

Tip

You'll hate 640 x 480 resolution for viewing Web pages, as most pages are designed with an 800 x 600 resolution in mind. If you use this technique to make your worksheets more legible, be prepared to set it back to 800 x 600 when you go to spend any time on the Web.

How to fix it

To change the resolution of your monitor, even if only for the time you're working in Excel, follow these steps:

1. Minimize all open windows to display the Windows desktop.

2. Right-click an empty spot on the desktop and then click Properties on the shortcut menu.

3. In the Display Properties dialog box, click the Settings tab. ▶

4. In the Screen Area section, drag the slider to the left to reduce the resolution to either 640 x 480 or 800 x 600.

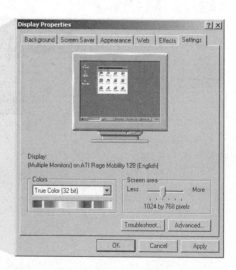

5. Click Apply. Windows tells you that your resolution will change and your screen might flicker. (You might even have to restart Windows for some of your applications to work properly.) Click OK.

6. After a few seconds, your screen resolution will change to the new setting. If the screen is legible, click OK when prompted to confirm the new resolution. You'll have 15 seconds to respond. If you don't, the resolution will revert to your old setting because Windows will assume you don't like the new setting.

Tip

If you want all of your text to be larger than 10 points on all worksheets, click Options on the Tools menu, and on the General tab, change the settings in the Standard Font and Size lists. Then click OK.

To increase the font size in your worksheet, follow these steps:

1. Select the cells that you want to change to a larger font.

2. On the Formatting toolbar, click the Font Size drop-down arrow, and click a larger font size. ▶

What you see is what you get...?

If your worksheet will be viewed on paper more often than on the screen, you might want to adjust the print scale settings before you actually print the worksheet. Because your worksheet might look dramatically different on the screen than it does on paper, you could be disappointed by the printed version of your worksheet after you spent so much time formatting it on the screen.

This doesn't mean you have to abandon the way you like to view the worksheet on the screen. You can print the worksheet larger than it appears on your monitor by increasing the scale at which it is printed. On the File menu, click Page Setup. In the Scaling section of the Page tab, increase the setting in the Adjust To box. The higher the percentage, the larger the worksheet content will appear when the worksheet is printed, without changing the worksheet's actual formatting. ▶

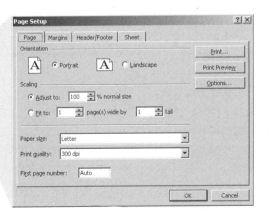

Warning

The one potential drawback to increasing the print scale of the worksheet is that the worksheet will print out on more pages. However, bear in mind that you might end up with those additional pages anyway, if you increase the font size in the worksheet.

The format of my text isn't consistent throughout my worksheet

Source of the problem

Not all worksheets are developed in a single session. For example, you sit down to set up the basic layout, enter your column and row labels, and enter some content. Then at a later time, you finish making your entries, create your formulas, and move things around as you reconsider your layout. Your process might vary, but unless you complete the entire worksheet and apply all the formatting in one session, you're likely to end up with some inconsistencies in your worksheet's appearance—a hodge-podge of fonts, text sizes, and styles, uneven application of number formats. (If other people work on your worksheet, they can introduce even more inconsistencies.) ▶

The larger your worksheet, the more likely these inconsistencies will occur because you can't see all of it at once. You might forget to make the labels bold in one section of the worksheet or change the font in one area and not in another. Why are these inconsistencies a problem? Because you don't want your piecemeal development process to be obvious, and because you want your worksheet to look as uniform and well planned as possible. Further, having consistent formatting throughout makes a worksheet easier to edit later because as you cut and copy text from place to place, the formatting will come with it.

	B	C	D	E	F
	Sales Analysis	2001			
	Second Quarter				
		Sales Revenue	Cost of Sales		
		Gross Sales	Sales Payroll	Advertising	Marketing
	TOTALS	208,826,923.00	2,657,910.00	758,341.00	
	New York	52,975,438.00	549,350.00	35,000.00	
	Philadelphia	43,892,359.00	450,670.00	25,450.00	
	Boston	33,489,123.00	325,650.00	45,670.00	
	Chicago	25,763,092.00	375,470.00	238,946.00	
	Houston	15,789,234.00	430,570.00	36,550.00	
	Phoenix	24,567,812.00	250,750.00	25,975.00	
	San Francisco	12,349,865.00	275,450.00	350,750.00	
	Sales Projections	2002			
	Second Quarter				
		Sales Revenue	Cost of Sales		
		Gross Sales	Sales Payroll	Advertising	Marketing
	TOTALS	250,083,407.00	250,083,407.00	250,083,407.00	250
	New York	62,975,438.00	62,975,438.00	62,975,438.00	62
	Philadelphia	53,892,359.00	53,892,359.00	53,892,359.00	53

Sheet1 / Sheet2 / Sheet3

> **Tip**
>
> If your worksheet is one of two or more that will have the same layout and formatting, group the worksheets first and then enter and format your labels and common content for maximum consistency throughout the workbook. (See "I don't want to have to build identical worksheets individually" on page 174.)

To correct the appearance of spotty formatting, you need to apply consistent styles throughout your worksheet. If, for example, you want all of your labels to be in a certain font and size, you need to apply the formatting to all of them at once. If you want totals and other important entries to stand out, choose attention-getting formats and apply them.

The following steps show you how to achieve consistently formatted worksheets.

Formatting text

How to fix it

Make a list of all the parts of your worksheet that require special formatting. One by one, go through the worksheet and select all of the content that needs a particular type of formatting—all the labels, for example, or all the totals. To select noncontiguous ranges of the worksheet, hold down the Ctrl key while you make your selections. With the cells selected, apply your formats using the buttons on the Formatting toolbar.

Ya gotta have style

If you've used a word processor such as Microsoft Word, you're probably familiar with the concept of styles. A style is a group of formats that can be applied to selected content with one command (the application of the style) rather than repeatedly applying several formats, step by step. By default, Excel has six different styles. You also create new styles of your own.

To edit an existing style, follow these steps:

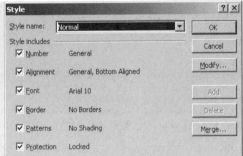

1. Click Style on the Format menu to display the Style dialog box. ▶

2. In the Style Name list, click the style you want to edit. Select the check boxes for the attributes—Number, Alignment, Font, Border, Patterns, and Protection—that you want the style to contain.

3. Click the Modify button to display the Format Cells dialog box and then apply the formatting you want for all the selected attributes.

4. Click OK to close the Format Cells dialog box, and then click OK again to close the Style dialog box and apply the style changes.

To create a new style, follow these steps:

1. Click Style on the Format menu and in the Style Name box, type a new style name to replace the name that is currently displayed.

2. Click the Modify button and in the Format Cells dialog box, apply all the formatting that the new style should include when it's applied to your worksheet.

3. Click OK to return to the Style dialog box; click the Add button to add your new style to the list of available styles for your workbook. Click OK.

Although you can apply the styles you created only in the workbook for which you created them, you can apply the Excel default styles from the Style Name list at any time. Select the cells to which you want to apply a style and click Style on the Format menu. In the Style Name list, click the style you want to apply and then click OK.

I'm not sure how to format paragraph text in my worksheet

Source of the problem

Many worksheets consist solely of numbers, with a brief amount of text to identify the numbers. Normally these worksheets track scientific or financial information and rarely, if ever, require any special formatting, other than to display numbers as currency or to make labels or important data bold. There are, however, worksheets that require a lot of text—rows of text-based data, labels between worksheet sections, and sometimes even paragraphs of text.

How can a worksheet, which is really just a grid of tiny cells, contain paragraphs? Easy. Because a worksheet is not designed for paragraph text, the tools to easily accommodate paragraph text aren't right there on the toolbars like the rest of the more commonly used tools. However, you can format any cell or range of cells to let text wrap within it. And by adjusting the width of a column, you can control both the width of the paragraph and the wrapping required to fit paragraph text into a cell. ▶

How to fix it

1. Select the cell or cells in which you want to wrap paragraph text.

2. Right-click the selection and then click Format Cells on the shortcut menu.

Tip

When a single cell contains a paragraph, it normally becomes taller. Its height increases to accommodate the amount of text in it and, in turn, the text wraps to accommodate the column width. Bear in mind that the height of the rest of the cells in that row will increase along with the affected cell, even if the other cells contain little or no content. If you later widen the column, you'll need to adjust the row height manually if all of the height is no longer needed. To adjust the row height, point to the bottom seam of the row's heading and then drag upward to decrease the row's height.

3. In the Format Cells dialog box, click the Alignment tab and in the Text Control section, select the Wrap Text check box. ▶

4. Click OK to close the dialog box and apply the format to the selected cell. Existing text or new text you enter will wrap within the column's current width.

5. As needed, widen the column by dragging the column heading's right seam to make the paragraph the width you need it to be.

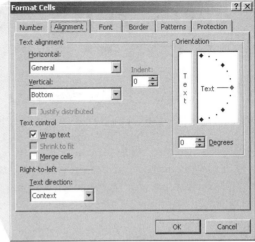

It's like you're floating

What if you don't want the paragraph to be in a specific cell? When you type a lot of text in a cell and you set the cell to wrap the text, the row the cell is in can get very tall, and the grid structure for that row might look weird with one cell filled with text and the rest of the cells overly tall for their contents. The alternative is to let the cell be yards long as a single string of text, which also looks weird.

How to avoid this phenomenon? Put the text in a text box. The text box will float over the surface of your worksheet, and you can place it wherever you want, even making its background clear so that if it overlaps any portion of the worksheet, the content underneath it isn't obscured. On the Drawing toolbar, click the Text Box button. (If the Drawing toolbar isn't visible, click the Drawing button on the Standard toolbar.) When the mouse pointer changes to a crosshair, click and drag to draw a rectangle the approximate size you think you'll need for your text. As soon as you release your mouse button, the insertion point is activated in the text box. Type your content, and the text will wrap to the confines of the box. ▶

You can always resize the text box by dragging its size handles—when the mouse pointer becomes a two-headed arrow, drag the corner handles outward to increase, or inward to decrease, the size of the box. You can also move the box by first selecting it and then, when the mouse pointer becomes a four-headed arrow, dragging it.

Tip

To make your text box transparent, select the box, click the arrow next to the Fill Color button on the Drawing toolbar, and then click No Fill.

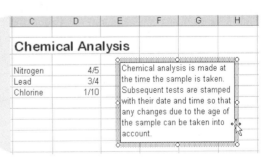

I can't center a title across the top row of my worksheet

Source of the problem

Your worksheet contains several rows and columns of data, and you've typed a title in one of the first cells. Now you want that title to be centered across the span of columns containing data or at least across the first screen of columns. A title is helpful, even if your worksheet is in a workbook with a file name that expresses the book's content, and even if your worksheet tab has a name on it. People often forget to read the sheet tabs unless they're leafing through looking for a particular sheet, and it's not a good idea to type really long tab names, anyway. What's more, the sheet tab name and the worksheet title may not be the same.

So you've got a title, and now you want to center it. ▶

How? Well, you don't move it to a cell that looks like it's roughly centered on the screen. Even if that were possible, if someone using a different size monitor or display resolution opens the file, the title won't appear centered for that person. If you print the worksheet, the title probably won't fall dead center, either.

The ideal method for centering a title across a span of columns is to use Excel's Merge And Center button. This way, the title will remain centered no matter how wide the columns are, or might become, due to future formatting.

	Last Name	First Name	Department	Date Hired	Bonus %	Insurance Y/N	Insurance Carrier
	Chambers	Rosemary	Accounting	11/15/1996	5.7%	Y	HMO
	Patrick	Kaitlin	Accounting	9/23/1995	5.8%	N	None
	Freifeld	Iris	Accounting	8/3/1993	6.2%	Y	HMO
	Balsamo	Anthony	Administration	2/27/1997	6.7%	N	None
	Geiger	Mary	Administration	4/30/1992	6.5%	Y	HMO
	Lambert	Harry	Administration	2/15/1998	7.0%	Y	BCBS
	Elmaleh	Miriam	Human Resources	8/24/1995	5.0%	N	None
	Ulrich	Lillie	Human Resources	12/15/1992	5.5%	Y	HMO
	Zerbe	Robert	Human Resources	11/27/1993	6.3%	Y	BCBS
	Fox	Seymour	Marketing	7/15/1993	6.0%	Y	BCBS
	Kline	Desiree	Marketing	3/15/1997	7.2%	Y	BCBS
	Miller	David	Marketing	9/24/1995	5.0%	N	None
	Talbot	Ann	Marketing	6/7/1997	5.0%	Y	BCBS
	Balinski	Joseph	Sales	9/2/1989	6.8%	Y	HMO
	Frankenfield	Daniel	Sales	5/25/1992	6.8%	Y	HMO

> **Tip**
>
> While you can make your worksheet title as long as you want, it's a good idea to be as succinct as possible when creating a title. For example, "Third Quarter Sales" is preferable to "Our Sales in the Third Quarter." By keeping the amount of text to a minimum, you can increase the size of the text to make it stand out and still not overwhelm the rest of the worksheet.

Formatting text

How to fix it

1. In the row containing your worksheet title, select the cells that span the distance across which you want to center the title. For example, if your worksheet fills columns A through H, and your title is in A1, select cells A1 through H1. ▶

2. Click the Merge And Center button on the Formatting toolbar.

Once your cells are merged and your title is centered, you can apply any formatting you wish, and any formatting already applied (other than alignment) will remain intact. If you add columns to your worksheet within the range of the merged cell, the cell will expand to center your title over all the columns. If you delete a column within the range, the merged cell will shrink to accommodate the new number of columns.

The cloud surrounding that silver lining

Merge And Center is very useful, and when people find out about it, it elicits a real "ooh, ahhh" reaction. There are, however, some drawbacks to it. The problems can occur not so much in using it, but in applying it too soon. Below is a list of things you can't do to a merged cell or to a column containing one. If you want to do these things, wait until after you've done them to use Merge And Center:

- Select an entire column and move it. If you try to move a column that includes the merged cell, a prompt appears indicating that you "cannot change part of a merged cell." In other words, by selecting the column, you've selected part of the merged cell, but that part can't be moved along with the rest of the cells in the column.

- Sort the data in a column that includes the merged cell.

- Apply formats from other areas of the worksheet with Format Painter. If you take formatting from somewhere else in the worksheet and attempt to apply it to a column that includes a merged and centered cell, a prompt tells you that you can't change part of a merged cell. The only way this can be done is if you apply the formats to the entire row that houses the merged and centered cell. Remember that in doing so, the merge and center format is removed and replaced by whatever new formatting you are applying.

People keep changing my text formatting, and I don't want them to

Source of the problem

You've taken the time to format your worksheet content just the way you like it. You've selected fonts, resized some of your text, created styles and applied them to headings and totals, and you've made your worksheet into a thing of beauty. Then what happens? Some joker opens your worksheet to look at it or do some editing, and the next thing you know, your formatting is changed. Maybe the other user copied content from one place to another and it came with formatting that doesn't belong where the content ended up. Or maybe he or she just didn't like your font and went ahead and changed it. The nerve!

Well, rather than strangling someone (or wasting your energy imagining such a thing), just prevent it from happening in the first place. Apply protection to your worksheet so that content can still be edited, but no one can ever fiddle with your formats again.

How to fix it

1. Select the entire worksheet by pressing Ctrl+A.

2. Right-click the selection and then click Format Cells on the shortcut menu.

3. In the Format Cells dialog box, click the Protection tab and clear the Locked check box. This will allow the cells in your worksheet to be edited after you apply protection, but other people won't be able to reformat your worksheet in any way. ▶

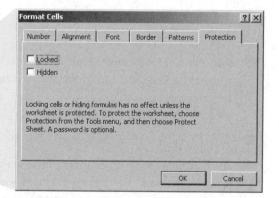

4. To apply worksheet protection, point to Protection on the Tools menu and then click Protect Sheet. In the Protect Sheet dialog box, type an optional password if you want and then click any check boxes in the Allow Users Of This Worksheet To list—the items you check are things you're letting people do in the worksheet—the fewer you check, the more control you retain. After your settings are in place, click OK.

Formatting text

Here an edit, there an edit

If you want to prevent not only formatting changes but edits to your worksheet, you can isolate areas and lock them. This process relies upon the fact that you turned off the locked status for the whole worksheet. Before applying protection, select the range of cells that you don't want anyone to edit, right-click the selection, and then click Format Cells on the shortcut menu. In the Format Cells dialog box, click the Protection tab, select the Locked check box, and click OK. Next, point to Protec-

tion on the Tools menu, and click Protect Sheet. Although the cells you didn't select can be edited, the locked range is protected from any editing. However, the entire work-sheet is completely pro-tected from changes to formatting. The entire For-matting toolbar is useless— the Formatting buttons are dimmed and clicking them produces no effect. ▶

And now, for the very cautious

If you want to keep people out of your worksheet entirely, seal the file with password protection. On the File menu, click Save As. ▶

For each password you type, a Confirm Pass-word box will appear, requiring you to reenter the password, just to make sure you didn't make a mistake the first time. Click OK to confirm each password and then click Save to close the Save As dialog box.

And the password is...

If you want to create a foolproof password but one that you won't forget easily, use the method Augustus Caesar invented: Take a word you wouldn't forget, such as your child's name or your mother's maiden name. Now, those don't seem too secure, because people who know you might be able to guess them. But wait! Think of a number—three, for example—and move each letter in your word three letters down in the alphabet. "Ann" becomes "DQQ," which no one is likely to guess. All you need to remember is the word and a single digit. You can even write the number somewhere, because no one will suspect that the "3" you wrote in the lower left corner of your calendar has anything to do with your password.

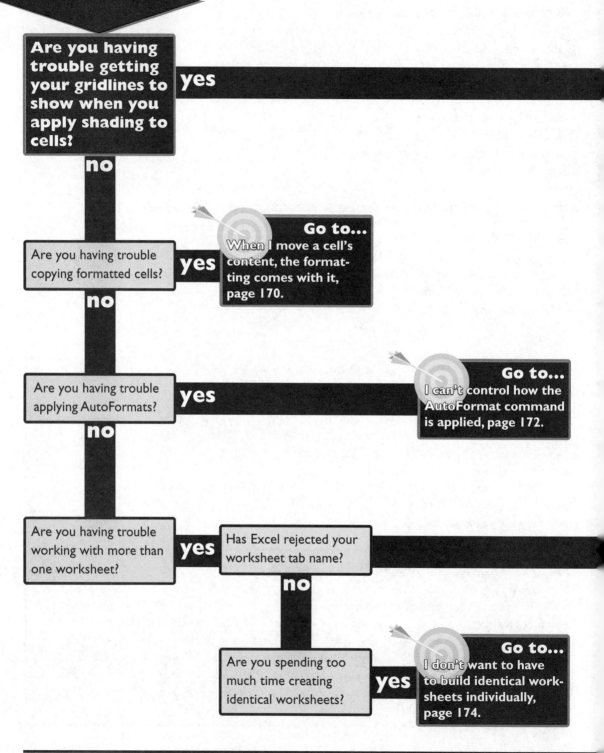

Forn

Are you having trouble getting your gridlines to show when you apply shading to cells?

yes

no

Are you having trouble copying formatted cells?

yes

Go to...
When I move a cell's content, the formatting comes with it, page 170.

no

Are you having trouble applying AutoFormats?

yes

Go to...
I can't control how the AutoFormat command is applied, page 172.

no

Are you having trouble working with more than one worksheet?

yes

Has Excel rejected your worksheet tab name?

no

Are you spending too much time creating identical worksheets?

yes

Go to...
I don't want to have to build identical worksheets individually, page 174.

168 **Troubleshooting Microsoft Excel 2002**

Quick fix

When you apply shading to cells, the gridlines are hidden by the shading color. To have visible gridlines and shaded cells at the same time, you need to apply cell borders. Select the cells in question, and right-click the selection. Choose Format Cells from the shortcut menu, and on the Border tab of the resulting dialog box, turn on both the Outside and Inside borders, and click OK.

Quick fix

To name a worksheet, double-click the tab, type a new name, and press Enter. The new name can have up to 31 characters, and can include spaces and punctuation, as well as numbers. The only characters you can't use are the slashes (/ \), the colon (:), square brackets ([ ]), or the question mark (?). If you attempt to use them, your new sheet tab name will be rejected.

If your solution isn't here, check these related chapters:

- Columns and rows, page 24
- Formatting numbers, page 146
- Formatting text, page 156
- Workspace customization, page 368

Or see the general troubleshooting tips on page xv.

When I move a cell's content, the formatting comes with it

Source of the problem

It's so simple to move cell content around on your worksheet—just click the cell, point to its border, and when your mouse pointer becomes a four-headed arrow, drag the content to a new cell. Easy, right? Well yes, unless you've already formatted your worksheet. If you've already applied borders, cell shading, text formatting, or a combination of any of these elements, all that formatting will move with the content. This can be a problem if the new location isn't meant to be formatted the same way. Furthermore, if you move content as opposed to copying it, you leave a formatting and content hole in your wake. As shown here, by moving the totals from cell C8 to C18, formatting is moved along with the total, and a hole is left where the shaded cell content used to be. ▶

What can you do about this particular problem? You have to change the way you move and copy content, changing from the aforementioned easy dragging method to one of two slightly more complex techniques. If you use the Paste Special command or a shortcut menu variant, you can choose what gets moved or copied—the content with the formatting, just the formatting, or just the content.

C18	▼	*fx*	=SUM(C9:C15)	
	A	B	C	D
1				
2				
3				
4		Sales Analysis	2001	
5		Second Quarter		
6			Sales Revenue	Cost of Sales
7			*Gross Sales*	*Sales Payroll*	Ad
8		TOTALS		2,657,910.00
9		New York	52,975,438.00	549,350.00
10		Philadelphia	43,892,359.00	450,670.00
11		Boston	33,489,123.00	325,650.00
12		Chicago	25,763,092.00	375,470.00
13		Houston	15,789,234.00	430,570.00
14		Phoenix	24,567,812.00	250,750.00
15		San Francisco	12,349,865.00	275,450.00
16				
17				
18		*SUMMARIES:*	208,826,923.00	

How to fix it

To use Paste Special, follow these steps:

1. Select the cell or range to be moved or copied.

2. Right-click the selection and then click Copy on the shortcut menu. Yes, you're going to copy the content even if you want to cut it. If you click Cut instead of Copy, the Paste Special command you'll use in step 4 will be unavailable on the shortcut menu. You can always go back and delete the original content after you've pasted it.

Tip

You can use the Paste Special technique between worksheets and workbooks as well. Select the content to be moved or copied, right-click the selection, click Copy, and then switch to the target cell in another sheet or another open workbook. Right-click the target cell, click Paste Special, click Values in the Paste section, and then click OK.

3. Right-click the cell (or first cell of the target range) where you want to paste the content and then click Paste Special on the shortcut menu.

4. In the Paste Special dialog box, click the Values option in the Paste section to indicate that you want to paste only the cell content. ▶

5. Click OK to paste the content to the new location.

6. If you don't want the original content that you copied, select the cells containing the content, and then press Delete. If you want to remove the original cell formatting as well as the content, select the original cells, point to Clear on the Edit menu, and then click All.

Tip

If you want to create a connection between copied content in its original location and the target cell, click the Paste Link button in the Paste Special dialog box. After creating this link, any updates to the original cell will be reflected in the target cell.

To drag the content of cells without moving the formatting, follow these steps:

1. Select the cell or cells to be copied.

2. Point to the cell or range border. When the mouse pointer changes to a four-headed arrow, hold down the right mouse button and drag the cell or range of cells to its new location.

3. Release the right mouse button and click Copy Here As Values Only on the shortcut menu to copy the content, but not the formatting. ▶

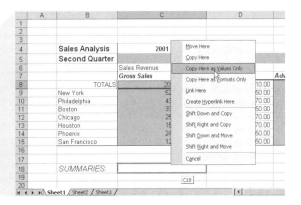

Just paint over it

The "fix" discussed in this section is more of a prevention than a cure. If you've already dragged a cell's content from one place to another and the formatting came with it, you can use the Format Painter to copy formatting from adjoining cells into the cell in which you pasted the content as well as into the cell in which the content originally resided. Select the cells containing the format you want to copy and then click the Format Painter button on the Standard toolbar. When the pointer changes to a paintbrush, drag through the cells that you want to apply the copied format to.

I can't control how the AutoFormat command is applied

Source of the problem

The AutoFormat command allows you to instantly apply a collection of formats to a range of cells. Using this command can save you a lot of time when compared to applying each format individually. Additionally, the AutoFormats that come with Microsoft Excel offer professional-looking, highly legible effects that you can apply to any of your worksheets that are constructed with AutoFormat in mind. ▶

So what could possibly go wrong? Lots of things, if you don't know how to control the way AutoFormat changes the appearance of your worksheet. By default, all AutoFormats can change the font, size, cell shading, borders, and column widths of the worksheet content to which you apply them. What if you've already adjusted your column widths and have them where you want them? Applying the AutoFormat can change them. What if you like everything about a particular AutoFormat except the font, and you've already chosen and applied the font you want to use? Your preferred font will lose out to the font included in the AutoFormat unless you customize the way the AutoFormat is applied.

	A	B	C	D	E	F	G	H
1								
2								
3								
4		Sales Analysis		2001				
5		Second Quarter						
6								
7			Sales Revenue Gross Sales	Cost of Sales Sales Payroll	Advertising	Marketing	Gross Profit	
8		TOTALS	208,826,923.00	2,657,910.00	758,341.00	88,057.00	205,322,615.00	
9		New York	52,975,438.00	549,350.00	35,000.00	1,450.00	52,389,638.00	
10		Philadelphia	43,892,359.00	450,670.00	25,450.00	25,650.00	43,390,589.00	
11		Boston	33,489,123.00	325,650.00	45,670.00	2,350.00	33,115,453.00	
12		Chicago	25,763,092.00	375,470.00	238,946.00	13,457.00	25,135,219.00	
13		Houston	15,789,234.00	430,570.00	36,550.00	2,750.00	15,319,364.00	
14		Phoenix	24,567,812.00	250,750.00	25,975.00	14,750.00	24,276,337.00	
15		San Francisco	12,349,865.00	275,450.00	350,750.00	27,650.00	11,696,015.00	
16								
17								

How to fix it

1. Select the portion of your worksheet you want to apply the AutoFormat to. To select the entire worksheet, press Ctrl+A.

2. On the Format menu, click AutoFormat.

3. In the AutoFormat dialog box, click once to select an AutoFormat from those displayed in the list box. Don't double-click the AutoFormat, or it will be applied without giving you the chance to customize it.

4. Click the Options button. The dialog box expands to offer a Formats To Apply section, which contains check boxes for AutoFormat features. Leave the check boxes selected for those formats

that you want to apply and clear the check boxes for those formats that you want to remove. For example, if you don't want your column widths or row heights to change, clear the Width/Height check box. ▶

5. When you've made all of the adjustments you need, click OK to apply the customized AutoFormat to the selected range of cells.

Yecch! I don't like this AutoFormat!

If you apply an AutoFormat and hate it, or if your worksheet content or layout changes and the format applied is no longer appropriate, you can remove it. No, you don't need to reformat the worksheet manually by removing shading and borders, or changing fonts—you can use None AutoFormat instead.

Simply select the range of cells that have an AutoFormat applied to them, click Auto-Format on the Format menu, and in the AutoFormat dialog box, click once on None in the list of sample AutoFormats. If you want to keep some of the formatting that's in place, such as column widths or borders, click the Options button, and clear the check boxes in the Formats To Apply section for features that you don't want changed. Then click OK to remove the AutoFormat.

Tip

You can also use the None AutoFormat to remove formatting you've applied manually. Suppose you've applied shading, borders, or fonts and tinkered with column widths, and now you want to return to the default worksheet appearance. Select the cells that are formatted, click AutoFormat on the Format menu, click None, and then click OK to remove the formats you don't want. Bear in mind that this will also get rid of numeric formatting, so if you've painstakingly applied (or even created) special date or other numeric formats, you may want to remove the other formatting—shading, fonts, and so on—manually.

Warning

You may find that your computer runs out of memory if you use the AutoFormat command on an entire worksheet. Although you can press Ctrl+A to select the whole sheet before issuing the Auto-Format command and applying a format, I don't recommend it—you may find that your system runs very slowly or that the Excel application has crashed (you'll get an error indicating that the program has stopped responding). If you must be able to format an entire worksheet with AutoFormat, consider increasing your system memory if you notice that Excel crawls anytime you attempt to AutoFormat a whole sheet.

I don't want to have to build identical worksheets individually

Source of the problem

Your workbook needs to contain two or more sheets with very similar content and layout, and you're grimacing at the thought of building Sheet1, then repeating yourself in Sheet2. Even if you've been crafty enough to think of copying content from Sheet1 to Sheet2 (to save yourself the typing and formatting), the process still feels like it's too much trouble.

Shouldn't there be a way to build several identical worksheets in the same workbook without redoing the work or copying and pasting between sheets? Yep, there should be, and there is! How's that for good news?

Creating multiple sheets is simple, requiring only that you group the sheets you want to mass-produce and then restrict your entries to the content that will be the same on all sheets. Say you want to create a series of department expense reports. You're in charge of three departments, and you want to build the same report form for each department. If you create three sheets (one for each department) and then group them, the column and row labels, formulas, and formats you build on any one of the three grouped sheets will appear on all three sheets.

However, you'll want to ungroup the worksheets before you enter material that is specific to one sheet so that changes you make don't end up on all sheets.

Mmm...making multiple mistakes

When your sheets are grouped, everything you do to one sheet—everything you type, every command you give, every formula you build—applies to the corresponding cell or cells in every sheet in the group. This includes mistakes!

If you find an error on one sheet that was part of a group when you worked on it, the error will appear on all the sheets that were originally grouped. To fix the error on all of the sheets, regroup them, and correct the mistake.

Of course this fix will work only if you haven't made erroneous edits separately to one or more of the sheets when they were ungrouped.

How to fix it

1. Click the first sheet tab that you want to include in the group.

2. Hold down the Shift key and click the last sheet tab in the series to be grouped. All sheets between and including the first and last sheets become grouped. ▶

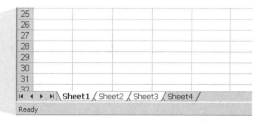

If you want to select nonconsecutive sheets, do the following:

1. Hold down the Ctrl key instead of the Shift key.

2. Click each sheet tab that you want to make part of the group. ▶

Name that worksheet

It's a good idea to name your worksheet tabs before grouping them, if only to make it easy for you to tell your sheets apart. This is especially important if you don't want to group all the worksheets in the workbook. If you have sheets that you don't want to be set up the same way as the ones you're building in the group, you might accidentally include them when you group your sheets. However, if you give your worksheet names and a generically named "Sheet4" shows up in the group, you'll know you've included a sheet you didn't intend to.

Shuffle sheets

When they're not grouped, you can rearrange your worksheets by clicking the tab of the sheet you want to move and then dragging the sheet icon that appears under the mouse pointer. A small triangle appears, indicating where the sheet will be moved to when you release the mouse button.

I don't want to have to build identical worksheets individually

(continued from page 175)

Breaking up is hard to do (well, not really)

Once you have entered the common material in all the sheets in a group, you'll want to ungroup the sheets so that you can start entering the content that's specific to the individual sheets. To ungroup sheets, use one of the following techniques:

- Click the tab of any sheet not in the group.

- Right-click any tab in the group and then click Ungroup Sheets on the shortcut menu. ▶

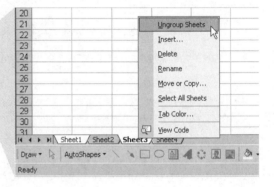

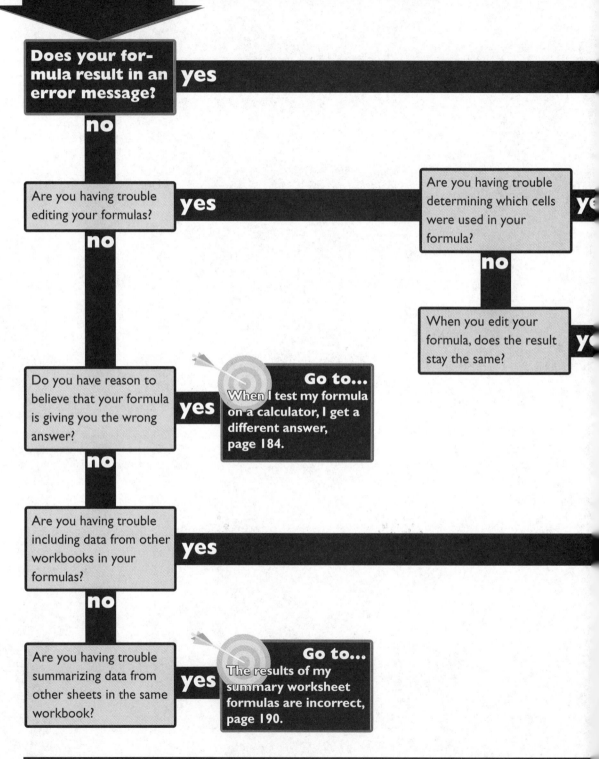

Does your formula result in an error message? — **yes**

no

Are you having trouble editing your formulas? — **yes**

no

Are you having trouble determining which cells were used in your formula? — **ye**

no

When you edit your formula, does the result stay the same? — **y**

Do you have reason to believe that your formula is giving you the wrong answer? — **yes**

Go to...
When I test my formula on a calculator, I get a different answer, page 184.

no

Are you having trouble including data from other workbooks in your formulas? — **yes**

no

Are you having trouble summarizing data from other sheets in the same workbook? — **yes**

Go to...
The results of my summary worksheet formulas are incorrect, page 190.

Formulas

Go to...
My formula causes an error message to appear, page 180.

Quick fix
To see your formulas instead of their results, choose Tools, Options and on the View tab, select the Formulas checkbox under Window Options. Click OK to close the dialog box, and you'll see your formulas in their cells. You can redisplay the results by reversing your steps. Uncheck the Formulas checkbox and the formula results reappear in their cells.

Go to...
When I edit the cells referenced in my formula, the result doesn't change, page 186.

Quick fix
To include data from other workbooks in your current worksheet, follow these steps:

1. Open the workbook containing the data you need and the workbook that will contain the formula that uses that data.

2. Start your formula by clicking in the cell where it will reside and start typing your formula.

3. When you're ready for the data from the other workbook, switch to that workbook and click in the cell containing the data you want.

4. Continue building the formula, clicking in cells and inserting operators and parentheses as needed.

If your solution isn't here, check these related chapters:

- Functions, page 192
- Macros, page 224
- Subtotal reports, page 336
- Templates, page 344

Or see the general troubleshooting tips on page xv.

My formula causes an error message to appear

Source of the problem

Formulas can be both the best part of Microsoft Excel and the most problematic. Not because they're difficult or they don't work reliably, but because they provide a place for everything that can go wrong to converge. Problems such as not knowing the right formula to use, which cells to include in the formula, or in what order the different parts of the formula should be calculated—not to mention making a simple error when you enter addresses and numbers to build the formula—can make formulas seem more troublesome than they are.

Any combination of these problems can occur and result in an error message when your formula is applied. The error message is helpful in that it gives you some tips on how to investigate the nature or cause of the problem. ▶

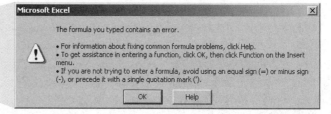

How to fix it

To correct the formula error, you can delete the offending formula and start from scratch, but the solution could be as simple as adding a missing parenthesis to complete the formula's proper structure. The solutions are as varied as the problems themselves. The good news—the solutions are generally straightforward and easy to implement. The table on the facing page lists the errors that might show up where you expect to see the results of your formulas and explains what you can do to fix these errors.

> ## An audit you'll actually enjoy
>
> Sometimes it helps to know how your worksheet material and its formulas relate to each other. Click a cell containing a formula, point to Auditing on the Tools menu, and then click Trace Precedents to highlight the cells that are used in the formula. Likewise, click a cell that might be referenced in a formula, point to Auditing on the Tools menu, and then click Trace Dependents. You'll see the formulas (if any) that reference the cell you're in.

Formulas

Error	How to fix it
#DIV/0!	This error appears if you try to divide by zero. Change the zero to some other number.
#N/A	This error means "not available." If cells referenced in a formula are unavailable, the error appears in the cell that contains the formula. Possible causes of this error include deleting a worksheet or workbook containing a cell referenced in a formula. To fix this, restore the missing material or edit the erroneous formula to reference identical material in a new cell or worksheet.
#NAME?	If text that Excel doesn't recognize appears in a formula, this error appears. This can be due to a misspelling or to using text without quotation marks around it (such as ="the total" is &G22 where G22 contains a total and the text in quotation marks is inserted with the number). You can also see this error if you forget the colon when referencing a range of cells, as in B12;G15. The solution? Click cells rather than type their names to insert them in a formula, and watch your punctuation.
#NUM!	This error message appears when the result of a formula is a number too large or too small to be displayed in Excel and indicates a problem with a number in the formula or in the result of the formula. To make sure you never see this error, your results must be between $-1*10^{307}$ and $1*10^{307}$, where * is the multiplication sign. That shouldn't be tough for most users!
#REF!	If your formula refers to cells that have been edited after you constructed the formula, or if the target cell reference is deleted, this error appears. When editing your worksheet, be careful not to replace referenced cell data with additional formulas. And when deleting content, make sure any formulas you have constructed don't reference what you're deleting.
#VALUE!	If you enter a nonnumerical character in a cell referenced in the formula, this error appears. This error might also appear if you enter a range (such as A3:B5) in a formula that requires only a single number or cell.
Circular Reference	When you include in a formula a cell that contains the formula itself, an error message appears notifying you of a circular reference. You need to edit the formula to remove the reference to the formula cell.

Formula dos and don'ts

- Do keep track of parentheses. There must be an even number of them in every formula. Make sure every left (open) parenthesis has a right (close) parenthesis mate.

- Do use colons to indicate a range of cells. A5:B6 means all the cells between and including A5 and B6. A5,B6 means that both A5 and B6 are arguments in a function. A5-B6 means A5 minus B6. Only the colon indicates a range.

- When referencing cells in another worksheet (in the same or a different workbook), do make sure the sheet name (even if it's just Sheet1) is enclosed in single quotation marks, followed by an exclamation point. If the sheet is in another workbook, that workbook's name is enclosed in brackets and appears before the sheet name within the single quotation marks.

My formula causes an error message to appear

(continued from page 181)

Keep a close watch

If you want to keep track of certain formulas in your worksheet, you can open the Watch window and tell Excel to watch one or more formulas in the worksheet. Once a formula is under watch, the following will appear in the Watch window: the name of the workbook the formula is in, the worksheet that contains it, any name you've applied to the formula cell, the cell address, the current value in the cell, and the formula itself. ▶

To open the Watch window and train the Watch feature's eyes on one or more of your formulas, choose Tools, Formula Auditing, Show Watch Window. Once the window is open, click the Add Watch button and then select the cell that contains the formula you want to watch.

Why watch a formula? If you have specific values in mind for a formula, you can keep an eye on the formula to make sure that other cells' content in the worksheet doesn't adversely affect your result. If your formula includes cells that are spread throughout the worksheet (or one or more workbooks), watching the formula lets you keep an eye on the result without having to look around to see how all the contributing cells are doing.

Book	Sheet	Name	Cell	Value	Formula
sales analysis.xls	Sheet1		C8	208,826,923.00	=SUM(C9:C15)

Tip

When you're finished watching a formula—after any editing that could affect the result has been completed, for example—select the formula in the Watch Window list and click the Delete Watch button. If the Watch window is no longer needed, choose Tools, Formula Auditing, Hide Watch Window.

Formulas

When I test my formula on a calculator, I get a different answer

Source of the problem

The big difference between how calculators and Excel formulas work with equations is that on the calculator, the math is done in the order you press the keys. If you press 5 - 2 * 3, the 2 is subtracted from the 5, and the result is multiplied by 3. If, however, you type =5-2*3 in a cell, Excel will multiply the 2 times the 3 first and then subtract that result from 5. Same formula, different answer. ▶

Why? Order of operations. Excel performs calculations within a formula in this order:

1. Parentheses
2. Exponents
3. Multiplication
4. Division
5. Addition
6. Subtraction

In school you might have learned to remember this standard mathematical order of operations with the phrase "Please Excuse My Dear Aunt Sally." Lame, maybe, but it worked. I'm remembering it an undisclosed number of years later, aren't I? Of course the operations are also done from left to right, so if there are two sets of a particular operation (two things to be multiplied, for example), the one on the left is done first. You could then expand the phrase to "Please Excuse My Dear Aunt Sally for Losing the Radishes."

So how would you tell Excel to subtract the 2 from the 5, and then multiply by 3? With appropriately placed parentheses! ▶

How to fix it

To edit an existing formula and change the order of operations, follow these steps:

1. Click the cell containing the formula that needs to be edited.

2. On the Formula bar, click to position your insertion point in the formula.

3. Using the left and right arrow keys as needed, reposition your insertion point where you want to insert the missing parentheses and then type the parentheses.

Formulas

To build a new formula, controlling the order of operations from the start, follow these steps:

1. Click the cell where you want to type the formula and type an equal sign to begin the formula.

2. Select cells to insert in a formula, or type cell references numbers, and operators to manually build a formula. Press Enter when you have completed building the formula.

3. As you build the formula, place parentheses around the portion of the formula that should be calculated as a separate entity. If more than one set of items needs to be calculated on its own, place the individual elements of the formula in order—from left to right and each element in parentheses. For example, as seen here, =6*10-4*2/2 will be seen as instructions to multiply 6 times 10, then 4 times 2, then that result divided by 2. Then that result is subtracted from 60 (the result of 6 times 10). The answer is 56. ▶

As seen in the next example, placing an extra set of parentheses around the two sets of operations— ((6*10)-(4*2))/2—makes sure that the division by 2 doesn't get calculated before the result of 6 times 10 is reduced by the result of 4 times 2. In this case, the answer is 26. ▶

Tip

Always make sure there is an even number of parentheses in your formulas. Make sure every left (open) parenthesis has a right (close) parenthesis to go with it. If even one is missing, your formula will display an error message. When the error message appears, click Yes if you want Excel to try to fix the parentheses for you or No if you want to fix the error yourself. See "My formula causes an error message to appear" on page 180.

When I edit the cells referenced in my formula, the result doesn't change

Source of the problem

One of the coolest things about an electronic spreadsheet is watching formulas get updated when cells are edited. A grand total in a series of summed columns? No big deal. But change one of the cells in the series and see that grand total change automatically? What a rush! OK, maybe I need to get a life, but if you have ever performed bookkeeping or data analysis on paper, you know the thrill of using a computer to do things faster and to not have to erase, recalculate, and rewrite the results when something changes in the data.

But where's the thrill if you edit the cells that are referenced in your formula and nothing happens? This can certainly be a letdown. In addition to being disappointed, you might be concerned about what's wrong with your formulas. If one isn't working, can you rely on any of the formulas you entered? Of course you can.

	B	C	D	E	F
1					
2		Travel Expenses by Department			
3					
4	Sales	Marketing	Info. Tech	Operations	Accounting
5					
6	2573.29	2135	58.65	298.75	125
7	2560.5	2400.5	204.38	302.5	54
8	4576.51	2986	350.11	306.25	320
9	3574.9	3411.5	495.84	310	88
10	=SUM(B6:B9)	=SUM(C6:C9)	=SUM(D6:D9)	=SUM(E6:E9)	=SUM(F6:F9)
11	4576.51	3837	641.57	313.75	185.5
12	5078.594	4278.5	787.3	317.5	201
13	5580.678	4720	933.03	321.25	216.5
14	6082.76200000001	5161.5	1078.76	325	232
15	6584.84600000001	5603	1224.49	328.75	247.5
16	=SUM(B11:B15)	=SUM(C11:C15)	=SUM(D11:D15)	=SUM(E11:E15)	=SUM(F11:F15)
17					

The problem is most likely a case of not knowing which cells are truly referenced by the formula in question, and it's easy enough to find out which ones are.

Excel calls the cells that are referenced in a formula *precedents*. The formulas that reference a cell are called *dependents*. These terms are based on the concept that the cells precede a formula,

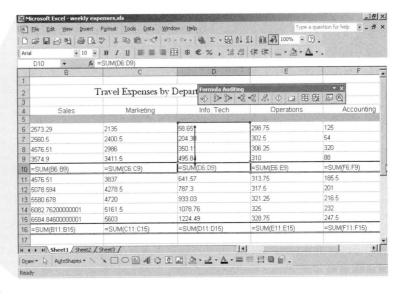

and the formula depends on the content of the cells. You can reveal the precedents and dependents for any cell or formula by using Excel's auditing tools to display arrows that point to and from the related content. These auditing tools even have their own toolbar, which you can display by choosing View, Toolbars, Formula Auditing. ▶

How to fix it

To reveal the cells that are referenced in a formula, follow these steps:

1. Click the cell containing the formula you want to examine.

2. On the Tools menu, point to Formula Auditing and then click Trace Precedents. An arrow points through all precedents to the cell containing the dependent formula. ▶

3. Look at the arrow that points from the precedent cells to the cell containing a formula. If the arrow doesn't point from cells that you want it to, the cells you intended to include in the formula aren't actually included. Edit the formula to refer to the cells you need to use in the formula's calculation.

When I edit the cells referenced in my formula, the result doesn't change

(continued from page 187)

To check for formulas that refer to a specific cell, follow these steps:

1. Click a cell that might be used in a formula in your worksheet.

2. On the Tools menu, point to Auditing and then click Trace Dependents. An arrow points from the cell to all formulas that depend on the cell. ▶

3. View the arrow that points from the cell you selected to its related worksheet formula.

> **Tip**
>
> To display the Auditing toolbar, point to Auditing on the Tools menu, and then click Show Auditing Toolbar. Strangely, this toolbar isn't listed when you point to Toolbars on the View menu to display the Toolbars submenu.

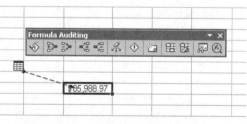

What's that little grid thingy?

If you see a precedents or dependents arrow pointing to or from a small grid icon, that indicates that the formula (dependent) or cell in the formula (precedent) is on another worksheet or workbook. ▶

To reveal the location of the external dependent or precedent, double-click the grid icon. The Go To dialog box appears, showing the address of the cell, including the workbook name and sheet name. (Don't worry if your dialog box looks a bit different from this one.) ▶

Select the address in the Go To box so that the address appears in the Reference box and then click OK to switch to the sheet containing the dependent or precedent.

Formulas

The results of my summary worksheet formulas are incorrect

Source of the problem

Formulas that summarize data from other worksheets can go wrong for a variety of reasons. The two most common are an error in the way the formula was created and a change in the sheets and data to which the summary formula refers. If your summary formula results in an error message, there's something wrong with the formula itself in a grammatical way—missing parentheses, cells not containing numbers referenced in the formula—and you should check "My formula causes an error message to appear" on page 180.

If, on the other hand, the result is just plain old wrong, the problem is that a cell or range is being referenced in error or the data that the formula references has moved or changed, and you're unaware of it. Either situation is easily straightened out through the use of Excel's auditing tools and some basic formula-creation tips.

If you're using a worksheet that someone else created or one you don't use that often, it's easy to forget how things relate to each other. You can use Excel's auditing tools to identify the cells referenced in a formula, as well as the formulas that reference a specific cell. So if the results of your summary worksheet are incorrect, you need to check your summary formula for the cells that are referenced in it.

> **Tip**
>
> To quickly see which cells are referenced in a formula, click a formula cell and check out the Formula bar. Although the cell in the worksheet contains the result, the Formula bar shows the formula that produces the result.

How to fix it

1. Click the cell containing the summary formula.

2. On the Tools menu, point to Auditing and then click Trace Precedents. You can also display the Formula Auditing toolbar (View, Toolbars, Formula Auditing) and click the Trace Precedents button there.

3. Examine the arrow that points to the summary formula. The arrow points from a small grid icon that indicates a cell reference outside of the active worksheet.

To view the external cell reference indicated by the grid icon, double-click the icon. The Go To dialog box appears, showing the address of the precedent (the cell reference contained in the formula) that's not on the active sheet. The address includes the workbook name and also the name of the worksheet on which the precedent can be found. (Don't worry if your dialog box looks a bit different from this one.) ▶

If you want to go to the cell that's referenced, select the address in the Go To box so that it also appears in the Reference box and then click OK. (You can also click Cancel to close the Go To dialog box after making a note of the address and then go to that workbook or worksheet on your own.) See "When I edit the cells referenced in my formula, the result doesn't change" on page 186.

Tip

For quick access to the Trace commands, display the Auditing toolbar. Point to Auditing on the Tools menu and then click Show Auditing Toolbar. This toolbar is not available when you point to Toolbars on the View menu and display the toolbars submenu.

One cell, many formulas

To check for the formulas (summary and otherwise) that refer to a specific cell, click the cell that you believe is referenced in your summary formula. On the Tools menu, point to Auditing and then click Trace Dependents. Examine the arrow pointing from the selected cell to the summary formula in question. Edit the formula if necessary so that it refers to the correct cells. ▶

Tip

If you want the cells to display your formulas instead of their results, click Options on the Tools menu. On the View tab of the Options dialog box, select the Formulas check box in the Window Options section and then click OK. All of the formula results in your current worksheet will appear as formulas until and unless you clear the Formulas check box in the Options dialog box.

Are you having trouble using functions?

yes

no

If you used Excel 2000 and previous versions, are you wondering where the Paste Function button went?

yes

Quick fix

Locate the Paste Function button. The Paste Function button has been renamed and moved. You'll find it on the formula bar, just to the right of the text box in which the active cell's content appears.

no

Do you want to build functions faster?

yes

no

Does your function result in an error message?

yes

Go to...

I get an error message when I enter my function, page 198.

no

Does your function require the use of cells from outside the active worksheet?

yes

Go to...

Cells I need to include in my function aren't in my active worksheet, page 200.

no

Are you having trouble editing a function?

yes

no

Do you need to use two functions together?

yes

Go to...

I'm not sure how to combine two functions in one formula, page 202.

Functions

Are you unsure how to build a function?

yes → **Go to...** I don't know how to construct the function I need, page 194.

no

Are you having trouble understanding how a function works?

yes → **Go to...** I don't know what to include in this function, page196.

Quick fix
Build functions yourself. Once you understand how a function is structured, you can build it manually, avoiding the entire Insert Function dialog box. Simply type an equal sign followed by the function name, and build the function piece by piece, cell by cell. For example, typing =AVERAGE(B5:B10) would average the range of cells from B5 through B10.

Quick fix
Rebuild your faulty function. If a function no longer works properly after you've edited it (or the cells to which it refers), it's often a good idea to simply delete the function and rebuild it, starting over with the Insert Function button and following the steps displayed in the resulting dialog box.

If your solution isn't here, check these related chapters:
- Formatting numbers, page 146
- Formulas, page 178

Or see the general troubleshooting tips on page xv.

I don't know how to construct the function I need

Source of the problem

You can determine the structure of most formulas by talking them through: "This cell should equal this other cell here, minus this cell, divided by three." So the formula is simple—subtract one cell from another and divide the result by three.

But what if you want to determine how much your car payment will be if you finance it for five years at an interest rate of 7 percent? What if you want to know how much an investment will be worth in 10 years, assuming a standard rate of return? Or how much an asset will depreciate before next year's taxes are due? Even if you understand the concepts of loan payments and interest rates and depreciation, the structure of the formulas to calculate them might not be so obvious. When you want to create a formula for a mathematical, statistical, scientific, or accounting procedure, you'll find what you need in Microsoft Excel's functions.

Functions are preset formulas that you can use by inserting information—cell addresses, numbers, even text—into prescribed positions. Excel provides a dialog box through which you can select the right function for the calculation you want to perform and learn how that function's formula is constructed. Once you find the function you need, you can proceed to set up that formula.

Tip

Don't be put off by some of the functions Excel offers. For example, one of the functions will return the hyperbolic cosine of a number. I admit that I understand only "the," "of," and "a number" in that last sentence, but I feel better knowing that Excel can help me if I ever need to use that function. Stick with the functions you need to use, and ignore the ones that make you scratch your head.

How to fix it

1. Click the cell in which you want to create a formula.

2. Click the Insert Function button on the Formula Bar.

3. In the Insert Function dialog box, click the Select A Category list and choose a function category.

4. View the selected category's list of functions in the Select A Function list. ▶

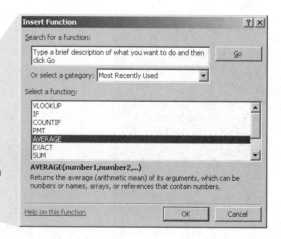

5. Because the function names don't always make it clear what a function is or does, you'll need to click them in the list to read a description of what they do and when they're used. The description appears in the dialog box below the lists of categories and functions.

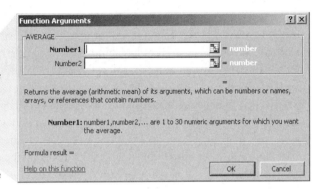

> **Tip**
>
> If you're not sure of the function name, use the Search For A Function text box to describe and search for the function that does what you need your formula to do.

6. When you find the function you need, double-click it. The Function Arguments dialog box appears. You can drag it anywhere on the worksheet so that it doesn't obscure the portions of the sheet you need to work with as you build your function. ▶

7. Enter a number or cell address in the Function Arguments dialog box's first argument box. (You can also select the information requested by clicking cells in your worksheet.)

8. To move to the next box, press Tab or click the box. The description of the argument changes to match the number for each box. As you fill in the requested information, a calculation result appears in the Formula Result section at the bottom of the Function Arguments dialog box. ▶

9. When you've filled in all the information the Function Argument dialog box asks for, click OK. The formula is built on the Formula bar, based on the information—cell addresses or numbers, or both—you entered into the argument boxes. ▼

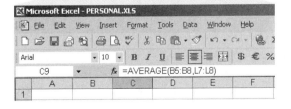

> **Tip**
>
> You don't have to fill in all of the information requested in the Formula palette argument boxes. If a box label is **bold**, an entry is required in that argument box. If the box label is plain text, you can skip entering a value in the box.

I don't know what to include in this function

Source of the problem

Your worksheet requires a rather complex formula, you've found the function that creates it, and you're ready to start building the formula using the Function Arguments dialog box. Despite the step-by-step process involved in selecting and building a function, you might have some trouble deciphering the descriptions in the Function Arguments dialog box. Each number, cell reference, or value that the function requires is explained, but sometimes the descriptions aren't terribly clear or they assume too high a level of familiarity with the accounting, statistical, or scientific concept on which the function is based. You might find out that you don't understand the function as you're building it, or when the function result turns out to be wrong.

In either case, all is not lost. You can use Excel's Help feature when you're really stuck. You can use Help proactively (before you attempt to create the formula) or reactively (when you're in the middle of building the function and smacking your forehead in frustration). You can also print Help pages for future reference.

Tip

A quick way to test a function is to build it with easy, round numbers so you'll know right off the bat if the result is wrong. If you're building a PMT (payment) function to determine a payment on a loan, test the function with simple numbers—10,000 for the loan amount, 10 months to pay it back, and 10% interest. Even the most mathematically challenged should be able to spot an error if the numbers are ones that you can calculate in your head.

How to fix it

1. On the Help menu, click Microsoft Excel Help.

2. Click the Index tab in the resulting Microsoft Excel Help window.

3. Type the name of the function into the Type Keywords text box. ▶

4. Click Search to see a list of Help articles in the Choose A Topic list. The first ones to appear should be the closest matches to your search criteria.

5. Click the article that matches the function you typed and view the article on the right side of the window. The help

may include pictures and hyperlinks, the latter taking you to additional articles pertaining to subjects mentioned in the main help file you're reading. ▶

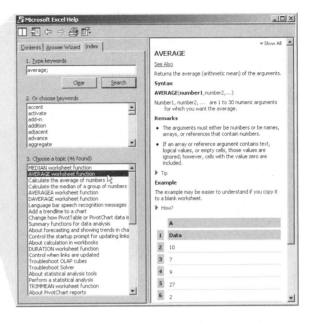

Hey, how about that question mark?

You noticed that, eh? Right there, in the Insert Function dialog box and again in the Function Arguments dialog box, there's a little question mark in the upper-right corner, lurking next to the Close button. What's that for? Well, you might have heard about it in the section of this book pertaining to Help, but for our purposes here, it serves a very useful role. It gives further explanation about the dialog box that's open and the text boxes, lists, and options within that dialog box. ▶

> To use this help feature, simply click the question mark button and note that your mouse grows a question mark of its own. Now, go click something in the dialog box—a text box, list, or option—and a yellow

ScreenTip box appears, showing you a complete explanation of the item in question.

> If that's not enough, click the Help On This Function hyperlink at the bottom of the Function Arguments dialog box. You'll be taken to the Microsoft Excel Help window, with the article pertaining to the selected function displayed and ready for reading or printing. ▶

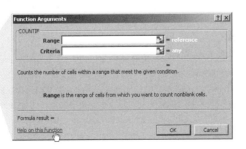

Tip

So you miss the Office Assistant? You're not alone, but your colleagues are few. Anyway, if you simply must see Clippit or The Genius or Links the cat, just choose Help, Show The Office Assistant. You can then click on the character to display a search box in which you can enter keywords and look for help. If you want to get rid of the assistant for a while, choose Help, Hide The Office Assistant or right-click the character and choose Hide from the shortcut menu.

I get an error message when I enter my function

Source of the problem

There's a difference between a wrong answer (15 when you were expecting 150) and an error. An error comes in the form of text in the cell that should contain a number and a small exclamation point icon, which, when clicked, displays your options for dealing with the error. ▶

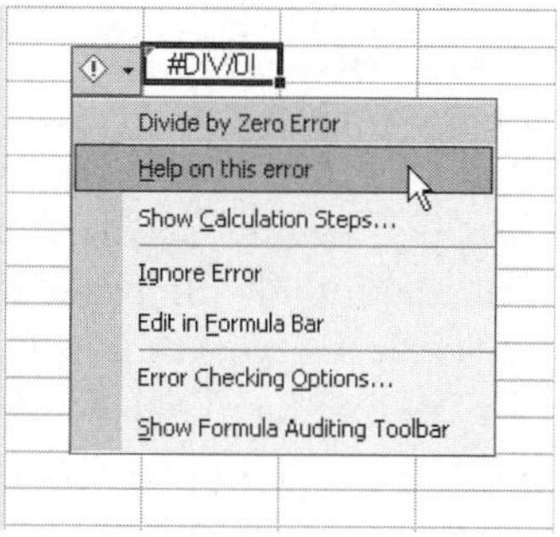

From the list that appears when you click the exclamation point icon (known as a *Smart Tag* in Microsoft Office XP), you can choose to ignore the error, edit it yourself in the Formula Bar (if you realize what went wrong), or get some help.

Errors in the cell come in seven varieties, and the solutions vary depending on the error. The solutions normally require editing the cell's formula by changing a cell reference or reducing the number of arguments you've included. If the editing seems to be too complex, just delete the cell contents and start over!

How to fix it

Here's a table describing the most common function errors in Excel:

Error	How to fix it
#DIV/0!	This error appears if you include the number zero in the function and other numbers within the function will be divided by that zero. References to a cell containing zero (if that cell is in a divisor position within the function) will also result in this error. Change the cell reference to a cell containing a number other than zero or edit the zero out of the function directly.
#N/A	If cells referenced in a function are unavailable, this error appears in the cell that contains the function. Possible causes include deleting a worksheet or workbook containing a cell that is referenced in a formula, or deleting the formula that the cell containing the error is trying to locate. To fix this, restore the missing material in the referenced worksheet or workbook or edit the erroneous function to reference identical material in a new cell or worksheet.
#NAME?	If text that Excel doesn't recognize appears in a function, this error appears. This can be due to a misspelling or to using text without quotes around it (in a Criteria argument, for example). You can also see this error if you forget the colon when you reference a range of cells, as in =AVERAGE(B12:G15). Be sure to always use a colon when referring to a range of cells in a function—or any formula for that matter.

Functions

Error	How to fix it
#NUM!	With regard to functions, this error normally indicates that the function was expecting a number and the cell referenced contains text. Check the cells your function references and either edit them or redirect the function to a cell containing a number.
#NULL!	If your function refers to two ranges that should intersect but don't, this error will appear. For example, if a SUM function refers to ranges B1:B10 and D1:D10, the lack of an intersecting cell will cause the #NULL! error to appear because Excel will try to find a cell that's in both ranges. Add a comma between the two ranges to tell Excel to add the two ranges separately and not to look for an intersecting cell.
#REF!	This is a "reference" error. If your function refers to cells that have been edited after you constructed the formula, or if the target cell has been deleted, this error appears. When editing your worksheet, be careful not to replace referenced cell data with formulas or additional functions, and when deleting content, make sure any formulas you have constructed with the function or functions don't reference what you're deleting.
#VALUE!	If you enter any nonnumeric characters in a cell referenced in the function and the function requires numeric content, this error appears. It might also appear if you enter a range in a function (such as A3:B5) when the formula requires only a single number or cell. The solution? Be sure not to use ranges when you need a single number (or a cell containing a single number), and check the content of all cells referenced in a function to make sure they contain what the function requires.

Put the "fun" back into functions

All this talk about errors can make functions seem unpleasant and difficult to use. However, if you understand a function's purpose in your worksheet, and you know what information the function needs to give you the result you want, you won't have any trouble. You might even enjoy the process, because Excel functions make creating complex formulas much easier than creating them "from scratch." Additionally, the process is relatively foolproof. (You can run into snags, however, if you work carelessly or don't pay attention to the "grammar" of a function.)

Remember that you must provide a series of arguments in the right order, containing the right stuff, and in precisely the way the function was designed to work. Always use a colon between cell addresses in a range (A1:B15), use a comma to indicate two separate ranges with no intersecting cell (A1:B6,B10:G25), and put quotation marks around criteria—as in =COUNTIF(A6:A16,"Atlanta").

Cells I need to include in my function aren't in my active worksheet

Source of the problem

Creating a function can be confusing enough without trying to reference cells from outside the active worksheet, right? Well, it's actually really simple to include cells from other worksheets in the current workbook or from another workbook entirely—the process is virtually the same as that the one you'd employ to include cells from another worksheet in a regular formula. You can reference these cells and ranges manually by typing the workbook or worksheet name (or both) and cell addresses in the formula. Or you can use the Function Arguments dialog box (which appears when you choose a function in the Insert Function dialog box) and select the cell ranges you need with your mouse pointer.

The keys to successfully referencing external cells are knowing which cells you want from which worksheets and workbooks before you get started and making sure that the cells you're referencing contain the sort of data the function requires. For example, be sure to use numbers, not text, if the cell is part of a calculation. Use single cells or numbers if a range won't work in the function you want (or, conversely, use ranges if single numbers or cells won't work), or use text or some other value in quotes if the function is looking for a comparison value.

Excel will alert you with an error message if you violate any of these rules (see "I get an error message when I enter my function" on page 198), so you'll know right away that you need to do something differently. You can always start over with a list of where to find the information you need—be it in the current worksheet, another worksheet or workbook, or obtained from someone or somewhere else (such as an interest rate or tax percentage that's not stored in a worksheet).

> **Tip**
>
> Another good reason to keep workbook file and sheet tab names short and simple is so that you can type them in formulas without serious risk of creating typos. If your file and tab names are complex, it might be difficult for you to refer to them manually as you build formulas and functions.

How to fix it

1. Click the cell that will house the formula and then click the Insert Function button.

2. In the Insert Function dialog box, select a function category in the category drop-down list and then double-click the function you need in the list of functions for that category.

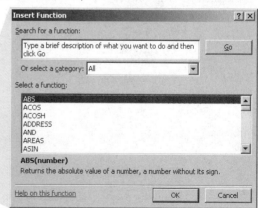

3. As soon as the Function Arguments dialog box appears on the worksheet, you can begin building the formula. Click the first box to type the cell reference or value. ▶

4. To include a reference to a cell outside the active worksheet, you have two options: To reference a cell within the active workbook but on a different sheet, click that sheet's tab. To reference a cell in another workbook, make sure the second workbook is open and click the workbook's name on the Window menu. When the workbook appears, click the tab of the worksheet containing the cell you want to reference.

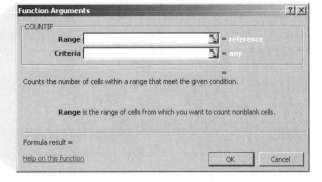

5. In the worksheet that contains the cell or range you want to reference, click the cell or drag through the range to select it. The Function Arguments dialog box is on the screen, so you can see the formula with the workbook, sheet, and cell references included. ▶

6. Continue building your function in the Function Arguments dialog box and click OK when you're done.

Don't forget the @!?*!! punctuation

If you decide to enter the external cell or range references manually, be sure to add the appropriate punctuation to the workbook and worksheet names. Workbook file names are enclosed in square brackets, and worksheet names are followed by an exclamation point. As you can see in the graphic above, the entire external location (workbook name and sheet name) is enclosed in single quotation marks.

Tip

When you've finished selecting a cell or range in a worksheet in another workbook, don't return to the original active worksheet until you've moved on to the next argument box in the Function Arguments dialog box. If the external reference is the last thing you need for the formula, click OK in the Function Arguments dialog box or press Enter. If you go back to any cell in the original active worksheet, you'll accidentally add that cell's address to the function.

I'm not sure how to combine two functions in one formula

Source of the problem

So one function isn't good enough for you, eh? You want two, three, maybe four functions all rolled up into one formula, and you don't know how to do it. Or maybe you've tried, and it didn't work. In either case, there are some key points to remember when building nested functions:

- Set some limits. The bottom line: You can't nest more than seven functions. If you are trying to nest more than that, there's your problem. The solution? Get rid of one of the functions by incorporating an already-calculated part of the formula in another cell and reference that cell in the function instead.

- If you've tried to combine or nest functions and an incorrect result or an error message appeared, the problem is most likely the function's structure. Where you insert the second-level function (say, a SUM function within an AVERAGE function) is important.

Tip

Want to find the Help file on nesting functions? Type *nest* in the Help window's Index text box and click Search. Scroll through the related topics to find "About nesting functions within functions."

- Be completely familiar with the proper way to build each of the individual functions you want to nest. Often, it's not the nesting that's gone wrong but the way one of the functions is set up.

With these considerations in mind, it's fairly straightforward to build a function that contains a second function within it—for example, a SUM function within an AVERAGE function.

How to fix it

1. Click the cell that will contain the formula.

2. Click the Insert Function button to display the Insert Function dialog box.

3. Select a category in the category list and then double-click the function you want in the list of functions. (If you're not sure which function to pick, try clicking All in the category list and then scrolling through the alphabetical list of functions to find one.)

4. When the Function Arguments dialog box appears, the Name box to the left of the Formula bar displays the function name. To supply the first argument (for example, the sum of a series of numbers), click the arrow to the left of the Function box, and, in the drop-down list, click the name of the function you want to nest inside the first function. ▶

5. On the worksheet, drag through the range of cells to be added. When you release the mouse button, both the nested function and range appear in bold on the Formula bar. ▶

6. Click the second argument box and then click the Function box to insert the displayed function.

7. Drag through the second range of cells. Again, a nested function and range appear on the Formula bar.

8. Click OK and view the results in your worksheet. For example, if you used the SUM function inside the AVERAGE function, you've averaged two sums. ▶

9. The correct formula appears in the Formula bar, and this combination of functions adds cells C9 through C19 and averages that result with the sum of M11 through M25.

Parenthetically speaking

The placement of parentheses is essential in forming nested functions, especially if you're entering the functions manually. There should be one set of parentheses around the nested function or functions and parentheses within each nested function if any ranges are referenced. If you type the function in the Formula bar and include the wrong number of parentheses, you'll see the pairs appear in color and the odd one (if you have a single parenthesis that's missing its mate) appear in bold. Get rid of the extra or give it a mate (whichever is appropriate), and the formula should work without an error message appearing.

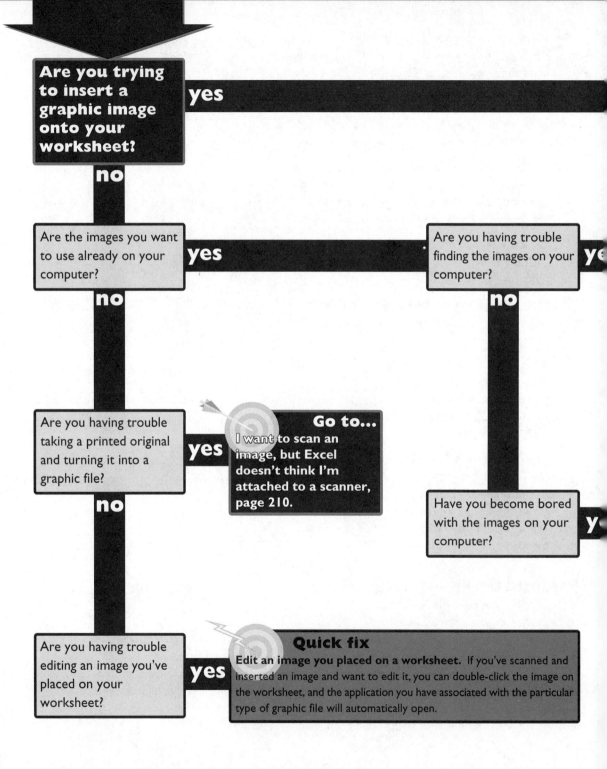

Are you trying to insert a graphic image onto your worksheet?

yes

no

Are the images you want to use already on your computer?

yes

no

Are you having trouble finding the images on your computer?

ye

no

Are you having trouble taking a printed original and turning it into a graphic file?

yes

Go to...
I want to scan an image, but Excel doesn't think I'm attached to a scanner, page 210.

no

Have you become bored with the images on your computer?

y

Are you having trouble editing an image you've placed on your worksheet?

yes

Quick fix
Edit an image you placed on a worksheet. If you've scanned and inserted an image and want to edit it, you can double-click the image on the worksheet, and the application you have associated with the particular type of graphic file will automatically open.

Graphics

Will the worksheet be displayed on the Web?

yes

Quick fix

Use the correct image format. If your images will wind up on the Web, be sure that you only use .jpg, .gif, or .png formatted image files. Web browsers won't recognize other file types, and if you tried to use other types (.bmp, .tif, .psd, etc.), the images won't appear on the Web page.

Are you using the Clip Gallery to search for images?

yes

Go to...
When I search for a graphic by keyword, none are found, page 206.

no

Do you have a lot of image files in many different folders on your local drive?

yes

Go to...
My clip art files are very disorganized, and I can't find the images I need, page 212.

Go to...
I'm tired of the images I have on my computer, and I want new ones, page 208.

If your solution isn't here, check these related chapters:

● Charts, page 2
● Drawing shapes and lines, page 96
● Saving, page 278

Or see the general troubleshooting tips on page xv.

When I search for a graphic by keyword, none are found

Source of the problem

Microsoft Office XP provides a new and improved tool for finding the right graphic for your needs—the Clip Organizer. The clip art that comes with Office XP is categorized and searchable by keyword, so that if, for example, you want a picture of flowers, you can type "flowers" and see a list of the images that are associated with that keyword. The Clip Gallery provides a specialized task pane for the purpose of searching for and viewing clip art images as representational thumbnails and tools for inserting the one you want into your worksheet, document, presentation, or Web page. ▶

The Clip Gallery in the Office XP interface is very user-friendly and logical. It works most of the time, but it can fail you—either the keyword you type isn't one of the keywords associated with any of the clip art images or the images associated with the keyword you typed are no longer where Office XP expected to find them. You might have also typed something wrong (spelling flowers as *floewrs*, for example).

But what if your keyword wasn't spelled incorrectly, and it is a perfectly acceptable word by which to search for images? What if the keyword worked before? The solutions to these scenarios lie in trying alternative keywords to see if the images will come up under another search and in checking the entire assortment of images to make sure that the one you want is really somewhere to be found.

How to fix it

A clear understanding of the way the Clip Gallery task pane works is a good start, and you'll need to familiarize yourself with it in order to test different keywords in search of the clip art you seek. Follow these steps:

1. If the task pane is displayed, click the drop triangle on its Title bar and choose Insert Clip Art to switch to the Clip Gallery. If the task pane isn't displayed, simply choose Insert, Picture, Clip Art, and the task pane will appear.

2. Type a keyword in the Search Text box and click the Search button.

3. View the resulting images. If no images are found for the keyword you typed, click the Modify button to begin your search again by replacing the current keyword with another one. ▶

Graphics

To make certain that all of your images are being searched when you enter the keyword, check the Other Search Options:

1. Click the Search In drop arrow to see the collections that are being searched. Check marks in the boxes next to the groups of images indicate that the collection will be searched; no check mark indicates that the collection isn't being searched. ▶

2. To include a collection in the search, click to place a check mark in the box next to the collection currently not being searched.

When the keys don't work, change the lock

You aren't stuck with the keywords that were assigned to your clip art images. To change or add keywords to any image, click the drop triangle next to the image (in the task pane, while the thumbnail image is displayed), and choose Edit Keywords. ▶

In the resulting window, you can view all the keywords associated with the image and move through the other images that met your search criteria, viewing their keywords as well. To add a keyword that isn't already associated with the image, click in the Keyword box and select the displayed word. Type the new keyword (which replaces the word that was in the box), and then click the Add button. You can repeat this process for as many keywords as you want to add to any particular image. ▶

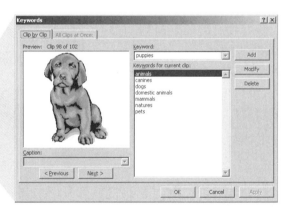

To delete a keyword, select it in the list and click the Delete button. It's best not to delete keywords unless they're words you added and you realize they're not appropriate—leave the default list intact.

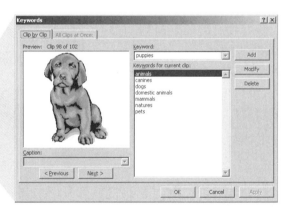

> **Tip**
>
> A rose isn't necessarily a rose...If you're searching for flowers and you typed the keyword *roses*, the lack of resulting images might be due to the fact that none of the flowers in the images are technically roses. Try general terms like *flowers* rather than specific ones.

I'm tired of the images I have on my computer, and I want new ones

Source of the problem

The Office XP suite comes with a fairly extensive assortment of clip art images, and if you're like most users, it's unlikely that you'd ever use all of them or use any of them so frequently that you'd tire of them. If, on the other hand, you create a lot of worksheets with graphic content, you may exhaust the supply of images in the categories you use most often—people, buildings, or business, for example.

If you feel the assortment of available images is limited, you have two choices—make sure you've installed all of the clip art that came with Office XP, or go to another resource (the Web, CD-ROM collections available at many stores) for a fresh supply of images.

How to fix it

If you didn't install all of the clip art that came with Office XP, you can go back and install it now, completing the assortment. To install the images you didn't install the first time, follow these steps:

1. Open the Control Panel by choosing Start, Settings, Control Panel.

2. In the Control Panel window, double-click the Add/Remove Programs icon.

3. In the Add/Remove Programs window, scroll to find Microsoft Office XP and click once on it to select it.

4. Click the Change button. ▶

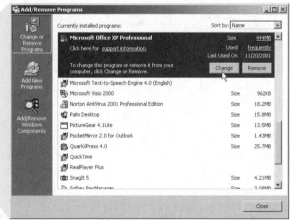

5. After a brief "Preparing To Install" prompt appears, the Microsoft Office XP Setup window appears. Click the Add or Remove Features option and click the Next button.

6. In the Features To Install list, if you see a minus sign next to Office Shared Features, click it to collapse the list of features and then click the minus sign next to Clip Organizer (if there is one). If plus signs appear next to these two items, you don't need to do anything.

7. Click the drop triangle next to Clip Organizer and choose Run All From My Computer. This tells the Setup utility that you want to install all of the Clip Organizer images and tools. ▶

8. Click the Update button.

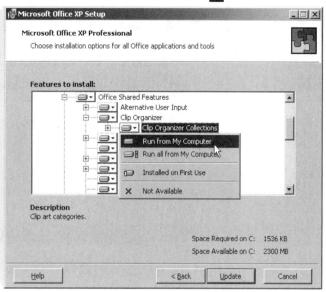

After you begin the update, you may be asked to insert the original Office XP CD-ROM, depending on your original installation process. If you're asked to insert it, place the CD-ROM in your computer's CD drive and follow the screen prompts until the installation is complete. The next time you run Microsoft Excel and attempt to insert clip art, the Clip Gallery's assortment of images will include the full collection.

Outside image sources

You can obtain lots of images on the Web, many for free, and many without any copyright restrictions. To find them, do a search through any search site (*www.google.com/*, *www.hotbot.com/*, *www.yahoo.com/*) typing "free clip art" or "free graphic images" into the search criteria box. From the resulting Web sites, you can download images or copy them to your computer by right-clicking them and choosing Save Picture As from the shortcut menu. ▶

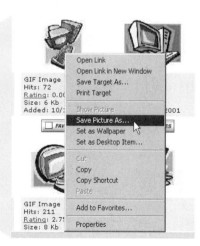

You can find CD-ROMs filled with clip art images in just about any office supply or computer store. You can install the images on your computer by following the instructions that come with the CD, or you can insert the CD each time you need an image and peruse the selection there for the image you want. The latter technique takes more time when you want to insert an image, but it also takes less of your hard disk space than copying the images from the CD to your C drive.

I want to scan an image, but Excel doesn't think I'm attached to a scanner

Source of the problem

You chose Picture, From Scanner or Camera from the Insert menu and were informed that Excel doesn't detect a scanner attached to your computer. The prompt suggested that you check your scanner's connection or reinstall the driver for your scanner, or both. But wait a minute, you're looking at the scanner, and you can see that it's attached to your computer. Maybe you've even used it before with another application, so you have no idea why Excel is so clueless. ▶

What's the deal? You can see you have a scanner, so why can't Excel see it? There can be any number of reasons for this problem, and here are a few of the more likely culprits:

- You installed Excel (or all of Office XP) before you set up your scanner.
- Your scanner isn't really connected—the cable could be loose, or the scanner could be off.
- The driver file that tells applications how to talk to your scanner is corrupt, missing, or has been moved and Excel can't find it.

How to fix it

If you installed your scanner after installing Office, you may need to run the Hardware Wizard through the System Properties dialog box (right-click the My Computer icon on your Desktop and choose Properties) or reinstall your scanner software—a CD or disk probably came with the scanner, along with installation instructions. ▶

If the driver is corrupt or missing, you can reinstall the scanner software, which installs the driver and overwrites the corrupted file. If your scanner isn't properly connected, check the

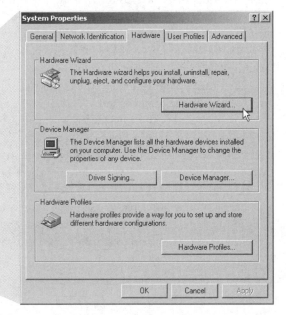

cable and make sure it's inserted into the right port and tightly connected to the computer and the scanner. Check to make sure the scanner is on, too—many a frustrated user has gone through reinstallations and a variety of other troubleshooting steps only to find that the device in question was off at the time.

The path of least resistance

If you find that you don't have the disk or CD that came with your scanner or that you don't have time to do a reinstall or to download a new driver from the scanner manufacturer's Web site, you can take a faster, somewhat roundabout method. If any other application—for example, Adobe Photoshop or CorelDraw—is able to see your scanner, scan the graphic you need and save the file. Then you can use the Insert, Picture, From File command to insert the image into your worksheet. ▶

Tip

If your graphic is on a worksheet bound for the Web, be sure to use the right graphic file type—.gif, .jpg, or for newer browser versions, .png. If you use any other format, the image won't display online.

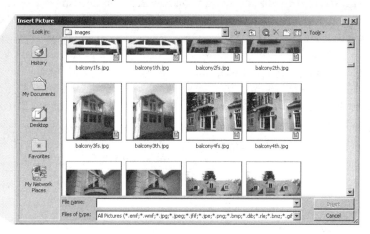

Many paths to the same end

You can also use the Control Panel's Add/Remove Hardware program to search for your scanner to make sure your computer "sees" it and to set it up for use if it is perceived by your system. Choose Control Panel from the Settings submenu in the Start menu and double-click Add/Remove Hardware. This starts the Add/Remove Hardware Wizard, the same one you encounter if you right-click the My Computer icon and choose Properties from the shortcut menu. The Hardware tab in that dialog box also offers the Hardware Wizard, which will coach you through the process of searching for the missing or unrecognized device.

My clip art files are very disorganized, and I can't find the images I need

Source of the problem

So you remember you had some images that would look great in the workbook you're setting up, and you know you saw them on your computer just the other day. Now you're creating the template and you're ready to add the images. Well, if you don't have an organized storage system, you're likely to lose things or to spend a lot of time looking for things that are right where you left them—the problem being you don't remember where you left them!

Office XP, and therefore Excel 2002, has a great tool for keeping all of your clip art images (and other graphics as well, such as scanned photos and drawings, or art for the Web) organized—the aptly named Clip Organizer. The Clip Organizer is opened through the task pane and appears in its own window, showing you all of your images, in all the drives and folders on your computer, or all those to which you have access if you're on a network.

Using the Clip Organizer is simple and requires nothing more than your refiling some of your images into logical folders and perhaps creating folders to store things in so you can keep images separate by type or content.

How to fix it

To access the Clip Organizer, follow these steps:

1. Display the task pane by choosing Task Pane in the View menu.

2. Click the drop triangle at the top of the task pane and choose Insert Clip Art. ▶

3. In the Insert Clip Art pane, look down at the bottom and click the Clip Organizer hyperlink.

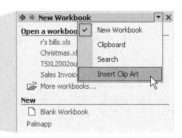

With the Clip Organizer window now open, you can go through your hard disk drive and folders and find your misfiled images and add them into any of the Clip Organizer folders. Follow these steps:

1. Click once on the folder into which the image(s) you want to add should be placed.

2. Choose File, Add Clips to Organizer, On My Own. This means that you'll be searching for the files yourself—choosing which ones to add and by your action in step 1, where they'll go.

3. In the resulting Add Clips To Organizer (preceded by the folder name you selected, such as Favorites), navigate to the folder that contains the first image(s) you want to add to the Clip Organizer. ▶

4. When you find the file(s) select it/them (you can use the Ctrl key to select multiple image files) and click the Add button.

5. Repeat steps 1 through 4 until you've located and added all the images you want to be able to access through the Clip Organizer.

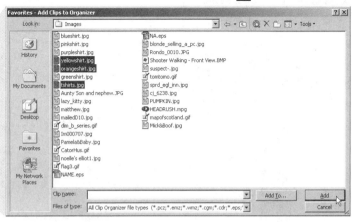

Tip

Remember that you can organize sound files, movie files, animated .gifs, as well as static graphics of any file format through the Clip Organizer. The name and its access through the Insert Clip Art pane in Excel might imply that it's just for pictures, but any media clip (the real derivation of the name) can be organized with the Clip Organizer.

I'm not a pack rat, I'm a *collector!*

If you feel that some of your images defy the existing folders (a.k.a. "collections"), you can build a new one of your own. In the Clip Organizer window, choose File, New Collection and in the resulting dialog box, choose a parent folder for the new collection folder, and then type a name for the collection. For example, you can create collections for individual clients (if you're a Web designer or use specific graphics for specific clients in some other capacity). ▶

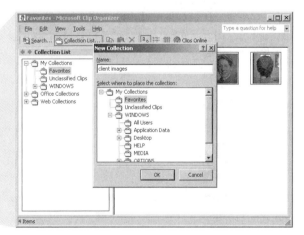

After you create the new collection folder, you can add existing images to it, and when you create, scan, or download new images that fall into this new category, you can add them to it, too. It's a good idea to begin thinking about your images not just in terms of where they are and how you'll use them, but how to store them. Taking the extra time to add them to the appropriate collection within the Clip Organizer will save you a lot of time as you work in the future.

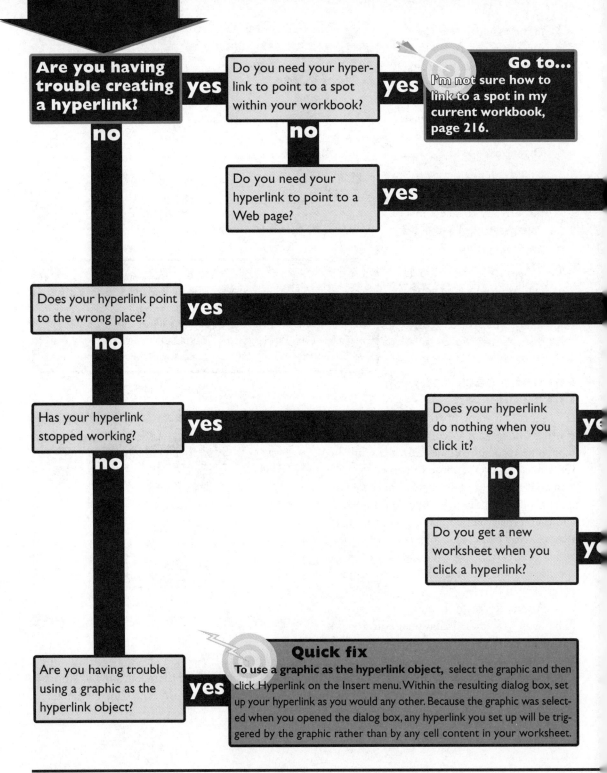

Are you having trouble creating a hyperlink? **yes** → Do you need your hyperlink to point to a spot within your workbook? **yes** →

Go to... I'm not sure how to link to a spot in my current workbook, page 216.

no ↓

Do you need your hyperlink to point to a Web page? **yes** →

no ↓

Does your hyperlink point to the wrong place? **yes** →

no ↓

Has your hyperlink stopped working? **yes** →

Does your hyperlink do nothing when you click it? **ye** →

no ↓

Do you get a new worksheet when you click a hyperlink? **y**

no ↓

Are you having trouble using a graphic as the hyperlink object? **yes** →

Quick fix

To use a graphic as the hyperlink object, select the graphic and then click Hyperlink on the Insert menu. Within the resulting dialog box, set up your hyperlink as you would any other. Because the graphic was selected when you opened the dialog box, any hyperlink you set up will be triggered by the graphic rather than by any cell content in your worksheet.

Hyperlinks

Go to...
I don't know the exact Web address that my hyperlink should point to, page 218.

Quick fix

If the target of your hyperlink has been moved, renamed, or deleted, the link won't work anymore. To make the hyperlink work again, you need to relocate the target and edit the hyperlink so that it points to the target's new location. Right-click the hyperlink and then click Edit Hyperlink on the resulting shortcut menu. In the Edit Hyperlink dialog box, type the new target location.

Go to...
I click a hyperlink in my worksheet, and nothing happens, page 220.

Go to...
When I click my hyperlink, it creates a new, blank workbook, page 222.

If your solution isn't here, check these related chapters:

- Drawing shapes and lines, page 96
- Graphics, page 204
- Saving, page 278

Or see the general troubleshooting tips on page xv.

I'm not sure how to link to a spot in my current workbook

Source of the problem

When most people think of hyperlinks, they think of text or graphics on a Web page that take you to other Web pages when you click them. Few people are aware that you can create hyperlinks that open new and existing documents or that move you to other locations within your current file.

Given the size of a Microsoft Excel workbook and the fact that data can be spread out over more than 16 million cells per sheet, it would be rather handy to be able to click one cell or a graphic image and be instantly taken to another cell on the same worksheet or on a different worksheet in the same workbook. Imagine the convenience of being able to turn a cell into a hyperlink that takes the user to supporting data somewhere else in the same workbook—making your worksheets easier to use and more informative, as well. Sadly, however, because people aren't aware of this capability within Excel (or Microsoft Word, for that matter), they usually have no idea how to make it happen.

Creating hyperlinks is simple, and it involves a very short series of steps, beginning with choosing the item that will serve as the link. In Excel, your choices are a cell, a chart, or a graphic object (for example, an AutoShape, a piece of clip art or some other image file, a WordArt object, or anything you've drawn using the Drawing toolbar). It's a good idea to have planned your hyperlinks before you sit down to create them. Jotting down a list of what links to what or at least planning it in your head, will save you a lot of time making changes and corrections.

> **Tip**
>
> When you're planning your intra-worksheet hyperlinks, remember that the target within your worksheet can be a cell, a range of cells, or a chart. You can also create hyperlinks that point to other workbook files and to specific worksheets within them.

How to fix it

1. Select the worksheet entry (a cell or range of cells) or object (graphic or chart) that will serve as the hyperlink object.

2. On the Insert menu, click Hyperlink. You can also click the Insert Hyperlink button on the Standard toolbar.

3. Click Place In This Document in the Link To section of the Insert Hyperlink dialog box.

> **Tip**
>
> Unlike Word, Excel won't allow you to turn text into a hyperlink. You can turn an entire cell (which can contain text) into a link, but you can't select text within a cell and create a hyperlink.

Hyperlinks

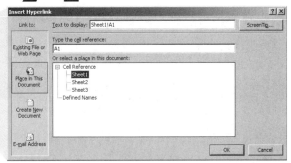

4. In the Type The Cell Reference box, type the cell or range that the hyperlink should point to. ▶

5. In the list of sheets provided in the Insert Hyperlink dialog box, select the sheet within your current workbook that the hyperlink should point to.

6. Click OK. When you point to the hyperlink object, the pointer becomes a pointing finger, indicating that clicking the link will access the target cell or range. ▶

Psssst! It's a ScreenTip

If you want some descriptive or instructional text to appear when people move their mouse pointer over a hyperlink, you can create a ScreenTip. Just like the little boxes that pop up when you point to a toolbar button, this

Tip

If you want to turn an empty cell into a hyperlink, type instructions such as "click here to view supporting data" in the Text To Display text box in the Insert Hyperlink dialog box. As soon as you click OK to create the link, the text you typed in the Text To Display box appears in the cell that was active when the hyperlink insertion process began.

ScreenTip will appear whenever anyone hovers a mouse pointer over the hyperlink for more than a second. Your ScreenTip might say "Click here to view the supporting data" or something like that—something that tells the person what to expect at the other end of the hyperlink.

To create a ScreenTip for an existing hyperlink, you can use the ScreenTip button in the Insert Hyperlink dialog box or, if you've already created the link and now realize a ScreenTip might be helpful, right-click the existing hyperlink object, point to Hyperlink on the shortcut menu, and then click Edit Hyperlink. In the Edit Hyperlink dialog box, click the ScreenTip button to display the Set Hyperlink ScreenTip dialog box. ▶

In the ScreenTip Text box, type the text you want to appear in the ScreenTip. You can use as many as 90 characters, but it's better to use 50 or fewer characters to keep it concise and easy to read. Click OK to return to the Edit Hyperlink dialog box and click OK again to implement the ScreenTip.

Tip

It's a good idea to test your hyperlink and its ScreenTip—make sure the hyperlink points to the location you want it to and that the ScreenTip is spelled and worded correctly—before making your workbook available to others. Better for you to spot a mistake than to have someone else tell you about it!

I don't know the exact Web address that my hyperlink should point to

Source of the problem

A hyperlink that points to a Web page can give your lowly worksheet a global reach. Whether the hyperlink points to your company Web page or to supporting or related information on someone else's site, it's important that the hyperlink work properly, taking users to the exact spot on the exact Web page you intended. This is especially important if the linked page contains sensitive or essential information that the worksheet user needs in order to interpret or make use of the worksheet data —sending them, however accidentally, on a wild Web goose chase will not make you a popular person!

But what if you don't know the exact Web address, right down to the page name? You may know the main address (*www.domain.com/*), but if the data is on a subpage of that site, you need to know that bit of the address as well—as in *www.domain.com/data.htm*.

It's a good idea to know this information before you start the hyperlink creation process, but if you're like me and don't read directions or plan ahead before set-ting out on a trip, you might find yourself sitting in front of the computer saying, "Wait a minute, I don't know where this hyperlink is supposed to point!" For the preparation-challenged, the Insert Hyperlink dialog box gives you the chance to browse the Web in search of the page your hyperlink should point to.

> **Tip**
>
> A Web address is also called a URL, which stands for Uniform Resource Locator. Some geeks pronounce it "Earl," but being a non-geek myself, I say the letters U-R-L. The choice is up to you, but if you choose the geek way, people might snicker at you behind your back.

How to fix it

1. Select the cell, range, graphic, or chart that will act as your hyperlink object.

2. On the Insert menu, click Hyperlink.

3. Click Existing File Or Web Page in the Link To section of the Insert Hyperlink dialog box. ▶

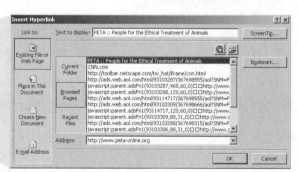

4. Click the Browsed Pages button to see pages you've been to recently (the sites stored in your History folder, through your default Web browser) and look through the corresponding list of sites to see if you can find the page you want.

5. Click once on the address you want to link to or, if you don't find it in the Browsed Pages, start your Web browser by clicking the Open Browser button (see the upper right corner of the window—the button looks like the Earth with a magnifying glass on it). You can also open your browser from the Desktop or Start menu. In either case, once the browser is open, navigate to the site.

6. In the Web browser window, once you're on the page to which you want to link, select the content of the Address bar by clicking once on the address—it will become highlighted—and then choose Edit, Copy or press Ctrl+C. ▶

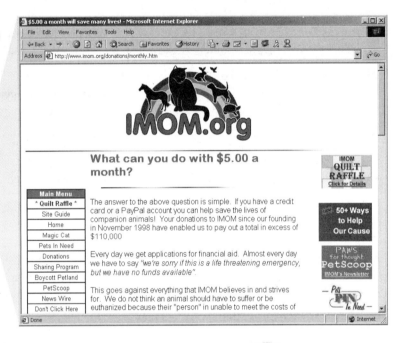

7. Back in Excel, where the Insert Hyperlink dialog box is waiting for you, click in the Address box at the bottom of the dialog box and press Ctrl+V to paste the address you just copied from the browser window.

8. Click OK to insert the hyperlink.

It's a good idea to test your hyperlinks immediately after setting them up and to continue to test them. Web sites close or get reorganized (which can change the address of a specific page within the site), and content moves from one page to another, potentially leaving your hyperlink connected to inaccurate or non-existent content.

Tip

Hyperlinks can also point to Web pages on your company's intranet. Some companies don't want to post the kind of data your worksheet might refer to on an Internet-based Web server, preferring to keep what could be confidential info in-house.

I click a hyperlink in my worksheet, and nothing happens

Source of the problem

You click a hyperlink, and you expect to be taken to a Web site or to a specific location in a worksheet. But it doesn't work. Isn't that aggravating? I hate it when that happens. The problem is easy enough to fix, but you'll want to know what happened so it doesn't happen again, right?

Before you get started solving the problem, here are some questions to consider:

- Are you sure what you're clicking is a hyperlink? If the hyperlink is the content of a cell, it should be in color (blue or purple, if you're using default settings for hyperlinks) and be underlined. Also, your mouse pointer should turn into a pointing finger when you point to it.

- When you point to the hyperlink (whether it's a cell's content or a graphic object), does a ScreenTip appear with the location of the hyperlink's target?

- Did the hyperlink work before? If so, could anything have changed?

Your answers can shed light on the nature and source of the problem. If the text in the cell isn't underlined or if your mouse pointer doesn't change when you point to a cell or graphic, the cell or graphic probably isn't a hyperlink. If everything looks as it should, perhaps the hyperlink points to itself. It's possible to link to the cell that's serving as the hyperlink object—not on purpose, but accidents happen! If the hyperlink used to work, something has to have changed. Perhaps the target file or Web site has moved. Whatever the cause, the solution is to edit the hyperlink. The following steps show you how.

How to fix it

1. Right-click the cell or graphic, point to Hyperlink on the shortcut menu, and then click Edit Hyperlink. Note! If the item you right-click results in a menu with a plain "Hyperlink" command, then you've right-clicked something that wasn't a hyperlink to begin with. The rest of these steps assume that the item was in fact a hyperlink. ▶

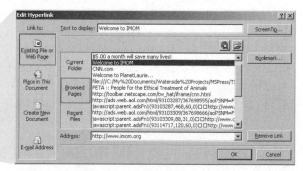

Hyperlinks

2. If the hyperlink is linked to a place within the worksheet (or to a cell or range within another worksheet or workbook), the address appears in the Type The Cell Reference box. If your link points to a Web site or another file (other than a different workbook), the address will appear in the Address box.

3. Examine the address in the box and then edit the hyperlink by either reestablishing a target for the hyperlink within the worksheet or reentering the name of the file or Web page to which the hyperlink should point.

4. When you've reset the hyperlink information, click OK.

No thanks, just browsing

If your hyperlink points to a Web site and you think the existing address is the correct one (despite the link not working), click the button that opens a new Web browser window (the button looks like a globe, just above and to the right of your list of Browsed Pages). ▶

When your browser opens, use a search site such as *www.yahoo.com/* or *www.google.com/* to search for the site or try entering the Web address you think is right, using the browser's Address or Location bar.

Once you locate the working Web site, switch back to Excel (where you left the Edit Hyperlink dialog box open), and you'll see that the address has been inserted in the Address box at the bottom of the Edit Hyperlink dialog box.

When I click my hyperlink, it creates a new, blank workbook

Source of the problem

This is one of those problems that isn't technically a problem. There is a certain type of hyperlink that is meant to open a new blank workbook. But if opening a new workbook isn't what you want your hyperlink to do or if you don't expect this result from a hyperlink someone else created, it can be an unpleasant surprise. In either case, if you don't know how to fix it, it's a problem.

Before we get started, let's clarify a few things. In addition to linking to files and Web sites, Excel hyperlinks can be set up to link to any of the following:

- a place in your existing worksheet (a cell or range thereof)

- a new blank workbook created at the time the hyperlink is clicked

- an e-mail address in a new message window

> **Tip**
>
> Before clicking a hyperlink, check its ScreenTip by moving your mouse pointer over the link. Even if the person who set up the hyperlink didn't create a custom ScreenTip, there should be a default one—probably the name of the file or Web site the link points to. If the ScreenTip doesn't list a Web site, a workbook file name that you recognize, or say "mailto: name@domain.com" (for an e-mail link), chances are that clicking the link will create a new blank workbook.

If the problem hyperlink is one that you created, it's relatively easy to see how you might have created this type of hyperlink by mistake—the version of the Insert Hyperlink dialog box that appears when the Create New Document button is clicked does ask for a file name and path to that file, so you might have thought you were setting up a link to an existing file.

If you're working with a hyperlink created by someone else, let's just assume they were sleepy or just not thinking straight at the time they created it and let it go. Take a deep breath and move on—you'll just fix the problem and have the satisfaction of knowing that you did a good deed!

How to fix it

1. Right-click the hyperlink that's generating a new workbook whenever it's clicked, and on the shortcut menu click Edit Hyperlink.

2. In the Edit Hyperlink dialog box, observe the panel of buttons in the Link To section. Most probably, the Existing File Or Web Page button is selected. To change the hyperlink to a different type—one that links to a Web page or a location in an existing worksheet or workbook or one that generates an e-mail message—click the appropriate button in the Link To section.

3. Type a file name and location or a Web address in the Type The File Or Web Page Name box or click an address in the Or Select From List section. Click Remove Link if you'd rather not link the selected cell or object at all. ▶

4. Click OK to return to your worksheet.

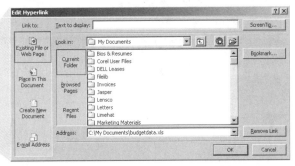

Now I want a new blank workbook!

I know, you didn't want one before, but now you see the merits. If your worksheet contains data that people test and play with, you can create a link that gives them a blank workbook into which they can copy the data. They can then play without risk of mangling the original data.

Click the cell, range, or object that will be the hyperlink object and on the Insert menu, click Hyperlink. In the Insert Hyperlink dialog box, click Create New Document in the Link To section. In the Name Of New Document box, type the name and extension of the file you want the link to create (*testdata.xls*, for example, for a workbook that is a testing location for data). ▶

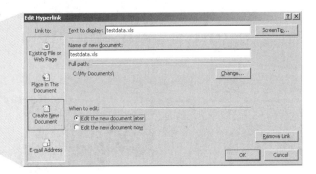

Click the Change button if you don't want the file to be stored in the My Documents folder, which is the default location. When the Create New Document dialog box appears, find where you want to store the new file, type the new file's name (including its extension) in the File Name box, and click OK. If you want to be able to keep working in the current worksheet after creating the link, click the Edit The New Document Later option. (Otherwise, the new file will open as soon as you click OK.)

Click OK to create the hyperlink and the new file that the hyperlink targets. If you clicked the Edit The New Document Later option, the new file won't open right away—it will be created and stored in the directory that you set in the Full Path section so that you can edit it at your leisure.

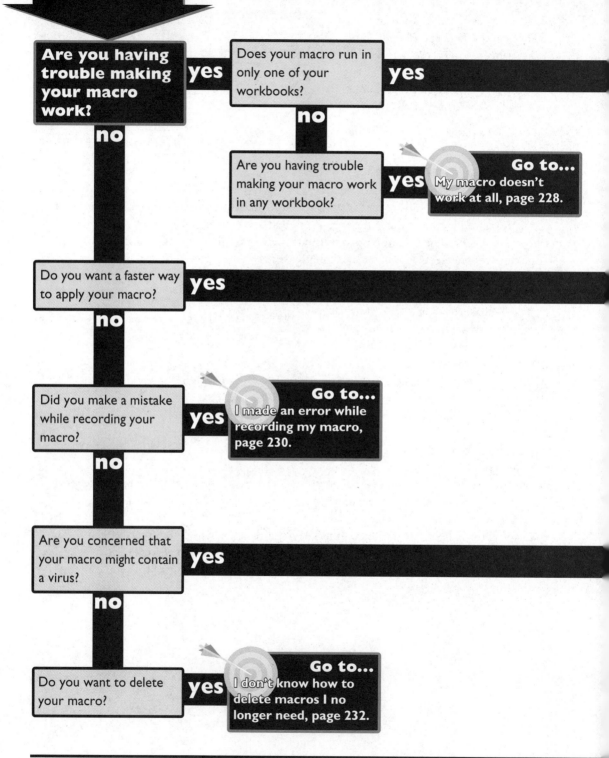

Are you having trouble making your macro work?

yes → Does your macro run in only one of your workbooks?

yes →

no →

Are you having trouble making your macro work in any workbook?

yes → **Go to...** My macro doesn't work at all, page 228.

no ↓

Do you want a faster way to apply your macro?

yes →

no ↓

Did you make a mistake while recording your macro?

yes → **Go to...** I made an error while recording my macro, page 230.

no ↓

Are you concerned that your macro might contain a virus?

yes →

no ↓

Do you want to delete your macro?

yes → **Go to...** I don't know how to delete macros I no longer need, page 232.

Go to...
My macro won't run in the active workbook, page 226.

Quick fix

To create a keyboard shortcut for your macro, follow these steps:

1. Choose Macro from the Tools menu and then click Macros from the submenu.

2. Click the Options button.

3. In the Options dialog box, type a letter (that will be pressed in conjunction with the Ctrl key) to run your macro.

4. Click OK to close the dialog box.

NOTE: You can add the Shift key when you press the letter to create a three-key shortcut.

Quick fix

Scan for viruses in macros. Computer viruses can be stored in macros and if you enable a macro in a worksheet that someone has sent you via email or on disk, you risk infecting your computer. Run your virus scan software on any downloaded files, and if they're not infected, go ahead and enable the macros when you open the workbook.

If your solution isn't here, check these related chapters:

- Printing, page 268
- Workspace customization, page 368

Or see the general troubleshooting tips on page xv.

My macro won't run in the active workbook

Source of the problem

You recorded a macro, but when you try to invoke it in your current workbook, nothing happens. If you assigned a keyboard shortcut to your macro, pressing the key sequence doesn't work. If you go to the Tools menu and click Macros, the macro isn't listed, so you can't even try to run it that way. What's going on?

The cause of your dilemma is most likely that you aren't working in the workbook in which you created the macro. When you create a macro, you specify a storage location for it—and the default location is This Workbook, which means the one you're working in when you create the macro. The Personal Macro Workbook is the location that you want to use if the macro you're recording should be available to all workbooks.

The simplest method of fixing the problem requires re-recording the macro and opting to save the new version to the Personal Macro Workbook. Yes, that sounds like a lot of work, especially if your macro is a long one, encompassing a lot of steps. Think of it this way, though—you'll know where to store your macros in the future, and you'll only have to rerecord a macro for this purpose once!

> ## That's getting rather personal
>
> So what's this Personal Macro Workbook? It's a workbook that opens as soon as you elect to store a macro in it during the current Microsoft Excel session. It isn't available from the Window menu, so it is essentially invisible unless you click Unhide on the Window menu and then click OK to unhide the workbook file (called Personal.xls by default). If you close this workbook before closing Excel, make sure you save any changes to it; otherwise the macros you recorded in the current Excel session will be lost! If you click Unhide and don't see Personal.xls listed (or if the Unhide command is unavailable on the Window menu), no macros were saved to the Personal Macro Workbook in your current Excel session.

How to fix it

1. In any open workbook (it doesn't matter which one, because you'll be storing the macro in the Personal Macro Workbook), point to Macro on the Tools menu and then click Record New Macro.

2. In the Macro Name box of the Record Macro dialog box, type a name for your macro, replacing the default generic name (such as Macro1).

3. Type a keyboard letter in the Shortcut Key box if you want to be able to invoke your macro by pressing a key combination. (Keep in mind that you must type a letter—you can't use special characters, symbols or numbers.)

Macros

4. Click Personal Macro Workbook in the Store Macro In drop-down list. ▶

5. Type a description to elaborate on the macro's purpose.

6. Click OK and begin recording your macro.

7. When you have finished recording your macro, click the floating Stop Recording button. Be sure to save changes to the Personal Macro Workbook if you either close the Personal.xls workbook or exit Excel.

Tip

Many Ctrl+[letter] combinations are used by application commands. To expand the possibilities when you create a keyboard shortcut for a macro, add the Shift key to the key combination, giving yourself 26 new keyboard shortcuts to choose from.

If you really don't want to rerecord...

Feeling adventurous? You can copy your existing macro—you know, the one you stored in a specific workbook and not in the Personal Macro workbook—and place a copy in the Personal Macro Workbook. Open the Microsoft Visual Basic editor and copy the macro from the open workbook into the Personal Macro Workbook. The macro will now be available in both the current workbook and in all other workbooks because it's stored in the Personal Macro Workbook.

In the workbook containing the macro you want to copy, point to Macro on the Tools menu and then click Macros. (Make sure Personal.xls is open, even if it's hidden.) Click the macro in the Macro Name list and then click the Edit button to display the Microsoft Visual Basic editor window. ▶

On the View menu, click Project Explorer to make sure that the Project panel is visible. With your macro's program code visible, look in the Project panel for the module that

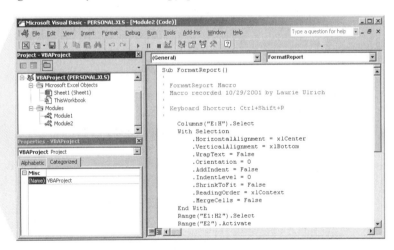

represents the macro you want to copy. If necessary, select the module and drag it to VBAProject Personal.xls. Close the Microsoft Visual Basic editor window by clicking the Close button in the upper right corner. Back in your open workbook, point to Macro on the Tools menu and click Macros. In the Macro Name list of the Macro dialog box, verify that your macro now appears listed with PERSONAL.XLS! in front of it, indicating that a copy of your macro is stored in that workbook. From now on, your macro will run in any workbook.

My macro doesn't work at all

Source of the problem

Unlike a macro that works in only one worksheet (see "My macro won't run in the active workbook" on page 226), a macro that won't run at all probably needs to be edited or rerecorded. When you run a macro that doesn't work, either nothing happens or you get an error message.

The causes of this problem with your macro include the following:

- The macro contains procedures that are in conflict with the current circumstances when you go to run it. For example, a macro that involves printing won't work if your computer can no longer access a printer, and a macro that hides a column will stop if the column is already hidden. Such a conflict results in an error message that alerts you to the problem the macro has encountered.

- The macro doesn't really exist. Perhaps you created and stored it in one workbook, and now that workbook is gone (or was never saved at all). If this is the problem, the macro won't be in the Macros dialog box list, and if you try to invoke it using a keyboard shortcut, nothing happens.

- The macro has been deleted by you (and you forgot) or by another user.

- The macro is stored in a workbook that you haven't opened, so you can't find it. If you want the macro to be available to all workbooks, you should store the macro in the Personal Macro Workbook. You can store an existing macro in this workbook by opening the workbook where the macro is currently located and then copying the macro to the Personal Macro Workbook. (See "My macro won't run in the active workbook" on page 226.)

> **Tip**
>
> Some macros work only partially—they do some of the things intended and then stop. In this case, rerecording the macro is your best bet. Unless you're a Microsoft Visual Basic programmer (or at least have some knowledge of Visual Basic), you'll spend more time editing the macro's programming code than you would recording it again.

> **Tip**
>
> When you exit Excel after you copy or store a macro in the Personal Macro Workbook, you'll be asked if you want to save changes to the Personal Macro Workbook. Click Yes. If you click No, the macros you just copied to or stored in the Personal Macro Workbook will be lost.

If you aren't sure of the cause, the quickest way to be able to perform whatever tasks the macro automated is to rerecord the macro. If the macro is gone, you can reuse the macro name and shortcut with no problem. If it still exists but has some error in it, you can replace the malfunctioning macro with the new one, and in doing so, make it possible to reuse the keyboard shortcut.

Before you go to the trouble, however, find out if the macro exists anywhere—in the Personal Macro Workbook or in any of your other saved workbooks.

How to fix it

To determine if the macro is still on your computer, follow these steps:

1. Open all the workbooks in which you might have created (and also stored) the macro you're looking for.

2. In any one of them, point to Macro on the Tools menu and then click Macros.

3. If necessary, click All Open Workbooks in the Macros In drop-down list. ▶

4. Select the macro in the Macro Name list and click the Run button. The macro will likely run fine.

Remember when...

If you have an idea of when you recorded the macro, view the list of your workbooks by the date they were created. In the Details view in Windows Explorer or My Computer, open the folder in which you save your workbooks and, in the right pane, click the Modified heading at the top of the Modified column. (Click Details on the View menu if you can't see a Modified column.) Find workbooks with dates around the time you think you created the macro. Open these workbooks when you begin your search for the missing macro.

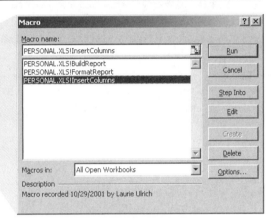

If your macro does exist and you need to copy it to the Personal Macro Workbook so you can run it from any worksheet, see "My macro won't run in the active workbook," on page 226.

If your macro exists and you can't make it work in the worksheet it was stored in, you can edit the macro if you know Visual Basic. Assuming you just said "Yeah, right," simply rerecord your macro by following these steps:

1. In any workbook, point to Macros on the Tools menu and then click Record New Macro.

2. In the Macro Name box, type the name of the macro you want to replace. If you want, type a letter in the Shortcut Key box. (Press Shift while typing the letter to expand your keyboard shortcut options.) You can then simultaneously press this letter key and Ctrl (and Shift, if you used that, too) to run the macro.

3. In the Store Macro In drop-down list, select Personal Macro Workbook so that the macro can be run from any worksheet.

4. If you want, type a description in the Description box and then click OK. Click Yes when the prompt appears asking if you want to replace the existing macro with the same name.

5. Record your macro and then click the floating Stop Recording button when you are finished. If for any reason the floating toolbar is missing, you can access the Stop command on the Tools menu.

I made an error while recording my macro

Source of the problem

If you made an error while recording your macro, the problem will make its presence known either as you're recording the macro or the first time you try to run the macro (and something undesirable happens). With the former, after you smack yourself in the forehead, you're faced with the decision—do I continue recording and then edit the macro later, or do I click Stop Recording now and start over? Well, that depends on the nature of the error.

If the error is fundamental—you opened the wrong file, or you set up the worksheet with an entirely inappropriate layout—it's probably best to rerecord the macro, reusing the name and keyboard shortcut. (See "My macro doesn't work at all" on page 228.) But perhaps the error is relatively minor. Did you misspell something when you inserted text? Did you enter the wrong number in a cell? Did you apply formatting and choose the wrong font or font size? These errors are all easy to edit, even if you're not a Visual Basic programmer, so you can probably fix the mistakes yourself by editing your macro.

If you've discovered the error after completing the macro-creation process, simple errors are still easy to fix.

> **Tip**
>
> Visual Basic might not seem so basic if you're not familiar with it. It's a simple programming language that uses standard instructions to complete a series of tasks. You can learn more about it by reading *Microsoft Visual Basic Professional 6.0 Step by Step* from Microsoft Press.

How to fix it

1. Open the workbook in which your macro is stored. (If it's stored in the Personal Macro Workbook, open any workbook.)

2. If you stored the macro in the Personal Macro Workbook, click Unhide on the Window menu and then click Personal.xls in the Unhide dialog box. Click OK to unhide the workbook. (You can't edit a macro that's stored in a hidden workbook.)

3. On the Tools menu, point to Macro and then click Macros.

4. In the Macro dialog box, click the macro you want to edit and then click the Edit button to display the Microsoft Visual Basic editor window.

5. In the Microsoft Visual Basic editor window, read the code in the Module window. ▶

6. The text or numbers you've typed appear in quotation marks. Edit them by positioning your insertion point in the text and typing a correction using the Backspace and Delete keys as needed. To correct formatting, find the

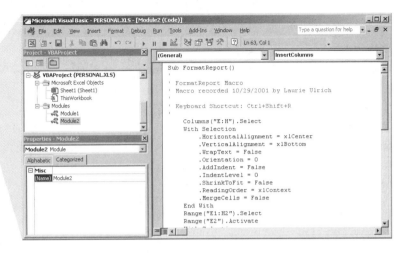

format setting and change the font, size, alignment, color, or other format. Type the new format (such as *Bold*) after the equal sign; if the original setting was in quotation marks, keep the quotation marks intact.

7. When you've completed your edits, press Ctrl+S to save the open macro.

8. Click the Close button at the right side of the title bar or choose File, Exit and Return to Excel. Either action returns you to the Excel application window, and the Visual Basic editor application is closed.

You'll want to test your macro right away to make sure your edits worked. If they didn't, go back and re-edit, repeating steps 3 through 8. If you're unable to solve the problem, you'll want to rerecord the macro from scratch. If the problem isn't resolved after two attempts at editing, it will take less time to start over than to keep editing, especially if you're unfamiliar with Visual Basic.

An ounce of prevention is worth a pound of rerecording
To avoid macro errors in the future, keep the following in mind as you record your macros:

- Planning is key. Write down the macro's tasks in the order they should be recorded. The order in which they're recorded is the order in which they'll be done when you run the macro.

- The macro recorder is recording *everything* you're doing, including making erroneous selections from menus, inserting typos that you backspace through and type again, creating formulas that don't work and have to be redone, moving content from cell to cell, and selecting elements with your mouse. Do a test run before you start recording so that you keep the mistakes (even those that you fix and that don't mess up the macro's performance) to a minimum.

- The Description box in the Record Macro dialog box is very handy, especially if others will be using your macros. The contents of that box will appear in the Visual Basic editing window and can help to clarify what your macro is supposed to do, long after you might have forgotten.

I don't know how to delete macros I no longer need

Source of the problem

There's no harm in keeping macros around after they're no longer useful, unless you want to reuse the keyboard shortcut assigned to one, or you are recording a similar macro and want to reuse the name or use one like it. Or, perhaps you're just very tidy and like to throw things away when you no longer need them.

What makes a macro obsolete? Maybe it was used for a particular set of circumstances, and those circumstances no longer exist. Perhaps you found a better way to do something, and the macro that automated the old way is no longer useful. Whatever the reason, macros are simple to delete.

Tip

Deleting macros might be *too* simple. Although the deletion process results in a prompt that you must respond to before the deletion occurs, many users quickly click OK to confirm prompts, without reading their messages. Be sure you're deleting the right macro, not the one above or below it in the Macro Name list!

How to fix it

1. If the macro you want to delete is stored in one of your workbooks, open that workbook. If the macro is stored in the Personal Macro Workbook, click Unhide on the Window menu, make sure Personal.xls is selected in the Unhide dialog box, and then click OK.

2. On the Tools menu, point to Macro and then click Macros.

3. In the Macro dialog box, click All Open Workbooks in the Macros In drop-down list. ▶

4. Click the macro you want to delete in the Macro Name list.

5. Click the Delete button. A prompt appears, asking you to confirm your intention to delete the macro. This is your chance to change your mind. If you really want to delete the macro, click Yes; if you decide you don't want to delete it, click No. ▶

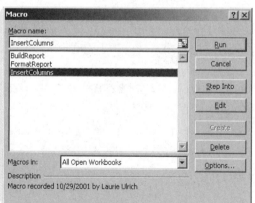

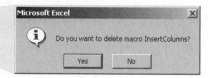

Macros

When you don't know where it's been

Sometimes you might want to delete macros that other people have created, just to make the workbook where the macros were stored safe to view and use. Why? Macros can contain viruses, which is why Excel might prompt you before it opens a worksheet containing macros, asking if you want to enable those macros when the file is opened. Choosing to disable them will prevent any infected macro from giving your computer a virus; choosing to enable them puts your computer at risk if you don't have virus protection software installed.

> ## Going, going, GONE!
>
> Once a macro is gone, it's really gone. You can't undo the deletion of a macro, so be very sure you want to delete it before you click Yes to confirm the deletion. If the macro was in the Personal Macro Workbook, you can't get the macro back, even by saying No to saving changes to the Personal Macro Workbook when you exit Excel—the deletion is permanent.

If someone has sent you a workbook, always scan it before you open it, using your virus protection software. This is a good rule of thumb even if you don't know if the workbook contains macros in the first place. If you don't have virus protection software, get some. Having the software, however, doesn't make you immune to viruses—new ones are being developed daily, so your virus protection software might not have the "cure" for the latest virus you might have caught.

Of course, you can open the file, choose to disable the macros, and then delete the macros from the file. This might result in limiting the workbook's functionality, especially if the macros are important to the way the author intended you to use the worksheets and their data. Deleting the macros won't limit your ability to view, edit, and work with the data, however.

> ## Warning
>
> If someone you don't know sends you a workbook and you didn't ask for it, don't even open it. Regardless of the sender, always scan any attachments to e-mail messages for viruses and always scan any files you download from the Internet.

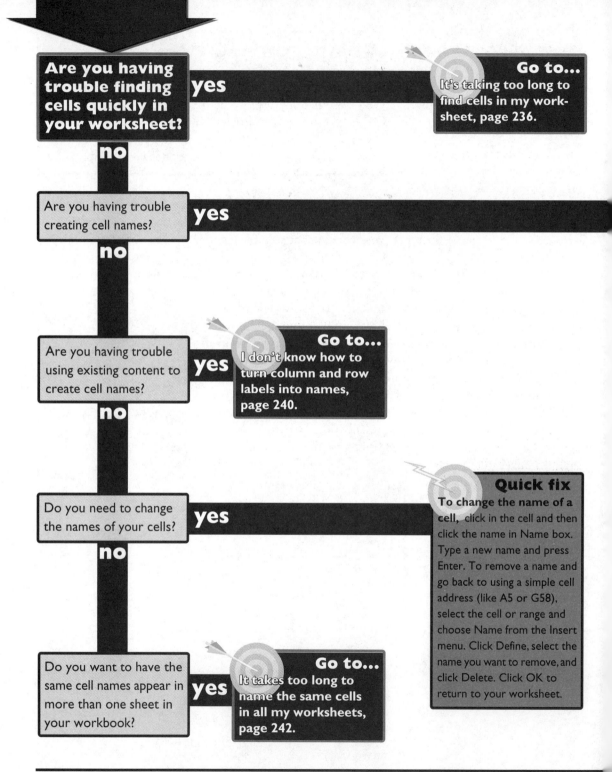

Are you having trouble finding cells quickly in your worksheet?

yes ⟶

Go to...
It's taking too long to find cells in my worksheet, page 236.

no

Are you having trouble creating cell names?

yes ⟶

no

Are you having trouble using existing content to create cell names?

yes ⟶

Go to...
I don't know how to turn column and row labels into names, page 240.

no

Do you need to change the names of your cells?

yes ⟶

no

Do you want to have the same cell names appear in more than one sheet in your workbook?

yes ⟶

Go to...
It takes too long to name the same cells in all my worksheets, page 242.

Quick fix
To change the name of a cell, click in the cell and then click the name in Name box. Type a new name and press Enter. To remove a name and go back to using a simple cell address (like A5 or G58), select the cell or range and choose Name from the Insert menu. Click Define, select the name you want to remove, and click Delete. Click OK to return to your worksheet.

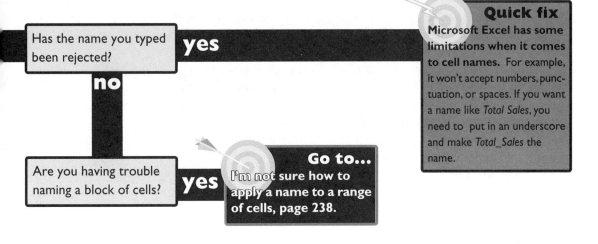

Has the name you typed been rejected?

yes

no

Are you having trouble naming a block of cells?

yes

Quick fix

Microsoft Excel has some limitations when it comes to cell names. For example, it won't accept numbers, punctuation, or spaces. If you want a name like *Total Sales*, you need to put in an underscore and make *Total_Sales* the name.

Go to...

I'm not sure how to apply a name to a range of cells, page 238.

If your solution isn't here, check these related chapters:

● Formatting worksheets, page 168

● Outlining, page 244

● Searching for data, page 290

● Workspace customization, page 368

Or see the general troubleshooting tips on page xv.

It's taking too long to find cells in my worksheet

Source of the problem

You've been searching for a particular worksheet entry, be it a number or text, by searching manually—looking through the worksheet for the missing content—or by clicking Find on the Edit menu and entering search criteria. Both methods, especially the first one, are time consuming, and with the latter approach, if you set up the Find criteria incorrectly, you might not find what you're looking for. There has to be a faster, more efficient way of finding worksheet content, right? Right, there is.

In Microsoft Excel, you can name cells in your worksheet, giving them logical names that you can use to look for them and to refer to them in formulas. If, for example, you have a number in the worksheet that's the total sales for all of your company's divisions, you can call it *corp_total* or something similar. Then you won't have to remember that the total is in cell H10. You can name the totals for each division as well, giving them names such as *sw_total* (for the total sales for the southwest division) or *philasales* (if your sales are by city rather than region). These names are a lot closer to what you call these cells in your mind than their cell addresses are. They are easier to remember than the part of the worksheet they're stored in.

So you can name cells. How does that help you find them? As long as you've appropriately named cells, you can use the Name box to find the named cells you need to locate. All you have to do is click a cell name in the Name box drop-down list, and that cell will become the active cell. ▶

To use the Name box feature to label cells so you can find them later, you must go through your worksheet and name important cells—cells you have looked for or think you'll need to look for in the future. Naming cells that you won't have trouble finding but that you know you'd like to refer to

in formulas is also a good idea. This can be helpful not only for you, but also for others who use your worksheet and might not be as familiar with its layout as you are.

Naming cells

How to fix it

To name a cell, complete the following steps:

1. Click the cell that you want to name.

2. In the Name box, click the cell address once. The address becomes highlighted and moves to the left side of the box. ▶

3. Type the name you want to give the cell.

4. Press Enter to confirm the name. If you click the named cell again, you'll see the name you typed in the Name box.

A cell by any other name...

You're not stuck with names you give to cells. If you think of a better name or more appropriate abbreviation for a cell name, you can edit it. You can also delete cell names if you've named the wrong cell or don't want a cell to be named anymore. To rename a cell, follow these steps:

1. Click the cell and then click the current name for that cell in the Name box once.

2. When the name becomes highlighted, type the new name over it.

3. Press Enter to confirm the new name.

Oddly, the old name remains in place, but if you click the Name box drop-down arrow, you'll see the new name in the list. So now you have to delete the old name so that only the new name points to the cell.

1. On the Insert menu, point to Name and then click Define.

2. In the Names In Workbook list in the Define Name dialog box, scroll as needed to find the name you want to get rid of and click it to select. ▶

3. Click the Delete button and then click OK.

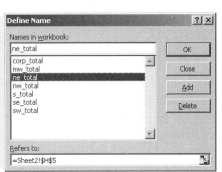

> **Tip**
>
> If you need to create the illusion of a space within your cell name, use an underscore. Total_Sales looks more polished to some people than TotalSales, and it's more legible in the Name box list. For simplicity's sake, you can also skip the use of capital letters and name the cell total_sales.

> **Tip**
>
> You can always keep both names for the cell rather than deleting the old one in favor of the new. In fact, it can be helpful to give certain cells more than one name to account for all the ways different users might want to refer to them.

I'm not sure how to apply a name to a range of cells

Source of the problem

Some individual cells in your worksheet are happily named, feeling all puffed up because they have real names, not just cell addresses. The other cells are jealous, and in the interest of worksheet harmony, you want to name cell ranges, creating groups of cells, both contiguous and noncontiguous, with names like Regional_Totals and List_of_Departments. Now your worksheet cells will work together—there's no stopping you now!

So how do you name a range? You can use the same technique you would employ to name a single cell (by using the Name box—see "It's taking too long to find cells in my worksheet" on page 236), and you can also use the Define command and the Define Name dialog box. You need to know both techniques because there are benefits to each, and you might find situations that make one preferable to the other. One requires you to select the range before you start the naming process; the other allows you to specify the range after you've created the name.

Home on the range

Naming ranges is a great way to turn your worksheet into a searchable database. Do you currently store a list of employees and keep that list in order by department? You can apply a name to the range of cells that lists all the employees in a given department and name the range using the department name. Do you need to see all the people in the Sales department? Choose Sales_Dept_Staff from the Name box list, and the information about people in that department is selected and ready to be viewed, copied to a worksheet, or printed out.

How to fix it

To name a range of cells using the Name box, follow these steps:

1. Select the range of cells that you want to name. You can select noncontiguous cells by holding down the Ctrl key as you drag through or click cells anywhere in your worksheet.

2. Click the Name box once. Don't worry that only one cell address—the first cell in the selected range—appears. It doesn't mean that you're naming only that cell. ▶

3. Type the name you want to apply to the selected range.

4. Press Enter to confirm the name.

	A	B	C	D	E	F	G	H
				Regional Sales				
				Sales in Millions of US Dollars				
		January	February	March	April	May	June	TOTALS
4	Midwest	5.2	4.5	3.8	3.1	2.4	1.7	$ 20.70
5	Northeast	5.4	4.3	3.2	2.1	1	-0.1	$ 15.90
6	Northwest	3.7	3.8	3.9	4	4.1	4.2	$ 23.70
7	South	1.8	2.1	2.4	2.7	3	3.3	$ 15.30
8	Southeast	3.9	3.7	3.5	3.3	3.1	2.9	$ 20.40
9	Southwest	2.7	2.6	2.5	2.4	2.3	2.2	$ 14.70
10	TOTALS	$ 22.70	$ 21.00	$ 19.30	$ 17.60	$ 15.90	$ 14.20	$ 110.70

Naming cells

5. Click the Name box drop-down list and then select the name you just created—the range of cells is instantly highlighted. ▶

To name a range of cells using the Define command, follow these steps:

1. In the worksheet containing the range you want to name, select the range and then point to Name on the Insert menu. On the submenu, click Define.

2. In the Names In Workbook text box of the Define Name dialog box, type the name you want to give to the range of cells.

3. If the cells listed in the Refers To text box are not the ones you want to name (perhaps you selected the wrong range in Step 1), you can click in the Refers To box and type a new range or move the dialog box aside and select the correct range—it will appear automatically in the Refers To box. ▶

4. Click OK to define the name and close the dialog box.

corp_jan_sales			fx	5.2			
	A	B	C	D	E	F	G	H
1			Regional Sales					
2			Sales in Millions of US Dollars					
3		January	February	March	April	May	June	TOTALS
4	Midwest	5.2	4.5	3.8	3.1	2.4	1.7	$ 20.70
5	Northeast	5.4	4.3	3.2	2.1	1	-0.1	$ 15.90
6	Northwest	3.7	3.8	3.9	4	4.1	4.2	$ 23.70
7	South	1.8	2.1	2.4	2.7	3	3.3	$ 15.30
8	Southeast	3.9	3.7	3.5	3.3	3.1	2.9	$ 20.40
9	Southwest	2.7	2.6	2.5	2.4	2.3	2.2	$ 14.70
10	TOTALS	$ 22.70	$ 21.00	$ 19.30	$ 17.60	$ 15.90	$ 14.20	$ 110.70
11								
12								

C4			fx	4.5				
	A	B	C	D	E	F	G	H	I
1			Regional Sales						
2			Sales in Millions of US Dollars						
3		January	February	March	April	May	June	TOTALS	
4	Midwest	5.2	4.5	3.8	3.1	2.4	1.7	$ 20.70	
5	Northeast	5.4	4.3	3.2	2.1	1	-0.1	$ 15.90	
6	Northwest	3.7	3.8	3.9	4	4.1	4.2	$ 23.70	
7	South	1.8	2.1	2.4	2.7	3	3.3	$ 15.30	
8	Southeast	3.9	3.7	3.5	3.3	3.1	2.9	$ 20.40	
9	Southwest	2.7	2.6	2.5	2.4	2.3	2.2	$ 14.70	
10	TOTALS	$ 22.70	$ 21.00	$ 19.30	$ 17.60	$ 15.90	$ 14.20	$ 110.70	
11									
12			Define Name - Refers to:					? X	
13			=Sheet2!$C$4:$C$9+Sheet2!$C$4:$C$9						
14									
15									

Tip

You don't have to be creating a cell or range name in order to use the Define Name dialog box. You can use it to edit existing names, review the cells and ranges to which the names apply, and delete obsolete names or names you don't want to give to cells or ranges anymore.

I don't know how to turn column and row labels into names

Source of the problem

You've taken the time to build your worksheet with column and row labels that clearly identify your worksheet content, and you wish you could somehow use those labels to create names for cells in your worksheet. It would be a big pain and a waste of time to go in and select each of the important cells or ranges in a worksheet and apply names to them individually. What's more, it would make it so much easier to use the worksheet names if they were the same as the labels that already exist.

Instead of creating names for individual cells, let Excel's Create Names feature build a series of names for the cells in your worksheet based on the column and row labels you already have. Using labels for names would help you and others who use the worksheet to find data and to use the names in formulas.

> ## When you call my name
>
> Did I say "use the names in formulas"? You bet I did. Rather than referring to cells by their cell addresses when using them in a formula, type the cell name, as in =SUM(Regional_Totals), where Regional_Totals is a column of numbers in a named range. If you plan to use names in formulas, keep them simple so that you can type them without risk of typos. Using names in formulas also helps other users of the worksheet decipher your formulas, instantly knowing what the calculation does by reading the formula itself.

How to fix it

1. Select the section of your worksheet that contains the column and row labels you want to use, plus the data to which they refer.

2. On the Insert menu, point to Name and then click Create.

3. In the Create Names dialog box, select the column and row check boxes that match the location of your labels. For example, if your labels appear in the worksheet both across the top and down the left side, select the Top Row and Left Column check boxes. ▶

4. Click OK. When you open the Name box drop-down list, you'll see your column and row labels listed.

	A	B	C	D	E	F
1		Regional Sales				
2		Sales in Millions of US Dollars				
3		January	February	March	April	May
4	Midwest	5.2	4.5	3.8	3.1	2.4
5	Northeast	5.4	4.3	3.2	2.1	1
6	Northwest	3.7	3.8	3.9	4	4.1
7	South	1.8	2.1	2.4	2.7	3
8	Southeast	3.9	3.7	3.5	3.3	3.1
9	Southwest	2.7	2.6	2.5	2.4	2.3
10	TOTALS	$ 22.70	$ 21.00	$ 19.30	$ 17.60	$ 15.90

Create Names ? ×
Create names in
☑ Top row
☑ Left column
☐ Bottom row
☐ Right column
OK Cancel

Naming cells

To use the label-based names in formulas or to quickly access and select a range of cells, select the name from the list. When you select, for example, the name based on the fourth label in the left column, the cell adjacent to that label will be selected. ▶

Northwest ▼		fx	3.7		
	A	B	C	D	E
1				Regional Sales	
2			Sales in Millions of US Dol		
3		January	February	March	April
4	Midwest	5.2	4.5	3.8	3.1
5	Northeast	5.4	4.3	3.2	2.1
6	Northwest	3.7	3.8	3.9	4
7	South	1.8	2.1	2.4	2.7
8	Southeast	3.9	3.7	3.5	3.3
9	Southwest	2.7	2.6	2.5	2.4
10	TOTALS	$ 22.70	$ 21.00	$ 19.30	$ 17.60	$
11					
12					

Give us their names

If you open someone else's worksheet and click the Name box drop-down list to see if there are any named cells or ranges, you won't be able to tell which cells or ranges the names refer to without selecting them, one by one.

Instead of going on such a wild goose chase, why not create a list of the workbook's names and the cells and ranges to which they apply? It'll save you opening the Define Name dialog box (in

Tip

The rules for acceptable cell and range names still apply, even when you use existing column and row labels to create them. Your names can't start with a number, you can't use spaces, and you can't use punctuation such as dashes and slashes. If, however, your labels contain any of these verboten elements, Excel will adjust the names accordingly by adding underscores in front of names that start with a number and in between words separated by spaces.

case you were thinking that was a convenient alternative), because there you have to click the names and view the Refers To information, plus shrink or move the dialog box aside to see the worksheet. No, it's much better to have a list of all the names and their cells in one place. You can squirrel the list away on a sheet that will never be printed or hide the column it's in if you don't want it to be visible until you need to refer to it. Note that if you move your named cells or ranges, the list you pasted with the Paste List feature won't change automatically. You'll have to delete the list and paste it again to reflect the named cells' or ranges' new locations.

Sold, even with that small caveat? Well, okay then. Click the cell at the beginning of the blank range where you want to stash the name list. Keep in mind that the list will occupy two cells per name: one for the name itself and one for the cell or range to which it refers. On the Insert menu, point to Name and then click Paste. In the Paste Name dialog box, click the Paste List button. Voilà—the list appears in your worksheet. ▶

14	corp_jan_sales	=Sheet2!$B$4:$B$9
15	corp_total	=Sheet2!$H$10
16	January	=Sheet2!$B$4:$B$10
17	Midwest	=Sheet2!$B$4
18	mw_total	=Sheet2!$H$4
19	ne_total	=Sheet2!$H$5
20	Northeast	=Sheet2!$B$5
21	Northwest	=Sheet2!$B$6
22	nw_total	=Sheet2!$H$6
23	s_total	=Sheet2!$H$7
24	se_total	=Sheet2!$H$8
25	South	=Sheet2!$B$7
26	Southeast	=Sheet2!$B$8
27	Southwest	=Sheet2!$B$9
28	sw_total	=Sheet2!$H$9
29	TOTALS	=Sheet2!$B$10

Tip

When you move a named cell or range from one place to another on a worksheet or to another worksheet within the same workbook, the address changes to point to the cell or range in its new location. If, however, you cut or copy a named cell to a new workbook or if you copy a named cell or range within the same workbook, the name for the pasted cell or range will have to be re-created in the cell's or range's new home.

It takes too long to name the same cells in all my worksheets

Source of the problem

Some workbooks contain two or more worksheets that have the same exact layout. Although the data might vary from sheet to sheet, the column and row labels are the same, and the worksheet is set up in the same cells on all of the sheets. You might have even created the worksheets at the same time by grouping them before entering the common content. (See "I'm tired of entering the same series of labels in my worksheets," on page 114 if you want to find out about creating worksheets with the same layout and labels).

If you're naming cells in these sheets, it can seem like a waste of time to go into each sheet and create names for the cells. In fact, you might have already spent a great deal of time doing just that, leading you to this very page in this book. Your belief that there has to be a better way is justified. There should be, and there is.

In Excel, you can create 3-D cell references, which means that names are created for cells in multiple worksheets at the same time. You need to create the names only once, but all the names will be created simultaneously in all the worksheets.

How to fix it

To create names that will apply to multiple worksheets, follow these steps:

1. On the Insert menu, point to Name and then click Define to display the Define Name dialog box. In the Names In Workbook text box, type the name you want to apply to the cell or cells in multiple sheets.

2. Click in the Refers To box and delete any current content by selecting any and all existing sheet and cell references and then pressing the Delete key.

3. Type = (an equal sign) in the Refers To Box.

4. Click the tab for the first worksheet to be used in the multiple-sheet reference. The sheet name appears in the Refers To box.

5. Hold down the Shift key and click the tab for the last worksheet to be included in the multiple-sheet reference. Any tabs between the first and last tabs you clicked are also included in the multiple-sheet reference. (The name of the last tab you clicked now appears in the Refers To box, with a colon separating it from the name of the first sheet tab you clicked.)

6. Click the individual cell or drag through the range of cells that you want to be referenced by the name you typed. The cell or range appears in the Refers To box, after the sheet tabs' reference. ▶

7. Click the Add button. The name is now stored, and it is associated with the cell or range you specified. (Note, however, that you'll be able to access the multiple-sheet name only through the Define Name dialog box; the name won't appear in the Name box or its drop-down list.)

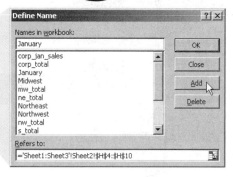

8. Repeat steps 2 through 8 for any additional names you want to create.

9. Click OK to close the dialog box and return to your worksheet.

To create names from column and row labels in all the identical worksheets in your workbook, follow these steps:

1. Group the sheets (if they're not currently grouped) by clicking the tab of the first sheet you want to include in the group, holding down the Shift key, and then clicking the tab of the last sheet you want to include in the group. (To select nonconsecutive sheets in a group, hold down the Ctrl key as you click sheet tabs.)

2. In any worksheet in the grouped sheets, select the range of cells that contains both the column or row labels and the data they identify. Excel assumes that the labels are the same in all of the grouped sheets and that the labels and data are in the same cells on all of the sheets.

> **Tip**
>
> After you're finished doing anything with grouped worksheets, always ungroup them. This will save you the pain and suffering that results from realizing too late that you've just entered text in, edited, or formatted all of the sheets in a group when you intended only to work on a single sheet.

3. On the Insert menu, point to Name and then click Create.

4. In the Create Names dialog box, select the Create Names In check boxes that match the location of your labels. In many worksheets, the column labels are in the top row of the selected range and the row labels are down the left side—therefore, you'd select Top Row and Left Column from the list of options. Click OK. ▶

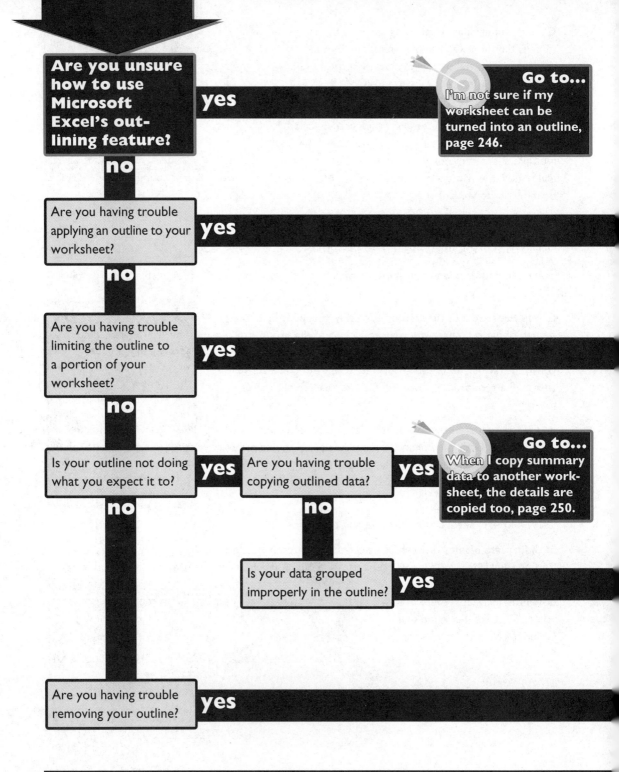

Are you unsure how to use Microsoft Excel's outlining feature?

yes

Go to...
I'm not sure if my worksheet can be turned into an outline, page 246.

no

Are you having trouble applying an outline to your worksheet?

yes

no

Are you having trouble limiting the outline to a portion of your worksheet?

yes

no

Is your outline not doing what you expect it to?

yes

Are you having trouble copying outlined data?

yes

Go to...
When I copy summary data to another worksheet, the details are copied too, page 250.

no

no

Is your data grouped improperly in the outline?

yes

Are you having trouble removing your outline?

yes

Go to...
When I use the Auto Outline command, I get an error message, page 248.

Quick fix
To restrict the outline to just some of your worksheet cells, select the range of cells to be outlined and choose Group And Outline from the Data menu. Choose Auto Outline from the submenu.

Go to...
My worksheet content doesn't fall into appropriate outline groups, page 252.

Quick fix
To get rid of an outline you no longer need, select the outlined portion of your worksheet and choose Group And Outline from the data menu. In the resulting dialog box, click Clear Outline.

If your solution isn't here, check these related chapters:
- PivotTables, page 254
- Sorting data, page 310
- Subtotal reports, page 336

Or see the general troubleshooting tips on page xv.

I'm not sure if my worksheet can be turned into an outline

Source of the problem

Obviously, not all worksheets can be broken down into levels of hierarchical or topical content in an outline, and you're wondering if your worksheet falls into the "Yep" or "Nope" category.

What makes a worksheet outline-worthy? The way it's structured and the data it contains. If it's a highly segmented worksheet that's not stored in regular rows and contains no totals or subtotals, nope, it can't be turned into an outline. If your worksheet is a list of records stored in rows, and the rows are in a specific order and are subtotaled within that sort order, yep, it can be turned into an outline. Worksheets that contain lists that are sorted by a column with many duplicate entries are the best outlining candidates. The worksheet shown here is sorted by Department column, in alphabetical ascending order, which creates groups according to the departments for which people work. ▶

Once you've determined, based on the considerations just mentioned, that your worksheet is indeed outline-worthy, you can go ahead and create the outline.

How to fix it

1. Sort your list by at least one column in your worksheet, preferably a column containing a lot of duplicates, which will break your list into groups of similar content.

2. Click any cell in the worksheet except the title. Point to Group And Outline on the Data menu and then click Auto Outline. Two outline level buttons appear to the left of the row numbers,

Tip

For a really dynamic outlined worksheet, you can subtotal the items in the sorted groups. Click Subtotal on the Data menu. In the Subtotal dialog box, click Sum, Average, or Count in the Use Function list and click OK. This process creates collapsible and expandable horizontal levels. If you want, you can then create vertical outline levels by grouping your columns.

above the column letters, or in both places, depending on the type of information and how it's arranged in your worksheet. ▶

	SocSec#	Last Name	First Name	Date Hired	Department	Job Title	Current Salary	Bonus %	Phone Ext.
					Employee Information				
3	123-45-6793	Blattner	Patricia	11/2/1999	Accounting	Clerk	$ 26,800.00	3%	192
4	249-781-1242	Reilly	Michael	7/2/1998	Accounting	Coordinator	$ 51,250.00	6%	176
5	123-45-6792	Schiller	Jo Ann	8/13/1995	Accounting	Manager	$ 75,400.00	8%	287
6	249-781-1243	Hodges	Roberta	9/5/1998	Human Resources	Coordinator	$ 51,500.00	6%	201
7	249-781-1240	Talbot	Susan	5/23/1996	Human Resources	Specialist	$ 48,250.00	5%	220
8	123-45-6790	Kline	Linda	12/15/1998	Marketing	Coordinator	$ 43,750.00	5%	138
9	123-45-6794	MacElyea	Blanche	8/15/1999	Marketing	Coordinator	$ 55,250.00	6%	135
10	201-672-9083	Pederzani	Jacob	6/15/1998	Marketing	Manager	$ 72,500.00	8%	189
11	123-45-6789	Chambers	Martin	6/15/1999	Marketing	Specialist	$ 46,500.00	5%	145
12	201-672-9084	Kovalcik	John	4/3/1990	Operations	Clerk	$ 25,200.00	3%	190
13	123-45-6791	Thomas	Gary	3/2/2000	Operations	Coordinator	$ 52,000.00	6%	231
14	201-672-9085	Miller	Pam	4/25/1997	Operations	Manager	$ 78,250.00	8%	258
15	201-672-9081	Balsamo	Anthony	3/25/1996	Operations	Specialist	$ 53,400.00	6%	167
16	249-781-1239	Elmaleh	Miriam	4/22/1997	Sales	Coordinator	$ 48,750.00	5%	234
17	249-781-1241	Ulrich	Joshua	5/2/2001	Sales	Manager	$ 65,000.00	7%	125
18	201-672-9082	Ashton	Steven	10/31/1997	Sales	Representative	$ 62,500.00	7%	158
19	249-781-1244	Maurone	Richard	5/2/1995	Sales	Representative	$ 65,700.00	7%	250
20	201-672-9086	Ulrich	Zachary	4/9/2000	Sales	Representative	$ 64,600.00	7%	232
21							$ 54,811.11	6%	

Break it down

Perhaps you were hoping to be able to collapse the outline at two or more points across the rows or columns, but there's only one outline level. What to do? Group your rows or columns in the outline with the Group command on the Group And Outline submenu, turning one or all of the groups into additional outline levels. Looking at your data, think which columns or rows you'd like to hide and select the headings of the rows or columns in a group that you'd like to isolate in the outline. ▶

Having selected the rows you want to group, point to Group And Outline on the Data menu and then click Group. A level indicator appears. To add another group, select the first group and then drag through the second group's row headings. On the Data menu, point to

Group And Outline and then click Group again. Another level indicator appears. You can expand a collapsed level by clicking the plus sign near the last row in the level. Conversely, you can collapse an expanded level by clicking the minus sign.

And break it down again

Having broken your sorted rows into groups, you can also break your columns into collapsible levels. Select the column headings, point to Group And Outline on the Data menu, and then click Group. You'll end up with horizontal and vertical outline levels that can be expanded and collapsed.

When I use the Auto Outline command, I get an error message

Source of the problem

"Cannot create an outline." Well, why the heck not? You thought you did everything right—you made sure your database had all the elements that are needed to turn a worksheet into an outline (see "I'm not sure if my worksheet can be turned into an outline" on page 246), and you pointed to Group And Outline on the Data menu and then clicked Auto Outline. But instead of seeing outline levels appear on your worksheet, you see an error message. Possible reasons for this message include:

- There's no real database. If Microsoft Excel doesn't detect a worksheet that's laid out as a database (if it has an inconsistent layout, blank columns or rows, or missing column and row labels), it won't create an outline.

- You didn't select the whole database. When you tried to select the entire database, you missed some of the cells, so Excel is confused as to what you want to outline. ▶

- You selected a cell that doesn't contain data or a label. If you select your worksheet title (usually in cell A1 or A2) rather than a data or label cell, the error message appears because Excel doesn't see any contiguous data that can be turned into an outline.

This is sort of a case of "Doctor, it hurts when I go like this." The doctor replies, "Well, then don't go like that!" The way to prevent this error message from appearing is to not do any of the things just listed—don't select the worksheet title or a range of cells within the database before issuing the Auto Outline command and make sure your worksheet contains data in a layout that's conducive to outlining.

How to fix it

1. Check your data for content or layout that will prevent the Auto Outline command from working. Make sure all of your labels are there and that no blank rows or columns are within the database.

2. Click a cell within the data—not the cell containing the worksheet title, but a cell containing a label or data.

3. On the Data menu, point to Group And Outline and then click Auto Outline to make two outline levels appear down the left side of your worksheet.

Just asking...

Another message that you might see when attempting to use the Auto Outline feature is one that asks, "Modify the current outline?" You'll see this when you've already used the Auto Outline command on the active worksheet or when you've used the Subtotals command on the Data menu to create a subtotal report using your data. Because the subtotal report breaks your data into levels (based on sorted rows), it's considered to be an existing outline. ▶

If you were unaware that an outline already existed (perhaps someone else applied it) and you want to remove this outline before applying a new one, click any cell in your data (other than the title cell), point to Group And Outline on the Data menu and, then click Clear Outline. However, if your data has been subtotaled, click Subtotals on the Data menu and, in the Subtotal dialog box, click the Remove All button to remove both the subtotals and the outline that resulted from subtotaling. In either case, any existing outline will be removed, and you can go ahead and use the Auto Outline command without fear of unexpected results.

Tip

For more information on using the Subtotals command to subtotal your database, see "Subtotal reports" on page 336.

When I copy summary data to another worksheet, the details are copied too

Source of the problem

You've collapsed a level in your worksheet by clicking the Outline button, successfully hiding some of your columns or rows. With this detail hidden, you want to copy the displayed data to another worksheet—perhaps to be e-mailed to someone who needs to see only the summary data or to be accessed through a network drive to which other users have access. When you select the displayed cells and copy them to another worksheet, you get more than you bargained for, however.

The outlined data comes complete with the hidden data, which is now displayed in your worksheet, even though you didn't want that detail to come along for the ride. What can you do? Excel gives you some special selection tools in the Go To dialog box with which you can select just the cells that are visible on-screen. By using this feature, you can copy only the cells that are showing, preserving the appearance of the data that you've achieved by collapsing your outline. In this example, the salary column was hidden in the source data, but it appears here. ▶

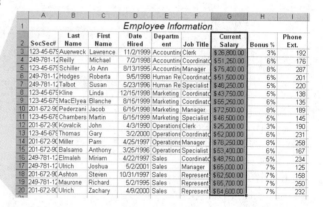

How to fix it

1. Collapse the levels of your outline so that only the portions of your worksheet that you want to copy are visible.

2. On the Edit menu, click Go To.

3. In the Go To dialog box, click the Special button to open the Go To Special dialog box.

4. In the Go To Special dialog box, click Visible Cells Only. ▶

5. Click OK. The dialog box closes, and though it appears that your entire worksheet is selected, only those cells that are displayed are actually selected—the hidden rows and columns are not included.

6. Press Ctrl+C to place the visible cells on the Clipboard.

7. Move to the target worksheet and click the first cell. Be sure that the worksheet contains no material that you want to save, because it will be overwritten by the visible cells that you copied, which include all the blank cells as well as the displayed entries in the source worksheet.

8. Press Enter to paste the visible cells in the target worksheet, unaccompanied by the hidden cells.

Error messages that make you want to slap your computer

Some situations will prevent you from using the Visible Cells Only option in the Go To Special dialog box. Among them:

- If a merged cell in the target worksheet is a different size than in the source worksheet or if the target worksheet has a merged cell containing a title, a message appears telling you that you can't "change part of a merged cell."

- If you've already selected cells using the Go To Special dialog box, a message appears telling you that a selection has already been made.

- If you select a range of cells that includes no hidden cells and then issue the Go To command, when you try to select Visible Cells Only, a message tells you that there's no hidden content.

Obviously, if you split up any merged cells in the target worksheet, click a cell to deselect a previous selection and make sure you select a range of cells containing hidden columns and rows, these messages won't appear. Equally obvious is the fact that despite your diligent efforts to avoid them, you will at one time or another see these messages and want to slap your computer.

Tip

If your worksheet is small or if your computer's memory seems overly taxed by copying and pasting an entire worksheet, you can select the range of cells that you want to copy before issuing the Go To command. When you select Visible Cells Only, Go To will select those cells in the range you've highlighted, leaving the rest of the worksheet untouched.

Tip

If you have applied an Auto-Filter to your worksheet (point to Filter on the Data menu and then click Auto-Filter) and only the rows containing data meeting your filter criteria are displayed, you can copy those rows and not the hidden records. Select the cells you want to copy, press Ctrl+G, click the Special button, click the Visible Cells Only option in the Go To Special dialog box, and click OK.

My worksheet content doesn't fall into appropriate outline groups

Source of the problem

You point to Group And Outline on the Data menu, then click Auto Outline, and voilà! The worksheet is turned into an outline, with handy collapsible levels that allow you to hide portions of your worksheet at will. Outlining is really a great feature. Or so you thought until you issued the Auto Outline command and ended up with outline levels that make no sense—sure, you could collapse your outline at various points, hiding columns or rows, but why these levels were placed where they were is a mystery. You ended up clearing the outline and starting over, probably with the same result. Now you're really confused.

To put an end to the confusion, it's important to understand how Excel chooses where to place those automatic outline levels. Excel looks for columns and rows containing totals or the results of formulas that use other columns or rows in the worksheet. If you have a column that totals the columns before or after it, that column will become a point at which the outline can be collapsed so that only the totals, not the columns that were totaled, are displayed. Same with a total in a row at the foot of several rows of data—that row will become an outline level, which you can collapse to see just the total of the rows in the list, not the rows that make up that list.

		B	C	D	E	F	G	H	I
	1			Employee Information					
	2	Last Name	First Name	Date Hired	Department	Job Title	Current Salary	Bonus %	Phone Ext.
	21		Count of Employees:	18		Avg Salary/Bonus:	$ 54,811.11	6%	
	22								

There are two approaches to fixing an outline that doesn't make sense—one proactive, the other reactive. To proactively solve this problem, make sure your totaled columns and the column containing the totals are contiguous. To reactively solve this problem, you can create your own groups, eliminating the need for Excel's Auto Outline rules to be satisfied by the order and relationship of your worksheet's columns and rows.

You can manually group columns and rows that don't result in or have any connection to totals in your worksheet but that simply contain details that you want to collapse—say, to simplify a worksheet visually or to hide confidential details.

Are you on the level?

If your column or row containing totals gets those totals from noncontiguous rows or columns in your worksheet, no level will be created. For example, if the numbers in column F are the result of adding columns D and E, column F becomes an outline level. If B and E are summed (or averaged or used in a formula), and the results appear in column F, column F isn't turned into a level. Think about this when planning the order of columns in a worksheet that will be turned into an outline.

How to fix it

1. If you'll be grouping rows, first sort your worksheet by a field that contains similar content. For example, in a list of classes, you can sort by topic, instructor, or price—anything that will put your list in ordered groups. ▶

2. Select a series of columns or rows on your worksheet by dragging through their column or row headings.

3. On the Data menu, point to Group And Outline and then click Group. If you're grouping columns, the group will encompass the selected columns, and the column to the right of them will represent the outline level. If you're grouping rows, the group will encompass the selected rows, and the row just below them will represent the outline level. ▶

4. Continue selecting groups by repeating steps 2 and 3. Be sure to select the rows or columns in the previous group or groups to get successive groups that don't overlap.

When these records are sorted by Application name, they can become outline groups.

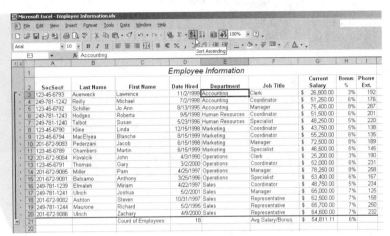

Tip

If you realize that you included too few or too many rows or columns in a group, and the resulting level is in the wrong place, point to Group And Outline on the Data menu and then click Ungroup. In the Ungroup dialog box, click either Rows or Columns and then click OK to remove the group.

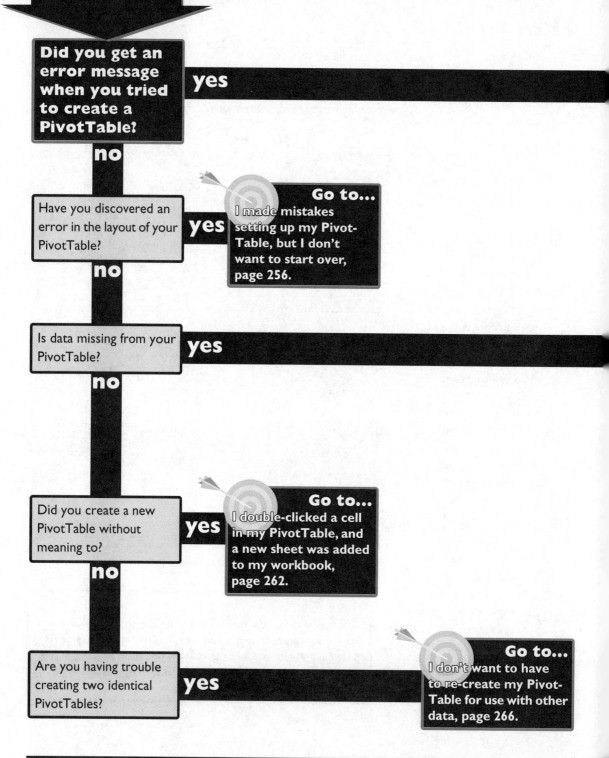

Did you get an error message when you tried to create a PivotTable?

yes

no

Have you discovered an error in the layout of your PivotTable?

yes

Go to...
I made mistakes setting up my Pivot-Table, but I don't want to start over, page 256.

no

Is data missing from your PivotTable?

yes

no

Did you create a new PivotTable without meaning to?

yes

Go to...
I double-clicked a cell in my PivotTable, and a new sheet was added to my workbook, page 262.

no

Are you having trouble creating two identical PivotTables?

yes

Go to...
I don't want to have to re-create my Pivot-Table for use with other data, page 266.

Quick fix

If your computer tells you there isn't enough memory to create a PivotTable, close any other open applications and then try again. If the problem persists, restart your computer and then check how much memory it has available. To do this, right-click the My Computer icon on your Desktop and choose Properties. On the Performance tab, check the percentage of free memory available. It should be at or above 80 percent.

Is the missing data related to records containing blank fields?

yes

Go to...

My data includes blank fields, but they're not showing up in my PivotTable, page 260.

no

Have you refreshed your PivotTable?

yes

Go to...

I refreshed my Pivot-Table, but the data still doesn't reflect my changes, page 264.

no

Quick fix

To include new or edited data in your PivotTable, click any cell in the table and then choose Refresh Data from the Data menu. Excel will take a look at your data range, and update the PivotTable accordingly.

If your solution isn't here, check these related chapters:

- Filtering records, page, 136
- Outlining, page 244
- Subtotal reports, page 336

Or see the general troubleshooting tips on page xv.

I made mistakes setting up my PivotTable, but I don't want to start over

Source of the problem

Unlike Microsoft Excel's other relatively automatic report-creation features (Subtotals and Outlines), PivotTable reports require some setup decisions before Excel can create the report you need. In making those decisions, mistakes and oversights can occur, resulting in a PivotTable report that doesn't include all the information you want or that displays the information less effectively than you might like. Starting from scratch is an option when the PivotTable is so out of whack that you can't use it at all, but if you have only a few changes to make—such as switching some of your fields from columns to rows or changing the calculation performed on the data—it can be easier to edit the PivotTable in place.

With the PivotTable Wizard, you can easily make the following changes to your PivotTable:

● Change the range of cells from which the PivotTable draws data.

● Change the layout of the PivotTable.

● Change the function applied to the Data portion of the PivotTable.

To make these changes, you can use the PivotTable Wizard or the PivotTable toolbar, which appears on the screen as soon as a new PivotTable is created.

How to fix it

To change the layout of your PivotTable using the PivotTable Wizard, follow these steps:

1. Click any cell in the PivotTable.

2. On the Data menu, click Pivot-Table And PivotChart Report. Excel displays step 3 of the PivotTable Wizard. ▶

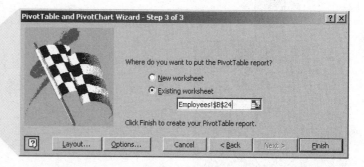

3. When the wizard's third step appears, click the Layout button to display a separate Layout dialog box and then make your edits. Click OK and then click Finish. ▶

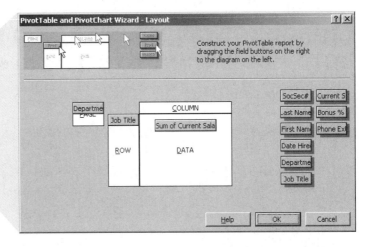

When editing the layout of your PivotTable, keep these pointers in mind:

● To change which fields are in which parts of the PivotTable, drag the field boxes to the desired locations within the layout diagram.

● To change the calculation performed on a field in the Data section of the PivotTable diagram, double-click the field name in the Data section. In the resulting PivotTable Field dialog box, choose a different function from the Summarize By list. ▶

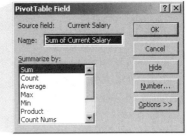

They don't call it a wizard for nothing!

If you correct the layout of your PivotTable using the steps provided, you'll want to make sure to click a cell directly in the PivotTable to make your changes most quickly. You could click any cell outside the PivotTable (provided the cell is on the same sheet as the PivotTable), but then you'd have to start the PivotTable And PivotChart Wizard from the beginning, as if you were creating a PivotTable from scratch. When the wizard's first step appears, all you have to do is click Next; but when prompted in the second step to select the data you want to use, you'll have to reselect the cells you used when originally building your PivotTable. That's why the PivotTable Wizard skips to the third step when you click a cell directly in the PivotTable—Excel acknowledges that you're just making changes to a PivotTable and saves you the hassle of going through the wizard's first two steps all over again. Smart, isn't it?

Tip

In the PivotTable Field dialog box, click the Number button to choose a number format for your data. You can select from the same number format options you'd have available if you clicked Cells on the Format menu. This feature is helpful when the data on which the PivotTable report is based was not formatted before the report was created.

I made mistakes setting up my PivotTable, but I don't want to start over

(continued from page 257)

To use the PivotTable Wizard to change the range of cells from which the PivotTable report draws data, follow these steps:

1. If the PivotTable Wizard is not displayed, click any cell in the PivotTable and click PivotTable And PivotChart Report on the Data menu. The wizard opens with its third dialog box displayed.

2. In the wizard's third step, click the Back button. This takes you back to the second step in the wizard and shows the current range of cells used to build your PivotTable. (Don't worry if your dialog box looks a little bit different from ours.)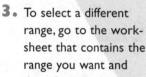

3. To select a different range, go to the worksheet that contains the range you want and drag through the cells that should be used to build the table.

4. Click Finish to exit the wizard and redisplay the PivotTable with the different or additional data included.

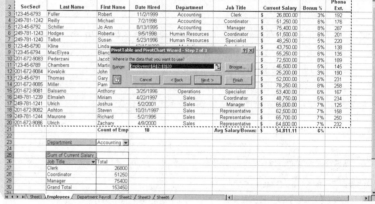

Tip

If you're adding to the existing range, hold down the Shift key and click at the end of the row or column you wish to add. This will add the cells between the original selection and the cell you just clicked to the range used to create the PivotTable.

Using the PivotTable Toolbar and Field List

If the problem with your PivotTable isn't so much that it contains a mistake as it is that you want to change your PivotTable's layout, you don't need to go to all the trouble of rerunning the Pivot-Table Wizard. Instead, you can make use of the PivotTable toolbar and Field List dialog box, both of which give you the ability to rearrange your table, add fields, and make formatting adjustments. ▶

Both items should appear as soon you click any cell in your PivotTable; however, if they don't, right-click the PivotTable and choose Show PivotTable Toolbar from the shortcut menu. Then repeat the process and choose Show Field List. You can also turn on the Field List from the PivotTable toolbar—the last button on it is Show (or Hide, if it's already showing) Field List.

Once the toolbar and list are displayed, click the PivotTable button on the toolbar and then click Table Options on the drop-down menu. In the PivotTable Options dialog box, you can select or clear check boxes to turn options, such as grand totaling rows or columns and applying AutoFormats, on or off. From this dialog box, you can also designate a special character to appear in empty cells in the PivotTable. ▶

To add fields to the table, drag the field names from the field list to the Page, Column, Row, or Data sections of the PivotTable. The mouse pointer changes into a table symbol when it's at a spot that's appropriate to drop the field. If the mouse pointer doesn't change into a table symbol, you won't be able to drop the field icon onto the PivotTable.

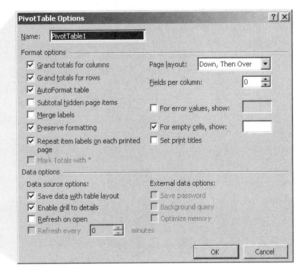

Tip

The PivotTable toolbar needn't be displayed for you to rearrange your table's fields. Simply drag the fields (the gray boxes with names) you want to move from one section of the table to another. In this way you can add another field to the Page section, for example, or move a field from the Row section to the Column section and vice versa.

My data includes blank fields, but they're not showing up in my PivotTable

Source of the problem

Depending on the nature of the data you're using as a basis for your PivotTable, the database might contain blank fields. For example, if you're listing the employees that work for your company and not all of the employees have met the requirements for earning a bonus, there will be blank fields in the Bonus % column for certain employees. These blanks don't affect the accuracy of your database and, unlike blank rows within your database, they aren't against the "rules" for good Excel database construction. ▶

If you want to see those blanks represented in your PivotTable—so that you know, say, how many people don't currently get a bonus or so you can check for blanks that are in error—it can be

	SocSec#	Last Name	First Name	Date Hired	Department	Job Title	Current Salary	Bonus %	Phone Ext.
1					Employee Information				
3	123-45-6793	Fuller	Robert	11/2/1999	Accounting	Clerk	$ 26,800.00	3%	192
4	249-781-1242	Reilly	Michael	7/2/1998	Accounting	Coordinator	$ 51,250.00	6%	176
5	123-45-6792	Schiller	Jo Ann	8/13/1995	Accounting	Manager	$ 75,400.00	8%	287
6	249-781-1243	Hodges	Roberta	9/5/1998	uman Resource	Coordinator	$ 51,500.00	6%	201
7	249-781-1240	Talbot	Susan	5/23/1996	uman Resource	Specialist	$ 48,250.00		220
8	123-45-6790	Kline	Linda	12/15/1998	Marketing	Coordinator	$ 43,750.00	5%	138
9	123-45-6794	MacElyea	Blanche	8/15/1999	Marketing	Coordinator	$ 55,250.00	6%	135
10	201-672-9083	Pederzani	Jacob	6/15/1998	Marketing	Manager	$ 72,500.00	8%	189
11	123-45-6789	Chambers	Martin	6/15/1999	Marketing	Specialist	$ 46,500.00	5%	145
12	201-672-9084	Kovalcik	John	4/3/1990	Operations	Clerk	$ 25,200.00	3%	190
13	123-45-6791	Thomas	Gary	3/2/2000	Operations	Coordinator	$ 52,000.00	6%	231
14	201-672-9085	Miller	Pam	4/25/1997	Operations	Manager	$ 78,250.00	8%	258
15	201-672-9081	Balsamo	Anthony	3/25/1996	Operations	Specialist	$ 53,400.00		167
16	249-781-1239	Elmaleh	Miriam	4/22/1997	Sales	Coordinator	$ 48,750.00	5%	234
17	249-781-1241	Ulrich	Joshua	5/2/2001	Sales	Manager	$ 65,000.00	7%	125
18	201-672-9082	Ashton	Steven	10/31/1997	Sales	Representative	$ 62,500.00		158
19	249-781-1244	Maurone	Richard	5/2/1995	Sales	Representative	$ 65,700.00		250
20	201-672-9086	Ulrich	Zachary	4/9/2000	Sales	Representative	$ 64,600.00	7%	232
21		Count of Emp	18			Avg Salary/Bon	$ 54,811.11	6%	

frustrating. By default, Excel's PivotTable feature doesn't include empty cells. You can include the blanks, however, by selecting an option in the PivotTable Field dialog box. When you choose to include blanks, your PivotTable becomes more accurate, because intentionally blank cells are part of the information your worksheet stores.

How to fix it

1. In the PivotTable, locate the box for the field that contains blank data (field names appear in a 3-D-looking gray box).

2. Double-click the box to open the PivotTable Field dialog box.

3. In the dialog box, select the Show Items With No Data check box. ▶

4. Click OK to close the dialog box.

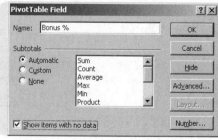

PivotTables

When in doubt, count

If the fields you drag into the Data section of the PivotTable layout diagram contain any blanks, Excel will apply the COUNT function by default. (To access the layout diagram, click a cell within the Pivot Table, click PivotTable And PivotChart Report on the Data menu, click PivotTable, and then click the Layout button in the PivotTable Wizard's third step.) For fields with no blanks, the default is SUM. You can easily change the function to SUM (or to COUNT, AVERAGE, or any other PivotTable function). To make these changes to the default (or previously chosen) calculations, right-click the PivotTable cell that represents the field for which you want to change the function. Click Field Settings on the shortcut menu. In the PivotTable Field dialog box, click the desired function in the Summarize By or Subtotals list (depending on which cell you clicked before opening the dialog box). ▶

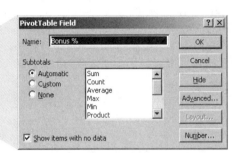

Click OK to close the dialog box. Back in the PivotTable, the numbers in that field will have changed to reflect the new function, and the heading for the numbers will also reflect the new function name.

Tip

You can customize the entry for blank cells based on the table's content. For example, if your PivotTable pertains to sales in various geographic regions, you can type No Sales Here, or words to that effect. Your entry in the For Empty Cells, Show box can have up to 255 characters.

Tip

If you're changing from a COUNT to a SUM function and the numbers your new function will display represent money, you might want to change the formatting of the results to Currency. In the PivotTable Field dialog box, click the Number button to open another dialog box, through which you can click Currency in the Category list. This dialog box has all the features found on the Number tab in the Format Cells dialog box, so you can also choose the number of decimals to display and the way negative numbers appear in your worksheet.

If you're still in doubt, insert an X

Another option available to you for dealing with blank entries is found in the PivotTable Options dialog box. Right-click any nonblank cell in your PivotTable and click Table Options on the shortcut menu. In the PivotTable Options dialog box, make sure the For Empty Cells, Show check box is selected, and then enter a character—an X, a zero, a dash, an asterisk, or anything other than a number, which would be confusing when viewing the table—and click OK. Any empty cells in your PivotTable will then contain the character you entered. ▶

I double-clicked a cell in my PivotTable, and a new sheet was added to my workbook

Source of the problem

This isn't so much of a problem as a surprise. You double-click a cell in the calculated portion of your PivotTable (the numbers created by the fields you placed in the Data section of the table's layout), and a new sheet is added to your workbook, containing data from the original database. Each time you double-click a cell in the Data portion of the PivotTable, the same thing happens—a new worksheet, containing data pertaining to the cell you double-clicked, is added to the workbook. You might want to rearrange the sheets after the new one is added, which you can easily do by dragging the sheet tabs to the left or right to place them in a more preferable order.

Although you can't stop this from happening (except by not double-clicking the cells), you can use it to your advantage. You can create worksheets for important records in your PivotTable data to easily isolate data you want to print or use as the beginning of a worksheet that can be edited to contain additional information related or relevant to the PivotTable data.

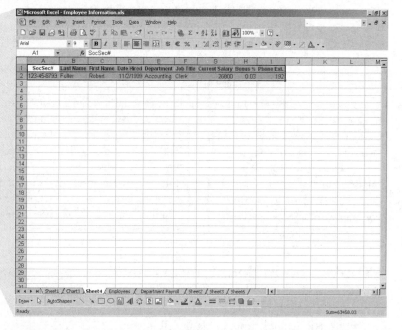

If you accidentally double-clicked a cell and don't want the resulting new sheet, simply remove the sheet from the workbook or delete the content and use the now blank sheet for something else.

How to fix it

1. Double-click the cell in your PivotTable that you want to use to create a new worksheet.

2. In the new worksheet, format the content as desired.

3. Name the worksheet by double-clicking the sheet tab and typing something that will identify and differentiate the worksheet from the others in the workbook.

Other stuff that happens automatically

If you want to create new PivotTable worksheets from a cell in the current one, click on any cell in the PivotTable and click the PivotTable button on the PivotTable toolbar. On the resulting menu, click Show Pages, and then click OK in the Show Pages dialog box. If you have more than one field in the Page section of the PivotTable, you can select which field the detail worksheets will be created for before clicking OK.

A worksheet is created for each item in the Pages list, showing the detailed data, with the sheet tabs automatically named for the items. For example, if you have a PivotTable listing employees by department, and the departments are the items you can select from the Page drop list, a worksheet will be created for each department. ▶

> **Tip**
>
> If you double-click a cell accidentally and don't want the resulting new worksheet, simply delete it. Make sure the sheet you want to delete is active, then right-click the sheet's tab and click Delete on the shortcut menu. When you're prompted to verify the deletion, click OK.

> **Tip**
>
> You can use the Show Pages feature to build several PivotTables and then delete the original PivotTable. This is a quick way to create several duplicate tables and name the worksheets that contain them.

I refreshed my PivotTable, but the data still doesn't reflect my changes

Source of the problem

The process of refreshing a PivotTable involves checking the PivotTable's source cells and changing the content of the PivotTable based on any changes to that range of source cells. If you've clicked the Refresh Data command on the Data menu and your PivotTable wasn't updated, the problem lies in the range of cells specified as the source of your table. If you've expanded the range of cells in your database—by typing new rows of records or by adding columns, for example—those new entries won't fall in the range that Excel is looking at when refreshing your table, so the content of the new cells won't be reflected in the table's cells.

What to do? Establish an expanded range for your PivotTable by rerunning the PivotTable setup process and inserting the new range of cells in the second step of the PivotTable Wizard.

How to fix it

1. Right-click any cell in the PivotTable, and click Wizard on the shortcut menu. Step 3 of 3 of the PivotTable And PivotChart Wizard appears.

2. Click the Back button once to access the second step of the wizard.

3. As needed, move the wizard out of the way or click the Collapse button at the end of the Range box.

4. Drag through the cells that you want to include as the source range for your PivotTable. The range you select appears in the Range box.

> **Tip**
>
> If the range of cells is too large to drag through easily, select the first row with your mouse, and then hold down the Shift key (if you're adding consecutive rows) or the Ctrl key (if you're adding nonconsecutive rows). Then click the row headings for rows you want to add until the entire range of cells is selected. You can also hold down the Shift key and select contiguous rows with the Up or Down Arrow keys, if you want. If the range is really huge, you can scroll to the end of the data range, hold down the Shift key, and click the last cell of the desired range. Everything from the first selected row to the last cell clicked will be selected as the source range for your PivotTable.

5. If you collapsed the wizard in step 3, click the Expand button to restore its size.

6. Click Finish to redraw the PivotTable, which will now be based on the range of cells you just specified.

What a refreshing idea

If you want your PivotTable to be refreshed each time you open the worksheet that contains the table, right-click any cell in your PivotTable, and click Table Options on the shortcut menu. In the Data Options section of the PivotTable Options dialog box, select the Refresh On Open check box, and then click OK. ▶

Once this option is turned on, each time you open the worksheet, Excel will check the source range for the PivotTable and update the table to reflect any new data in that range of cells.

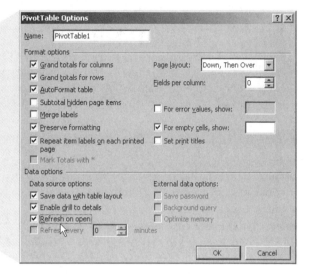

Refresh with caution

One potential problem with using the Refresh On Open option is that if others have been editing your worksheet and have made changes to the source cells for your PivotTable, your table could change in an undesirable way. If, for example, someone has deleted a column or altered a label, or added erroneous data, your table might change in a way that you don't want. If you really need to use the Refresh On Open option and others have access to your worksheet, consider protecting the source range of cells. (For more information on protecting cell ranges from changes, see "When I put Excel content into a Microsoft Access database, I have trouble with the date formats" on page 84.)

I don't want to have to re-create my PivotTable for use with other data

Source of the problem

Suppose you've got the perfect PivotTable, and you have another worksheet that could use the very same PivotTable setup. Or suppose you want to have two, or more than two, PivotTables side by side, each showing a different aspect of the same target data. In either case, the prospect of starting from scratch to build a new PivotTable doesn't sound terribly appealing. I'm with you!

If you need to use an existing table with different data on a different worksheet or in another spot on the same worksheet, the solution requires that you copy the table to a new spot and edit its setup to reflect a different range of source cells. If you want to duplicate a table using the same data as the original so that you can display a different portion, all you have to do is copy and paste the original, and then make a few minor adjustments to the duplicate. In this example, the tables are identical except for which department's salaries are shown in detail. ▶

Department	Accounting ▼		Department	Marketing ▼
Sum of Current Salary			Sum of Current Salary	
Job Title ▼	Total		Job Title ▼	Total
Clerk	26800		Coordinator	99000
Coordinator	51250		Manager	72500
Manager	75400		Specialist	46500
Grand Total	153450		Grand Total	218000

How to fix it

To copy a PivotTable, follow these steps:

1. Right-click the PivotTable you want to copy, point to Select on the short-cut menu, and then click Entire Table.

2. With the PivotTable selected, press Ctrl+C to copy the PivotTable to the Clipboard.

3. Move to the target location for the duplicate PivotTable, and press Enter. The table appears in the new location. (You might have to adjust the layout, formatting, and column widths of the pasted copy to match the original.)

> ### Tip
> When you copy a Pivot-Table, clicking Entire Table is much easier than dragging through the table's cells, no matter how small the table is. If you try to drag through the table's cells, you can't start from the first cell, because that's typically a button—clicking it might drop down a list instead of simply selecting the cell. You'd have to start the selection from the last cell in the last column.

A table so nice, they used it twice

Placing PivotTables side by side on a worksheet is a good way to look at the same data from different perspectives. For example, if your data shows the detail of employees by department (with the Department field in the Page section of the PivotTable layout), you can have the first table display the salaries (or number of employees, or average bonus, whatever) for one department, and then in the duplicate, show that same data for a different department. Create duplicates for each of the departments and then an additional table for showing all departments' data combined in a single table.

Why not just use the Page section drop-down list in a single table and choose a different department? Because with only one PivotTable, you can see the table from only one perspective at a time, and you can't make easy visual comparisons.

Making an attractive PivotTable

Useful for many PivotTables and especially helpful for closely placed duplicates, the Format Report command allows you to choose from a series of preset table formats—cell shading, fonts, or table layouts—that can help you quickly create a professional look for your Pivot-Table. In the case of side-by-side duplicates, having each version of the table in a different color helps you tell them apart. ▶

To use this feature, click any cell in the PivotTable, and when the PivotTable toolbar appears (it should appear automatically, but if it doesn't, right-click the table and choose Show PivotTable Toolbar) click the PivotTable button. Choose Format Report from the resulting menu, and then pick a format from the AutoFormat dialog box.

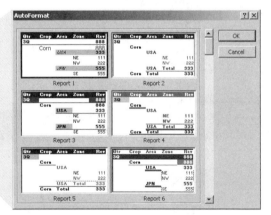

Tip

If you want to use a different range of cells as the source data for a duplicate table, right-click the table and click Wizard on the shortcut menu. In the PivotTable And PivotChart Wizard, click the Back button to access the wizard's second step, and then establish a different range for the PivotTable. Complete instructions for this process are found in "I refreshed my PivotTable, but the data still doesn't reflect my changes" on page 264.

Tip

One potential drawback to applying preset table formats is that applying these formats can change the layout of your PivotTable and alter the way the PivotTable content is displayed. Be prepared to click Undo to get rid of the formatting if any undesirable change occurs. If you can't undo a change (because you made the change too many actions ago, or you just opened the file), click None in the AutoFormat dialog box (it's the last sample in the dialog box), and then click OK to return the table to its original state.

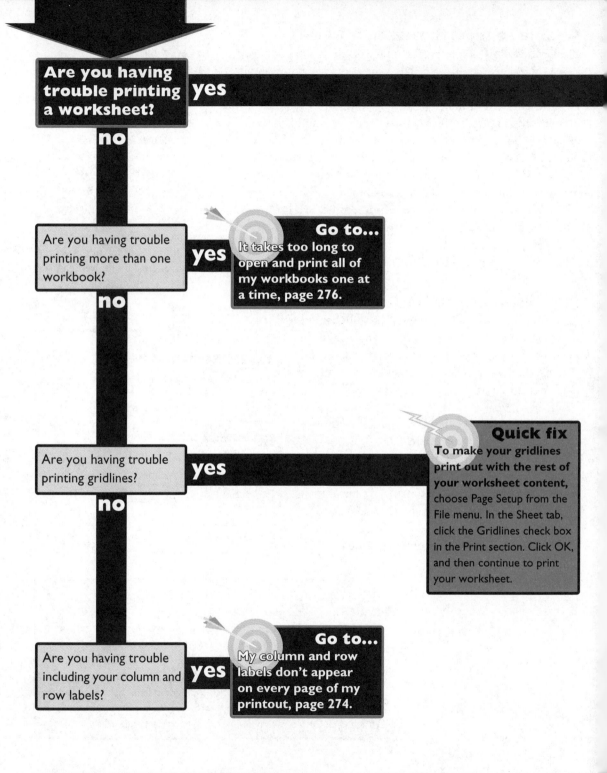

Are you having trouble printing a worksheet? **yes**

no

Are you having trouble printing more than one workbook? **yes**

Go to...
It takes too long to open and print all of my workbooks one at a time, page 276.

no

Are you having trouble printing gridlines? **yes**

Quick fix
To make your gridlines print out with the rest of your worksheet content, choose Page Setup from the File menu. In the Sheet tab, click the Gridlines check box in the Print section. Click OK, and then continue to print your worksheet.

no

Are you having trouble including your column and row labels? **yes**

Go to...
My column and row labels don't appear on every page of my printout, page 274.

Printing

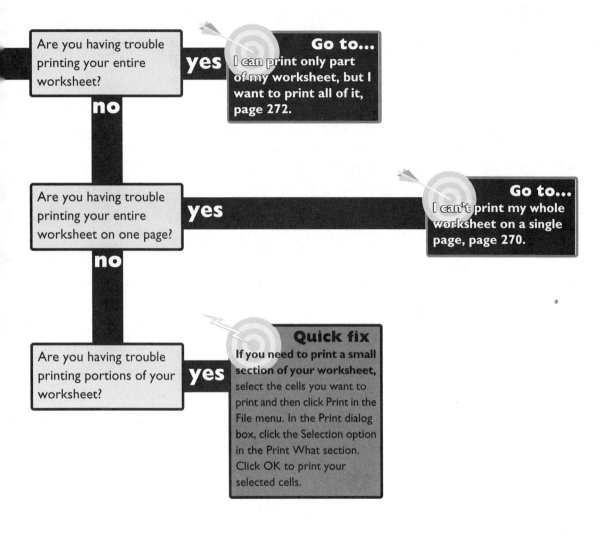

Are you having trouble printing your entire worksheet?

yes → **Go to...** I can print only part of my worksheet, but I want to print all of it, page 272.

no

Are you having trouble printing your entire worksheet on one page?

yes → **Go to...** I can't print my whole worksheet on a single page, page 270.

no

Are you having trouble printing portions of your worksheet?

yes → **Quick fix** If you need to print a small section of your worksheet, select the cells you want to print and then click Print in the File menu. In the Print dialog box, click the Selection option in the Print What section. Click OK to print your selected cells.

If your solution isn't here, check these related chapters:

- Formatting worksheets, page 168
- Workspace customization, page 368

Or see the general troubleshooting tips on page xv.

I can't print my whole worksheet on a single page

Source of the problem

By default, Microsoft Excel will print your entire worksheet (all the cells containing text and numbers as well as any empty rows and columns between those cells) at 100 percent of its size, on as many sheets of paper as it takes to print everything. This can be frustrating, especially if the working part of the worksheet fits nicely on your computer screen. It should fit as nicely on a single sheet of paper, right?

Regrettably, this assumption can be wrong much of the time. Depending on your monitor's resolution, you might be able to see many more columns across and rows down than could possibly fit on a single sheet of paper. Even a worksheet that uses only six or seven columns might require two sheets of paper, with a stray column or row printing on the second sheet.

The solution requires telling Excel that you want your worksheet to fit on one sheet. This is easy to do using the Page Setup dialog box. There are a few negative consequences, however, depending on how much of your worksheet doesn't fit on one sheet naturally. For example, by reducing the worksheet size to fit on one sheet, you can end up with tiny, illegible content. We'll work to minimize and help you work around these possible negatives, though!

> **Tip**
>
> Before wasting paper, always check Print Preview. This will show you how many pages the printout currently requires, and you can then use the Page Setup dialog box to adjust the printed output.

How to fix it

1. If you're in Normal view (as opposed to Print Preview), click Page Setup on the File menu.

2. In the Page Setup dialog box, make sure the Page tab is visible.

3. Click the Fit To option in the Scaling section of the dialog box and check the number that appears in both the Pages Wide By and Tall boxes. The default setting is 1; if another number appears, overwrite it by selecting it and typing 1.

4. Note that using the Fit To option will change the Adjust To setting; in this example it's been changed to 78 percent. That's the total reduction required for this particular worksheet to fit on one page. ▶

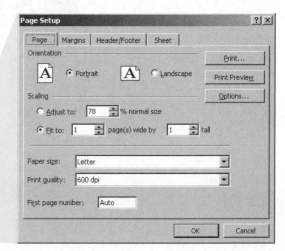

5. Click OK to apply any changes and close the dialog box.

6. Click Print Preview on the File menu to verify that your worksheet will fit on one page, and then print it.

Feeling disoriented?

If your worksheet is printed on two pages because it's too wide, and only one or two columns end up on that second page, try turning the paper on its side so that the worksheet is printed in landscape orientation. This could eliminate the need to reduce the scaling of your worksheet or require less reduction of your worksheet content because the worksheet has a wider area on which to be printed. If your worksheet is too long for a regular sheet of paper in portrait orientation (the default), changing to landscape orientation won't help. But you can change your paper's orientation and then check to see if the change does the trick.

On the File menu, click Page Setup to open the Page Setup dialog box, making sure the Page tab is visible. In the Orientation section of the dialog box, click the Landscape option and then click OK. You can't see what your printed worksheet will look like while it is in Normal view, so click Print Preview on the File menu to see how it will look when you print it. If the Next and Previous buttons in the Print Preview window are unavailable, your worksheet will be printed on one sheet of paper. If either or both of the buttons are available, click them (one at a time, of course) to see which parts of the worksheet still stray onto extra pages. ▶

If your worksheet still won't fit on one page, you can reduce the scaling percentage or change the Fit To settings in the Page Setup dialog box as needed.

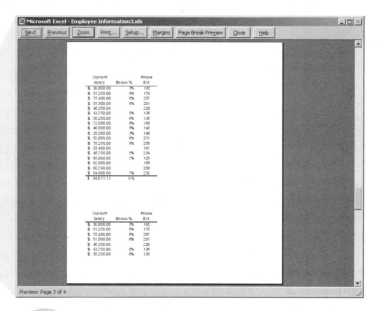

> **Tip**
>
> When you are in Print Preview, you can click the Setup button to display the Page Setup dialog box. After you make your selections in the dialog box, clicking OK returns you to Print Preview.

> **Tip**
>
> As a general rule, reducing the scaling percentage below 75 percent can result in a worksheet that's difficult to read. If your worksheet doesn't fit on one page without reducing it to Lilliputian proportions, you might have to stick with printing it on more than one page.

I can print only part of my worksheet, but I want to print all of it

Source of the problem

The Print dialog box offers the All option in its Print Range section, and one would assume that the entire worksheet would be printed if that option were selected. A generally reliable assumption, but if you're reading this part of the book, something tells me you feel as though the Print dialog box duped you—you saw the All option selected (it's the default, after all), and you clicked the OK button. You waited for your worksheet printout to emerge from the printer, and sadly, parts of it weren't included in the print job. What gives?

Allow me to introduce you to a very convenient feature that, once used, can be a real nuisance. The feature gives you the ability to select a section of the worksheet and set it as the *print area*. It's convenient in that it allows you to select an area as small as a single cell and print just that—nothing confidential, nothing that's still being worked on, nothing you don't want committed to paper. No need to hide columns or rows, no need to copy sections of the worksheet to another worksheet just to print them on their own. So where's the downside, and how does this have anything to do with the All option not working?

If you've set a print area in your worksheet, it remains set as the print area until and unless you clear it. That means that if you set a print area at 10 A.M., when you go back at 3 P.M. and click Print on the File menu, the only part of your worksheet that will be printed is the content within that previously established print area. This is true even if All is selected in the Print dialog box's Print Range section. Even if you really, really wanted to print the whole worksheet.

The solution? Clear your print area before attempting to print a worksheet. Even if you didn't set one, someone else might have. There's no harm in clearing it before printing your worksheet—you'll save yourself the aggravation and paper for an unusable partial printout.

How to fix it

1. On the File menu, point to Print Area and then click Clear Print Area. Any print area that was set is removed.

2. On the File menu, click Print. In the Print dialog box, make sure that All is selected in the Print Range section.

3. Click OK to print the entire worksheet.

> **Tip**
>
> To print a small portion of your worksheet without creating a print area, select that portion and click Print on the File menu. In the Print What section of the Print dialog box, click Selection and click OK. Only the content of the selected cells will be printed.

What print area??

How can you tell if a print area has been set? By the appearance of a dashed border around the print area itself. This should not be confused with the flashing dashed border that appears when you select a range of cells and copy or cut them to the clipboard. This is a static, thin dashed border around the cells you selected before pointing to Print Area on the File menu and clicking Set Print Area.

If you're thinking that you have to do a preemptive clearing of the print area before you print anything, that's not necessarily the case. If the entire working area of the worksheet can be seen without a lot of scrolling up and down, you can easily see if a print area has been set. If your data is voluminous and spread all over the worksheet, then clearing the print area before any print job is probably a good step to take, just to avoid having to scroll around looking for a previously set print area or wasting paper on a partial printout when you wanted the whole thing.

	A	B	C	D	E	F	G	H	I
1	Regional Sales								
2	First and Second Quarter Sales								
3		January	February	March	April	May	June	TOTALS	
4	Midwest	4265389	4567281	4869173	5171065	5472957	5774849	30120714	
5	Subtotal	4265389	4567281	4869173	5171065	5472957	5774849	30120714	
6	Northeast	5489282	4389188	3289094	2189000	1088906	4629991	21075461	
7	Northwest	3789202	3872098	3954994	4037890	4120786	4203682	23978652	
8	Subtotal	9278484	8261286	7244088	6226890	5209692	8833673	45054113	
9	South	1789288	2178491	2567694	2956897	3346100	3735303	16573773	
10	Southeast	3849991	3764902	3679813	3594724	3509635	3424546	21823611	
11	Southwest	2789376	2679125	2568874	2458623	2348372	2637772	15482142	
12	Subtotal	8428655	8622518	8816381	9010244	9204107	9797621	53879526	
13	TOTALS	21972528	21451085	20929642	20408199	19886756	24406143	129054353	
14									
15									
16	Regional Sales								
17	First and Second Quarter Sales								
18		January	February	March	April	May	June	TOTALS	
19	Midwest	4265389	4567281	4869173	5171065	5472957	5774849	30120714	
20	Subtotal	4265389	4567281	4869173	5171065	5472957	5774849	30120714	
21	Northeast	5489282	4389188	3289094	2189000	1088906	4629991	21075461	
22	Northwest	3789202	3872098	3954994	4037890	4120786	4203682	23978652	
23	Subtotal	9278484	8261286	7244088	6226890	5209692	8833673	45054113	
24	South	1789288	2178491	2567694	2956897	3346100	3735303	16573773	
25	Southeast	3849991	3764902	3679813	3594724	3509635	3424546	21823611	
26	Southwest	2789376	2679125	2568874	2458623	2348372	2637772	15482142	
27	Subtotal	8428655	8622518	8816381	9010244	9204107	9797621	53879526	
28	TOTALS	21972528	21451085	20929642	20408199	19886756	24406143	129054353	
29									

Maybe you don't need to have it all

When you get to know Excel's Print Area command, you'll find that it's useful for printing what appears to be "all" of your

Take another look at it

Another way to tell if there's a print area set anywhere in your worksheet is to view the sheet in Page Break Preview mode. On the View menu, click Page Break Preview, and you'll see the print area mapped out with a thick blue border around it on a gray field. To expand or reduce the print area, drag the border out to increase the print area's size, or drag it in to reduce it. Switch back to Normal view, and you'll see the print area has changed to match the dimensions you designated.

worksheet. However, it's actually only the sections that contain information you want to print—you can skip blank sections or cells that contain repetitive or uninteresting data.

Using your Ctrl key, select all the areas of your worksheet that you want to print. (They needn't be contiguous, and single cells all around the worksheet can be included in the mass selection.) When the areas are selected, point to Print Area on the File menu, and then click Set Print Area. Any previously set area will be removed in favor of the new designated area, and when you choose to print all of the worksheet, you'll really be printing all of the worksheet that you're interested in, leaving out the cells and ranges that aren't important. Note, however, that if your selected areas are not contiguous, each of them will be printed on a separate page—you knew there had to be a catch, didn't you?

My column and row labels don't appear on every page of my printout

Source of the problem

When your worksheet takes up more than one screenful of cells, it can be hard to follow the content if the column labels and row labels don't repeat throughout the worksheet. For that reason, it's very convenient to freeze the label row at the top of a long database (or the headings column on the far left) and have those labels stay on the screen no matter how far down into (or across) the worksheet you might scroll. Now imagine a long or wide (or both) worksheet that prints out on several sheets of paper. Having those labels and headings remain on each page of the printout can be very helpful as well, just as they help if they stay on screen.

Now before you ask, no, you don't have to figure out where your page breaks will occur and retype the labels at that point in your worksheet—in fact if you do that, you can render your worksheet useless if it's a database, because in so doing, you'd be making it impossible to sort and use AutoFilter properly.

The solution, you'll be happy to hear, is much simpler, and it won't compromise your worksheet in the slightest. You merely need to tell Excel that you want your column and row labels to print on each page and make sure Excel knows in which cells those labels are currently found. It's important to note, however, that Excel will repeat your column and row labels only on pages that print the content from the sections of your worksheet that the labels apply to. (This sounds like a limitation, but it's not. If your worksheet contains information that doesn't pertain to or fall under the labels, you don't want the labels to appear on those pages and confuse someone reading the printout.)

For example, if your column labels are in cells A3 through H3, only pages containing cells from columns A through H will have the labels printed on them. If your row labels are in cells A4 through A20, only pages containing the cells between row 4 and row 20 will contain the labels. In this example, the employee's social security numbers are row labels, and the column headings identify what's found in each record in this database.

	A	B	C	D	E	F	G	H	I	J
1				*Employee Information*						
2	SocSec#	Last Name	First Name	Date Hired	Department	Job Title	Current Salary	Bonus %	Phone Ext.	
3	123-45-6793	Auerweck	Lawrence	11/2/1999	Accounting	Clerk	$ 26,800.00	3%	192	
4	249-781-1242	Reilly	Michael	7/2/1998	Accounting	Coordinator	$ 51,250.00	6%	176	
5	123-45-6792	Schiller	Jo Ann	8/13/1995	Accounting	Manager	$ 75,400.00	8%	287	
6	249-781-1243	Hodges	Roberta	9/5/1998	Human Resources	Coordinator	$ 51,500.00	6%	201	
7	249-781-1240	Talbot	Susan	5/23/1996	Human Resources	Specialist	$ 48,250.00	5%	220	
8	123-45-6790	Kline	Linda	12/15/1998	Marketing	Coordinator	$ 43,750.00	5%	138	
9	123-45-6794	MacElyea	Blanche	8/15/1999	Marketing	Coordinator	$ 55,250.00	6%	135	
10	201-672-9093	Pederzani	Jacob	6/15/1998	Marketing	Manager	$ 72,500.00	8%	189	
11	123-45-6789	Chambers	Martin	6/15/1999	Marketing	Specialist	$ 46,500.00	5%	145	
12	201-672-9084	Kovalcik	John	4/3/1990	Operations	Clerk	$ 25,200.00	3%	190	
13	123-45-6791	Thomas	Gary	3/2/2000	Operations	Coordinator	$ 52,000.00	6%	231	
14	201-672-9095	Miller	Pam	4/25/1997	Operations	Manager	$ 78,250.00	8%	258	
15	249-781-9081	Balsamo	Anthony	3/25/1996	Operations	Specialist	$ 53,400.00	6%	167	
16	249-781-1239	Elmaleh	Miriam	4/22/1997	Sales	Coordinator	$ 48,750.00	5%	234	
17	249-781-1241	Ulrich	Joshua	5/2/2001	Sales	Manager	$ 65,000.00	7%	125	
18	201-672-9082	Ashton	Steven	10/31/1997	Sales	Representative	$ 62,500.00	7%	158	
19	249-781-1244	Maurone	Richard	5/2/1995	Sales	Representative	$ 65,700.00	7%	250	
20	201-672-9086	Ulrich	Zachary	4/9/2000	Sales	Representative	$ 64,600.00	7%	232	
21			Count of Employees:	18		Avg Salary/Bonus:	$ 54,811.11	6%		
22										
23										
24										

How to fix it

1. On the worksheet you intend to print, click Page Setup on the File menu.

2. Click the Sheet tab.

3. In the Print Titles section of the dialog box, click in the Rows To Repeat At Top box to place your insertion point there.

4. Outside of the dialog box (move it aside as needed), drag through the row or rows that contain your column headings. Note the range of cells that appears in the Rows To Repeat At Top box.

5. Click in the Columns To Repeat At Left box to place your insertion point there.

6. Again, outside of the dialog box, drag through the column or columns containing your row labels. Note the range that appears in the Columns To Repeat At Left box. (You might have to adjust the column settings Excel selects by retyping the letter of the column that "finishes off" your row labels.) ▶

7. Click OK.

8. Although you don't need this last step to make this feature work, you might still want to take it as a wise final pre-printing step. On the File menu, click Print Preview to see how your worksheet will look when you print it, and make sure your labels are where you want them, on the pages you need them. If all's well, go ahead and print your worksheet whenever you're ready.

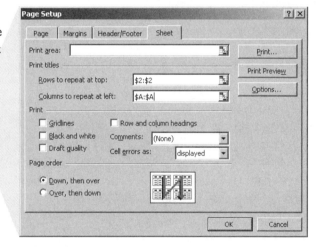

Tip

If your column and row labels appear on more than one of your worksheets, it becomes more important than ever that they be spelled correctly, that they use well-known abbreviation forms, and that they're formatted attractively—bold to make them stand out, for example, or in a different color so that you can distinguish them from the rows and columns containing data.

Tip

If your worksheet has a merged cell at the top (housing the worksheet title, for example), when you click the first column of the worksheet to designate it as the source for Columns To Repeat At Left, you'll get the entire column span of columns that are included in the merged cell—say $A:$G if the merged cell spans columns A through G. To remedy this, simply retype the column letter after the colon in this Page Setup dialog box field so that the single column you want is the one that's repeated on your printout.

It takes too long to open and print all of my workbooks one at a time

Source of the problem

For people who work with several different workbooks on a consistent basis, it can be a pain to open each of them, one at a time, whenever you need them all open. If you also need to print them, that's another step that has to be repeated for each open workbook. There has to be a better way, right? Yes, and unlike some procedures that should be easier but they aren't, this one can be!

Excel's Open dialog box allows you to select multiple workbooks from within the same folder and open them all at the same time. Moreover, you can choose to open and print all of them at the same time, saving a lot of redundant effort.

Tip

The quick procedure described in this section works only for workbooks that are stored in the same folder. If you want to open all of your workbooks at once, move or copy them to the same folder, and then follow the steps in this section. If the workbooks must remain in separate folders, you'll have to open and print groups of workbooks in each of the separate folders.

How to fix it

1. Make sure your printer is on and ready, with enough paper for the entire print job. On the File menu, click Open.

2. As needed, navigate to the folder containing the workbooks you want to open and print.

3. When the desired workbooks are displayed in the dialog box, click the first one you want to open.

Respond to prompts promptly

If there are any problems printing any of the workbooks you've selected, appropriate print error messages will appear. If, for example, one of the workbooks is empty, a "Nothing to print" message will appear. If one of the workbooks contains worksheets set to landscape orientation, a prompt will appear asking if you want the printer to change its orientation automatically. Respond to these prompts so that the print process can continue for the remaining workbooks with printable content.

4. Hold down the Ctrl key and click each of the other workbooks you want to open and print once. (Don't worry if your dialog box looks different from ours.)

5. Click the Tools button and then click Print on the drop-down menu that appears. Without the Print dialog box opening, each of the selected workbooks will be opened, all the contents of all

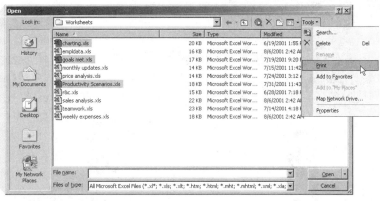

worksheets will be sent to the default printer, and the workbooks will be closed when the print operation is complete. ▶

Open (and close) sesame

You can use a variation of this procedure to open a series of workbooks without printing them. To open several workbooks at once, click Open on the File menu, and in the Open dialog box, move to the folder containing the workbooks you want to open. (Again, they must all be in the same folder.) Use the Ctrl key to select multiple files, and then click Open. All of the workbooks will open, and each will be listed on the Window menu.

After the workbooks are open and you've done whatever reviewing and editing they require, you will probably want to save and close them. If you don't want to exit Excel at the same time, there's a trick that allows you to close all open workbooks. (You'll get a prompt to save any workbooks that haven't been saved since their last edits.) Press the Shift key as you click the File menu, and you'll notice that the Close command has changed to Close All. Click that command, and each workbook will be closed in turn. If a prompt appears asking if you want to save changes, click Yes to save them or No to close the workbook in question without saving changes. (To abandon the group closing process, click Cancel.) ▶

Tip

If any of the workbooks you want to open are already open, when you try to open them again in the Open dialog box, a prompt appears, warning you that if you choose to reopen the file, all changes made since the file was previously opened will be lost. Click Yes to reopen the workbook and lose the changes or No to leave the currently open copy intact—that is, to ignore your instruction to reopen the file.

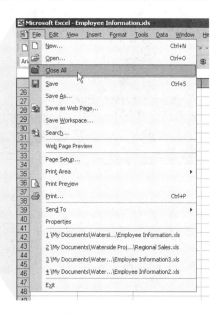

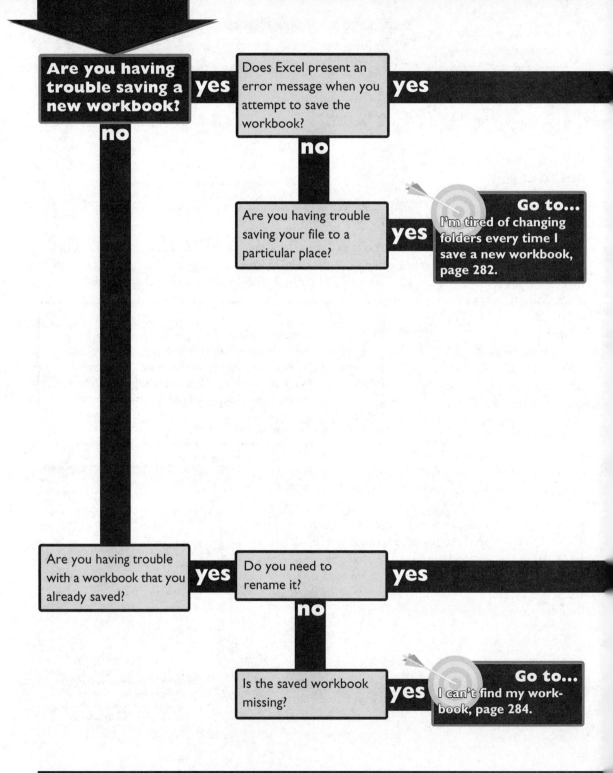

Are you having trouble saving a new workbook?

yes → **Does Excel present an error message when you attempt to save the workbook?**

yes →

no ↓

Are you having trouble saving your file to a particular place?

yes → **Go to...** I'm tired of changing folders every time I save a new workbook, page 282.

no ↓

Are you having trouble with a workbook that you already saved?

yes → **Do you need to rename it?**

yes →

no ↓

Is the saved workbook missing?

yes → **Go to...** I can't find my workbook, page 284.

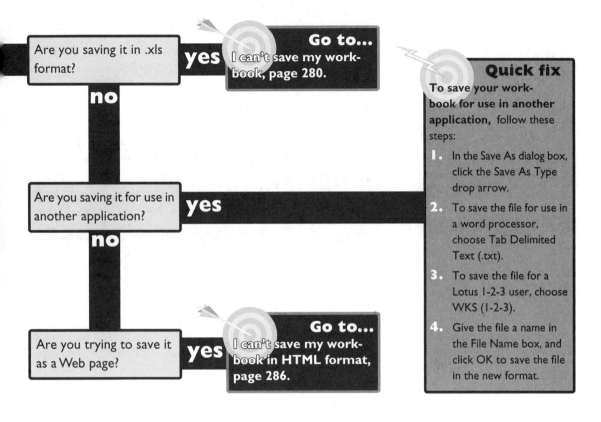

Are you saving it in .xls format?

yes → **Go to...** I can't save my workbook, page 280.

no

Quick fix

To save your workbook for use in another application, follow these steps:

1. In the Save As dialog box, click the Save As Type drop arrow.

2. To save the file for use in a word processor, choose Tab Delimited Text (.txt).

3. To save the file for a Lotus 1-2-3 user, choose WKS (1-2-3).

4. Give the file a name in the File Name box, and click OK to save the file in the new format.

Are you saving it for use in another application?

yes →

no

Are you trying to save it as a Web page?

yes → **Go to...** I can't save my workbook in HTML format, page 286.

Quick fix

To rename your previously-saved workbook, close the workbook, but leave Excel open. Then, choose Open from the File menu, and in the Open dialog box, navigate to the folder containing the file you want to rename. Right-click the file, and choose Rename from the shortcut menu. Type a new name for the file (don't forget to keep the extension!) and press Enter.

If your solution isn't here, check these related chapters:

- Exporting and importing, page 120
- Templates, page 344
- Web tools, page 358

Or see the general troubleshooting tips on page xv.

I can't save my workbook

Source of the problem

If you open an existing workbook file and try to resave it, Microsoft Excel will stop you if the file is protected from modifications by a password, if the file is open twice on your computer and the copy you're working with is open as read-only, or if the name you're attempting to give the file is already used by another workbook in the same folder.

When Excel refuses to let you save the open workbook, it should explain why. It doesn't merely say "No!" and leave you in the dark—it gives you a message telling you what the problem is. Based on the message you receive, you can act accordingly—provide the password that's required, close the extra version of the file you have open, or edit the name you're trying to use so that it isn't the same as the existing file. ▶

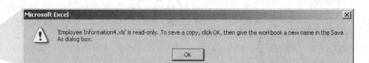

How to fix it

- If you need a password for the file you want to save, you'll have to go to the person who password-protected the file. He or she could have done it using the commands on Excel's Protection submenu or during the saving process. In either case, ask the person for the password and enter it when you're prompted to do so. If the person won't give you the password or you can't find the person who protected the file, save the file with a different name. You can then bypass the password because the original file won't be overwritten.

- If the file you're trying to save is already open but the copy you're using is read-only, you must either open the Window menu, switch to the other open version of the file, and then close it, or save the read-only version with a different name so that the other open version isn't affected.

- If the file name you want to use for the workbook is already used by another workbook in the folder that you're saving the file to, either give the file you're saving a different name or save it to a different folder.

> **Tip**
>
> The password-protection feature should not be confused with the Protection submenu's commands in Excel—the former is available in all the Office applications and pertains to the file, not its contents.

So how'd they do that password thing?

You can use the password-protection feature yourself to protect your files from being opened or modified by people you don't want using them. You can apply a password to a file to prevent people from opening the file without authorization or to force them to supply another password when they try to save changes to the file once it's open. This ensures that your file will be the same as the last time you saved it.

To apply a password, click Save As on the File menu. If the file is being saved for the first time (its current name is Book1 or Book2, and so on), you can click Save on the File menu. In the Save As dialog box (which opens in either case), navigate to the folder you want to save the file in, and enter a name for it in the File Name box. Click the Tools button and click General Options on the drop-down menu. ▶

In the Save Options dialog box, enter a password in the Password To Open text box if you want to keep people from opening the file without a password. To prevent people from guessing your password, make it at least four characters long and include both numbers and letters. Don't use your kids' names, your birth date, or the insulting name everyone calls the boss behind his or her back—they're all too easy for someone to figure out. ▶

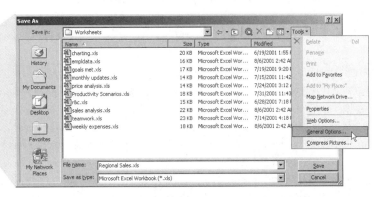

To prevent people from saving the file (with or without any changes) unless they give it a new name (thus creating a new file), type a password in the Password To Modify text box. If you want to further protect the file, select the Read-Only Recommended check box if you want Excel to display a recommendation to users that they open the file as read-only. Click OK. For each password you enter, a Confirm Password dialog box appears, asking you to retype the password you created. Type the password again in each successive box, and click OK. Back in the Save As dialog box, click Save to complete the saving process.

Tip

What happens if you click the Advanced button in the Save Options dialog box? You get a list of encryption options that make it even more difficult for people to hack your password-protected worksheet. If you choose a CryptoAPI encryption method, you can apply passwords as long as 255 characters, which makes them much more difficult to guess.

Five sons named George?

Having files with the same name, even if they're in different folders, is risky. It's easy to confuse them and edit or print the wrong file. If you want two or more files to have the same name, consider adding a character to the end of the name, such as Sales Analysis A.xls, Sales Analysis B.xls, and so on. When you have a lot of similarly named files, also remember to check the modified date for the files to make sure you're using the right file. In the Windows Explorer or My Computer window, click Details on the View menu and check the date the files were last modified.

I'm tired of changing folders every time I save a new workbook

Source of the problem

By default, Excel saves new workbooks in the My Documents folder. If you click Save on the File menu or click the Save button and do nothing other than enter a file name for the new workbook, the default file location is applied. Of course it's no problem to choose a different folder for the odd workbooks that don't belong in the My Documents folder, but if every workbook you create belongs in another folder, switching from My Documents to that folder every time you save a new file can certainly be tedious.

The solution to this problem lies in changing Excel's default location for new workbook files. When you choose a new default folder, choose one that's the likely home for the vast majority of your workbooks, not just the one you're dealing with at the time. If you categorize your workbooks by placing them in folders by subject or content and you aren't sure which one of the folders is the most frequently used, make them subfolders of the My Documents folder and leave that as the default. ▶

At the most, you'll have to double-click one of the folders listed in the default folder, adding just one double-click to the process of saving your files.

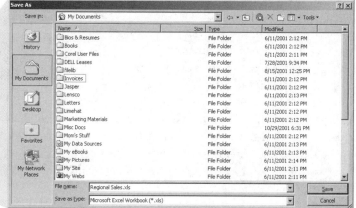

How to fix it

1. On the Tools menu, click Options.

2. In the Options dialog box, click the General tab.

> **Tip**
>
> If you decide to create a new folder and make that the default folder for saving workbooks, create one just for workbooks, such as "My Workbooks," which can be a subfolder of My Documents. Give your folders relevant names and create a folder hierarchy that makes sense according to the relationships between the folders and the files within them.

3. Click to position your insertion point in the Default File Location box. The box should display the name of the default folder to which new files are saved. ▶

4. Using the arrow keys and the Backspace and Delete keys as needed, edit the contents of the box to show the complete path of the default folder you want to use. The path includes the drive letter (most likely C:\), as well as the full and accurate names of any folders that contain the default folder you want to use.

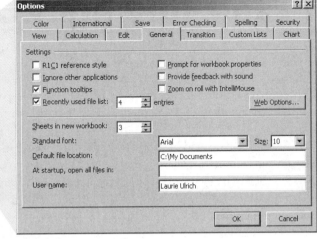

5. Click OK to put your change into effect and close the dialog box.

While you're there...

The next time you find yourself on the General tab of the Options dialog box, you can also adjust the number of recently used files displayed at the foot of the File menu. The default is four, but you can change that to anything from zero (which turns off the feature altogether) to nine by clicking the up or down arrows in the Entries box to the right of the Recently Used File List option.

Why bother tinkering with this feature? If you want to make it harder for people who share your computer to tell which files you used last, it's a good idea to display no recently used files on the File menu. Or, if you tend to open the same group of workbooks throughout an average workday, it can be very convenient to have a longer list of files on the File menu. Opening files through this list is a lot faster than clicking Open on the File menu and locating the files in the Open dialog box.

How does this relate to saving files? If the file you click at the bottom of the File menu won't open (indicated by an error message that says the file isn't found), it's because the file no longer exists where it was saved the last time you had it open. You might have renamed the file, or you might have moved the file to a different folder. In this case you'll have to press Ctrl+O and open the workbook from the Open dialog box. The File menu will be updated the next time you save and close the workbook.

> ### Tip
> Before opening a file from the recently used file list on the File menu, check the Window menu to make sure the file isn't already open. If you open a file that's already open, you'll be surprised when you're unable to save the file without giving it a new name.

I can't find my workbook

Source of the problem

We've all experienced that sinking feeling when we go to open a file from the folder where we just *know* we saved it, and it isn't there. Panic sets in, accompanied by the sinking feeling that you might have lost hours, days, perhaps weeks of work—or more. Where could the file be? How did it get lost?

Unless you deleted or moved the file since saving it, it's right where you left it. The problem lies in your memory of where it was saved. While it's possible that you or someone else did rename, move, or delete it since you saved it, if you're the only person using your computer and your memory doesn't usually leave you in the lurch, the file is simply saved in a different folder than the one you remember.

The solution? Find it. Before you say, "Well, duh!" what I mean is, let Excel find it for you. In the Open dialog box (where you might already be, if you're trying to open a file and can't find it), use the Find command to search your entire computer or perhaps just a specific group of folders for the file that's not where you thought you left it.

How to fix it

1. If the Open dialog box isn't already open, click Open on the File menu to display it.

2. Click the Tools button and then click Search on the drop-down menu.

3. In the resulting dialog box (on the Basic tab), click the Search In drop-down arrow, and choose My Computer on the drop-down list. This searches all your drives—the A drive, your local C drive, and any other drives attached to or inside your computer. It's better to look everywhere within your local drives than to narrow the search from the beginning and risk missing the file's actual location.

4. Type a keyword or phrase—something that's unique to the missing file—in the Search Text text box. For example, use a field name if the file is a database or a product number if the missing file contains a list of products.

I just had it...

If you recently worked on the file you're looking for, use the list of recently used files at the foot of the File menu to reopen it. No matter where you really saved it, this list will point to the file in its current location, and clicking the file will open it. You can then click Save As on the File menu to see where the file is stored. If the file isn't in the list of recently used files but was used in the last day or so, try the Start menu's Documents menu. (Click Start, and then point to Documents.) If the file is listed on the Documents menu, you can open it from that shortcut, and, again, you can click Save As on the File menu to see where it's stored.

Tip

If more than one file meets your Search criteria, click the Size, Type, and Modified columns in the Open dialog box to refocus the list by criteria that might help you find the file.

---

5. Click the Results Should Be drop-down list and choose the file type(s) to look for. Removing the checks from those that are not needed, such as documents and image files, will reduce the time it takes to search for your workbook. ▶

6. Click the Search button. The word "Searching..." appears in the Results box as long as the search is ongoing. When the search is complete, the files that contained your search text appear in the Results box instead. If no files meet your search criteria, "No Files Found" appears in the Results box. ▶

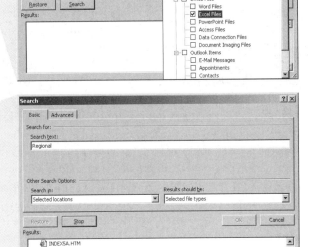

And what if I still can't find it?

There's always the possibility that your file has been deleted. Before leaping to that upsetting conclusion, however, there are other search features in the Search dialog box that can help you find a file that's been renamed or whose name you don't remember. You can search for your file based on its contents, creation date, last modification date, size, the template used to create it, or virtually any field you might have filled in (such as Author or Title) in the file's Properties dialog box. (For more information about the Properties dialog box, see "I don't want my name to appear in the comment box" on page 38.)

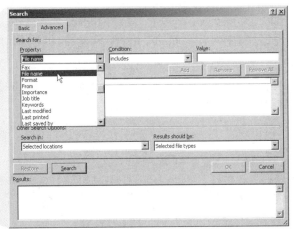

To make use of these tools, click the Advanced tab in the Search dialog box. Choose a Property to search for (File Name is a good choice or Author, if the file was created by you on a computer where you're listed as the author in the Properties dialog box), and then select a condition option and enter the appropriate text in the Value box. ▶

I can't save my workbook in HTML format

Source of the problem

You want to use the global reach of the Web so that clients and colleagues can view and interact with your worksheet data—that's great! What's even greater? Excel gives you the tools to do it. You can save your entire workbook, a single worksheet within the workbook, or even a section of a worksheet in Hypertext Markup Language (HTML) format and post it as a page on the Web. You can add interactivity, which means people can click the worksheet content and use Excel tools (which appear with the worksheet content on the Web page) to edit and use the data. Those changes won't affect the actual data stored on the Web—they'll be using a local copy of the content stored in their computer's memory, and any changes they make won't affect the actual Web page. Your visitors can save the content they edit to their local computers or copy your content to their own locally stored workbook so they can use it again and again on their own.

Tip

When you name your file, don't use spaces. Although Excel won't prevent you from using them, most Web browsing software doesn't support file names with spaces in them, and your page might not be displayed properly if you include spaces in the file name. If you want the appearance of a space, use the underscore character. (Hold down the Shift key and then press the hyphen [-] key.)

Sounds wonderful, huh? Well, it is, but sometimes saving your Excel data in HTML format can present problems. When you try to save a workbook, a worksheet, or a section thereof in HTML format, you might get an error message indicating that the file name you're trying to apply isn't accessible. If this occurs, one of the following situations must exist:

- You're trying to use a name that's already being used for an HTML file in the same folder.

- You're trying to save the file to a location on the network that's not available or to a nonexistent local drive or folder.

- You're trying to save too much data. If the amount of data exceeds the limit that can be accurately saved in HTML format, Excel won't let you complete the process.

The solutions to the first two problems require that you use a different name, location, or both for the HTML version of your content. In the last case, you must save a smaller section of your worksheet.

How to fix it

To save your file with a different name or to another folder, follow these steps:

1. Click Save As on the File menu.

2. To save the file with a different name, type the new name in the File Name box of the Save As dialog box. If you need to save the file to a different location (because the one you've selected is unavailable), click a different folder in the Save In drop-down list.

If you're trying to save too much data in HTML format, follow these steps to reduce the amount of data you're saving:

1. Select the range of cells on a single worksheet that contains the data you want to publish on the Internet.

2. On the File menu, click Save As Web Page.

3. In the Save As dialog box, click the Selection option, which is defined as the range of cells you selected. (If you selected the entire sheet, the word *Sheet* appears next to this option.) If you want, select the Add Interactivity check box so that you will be able to play with a local copy of the worksheet data (using Excel tools that will appear with the data) when you view the data on the Web. ▶

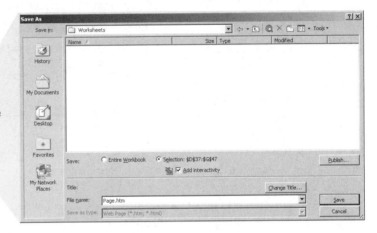

4. Designate a file location for the new Web page in the Save In drop-down list and then type a name for your page in the File Name box.

5. Click the Save button. The page is created, and the dialog box closes, leaving your worksheet open in Excel format.

You can open your new Web page by pressing Ctrl+O, making sure All Files (*.*) appears in the Files Of Type box, and then double-clicking the name of the file you just saved. (The page name should appear with an .htm file extension.)

You're published!

Want to see what your new Web page looks like after you create it? Instead of clicking Save in the Save As dialog box, click Publish. In the resulting Publish As Web Page dialog box, you can confirm selections you might have already made. In addition, you have the opportunity to view the new Web page in your default browser right after it's created. In the Publish As Web Page dialog box, select the Open Published Web Page In Browser check box, and then click Publish again to launch your default browser and display the new Web page as it would appear on the Internet.

I can't save my workbook in HTML format

(continued from page 287)

Don't just sit there, do something!

Your Excel data can be a handy addition to any Web site, but you can increase its usefulness by adding interactivity to the published content. Interactivity lets you work with the data on the Web page, making changes to the data and editing or adding formulas. ▶

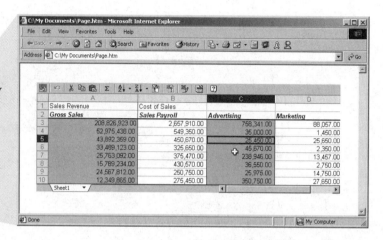

Of course you're interacting with only your copy of the content, not the data as it's stored on the Web server that provides the Web site content—when you close the page or hit the Back button in your browser, all changes are lost.

If you want to keep the data and your changes, you have to save the page to your local drive, which will create an .html file from the data including any edits you've made. This file can be reopened in any browser window (even if you're offline), in Excel, or even in Microsoft Word.

Tip

You can also copy the Web content to the clipboard, paste it in an open workbook on your local computer, and then play with the data there.

Caution! Clashing colors cause conflict

When you publish your content to the Web, whatever formatting you've applied—text and numeric formatting, cell shading, text colors—will appear on the Web as it appeared in your worksheet. It's a good idea, therefore, to take a look at the rest of the Web site to which your Excel-based page will be added. If you or your company employed a designer to create your site (or if you took the time to design it yourself), you don't want to add content that will clash with your color scheme or overall tone.

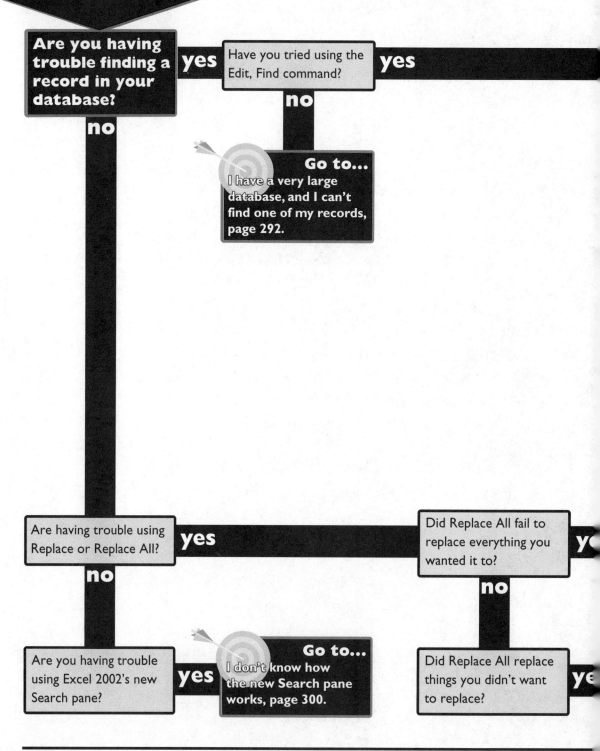

Are you having trouble finding a record in your database? — yes → Have you tried using the Edit, Find command? — yes →

no ↓

Go to...
I have a very large database, and I can't find one of my records, page 292.

no ↓

Are having trouble using Replace or Replace All? — yes → Did Replace All fail to replace everything you wanted it to? — y[es]

no ↓

no ↓

Are you having trouble using Excel 2002's new Search pane? — yes →

Go to...
I don't know how the new Search pane works, page 300.

Did Replace All replace things you didn't want to replace? — ye[s]

Searching for data

Did the Find command result in an error message?

yes →

Go to...
When I use the Find command, I get an error message, page 294.

no ↓

Do you need to search on more than one field in your database?

yes →

Go to...
The Find command doesn't allow me to search by example, page 298.

no ↓

Are you unsure which worksheet contains the content you need to find?

yes →

Quick fix

To be sure that your Find process searches all of your worksheets, follow these steps:

1. Group your worksheets by clicking the first one and, with the Shift key pressed, clicking the last one.

2. Perform your Find process—you'll notice that the repeated use of the Find Next button will search all of your worksheets.

3. To ungroup your sheets after having found the missing content, right-click any of the grouped sheets and choose Ungroup Sheets from the shortcut menu.

Quick fix

To resolve a problem with your Replace All procedure, you need to check your Find What settings to make sure that you weren't looking for things that aren't there. Make sure Match Case and Find Entire Cells aren't turned on unless they're appropriate, check for typos in the Find What box, and repeat the Replace All procedure.

Go to...
I used Replace All, and now I wish I hadn't, page ###.

If your solution isn't here, check these related chapters:

- Entering data, page 108
- Filtering records, page 136
- Sorting data, page 310

Or see the general troubleshooting tips on page xv.

I have a very large database, and I can't find one of my records

Source of the problem

Any Microsoft Excel worksheet can have thousands of rows (65,535 of them, to be exact), each one a record in a database. The more records you have, the more likely you are to have to rely on Excel to find one of them when you can't seem to locate it by scrolling through the list. Imagine you have a contacts database, and you need to find the guy who installed the skylight in the office last year so you can call him about a leak that's developed. You don't remember his name, and it's unlikely that his company name is Skylights, Inc. How do you find him?

Excel has a variety of tools that you can put into service to help you find records in your database. Depending on the columns, or fields, in your database, you might or might not be able to use all of them.

For example, if you have a column with Contact Type as the label, you might be able to find the skylight installer (or at least distill the list down to a smaller number of candidates) if you have entered Contractor in the Contact Type field of his record. You could find him by using AutoFilter to filter that field for Contractor. If you have a Date Of Last Contact field, you could sort the records by that field and look for records dated around the time you called him last year to install the skylight. If your database contains a Memo field into which you typed notes about each contact, you could select that column, click Find on the Edit menu, and search on the word *skylight*, which should be in that field for this person's record.

So, you have three options for finding your missing record: use AutoFilter, Sort, and/or Edit, Find. Why "and/or"? Because if you try one and come up dry, you can always try another option. At least one of the tools described here will find a missing record in virtually any database, unless that record has been deleted.

"Filtering records" on page 136 and "Sorting data" on page 310 cover the use of AutoFilter and sorting, respectively, and you can refer to those chapters to use those tools to locate your missing data. But the Find feature is probably the most effective of the tools you can use to locate a missing record, provided you know a word (or portion thereof) or a number in that record that you can use for the search.

> **Tip**
>
> You don't need to type a whole word or phrase to find the text you're looking for. If, for example, you wanted to find the guy who installed the skylight, you could type *sky* in the Find What box, and aside from stopping at skywriters or Skye terrier breeders, you're likely to turn up the missing skylight installer in no time.

Searching for data

How to fix it

1. If you're sure which column contains the word or number you're searching for, select that entire column by clicking the letter in the column heading. If you're not sure which column contains the word or number you're searching for and you're willing to look through the entire list, hopping from each incident of the word or number as it occurs in any field, click any cell within the database.

2. Click Find on the Edit menu to open the Find dialog box (you can also press Ctrl+F). ▶

3. Enter the word or number you need to find and click the Find Next button. The cell containing the first instance of the value in the Find What box is highlighted. (If your database contains no matches of the Find What text, a message appears telling you that no records were found. See "When I use the Find command, I get an error message" on page 294.)

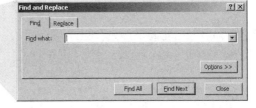

4. If the first result of the search isn't the record you were looking for, click Find Next again, and continue to do so until the data you're looking for is highlighted.

5. Click Close to close the dialog box and end the Find session.

Hide and seek

You can use the Find dialog box's Match Case and Find Entire Cells Only options to refine your search and eliminate stopping on cells that don't really match your criteria. To display these options, click the Options button in the Find dialog box—the dialog box changes, offering directional and content refinement options to narrow your search. Selecting the Match Case check box allows you to enter a value in the Find What box in lower, upper, title, or sentence case so that only those cells containing your entry in that same case will be found.

Select the Match Entire Cell Contents check box to restrict your results to cells containing the exact entry—no more, no less—that you typed in the Find What box. ▶

For example, if you were looking for the year 1998, you'd want to select the Find Entire Cells Only check box to avoid finding cells containing entries such as "$51,998.62."

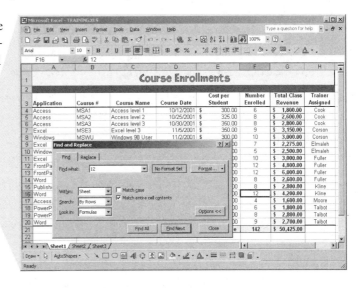

When I use the Find command, I get an error message

Source of the problem

You use the Find command to search for a record, and when you click Find Next in the Find dialog box, an error message tells you that none of the records meet your search criteria. You can click OK to make the error message go away, but that only removes the tedious reminder of your problem. You still haven't been able to find the record you were looking for. ▶

The problem stems from one of two situations:

Microsoft Excel ⊠

Microsoft Excel cannot find the data you're searching for. Check your search options, location and formatting.

[OK]

- The data you seek simply isn't in the database.

- Your Find criteria are faulty.

In the first situation, the problem isn't solvable, unless you enter the data you need in the database, in which case the data is not only back in the database, but you know precisely where it is! In the second situation, the solution is to check your criteria and fix typos or turn the Find options on or off, depending on whether or not you're using them and whether they're appropriate.

How to fix it

1. Choose Find in the Edit menu, or press Ctrl+F to display the Find dialog box, and then clear the check boxes for any Find options (such as Match Case and Match Entire Cell Contents) that you might have selected during your first Find attempt.

2. Check the spelling of the text you entered in the Find What box. If you entered a number, make sure there's no transposition or other typo.

3. After correcting any errors, click Find Next again.

4. If the desired data still isn't found, try entering a likely error in the Find What box. For example, if you're looking for the city of Phoenix, type *Pheonix*, a common misspelling of the word.

5. If that doesn't work, try making the Find What entry less specific. This will increase the number of unwanted hits as you click Find Next, but if you're looking for Phoenix and can't find it with the correct spelling (Phoenix) or the common misspelling (Pheonix), typing a simple Ph in the Find What box will flush out the data if it has been incorrectly entered as, say, *Phenix*.

Tip

Make sure that you don't have a section of your worksheet selected while your search is going on. If you select one or more columns or rows before issuing the Find command, the search will be restricted to those cells. If you want to search the whole database, make sure you don't have a range selected when you try to find your data.

Searching for data

Looking for data in all the wrong places

Other Find dialog box features that can unintentionally sabotage your search are the Within, Search, and Look In drop-down lists, which appear when you use the Options button in the Find dialog box. You should make sure these lists aren't set so as to undermine your attempts to find your missing data, and that starts with understanding what these options do. ▶

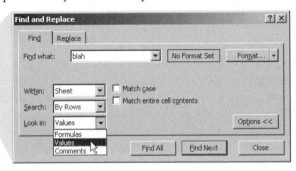

- The Within option gives you the choice of Sheet or Workbook. A database should only reside in a single worksheet, but if your workbook is made up of two or more individual databases (each on their own sheet), the Workbook option will allow you to search all of them.

- The Search option offers By Rows or By Columns. If you want to restrict your search to a particular column, you shouldn't have By Rows chosen, and if you want to search all of the records and all of the fields within them, By Columns isn't a good idea.

- The Look In option asks you to choose from Formulas, Values, or Comments. For a database, Values is the best bet.

Now that you know how the options work, you can make better use of them or at least prevent their ruining your search.

Search me...

By default, Excel's Find command works only in the active worksheet—you can, of course, choose Workbook from the Within option, but that will search the entire workbook, all of its sheets included. If the data you're looking for could only be in one of two or three sheets in your workbook (and there are other sheets you don't want to search), group the sheets you want to search before commencing the search, and leave the Within option set to Sheet.

To group the sheets you need to search, click the tab for one of the sheets you want to group, hold down the Ctrl key, and continue to click the other sheet tabs until all the sheets you want to group are selected. (When the sheets are grouped, their tabs will all be white.) Then click any cell on any of the grouped sheets, click Find on the Edit menu, and begin your search. When the desired data is found, you can ungroup the sheets by right-clicking any one of the sheet tabs and clicking Ungroup Sheets on the shortcut menu.

I used Replace All, and now I wish I hadn't

Source of the problem

Replace All is a very powerful feature. It's great for making sweeping changes to a large worksheet, saving time and reducing the margin for error. You shouldn't expect to spot every incident of X and replace it with Y on your own, as it's very likely you'll miss at least one of the X's. Imagine needing to edit your worksheet so that all of the serial numbers that currently start with B change to begin with R. You could sort the list of products by serial number and then, with all the B's together, edit them manually, or you could let Excel do the work. Wait a minute. What's that? You say you let Excel do the work with Replace All, something went awry (a spelling error is this example), and now your worksheet is a mess?

Well, I'm not surprised. Many people use Replace All and end up regretting it. Why? Either because the entries in the Find What or Replace With boxes were wrong, and the wrong stuff ended up being replaced (or was replaced with the wrong stuff); or because some of the cells that met the Find What criteria should have been left alone. What do you do when you've clicked the Replace All button and now you wish you hadn't?

	A	B	C	D	E	F	G	H
1			Course Enrollments					
2								
3	Application	Course #	Course Name	Course Date	Cost per Student	Number Enrolled	Total Class Revenue	Trainer Assigned
4	Access	MSA1	Access Level 1	10/12/2001	$ 300.00	6	$ 1,800.00	Cook
5	Access	MSA2	Access Level 2	10/25/2001	$ 325.00	8	$ 2,600.00	Cook
6	Access	MSA3	Access Level 3	10/30/2001	$ 350.00	8	$ 2,800.00	Cook
7	Excel	MSE3	Excel Level 3	11/5/2001	$ 350.00	9	$ 3,150.00	Corson
8	Windows	MSWU	Windows 98 User	11/2/2001	$ 300.00	10	$ 3,000.00	Corson
9	Excel	MSE2	Excel Level 2	10/20/2001	$ 325.00	7	$ 2,275.00	Elmaleh
10	Windows	MSNTA	Windows NT Administration	11/8/2001	$ 500.00	5	$ 2,500.00	Elmaleh
11	Excel	MSE1	Excel Level 1	10/8/2001	$ 300.00	10	$ 3,000.00	Fuller
12	FrontPage	FPWD1	Web Design w/FrontPage, lev 1	11/5/2001	$ 400.00	12	$ 4,800.00	Fuller
13	FrontPage	FPWD2	Web Design w/FrontPage, lev 2	11/15/2001	$ 500.00	12	$ 6,000.00	Fuller
14	Word	MSW2	Word Level 2	10/15/2001	$ 325.00	8	$ 2,600.00	Fuller
15	Publisher	MSPUB	Publisher Basics	11/13/2001	$ 350.00	8	$ 2,800.00	Kline
16	Word	MSW3	Word Level 3	11/1/2001	$ 350.00	12	$ 4,200.00	Kline
17	Access	MSAD1	Access Application Development	11/10/2001	$ 400.00	4	$ 1,600.00	Moore
18	PowerPoint	MSP1	PowerPoint Level 1	10/15/2001	$ 300.00	6	$ 1,800.00	Talbot
19	PowerPoint	MSP2	PowerPoint Level 2	10/30/2001	$ 350.00	8	$ 2,800.00	Talbot
20	Word	MSW1	Word Level 1	10/5/2001	$ 300.00	9	$ 2,700.00	Talbot
21					Total Revenue	142	$ 50,425.00	
22								

The first thing to try is clicking Edit, Undo. If Replace All was your last action, Undo will revert the worksheet to its status prior to the Replace command being issued. If Undo doesn't work—maybe because there have been too many changes since you made your mistake, and the Replace All command is too far back in the worksheet's history—you can retrace your steps to reverse your replacement. If you replaced X with Y, and now you want the X's back, use the Find Next and Replace buttons to replace the Y's with X's. By using Replace rather than Replace All, you avoid creating additional problems if some of the Y's were already there (before the original Replace All fiasco) and you want to keep them.

Searching for data

How to fix it

1. If you applied the Replace All command to an entire workbook or to a specific area of a worksheet, recreate that situation by selecting Workbook from the Within option (see the Replace dialog box, with the Options button clicked) or selecting the range in which the reversal should occur.

2. On the Edit menu, click Replace. The Replace dialog box opens. Click the Options button to display all of the dialog box features. ▶

3. In the Find What box, enter the content that replaced your original content.

4. In the Replace With box, type the original entry that the Replace All replaced. For example, if you accidentally replaced every instance of the number 2000 with 2002, and you meant to replace it only where 2000 represented the year 2000, type *2002* in the Find What box and *2000* in the Replace With box.

Find and Replace	? X

Find | Replace

Find what: | Leval | ▼ | No Format Set | Format... ▼
Replace with: | Level | ▼ | No Format Set | Format... ▼

Within: Sheet ▼   ☐ Match case
Search: By Rows ▼   ☑ Match entire cell contents
Look in: Formulas ▼   Options <<

Replace All | Replace | Find All | Find Next | Close

5. Be sure to select the check boxes for any Find options (such as Match Case or Match Entire Cell Contents) that you might have selected originally or that will help your reversal take place. For example, if the Match Case check box wasn't selected the first time the Replace All command was used, selecting this check box for the reversal will narrow its results and fail to fix the cells that shouldn't have been originally replaced.

6. Use the Find Next and Replace (rather than Replace All) buttons to move through your worksheet and edit the cells that need fixing.

How WOULD you change all the *B*'s to *R*'s?

Replace All can be used safely if you set up your Find What and Replace With entries properly. To use the serial number change as an example, imagine that all serial numbers starting with *B* have to change so that they start with *R* due to changes in product labeling. The thought of changing every *B* manually and perhaps missing at least one is daunting, so you decide to use Replace All—but you need to set it up to work properly.

To set up Replace All, start by selecting the column (for example, the Serial Number column) so that no other entries that start with the letter *B* are edited. On the Edit menu, click Replace, and in the Find What box, type the letter *B*. In the Replace With box, type the letter *R*. Select the Match Case check box so that capital or lowercase letters in the middle of words aren't affected, and then click Replace All. The replacements will be made only in the column you selected.

The Find command doesn't allow me to search by example

Source of the problem

You used a data entry form to build your database, and now you'd like to use it to scroll through your records, looking (or rather, allowing Excel to look) for records that have one or more common elements. Although you search through a single sheet or an entire workbook for a specific letter, word, or number, Excel might find lots of cells that contain what you're looking for if the Find What value is too broad or if it's searching everywhere and not just in certain fields (or columns) in your database. If you focus the Find command on a particular field, you'll find only those records with that entry in that particular field—you can't search for multiple entries in multiple fields in one Find session.

Although I might sound like I'm saying the Find tool isn't terribly useful, that's not my goal—Find is a very useful tool. It's just a little limiting if you want to find one particular record that has very specific entries in two or more fields.

For a more sophisticated level of searching, known in database terminology as *searching by example*, you really need to use a form. Even if you didn't use a form to enter your list's records, a form exists for your database, listing all the fields (your column labels) and allowing you to view each record individually in a Form dialog box. The form also allows you to enter example data into specific fields and view only the records that match the example field-for-field. It's a rather handy little device! ▶

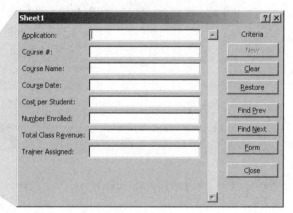

How to fix it

1. Click any cell that contains data in your list.

2. On the Data menu, click Form. The Form dialog box opens, displaying boxes for all of your database fields.

3. Click the Criteria button. The boxes for the fields are cleared so you can enter example data for each field on which you wish to search.

Searching for data

4. Enter the example data in the fields you want to use for the search. Using a database of courses as an example, you could enter a Course # (or a portion thereof), and a price in the Cost Per Student field to list all the classes with the same or similar course code (in our example, FP restricts the list to FrontPage courses) that have a certain cost. ▶

5. Click either the Find Next or Find Prev button to view the first record that meets your criteria.

6. Click either the Find Next or Find Prev button to view the rest of the records that meet your criteria, one click at a time. When you've seen them all, your computer will prompt you to indicate that there are no more records that meet your criteria.

My criteria are greater than your criteria

When you use the form to search for records, you can enter search operators, such as > for greater than, < for less than, and = for equals. This obviously works well for numbers, dates, and times. If you use it for fields that contain text, it works alphabetically, so >A means words starting with the letters B, C, D, and so on, but not A; and >M means words starting with the letters N, O, P, and so on, but not M. Got it?

You can also use the asterisk to indicate "anything." Using the course database as an example, to find all the classes pertaining to Excel, you could type E* in the Application or Course Name box and click Find Next or Find Prev to see all the records for classes starting with the letter E. What good is this? It saves you typing the whole word *Excel*, and for fields with long, possibly hard-to-spell names or terms in them, it's very convenient.

> **Tip**
>
> There's one problem with using a form to look for records. It's a tiny problem, not to be confused with a huge, unacceptably horrible problem. If none of your records meet the criteria you've set, the first record in the database will appear in the form as soon as you click the Find Next or Find Prev button. If you're not paying attention, you might think that the displayed record is the right result of your search.

> **Tip**
>
> When searching fields that contain currency-formatted numbers, there's no need to type the dollar signs or commas. For example, to see all the courses with Total Class Revenue in excess of $1,800, you'd type >1800 in the field's box.

I don't know how the new Search pane works

Source of the problem

You've noticed the new Task Pane that comes with Microsoft Office XP—the first time you opened Excel 2002 (or any other application in the suite), you probably noticed it there on the right side of the application window. You probably closed it right away, too. It pops up on its own when you issue certain commands (like File, New), but the rest of the time it just takes up valuable workspace real estate.

So what's it good for? Well, one version of this pane is for searching for documents, and it can help you search for files that contain certain text, which can help you locate a database that contains a specific record. It won't help you search an open database for a record you know is in that database, but if you have multiple databases (or any other sort of worksheet) and you can't find which one contains a particular bit of content, the Search version of the Task Pane can be rather handy. ►

The key, then, to using this version of the Task Pane is to display it and to navigate its features to perform a successful search. Once you understand how it works, you'll be able to use it in Excel, Microsoft Word, and Microsoft PowerPoint to find specific files based on their content.

How to fix it

It's not so much fixing it as understanding how it works. To display and use the Search pane, follow these steps:

1. If the Task Pane isn't currently displayed, choose Task Pane from the View menu. The pane appears on the right side of the open workbook window. ►

2. Click the Other Task Panes triangle on the right side of the top border of the pane and choose Search from the resulting menu. ▶

3. In the resulting Search pane, type the data you wish to find in the Search Text box. This can be someone's name if you're looking for a record in your name and address database, or a product number listed in an inventory database. It can be anything you know to be in one of your workbooks, whether that workbook is open now or not.

4. Click the first drop-down list (Selected Locations) in the Search In section of the dialog box. This allows you to choose which drives and folders will be searched. By default, the search will encompass every folder on every drive in your computer. To restrict the search to specific areas, remove the checkmarks in the boxes next to drives and folders you know don't contain the missing data.

5. Click the Selected File Types drop-down list and choose which types of files to look for. By default, all Office file types will be included in the search. Again, use the check boxes to indicate which file types to search for. If you're looking solely for data in an Excel worksheet, make sure nothing but Excel Files is selected in the Office files category. ▶

6. When your search text, locations, and file types are set, click the Search button. The search may last several seconds—the length of time depends on how many workbooks you have in the folders you specified for the search.

7. When the search is complete, the list of files that contain the text you were looking for display in the pane. If the file isn't already open, double-click the file, and it opens in the Excel window. ▶

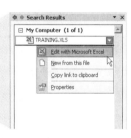

Now, sadly, the file won't open with the sought-after record highlighted. That would be very convenient, but it still remains for you to use the Find dialog box to search the now-open file for the record you seek. At least you know you're looking in the correct place though, right?

Tip

While the Search pane is open, the Find In This Document button at the foot of the pane will open the Find dialog box.

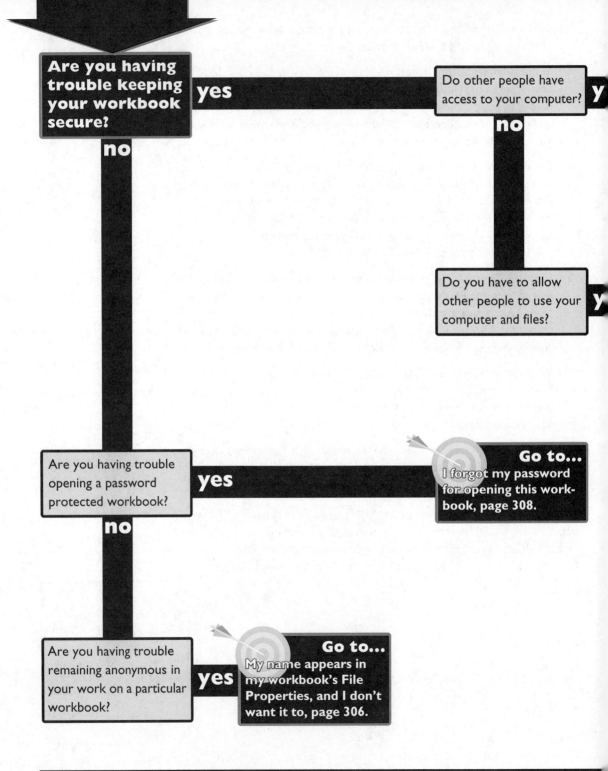

Are you having trouble keeping your workbook secure? yes

no

Do other people have access to your computer? **y**

no

Do you have to allow other people to use your computer and files? **y**

Are you having trouble opening a password protected workbook? yes

no

Go to...
I forgot my password for opening this workbook, page 308.

Are you having trouble remaining anonymous in your work on a particular workbook? yes

Go to...
My name appears in my workbook's File Properties, and I don't want it to, page 306.

Do you wish you could control access to your workbooks?

yes

Go to...
I want to keep people from opening my workbook, page 304.

Quick fix

If you can't keep people out of your files, you can at least keep a copy for yourself that no one can possibly edit or delete. Save the file to a network drive to which only you have access (if you're on a network), or save to diskette or zip disk. Keep the removable media with you, and take it with you when you go home at the end of the day. To keep the files separate, use different file names for your copy and the one that others need access to and that you therefore can't protect.

If your solution isn't here, check these related chapters:

- Entering data, page 108
- Saving, page 278

Or see the general troubleshooting tips on page xv.

I want to keep people from opening my workbook

Source of the problem

People can be a real pain, can't they? Taking forever to make left turns, reclining their seat on the airplane so that you spend an entire flight looking at their scalp, and opening your workbooks when you don't want them to. Well, I can't make anyone a better driver or teach traveler's etiquette to the masses, but I can help you keep other people's grimy paws out of your workbooks.

If you're reading this page out of curiosity and not because your own workbooks have, against your will, become public domain, you may be wondering why having others open your workbooks could be a problem. Consider these negative outcomes:

- The person who opens the workbook makes changes to the data that are incorrect or unwanted at the time.

- The person who opens the workbook sees confidential or sensitive data and is now in possession of information he or she shouldn't have.

- The person who opens the workbook saves it to a new location and now there are two versions that are difficult to tell apart.

- The person deletes the workbook because it doesn't seem useful.

Imagine your delight if any of these things happened to your workbooks! How can you keep these disasters from happening? By denying access to your workbooks through the use of passwords. You can lock people out of any workbook you create and/or require them to create a new version of the workbook (with a new name) if they do open it and make any changes.

Now, there are times when we need to work as part of a team, and you'll have to let others open and even edit the workbooks you create. If your workbook, for example, contains a sales report and you don't have the quotas for next month's sales, you may need someone else to either give you that information or enter it on his or her own. But you can prevent everyone but that person from opening the workbook with the aforementioned use of passwords and by using techniques covered in the chapters on security (protecting chart and worksheet data) and formatting text (preventing changes to worksheet format-ting). With these features, you can keep the one person who can open your workbook from mak-ing changes to any cells other than those for which he or she is directly responsible.

And don't you forget it!

When you set up a password, make sure it's something you'd never forget—like your PIN to access an ATM, your grandmother's maiden name, or your first dog's name. Of course you want the password to be easily remembered by you but not easily figured out by other people—your spouse or children's names aren't a good idea, and neither is your birthday.

How to fix it

To apply a password to your workbook so that only someone with the password can open it, follow these steps:

1. For a new or existing (previously saved) workbook, choose Save As from the File menu.

2. Click the Tools button at the top of the Save As dialog box and choose General Options from the menu.

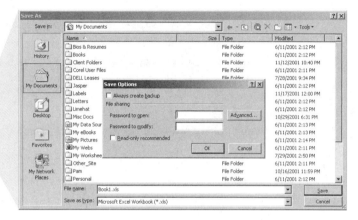

3. In the Save Options dialog box, type a password in the Password To Open text box. ▶

4. If you want those who open the file to have to supply a password before they save the file with any changes, type a password in the Password To Modify text box.

5. If you want the file to open as Read Only, check the Read Only Recommended check box. This will suggest to the person who opens it that they open it as Read Only, and if they comply, they'll have to save the file with a new name in order to save any of their changes or additions.

6. Click OK to apply your password(s) and then respond to the resulting prompts by retyping the passwords you assigned—a confirming box will appear for both the Open and Modify passwords if you set both up. ▶

7. Click OK to apply your confirming entry and then proceed to save your file with the name and in the location you desire.

Cryptography 101

If you want to use a word that's easy to remember but you think other people will be able to figure it out (like your spouse's name or the nickname everyone calls the boss behind her back), try this to disguise it:

Pick a number—three, for example—and apply it to each letter in the word or name. For example, if your spouse's name were Robert, the password would be UREHUW. How's that? If you take each letter in Robert's name and move forward three letters in the alphabet, you come up with this new word. As a result, if people try typing your spouse's name as the password, it won't work because they won't know your number "key" and won't be able to provide the actual password that will open the file.

My name appears in my workbook's File Properties, and I don't want it to

Source of the problem

On the face of it, having your name appear in a dialog box isn't such a big deal—who even looks at your file's properties? Well, other people do. People who open your file and people who simply right-click your file in a list of files through My Computer or the Windows Explorer. They can see your name, listed as the author of the workbook. ▶

So if someone looks at your file properties, they see your name. What's the problem with that? Well, maybe you aren't really the author. Or maybe you are and have no trouble accepting that role, but the name that appears in the Author box isn't yours and you don't want to imply that someone other than you created the workbook. If you want to change the author name in the File Properties dialog box, it's a simple process of retyping the name.

How to fix it

1. In the workbook in which you want to change or remove your name as it appears in the File Properties dialog box, choose Properties from the File menu.

2. Click the Summary tab to view the current author of the workbook.

3. Select the name that appears there and press Delete to get rid of it and leave no name in the box.

4. If you wish to change the name—perhaps removing your last name or changing your first name to a nickname or shorter version of the current name—select and then retype the author name as you want it to appear in this box, for this workbook, from now on. ▶

5. Click OK to save your changes.

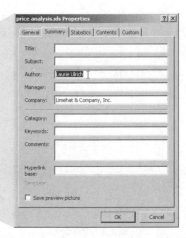

So what have you accomplished? You've deleted or changed the name in this box, and now if someone else opens the Properties dialog box for the workbook, they'll see the new name or no name at all. While you were there in the Properties dialog box, you could also have made the following Properties changes:

- Inserted a title for the workbook.

- Added a subject—typically, a word or phrase that describes the purpose of the workbook, such as "Budget" or "Expense Analysis."

- Typed a manager name, if someone other than the author is responsible for the content of the workbook and perhaps in charge of a team of contributors.

- Entered category, keyword, or description text (or all three) to enable you or someone else to search for the workbook based on these entries.

Keyword, schmeeword

So what's this keyword? How is it used? If you make use of this feature, typing keywords into the Properties dialog box for all your workbooks, you make it possible to search for workbooks based on those keywords—much the way you'd search the Web for sites that pertain to specific topics. When it comes to workbooks, keywords such "sales," "accounting," "data," and other words you think people would associate with the given workbook and its content are useful.

To search for workbooks based on the keyword or words typed into the Properties dialog box, follow these steps:

1. Click the Search button on the Standard toolbar and view the Basic Search task pane that appears. ▶

2. Click the Advanced Search link at the bottom of the pane.

3. Click the Property drop-down list and scroll to and select Keywords so that the search you do, based on criteria you enter, will look in the Keywords field for matches.

4. Type the keyword in the Value text box.

5. Click the Add button to add this criteria to the search. ▶

6. Click the Search button. Excel searches for workbooks with the keyword you entered, and your results appear in the large box below the Search button.

I forgot my password for opening this workbook

Source of the problem

Well, this is a big problem. When you read the next couple of sentences, you may want to grab some of your hair and... no, don't do that. Hey, it's only a workbook—but one that you can now forget all about using because you forgot the password. Remember on page 304 when I said that you wanted to pick a password that's really easy to remember? This is why. Because if you forget your password, you can't open the workbook. Ever again. ▶

Okay, you've noticed that the next heading on this page is "How to fix it," so you're thinking there must be a way around this apparently hard and fast rule—no password, no opening the secured file. I'm sorry to tell you that as you read on, the "fix" is more preventative than restorative. I won't be telling you a way to hack your password from some encrypted file. I won't, because I can't, because the only way to open a file that has a password is to know the correct password.

> **Microsoft Excel**
>
> ⚠ The password you supplied is not correct. Verify that the CAPS LOCK key is off and be sure to use the correct capitalization.
>
> OK

How to fix it

As I said, this solution is more about prevention than cure. If you've password-protected a file to prevent people opening it and now you're unable to open it because you forget the password, you will want to adopt some or all of these behaviors to prevent (yes, that word again) this from happening again. If you're reading this because you really can't open a file and you really can't remember the password, I believe I have your undivided attention when I suggest:

- Always assign passwords that you could never forget, other than if you suffer from amnesia. These include your mother's maiden name, the name of your first pet, the name of your favorite teacher in college. You don't want to go with things that are so obvious that other people (you know, the people you're trying to keep out of your file) will be able to figure out the password, but you want the word to be something that would never slip your mind.

- Write your passwords down. Now this probably sounds stupid—you may be saying, "Yeah, but then people can find the list and then use the passwords to open my files!" and you'd be right. But not if you put the list somewhere that other people don't generally poke around—your wallet, your handbag, or somewhere else that your coworkers don't generally look. If you do choose to write your passwords down, it might be a good idea to choose completely unique passwords—in the event someone *does* find your written list, you wouldn't want to have inadvertently given them your ATM password or the password for your voicemail box.

- Use a small group of passwords all the time. This, too, might sound like an insecure security method—if someone figures out one of those passwords, that person can get into more than one of your files. If you use a group of no more than four different passwords all the time, however, this makes it a challenge for people to guess which one you're using, yet you only have three possible duds when you're typing in the password yourself.

When in doubt, duplicate

Are you absolutely sure you're going to forget your password? Have you done it so many times that you feel like it's hopeless, even using allegedly unforgettable words and numbers and having cheat-sheets around? Then the answer to your dilemma may lie in duplication. If there's a workbook that's so important that you can't risk losing access to it by forgetting your password, and the workbook is also so important that you can't let others open it (perhaps a workbook that contains people's salary data or the notes or ratings from employee reviews), then make a duplicate of the workbook you're protecting with a password and don't password-protect the duplicate.

Of course this means that the duplicate is vulnerable—people can find it and open it. But they're not likely to do so if you name it something that belies what it really contains. A database of sensitive employee data called "Salaries and Ratings.xls" is going to pique people's interest if

they see it in a folder on the network or listed in the Windows Explorer window open on your desktop. Unsavory types may try to hack their way in, attempting to guess your password. If, however, you name the duplicate file "Car Repair History," no one but your mechanic will care to crack open the file. ▶

Another solution? Keep the duplicate on floppy disk, Zip disk, or CD; keep that item in your briefcase; and keep your brief-case locked.

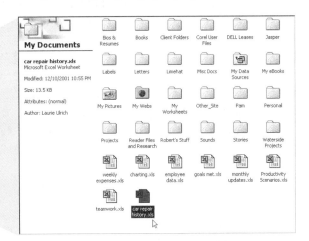

Hide in plain site

Hide your password list (the three or four passwords you use all the time) somewhere that no one would ever suspect. For example, tack what looks like a phone message to your bulletin board or write an appointment in your calendar with a sentence such as "Mr. Talbot called about Bingo, call him back at 215-555-3498." This sentence reminds you that your favorite teacher was Mr. Talbot, your first dog's name was Bingo, your nephew's birth date is March 4, 1998 (3/4/98), and that these are the passwords to try should you forget which password you assigned to the file.

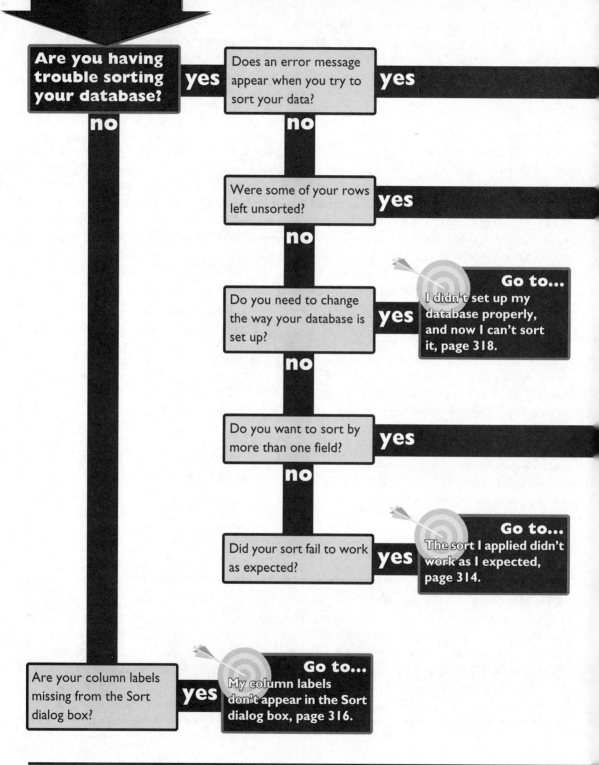

Are you having trouble sorting your database?

yes → Does an error message appear when you try to sort your data?

yes →

no ↓

Were some of your rows left unsorted?

yes →

no ↓

Do you need to change the way your database is set up?

yes → **Go to...** I didn't set up my database properly, and now I can't sort it, page 318.

no ↓

Do you want to sort by more than one field?

yes →

no ↓

Did your sort fail to work as expected?

yes → **Go to...** The sort I applied didn't work as I expected, page 314.

no ↓

Are your column labels missing from the Sort dialog box?

yes → **Go to...** My column labels don't appear in the Sort dialog box, page 316.

Sorting data

Quick fix

If you get an error message after attempting to sort, it's usually because Microsoft Excel doesn't see your worksheet content as a database. In order for a worksheet to be considered a database, it must have two or more rows with common content in a series of columns. Check to make sure that your worksheet is set up properly to function as a database, and then click in a single cell within that data. Then try your Sort again!

Quick fix

If only a portion of your database was sorted, it's either due to a blank row within your rows of data, or because you had a range of records selected before you performed the sort. Delete any blank rows (you can have blank fields in any row, but no entirely blank rows), and make sure that you have no block of cells selected before issuing the Sort command from the Data menu or using the Sort Ascending or Sort Descending buttons on the toolbar.

Go to...

I'm not sure how to sort my database by more than one field, page 312.

If your solution isn't here, check these related chapters:

● Filtering records, page 136

● Searching for data, page 290

Or see the general troubleshooting tips on page xv.

I'm not sure how to sort my database by more than one field

Source of the problem

A quick sort of your database by a single field (a column) is very simple—click any cell in that field and click the Sort Ascending or Sort Descending button. Done. But what if you want to do a more complex sort? One that puts the database in order by two or more fields so that you can, for example, see a list of upcoming courses by topic and then, within those topic groups, by date? You can't do it with the Sort buttons on the toolbar, because after you've sorted by one field, sorting by another throws out the first sort in favor of the second. If, for example, you sort by course topic and then by date, the database ends up in date order, with no regard for the topic.

What can you do? Microsoft Excel offers a Sort dialog box that allows you to sort your database by up to three fields. Only three? Yes, only three. That might sound limiting, but for the type of databases that are stored in Excel (or that should be stored in Excel), three is generally plenty. If your database is so complex that you wish you could sort by five or six different fields, you probably want to use Microsoft Access, if only for the sorting capabilities.

> **Tip**
>
> Sort an Excel database in Access? Absolutely. Check out "Exporting and importing" on page 120. You can paste your Excel database in an empty Access data table and then use the Access tools to sort by as many fields as you have in the database.

How to fix it

1. Click any single cell in the database.

2. On the Data menu, click Sort. The Sort dialog box appears, showing three possible sorting levels: Sort By, Then By, and another Then By. ▶

3. Click the Sort By drop-down arrow and select the field (column) you want to sort by first. (By default, Excel selects the database's first field, but you can change this if you want.)

4. Click either Ascending or Descending for the sort order.

5. Click the second field you want to sort by in the first Then By drop-down list and click either Ascending or Descending for this field.

6. If you need to, click a third field in the last Then By drop-down list and click either Ascending or Descending.

7. Click OK to perform the sort. The dialog box closes, and your database is sorted by the fields you chose, in the order you selected them. This list is sorted by Application, then by the cost of the course, then by the number of students enrolled. ▶

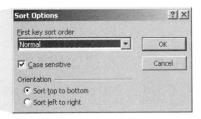

	A	B	C	D	E	F	G	H
1				**Course Enrollments**				
2								
3	Application	Course #	Course Name	Course Date	Cost per Student	Number Enrolled	Total Class Revenue	Trainer Assigned
4	Access	MSA1	Access Level 1	10/12/2001	$ 300.00	6	$ 1,800.00	Cook
5	Access	MSA2	Access Level 2	10/25/2001	$ 325.00	8	$ 2,600.00	Cook
6	Access	MSA3	Access Level 3	10/30/2001	$ 350.00	8	$ 2,800.00	Cook
7	Access	MSAD1	Access Application Development	11/10/2001	$ 400.00	4	$ 1,600.00	Moore
8	Excel	MSE1	Excel Level 1	10/8/2001	$ 300.00	10	$ 3,000.00	Fuller
9	Excel	MSE2	Excel Level 2	10/20/2001	$ 325.00	7	$ 2,275.00	Elmaleh
10	Excel	MSE3	Excel Level 3	11/5/2001	$ 350.00	9	$ 3,150.00	Corson
11	FrontPage	FPWD1	Web Design w/FrontPage, lev 1	11/5/2001	$ 400.00	12	$ 4,800.00	Fuller
12	FrontPage	FPWD2	Web Design w/FrontPage, lev 2	11/15/2001	$ 500.00	12	$ 6,000.00	Fuller
13	PowerPoint	MSP1	PowerPoint Level 1	10/15/2001	$ 300.00	6	$ 1,800.00	Talbot
14	PowerPoint	MSP2	PowerPoint Level 2	10/30/2001	$ 350.00	8	$ 2,800.00	Talbot
15	Publisher	MSPUB	Publisher Basics	11/13/2001	$ 350.00	8	$ 2,800.00	Kline
16	Windows	MSWU	Windows 98 User	11/2/2001	$ 300.00	10	$ 3,000.00	Corson
17	Windows	MSNTA	Windows NT Administration	11/8/2001	$ 500.00	5	$ 2,500.00	Elmaleh
18	Word	MSW1	Word Level 1	10/5/2001	$ 300.00	9	$ 2,700.00	Talbot
19	Word	MSW2	Word Level 2	10/15/2001	$ 325.00	8	$ 2,600.00	Fuller
20	Word	MSW3	Word Level 3	11/1/2001	$ 350.00	12	$ 4,200.00	Kline
21					Total Revenue	142	$ 50,425.00	
22								

So what are those options about?

The Sort dialog box's Options button is used most often to allow you to do case-sensitive sorts. When placing items in order, items in lowercase should precede those in uppercase, if you're doing an ascending sort. The case of your worksheet content is ignored if you don't turn on this option, but if you need to take case into account as you perform the sort, click the Options button in the Sort dialog box and select the Case Sensitive check box. ▶

To proceed, click OK and then, in the Sort dialog box, set up your sort as needed. Click OK to perform the sort, and you'll see your lowercase items (if they're in a sorted field) appear first if you're sorting in ascending order, or last if you're sorting in descending order.

The sort I applied didn't work as I expected

Source of the problem

This raises the question, "What were you expecting?" If you were expecting the database to be placed in some alphabetical or numerical order and it didn't end up that way, the source of the problem could be that you were sorting on a single field (a column) in your database using the Sort Ascending or Sort Descending button on the toolbar, and you accidentally sorted a different field than the one you thought you had. Or perhaps you meant to sort in ascending order and clicked the Sort Descending button instead. If you were using the Sort command, you might have chosen a different field to sort by than you'd intended to use. And if you were sorting by more than one field, you might have chosen to sort them in the wrong order.

With this many variables, it makes sense to sit back and review exactly what it is you want to accomplish with your sort, which tools are the best to use to achieve that result, and how those tools are meant to be used. Then you can try again. If the sort you just did made a real mess of your records, click Undo to reverse whatever happened. You can also close the file without saving, if that won't lose any entries or edits you made since you last saved. Once you've decided what you want and have thought about how to get it, try your sort again.

How to fix it

1. Click any cell in the field you want to sort by. In this example, the active cell would cause the list to be sorted by the number of students enrolled. ▶

	A	B	C	D	E	F	G	H
1			Course Enrollments					
2								
3	Application	Course #	Course Name	Course Date	Cost per Student	Number Enrolled	Total Class Revenue	Trainer Assigned
4	Access	MSA1	Access Level 1	10/12/2001	$ 300.00	6	$ 1,800.00	Cook
5	Access	MSA2	Access Level 2	10/25/2001	$ 325.00	8	$ 2,600.00	Cook
6	Access	MSA3	Access Level 3	10/30/2001	$ 350.00	8	$ 2,800.00	Cook
7	Access	MSAD1	Access Application Development	11/10/2001	$ 400.00	4	$ 1,600.00	Moore
8	Excel	MSE1	Excel Level 1	10/8/2001	$ 300.00	10	$ 3,000.00	Fuller
9	Excel	MSE2	Excel Level 2	10/20/2001	$ 325.00	7	$ 2,275.00	Elmaleh
10	Excel	MSE3	Excel Level 3	11/5/2001	$ 350.00	9	$ 3,150.00	Corson
11	FrontPage	FPWD1	Web Design w/FrontPage, lev 1	11/5/2001	$ 400.00	12	$ 4,800.00	Fuller
12	FrontPage	FPWD2	Web Design w/FrontPage, lev 2	11/15/2001	$ 500.00	12	$ 6,000.00	Fuller
13	PowerPoint	MSP1	PowerPoint Level 1	10/15/2001	$ 300.00	6	$ 1,800.00	Talbot
14	PowerPoint	MSP2	PowerPoint Level 2	10/30/2001	$ 350.00	8	$ 2,800.00	Talbot
15	Publisher	MSPUB	Publisher Basics	11/13/2001	$ 350.00	8	$ 2,800.00	Kline
16	Windows	MSWU	Windows 98 User	11/2/2001	$ 300.00	10	$ 3,000.00	Corson
17	Windows	MSNTA	Windows NT Administration	11/8/2001	$ 500.00	5	$ 2,500.00	Elmaleh
18	Word	MSW1	Word Level 1	10/5/2001	$ 300.00	9	$ 2,700.00	Talbot
19	Word	MSW2	Word Level 2	10/15/2001	$ 325.00	8	$ 2,600.00	Fuller
20	Word	MSW3	Word Level 3	11/1/2001	$ 350.00	12	$ 4,200.00	Kline
21					Total Revenue	142	$ 50,425.00	
22								

Tip

If your numerical data contains negative numbers, an ascending sort will put those numbers first in the database, followed by records with a zero in the sorted field, followed by positive numbers. If the field by which you're sorting has blank cells, those records will appear last in an ascending sort.

2. Click the Sort Ascending button on the Standard toolbar. The database should be placed in order by the field containing the active cell, in A–Z order if the content is text. If the field contains numerical content or if the database is in numerical order, lowest numbers will appear first.

If the problem arose from a multiple-field sort, you need to think about your fields and what data they contain, and let that guide your sort order. Here are some guidelines:

● For the first sorted field, choose a field that has the most duplicate entries in it. In a list of computer course offerings, the Application field would contain a lot of duplicates. Why are duplicates important? Because sorting by a field with few unique entries turns the database into a series of groups, and then the next fields you sort by will put the records in those groups in order. This database is sorted by the Application field, creating alphabetized groups. ▶

	A	B	C	D	E	F	G	H
1			Course Enrollments					
2								
3	Application	Course #	Course Name	Course Date	Cost per Student	Number Enrolled	Total Class Revenue	Trainer Assigned
4	Access	MSAD1	Access Application Development	11/10/2001	$ 400.00	4	$ 1,600.00	Moore
5	Access	MSA1	Access Level 1	10/12/2001	$ 300.00	6	$ 1,800.00	Cook
6	Access	MSA2	Access Level 2	10/25/2001	$ 325.00	8	$ 2,600.00	Cook
7	Access	MSA3	Access Level 3	10/30/2001	$ 350.00	8	$ 2,800.00	Cook
8	Excel	MSE2	Excel Level 2	10/20/2001	$ 325.00	7	$ 2,275.00	Elmaleh
9	Excel	MSE3	Excel Level 3	11/5/2001	$ 350.00	9	$ 3,150.00	Corson
10	Excel	MSE1	Excel Level 1	10/8/2001	$ 300.00	10	$ 3,000.00	Fuller
11	FrontPage	FPWD1	Web Design w/FrontPage, lev 1	11/5/2001	$ 400.00	12	$ 4,800.00	Fuller
12	FrontPage	FPWD2	Web Design w/FrontPage, lev 2	11/15/2001	$ 500.00	12	$ 6,000.00	Fuller
13	PowerPoint	MSP1	PowerPoint Level 1	10/15/2001	$ 300.00	6	$ 1,800.00	Talbot
14	PowerPoint	MSP2	PowerPoint Level 2	10/30/2001	$ 350.00	8	$ 2,800.00	Talbot
15	Publisher	MSPUB	Publisher Basics	11/13/2001	$ 350.00	8	$ 2,800.00	Kline
16	Windows	MSNTA	Windows NT Administration	11/8/2001	$ 500.00	5	$ 2,500.00	Elmaleh
17	Windows	MSWU	Windows 98 User	11/2/2001	$ 300.00	10	$ 3,000.00	Corson
18	Word	MSW2	Word Level 2	10/15/2001	$ 325.00	8	$ 2,600.00	Fuller
19	Word	MSW1	Word Level 1	10/5/2001	$ 300.00	9	$ 2,700.00	Talbot
20	Word	MSW3	Word Level 3	11/1/2001	$ 350.00	12	$ 4,200.00	Kline
21					Total Revenue	142	$ 50,425.00	
22								

● For the second sorted field, choose a field with fewer possible duplicates. Again, think of the course enrollment database. After sorting by the Application field, sorting by the Trainer Assigned field would be good, because there could be some duplicate trainers per application, but there might not be. If you're only sorting by two fields, Number Enrolled is another good choice.

● For the third sorted field, choose a field that's likely to be all unique entries, such as Course Number for the course enrollment list shown or Last Name for an employee database.

When performing a multiple-field sort, click any cell in your database, click Sort on the Data menu, select your fields as just described, and then examine your selections in the Sort dialog box to make sure you've selected them in the right order—first field in the Sort By box, second in the first Then By box, and third in the last Then By box. After doing this check, click OK to perform the sort.

And for our next selection...

Be careful not to select any cell ranges before opening the Sort dialog box. If you select a series of rows, only those rows will be sorted. If you select a block of cells that is outside the range of cells that actually contain your data, Excel might not see your column labels, and they won't appear in the dialog box. In short, before a sort, click carefully in the database so that you're not misdirecting Excel as to which records or database you want to sort.

My column labels don't appear in the Sort dialog box

Source of the problem

By default, Excel recognizes the first row in a database (the column labels) as the field names—the names that identify the pieces of each record in the database. When you click Sort on the Data menu, those field names show up in the Sort dialog box so that you can choose which fields to sort your database by. There are situations, however, where Excel doesn't see the first row as your field names and instead offers Column A, Column B, and so on, as the field names. ▶

Why does this happen? If in your zeal to tell Excel which cells contain your database, you select a column that's not part of the database—such as column G when your database resides in only columns A through F—Excel won't see a field name in that column and therefore won't see your other field labels.

This is yet another case of "Doctor, it hurts when I go like that." The doctor responds, "Don't go like that." The key to letting Excel see your column labels is in not selecting any of the database prior to issuing the Sort command.

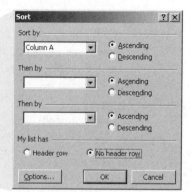

How to fix it

1. Click any cell in your database. Don't select any range of cells and don't click an empty cell outside of the range of records occupied by the data you want to sort.

2. On the Data menu, click Sort. The Sort dialog box appears, with one of your field names in the Sort box.

3. Click the Sort By drop-down arrow, click a field name to sort by a different field (if desired), and then click the Ascending or Descending option.

4. As needed, select sort fields in the two Then By drop-down lists. For both options, don't forget to click either the Ascending or Descending option.

5. Click OK to perform the sort.

> **Tip**
> If you sort your database while the generic field names (Column A, Column B, for example) are in the Sort By drop-down list, when your database is sorted, the real field names will be sorted in with the data. If you don't see your field names in the drop-down list, click Cancel.

Sorting data

A field by any other name

When you build your database, it's important to have field names for all of the columns that will contain data—don't leave any out. If you do, you'll run into a modified version of the problem of no field names appearing in the Sort dialog box. When one or more of your fields has no name (no column label), the Sort dialog box will list Column A, Column B, and so on, in the Sort By and Then By drop-down lists. If you click the Header Row option, Excel will say, "Ah ha! There they are!" and list the field names it sees in the top row. Except for the blank fields. Those will continue to appear in the list of field names as their column letters. ▶

If you select the Header Row option, you'll be able to sort your database without your field names being sorted in with the data, so you can complete the sorting process if this situation exists. However, it will be difficult to sort by any of the unnamed fields because you can't easily tell what kind of data the unnamed columns contain.

Tip

Clicking the Header Row option in the My List Has section of the Sort dialog box won't always make Excel see the field names in your database. If you click it and your field names don't appear in the Sort By drop-down list, click Cancel to get out of the dialog box and then click a single database cell before clicking Sort on the Data menu again.

This column heading is missing and appears as Column A in the Sort dialog box.

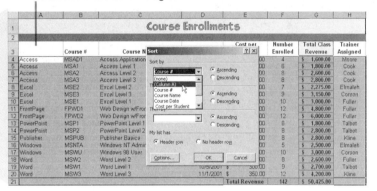

Tip

The Sort dialog box is a big part of the reason it's a good idea to keep your field names short. The Sort By and Then By drop-down lists don't show the full name of the field if the name exceeds 16 characters. Keep the names short and to the point so that no matter where you're seeing them, you can read most or all of the field names.

I didn't set up my database properly, and now I can't sort it

Source of the problem

You know the old saying, "Anything worth doing is worth doing right." Annoying when someone says this after you've done something wrong, isn't it? In this case, though, it's not so much that you've done something wrong as that you weren't aware of Excel's requirements for database structure and content. Some problems you might run into include:

- Your database won't sort at all—Excel throws an error message at you when you use the Sort buttons or issue the Sort command. The simple reason is likely that you're not in your database when you try to sort, and Excel can't see the database. So the simple solution is to click a cell within the database before trying to sort. If a single database cell is already selected, then the structure of your database is the culprit—a more complex problem.

- You're able to sort, but the sort comes out wrong. The problem lies either with your sort setup (maybe you asked Excel to sort by the wrong fields, or columns, or by the right fields but in the wrong order) or with the way your database is structured. Again, I'm using the S word— STRUCTURE. The way you set up your Excel database is key to it working properly. "Working properly" means that you are able to sort it, filter it, and use things like subtotal reports and PivotTables with it. (See "Filtering records" on page 136, "Subtotal reports" on page 336, and "PivotTables" on page 254.)

Assuming none of the easy solutions solved the problem, the solution to your sorting problem lies in fully understanding what Excel needs from you in terms of database layout and content. Once you have a sense of this, you can edit your database accordingly. Your future databases will fall together quickly and work seamlessly with whichever data command you choose to apply.

How to fix it

Excel databases have some very basic structural requirements—in fact, there are only two:

- There can be no blank rows between your column labels and the last record in your database. Don't skip a row, add visual space with blank rows, or manually insert a subtotal row at any point in the database. Blank rows throw off sorts and filters.

- There can be no blank columns between the first and the last columns in a database. If the first column in your database is B, and your database has seven fields, H has to be the last column— don't skip any columns, for any reason. To delete a blank column, select the column by clicking its heading. Then right-click the selected column and click **Delete** on the shortcut menu. ▶

In addition to these structural requirements, Excel has some database requirements for content:

- Don't leave any column labels blank. Every column in your database is a field, and every field must have a name.

- Don't leave any rows blank. Although you can have blank fields in a record, you can have no blank records. This includes deleting the content from a row in order to edit the record and accidentally leaving it blank. If you want to delete a record, select the row, right-click the selected row, and click Delete on the shortcut menu. The entire row will go away (and the content below it will move up to fill the empty spot), and you can properly sort the data as you want.

- Use consistent terminology. If you're listing a series of departments in an employee database, decide on the abbreviations you'll use right up front. Don't type "Mktg." in one record, and "Marketing" in another. Why? Because if you filter by department, the Marketing people will come before the Mktg. people, and if you're going to go on and do a subtotal report, that will be a problem.

If you stick to these very simple rules, you'll be able to easily sort your database, filter it, subtotal it, and turn it into a PivotTable as needed. If your database is in violation of any of these rules, you can fix it—add column labels where any are missing, delete blank rows, and delete blank columns. Go through and edit inconsistent spellings and abbreviations. After you've cleaned up your worksheet's structure and content, you'll be able to sort it properly, and any problems that do occur should be solved by the other solutions in this chapter!

Be a control freak

If you want to make sure no one enters "Mktg" in one record and "Marketing" in another (or any other undesirable combination of possible abbreviations), create some rules for the column containing the data that's likely to be entered inconsistently. Select the column(s) in question and choose Validation from the Data menu. In the resulting dialog box, choose List from the Allow drop-down list on the Settings tab; in the Source text box, type the list of acceptable entries for the column in question. You can use the Input Message and Error Alert tabs in the dialog box to create instructions for users and the chastisement they'll receive if they mess up.

Are you having trouble entering data with Microsoft Excel's Speech Recognition tools?

yes → Have you tried training the Speech Recognition tools?

yes → Are you having trouble with the Training process?

no

no →

Quick fix

Training is first and foremost in using Speech Recognition. Display the Speech Recognition toolbar (choose Speech from the Tools menu) and from the Tools button on the toolbar, choose Training to run through the training program. The program is quick, easy, and all you have to do is read to your computer so that it learns the sound of your voice and the way that you speak.

no

Does Excel misunderstand you when you speak? → **y**

no

Are there certain words that Excel doesn't recognize when you say them? → **y**

no (from first box) ↓

Are you having trouble issuing menu commands?

yes →

Quick fix

To issue menu commands (rather than dictate worksheet entries), switch to Voice Command using the Options button on the far right end of the Speech Recognition toolbar. If you're in Dictation mode, you're entering data—only Voice Command will access menus, commands, and options within dialog boxes.

Go to...
I can't seem to train Excel to understand my speech, page 322.

Go to...
When I dictate worksheet entries, the wrong data appears, page 324.

Go to...
I'm using new terminology, and the terms aren't being recognized, page 326.

If your solution isn't here, check these related chapters:

- Entering data, page 108
- Spelling, page 328

Or see the general troubleshooting tips on page xv.

I can't seem to train Excel to understand my speech

Source of the problem

You want to give your poor carpal-tunnel-syndrome-afflicted wrist a vacation and dictate the content of your worksheet. You also want to give menu commands, telling Microsoft Excel what to do. That's great—and Excel 2002 is poised to accommodate you with the speech recognition tools that come with it (as part of the Microsoft Office XP suite). Wait a minute, what's that? Excel needs to be trained to understand you, and the training isn't going well? You mean you can't get the training to work at all? That's annoying, but fixable. Check this list of possible causes, and then we'll see if we can get you up and speaking.

- Your computer's microphone is inadequate and Office XP has detected that fact.

- Your hands-free microphone isn't connected properly.

- Your environment is so noisy that the training application is picking up extraneous sounds in addition to your voice.

- Speaking to the training module makes you nervous, and you're not speaking in a normal, relaxed way.

Each of these problems has an obvious solution—from checking to see if your microphone is plugged into the right place to asking someone sitting nearby to clam up, please. Read on for more specific and somewhat higher-tech solutions.

How to fix it

- If your computer's built-in microphone isn't good enough, get an external microphone that is better. It shouldn't cost you very much to get a microphone that includes earphones and an adjustable mike to speak into. You always wanted to look like an air-traffic controller, didn't you?

- If you sound wooden and speak like a robot during the training period, the speech recognition software may not properly interpret your normal speaking voice when you use it under normal circumstances. Keep training and retraining until you feel comfortable enough to speak in a normal voice. Ask someone to tell you if you're still sounding wooden—you may not be able to judge.

I'm sorry, can you repeat that?

If you speak with a thick accent or have a speech impediment of some kind, don't give up. You can train Office XP (and therefore Excel) to understand you. As long as your speech is consistent—you say the same things the same way every time—you can train the software to interpret you accurately. The key lies in completing the basic training and doing all the extra training you can if you see that Excel (or any other application) isn't "getting you" all the time.

The rain in Spain falls mainly on the plain

So how does the training work? If you've never used speech recognition with Excel before, follow these steps:

1. Choose Tools, Speech, Speech Recognition. A prompt appears, indicating that you need to begin the training process and that you need to configure your microphone. ▶

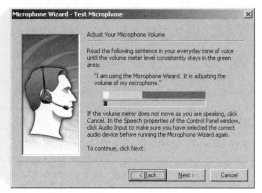

2. Click Next to start the Microphone Wizard, which will set up the speech recognition tools to work with the microphone that's installed in your computer or that you've plugged in externally. Generally, external mikes with headphones work better than yelling into the speaker on your laptop or the mike sitting on top of your monitor.

3. Click Next again and then read the line you're asked to read. You'll see a colored bar respond to the loudness of your voice. ▶

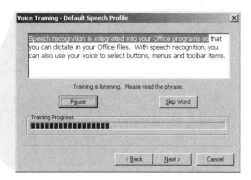

4. Click Next and then read the "papaya" sentence that tests for *p* sounds that are more like spitting or puffing. When it sounds good when played back to you, click Finish.

5. Now you'll click Next again to begin training. In the dialog boxes that follow, read the paragraphs, watching the text turn blue as your speech is recognized as matching the text. A progress bar shows your overall training progress, and new paragraphs appear as each one is successfully read. Click Next when you feel you've completed the training, and you can move on and complete the wizard. ▶

6. If you let the training paragraphs keep coming naturally and you wait until the Training Progress bar reaches the end, you'll be told you can always go back and retrain or train some more. Then your voice profile is created based on the training you've just performed. ▶

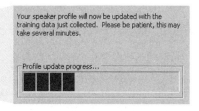

When I dictate worksheet entries, the wrong data appears

Source of the problem

Boy, that's annoying. You say *ten* and the word *tin* appears in the cell, or you say *sales quota* and *jails boating* is entered instead. What's the problem? You did the training, and the software seemed to recognize everything you said. Why doesn't it understand you now?

Speech recognition is a funny thing. It's very powerful in that it really can learn to understand anyone, even people with strong accents. It can be used to dictate file content as well as give menu and dialog box commands. But it can also be "distracted" easily, especially if the conditions you're working in are not identical (or quite similar) to those under which the training was performed.

What do I mean? Well, imagine that you trained the speech recognition software in your office, with the door shut, and you turned the ringer off on your phone, which also disables the intercom. Now, when you're working, your office door is open (people need to be able to stick their head in or talk to you from the outer office), your phone is ringing, and there's a lot of paging going on over the intercom system. Does it still seem like a mystery that your dictation isn't being correctly interpreted?

Another thing—were you completely honest when you said you did the training? Did you do *all* the training? Or did you read a few paragraphs and click Next to move on and have the software build a profile on your voice before the entire Training Progress was completed? Many people do this, thinking that if the software is recognizing your speech quickly and without your having to repeat anything, that whatever training you've done to that point is "enough." Well, it may be, but it probably isn't. Don't click Next too soon—let the progress bar make it to the end so that the software can base your voice profile on as much of your voice as possible. ▶

How to fix it

So it's clear you need to retrain. How do you do that? Follow these steps:

1. Display the Speech Recognition toolbar if it isn't already showing.

2. Click the Tools button and choose Training from the drop-down list. ▶

---

3. The training process will begin again, offering you a series of book excerpts to read and retrain the software to understand you. ▶

4. As the retraining progresses, keep reading the paragraphs that appear onscreen, allowing the progress bar to reach the right end of the box. Don't stop too early (by clicking Next to build a new profile) or you won't get the full benefit of additional training.

5. When you have completed the process, a new dialog box appears, indicating that your profile is being built. When that's complete, you're ready to start using speech recognition again. ▶

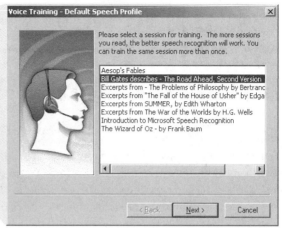

After this additional training, and if you're able to provide a dictation and command-giving environment close to that in which your training was performed, you will help the accuracy of the speech recognition software. No more jails boating!

And a one and a two...

While dictating your numerical entries for a worksheet, be careful to speak them exactly as you want them to appear. For example, if you say *A hundred dollars*, $100.00 won't appear in the cell. First of all, it's ONE hundred dollars, and you shouldn't mention the dollars if you don't want the word *dollars* to appear in the cell. Be specific, be clear, and leave out anything other than the numbers. When it comes to commas, dollar signs, decimal places, and other numerical formatting, don't refer to it while you're dictating the content of the cells. Save formatting for later, using the command mode to open menus and dialog boxes to change the appearance of content.

I'm using new terminology, and the terms aren't being recognized

Source of the problem

You're trying to build an inventory database, and the names of your products are eluding the speech-recognition software. When you say *Gizmo*, the words *gives more* or *kids mow* appear in the cell, and although it was amusing the first couple of times, it's not funny now that you realize that you'll have to type all the product names. It's not that there are that many of them that aren't actual words or phrases (the ones that are made from common words dictate just fine); it's just that you'll be using the odd names frequently in your worksheets, and it's a pain to have to type them. ▶

There's a solution to this problem, you'll be happy to hear. And it's a simple one that doctors, lawyers, and anyone else who uses esoteric terminology or "made up" product names will find easy to

	C8	▼		*fx* a per cut jam		
	A	B	C	D	E	F
1						
2			Product List			
3				Sold Last Year	Sold This Year	Difference
4			Orange Marmalade	534		
5			Raspberry Preserves	654		
6			Lemon Curd	267		
7			Strawberry Delight	982		
8			a per cut jam			
9						

use. When a word or phrase isn't recognized by Office's speech recognition software, you have to teach it—adding the word to the software's dictionary.

How to fix it

1. In the worksheet that's causing problems (or in any open worksheet), click the Tools button on the Speech Recognition toolbar.

2. From the drop-down list, choose Add/Delete Word(s).

3. In the resulting dialog box, type the word or phrase that the software doesn't currently recognize. You'll notice that the list below (the list of words in your Office dictionaries) moves to the first word beginning with the first letter of the word or phrase you typed. ▶

4. With your microphone on, click the Record Pronunciation button and say the word or phrase. The Record Pronunciation button is dimmed while the software "considers" your entry and its pronunciation.

5. As soon as the word is recognized, it appears in the list, and the button changes to Cancel Recording. If you need to say it again in order for the software to understand it and add it to the list, the Record Pronunciation button will become available again—click it and repeat the word until it's understood.

And what if I want to get rid of a word?

To delete a word from the dictionary, simply choose Add/Delete Word(s) from the Tools drop-down list (on the Speech Recognition toolbar, not the regular Tools menu) and click once on the word to be deleted. With the word highlighted, click the Delete button—all gone!

That's easy for you to say

As you view the list of words in the Add/Remove Word(s) dialog box, you can click on them and listen to the computer (in the form of Michelle or Michael, the two different "voices" available) speak the words. If you find one that's being pronounced incorrectly, you should retrain the software to say it correctly. Why? So that when you say it correctly, the speech recognition software recognizes what you've said and inserts the correct word.

If you're having trouble understanding the computer voice, you can tweak its speed and even change the gender of your computer's voice.
Follow these steps:

1. Click the Tools button on the Speech Recognition toolbar.

2. Choose Options from the drop list and view the Speech Properties dialog box. ▶

3. Click the Text To Speech tab and click the Voice Selection drop-down list to change from Michelle to Michael (or from Michael to Michelle).

4. Using the Voice Speed slider, drag the indicator toward Slow or Fast, depending on the effect you want to achieve. To test your results, click the Preview Voice button and hear the voice at the current speed.

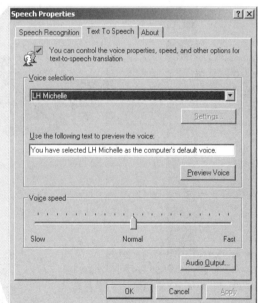

Once you've tinkered with the voice, you can go back to the Add/Delete Word(s) dialog box to listen to more words and fix the pronunciations or keep adding new words and phrases so the software will be ready for you the next time you use those names or terms.

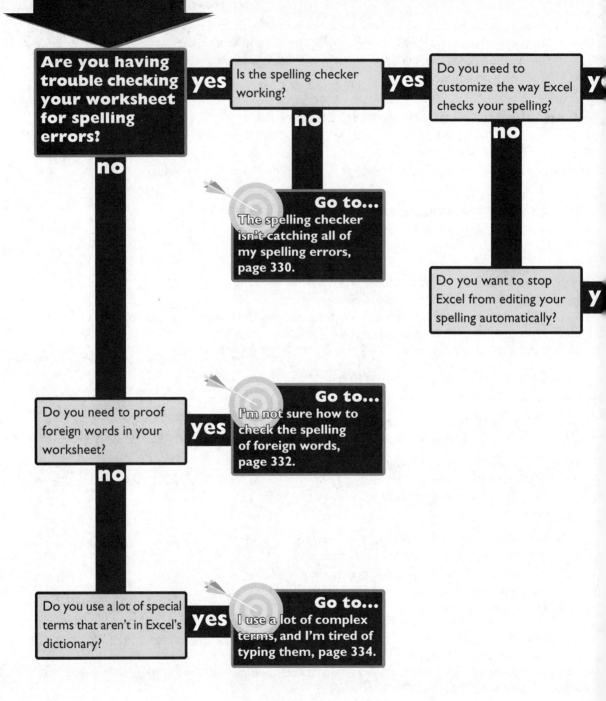

Are you having trouble checking your worksheet for spelling errors?

yes → Is the spelling checker working?

yes → Do you need to customize the way Excel checks your spelling? **y**

Is the spelling checker working? **no** →

Go to...
The spelling checker isn't catching all of my spelling errors, page 330.

Do you need to customize the way Excel checks your spelling? **no** →

Do you want to stop Excel from editing your spelling automatically? **y**

Are you having trouble... **no** →

Do you need to proof foreign words in your worksheet? **yes** →

Go to...
I'm not sure how to check the spelling of foreign words, page 332.

Do you need to proof foreign words in your worksheet? **no** →

Do you use a lot of special terms that aren't in Excel's dictionary? **yes** →

Go to...
I use a lot of complex terms, and I'm tired of typing them, page 334.

Quick fix

You can customize Excel's spell checking process by invoking some exceptions. For example, if you don't want text in CAPS to be checked, go to the Tools menu and choose Options. On the Spelling tab, place a checkmark next to the Ignore Words in UPPERCASE option. You'll see other adjustments you can make to the way Excel checks your spelling on this tab—click OK when you've completed your changes.

Quick fix

Turn off unwanted spelling corrections. Although Auto-Correct is extremely helpful, there are times you don't want it to help you so much. To turn off certain AutoCorrect actions, choose Tools, Auto-Correct Options, and remove the checkmark next to any options you want to turn off. Then scroll through the Replace and With columns to delete individual entries.

If your solution isn't here, check these related chapters:

- Entering data, page 108
- Naming cells, page 234
- Speech recognition, page 320

Or see the general trouble-shooting tips on page xv.

The spelling checker isn't catching all of my spelling errors

Source of the problem

Unlike in Microsoft Word, where your spelling errors are marked as soon as you make them, in Microsoft Excel you have to wait until you use the spelling checker to find your errors. So you click Spelling on the Tools menu (or click the Spelling button), and the Spelling dialog box appears. A few errors are presented, one by one, and you choose to change a spelling to a suggested alternative, ignore a perceived error (because it's an esoteric term or name, and you know it's spelled correctly), or add a word to the dictionary. Then, just when you think that your worksheet must be free of errors, you happen to spot some.

Why didn't Excel catch them? There are a few possibilities. Perhaps the misspelled word is in all capital letters, and you have your spelling checker set to ignore words in uppercase. Maybe a word that was spelled incorrectly was added to the dictionary, so now Excel thinks it's correct as is. Or perhaps the misspelled words were on another worksheet, and Excel checks the spelling on only the active sheet.

These are all fixable problems. You can turn off the option to ignore words in caps, and you can remove a misspelled word from the dictionary so that an accurate dictionary checks your spelling. If your spelling errors are in another sheet, you can use the spelling checker on that sheet or you can group the sheets before checking your spelling.

How to fix it

To adjust the way Excel checks the spelling in your active sheet (or in a group of sheets in the open workbook) so that words in uppercase are not ignored, follow these steps:

1. On the Tools menu, click Spelling.

2. In the Spelling dialog box, click the Options button, and in the resulting dialog box, clear the Ignore Words In UPPERCASE check box. As you continue to check your spelling, words in all capital letters won't be skipped. ▶

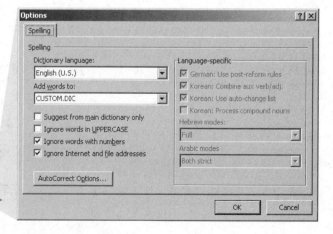

To remove a misspelled word from the dictionary, follow these steps:

1. Open Word to display a blank document.

2. On the Tools menu, click Options and then click the Spelling & Grammar tab.

3. Click the Custom Dictionaries button. ▶

4. Without clearing its check mark, select the CUSTOM.DIC dictionary. If you know your word was added to a different dictionary, select that one instead.

5. Click the Modify button and view the list of words, in a single column, that opens in a new dialog box.

6. Find the word you want to remove from the dictionary. Select it and press the Delete key. ▶

7. Click OK to close the Custom.Dic dialog box.

8. Click OK to close the Custom Dictionaries dialog box, and then click OK to exit the Options dialog box.

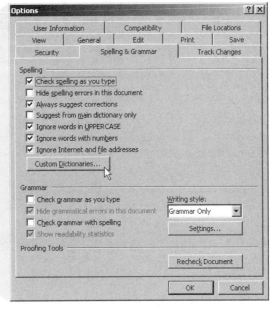

I'm not sure how to check the spelling of foreign words

Source of the problem

Suppose you work for a multinational company or belong to an organization that has members all over the world. Or suppose you run an international export/import business. No matter why you're sharing information with people around the world, your worksheets contain information provided or intended for use by people who don't speak your native language. You don't want to offend anyone by leaving misspellings in the worksheet, and you don't want the spelling checker to stop on the foreign words every time you check the spelling of the portions of the worksheet that are in your own language. What to do? ▶

In a standard installation of Excel 2002 (or Microsoft Office XP, if you installed the whole suite), English, Spanish, and French dictionaries are installed. You can install other dictionaries by making selections during installation. Once these dictionaries are installed, you can switch to them to check individual words, cell ranges, entire worksheets, or groups of sheets in a workbook. After checking the words, you can switch back to the dictionary of your native language and continue using that dictionary to check the spelling in the rest of your documents.

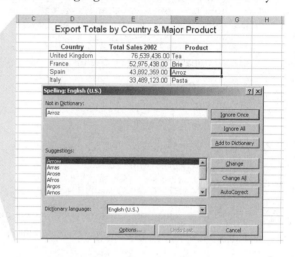

If the dictionary you need to use isn't installed, insert your Office CD-ROM and use the Add/Remove programs option in the Windows Control Panel to install the dictionary you need. The installation process will vary depending on the version of Office you're using.

Oui, oui, señor

There are subtle differences in the same language as it is used in different countries. When choosing a French dictionary, for example, be sure to select the right one—for France, Canada, or whichever French-speaking region your material is targeted to. When using an English dictionary, remember that English in Australia, Canada, the United Kingdom, and so on, is different than English in the United States. Choose the version of the language that matches the origin of the people who will be using your worksheet so as not to offend anyone with an inappropriate use or spelling of a word.

Spelling

How to fix it

If you want to check your spelling using a different language dictionary, try this technique:

1. In the worksheet containing the words you want to check, click Spelling on the Tools menu.

2. In the Spelling dialog box, click the Dictionary Language drop-down arrow and choose the language of the words you want to check. ▶

3. A prompt appears, indicating that you have to restart the spelling checker in order for the dictionary change to take effect. Click OK to close the prompt.

4. Close the Spelling dialog box so that you can restart the spelling checker.

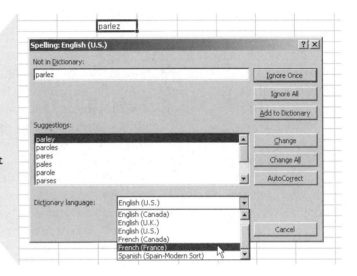

5. On the Tools menu, click Spelling again. Because you're checking spelling in a different language, words in your native language will probably be flagged as misspelled. Click Ignore to go past them—you can always check spelling in your own language later.

6. If foreign words come up as misspelled, use the Change or Change All commands to apply a suggested correction to the text or type the correction if you know it.

7. Move through the text, dealing with any other errors. Click OK when Excel tells you that the spelling checker has finished.

8. When all the words have been checked and corrected as needed, return to the dictionary of your own language by repeating steps 1 through 4.

I use a lot of complex terms, and I'm tired of typing them

Source of the problem

If your worksheets are loaded with legal, political, medical, scientific, or other types of specialized terminology, you probably do get very tired of typing complex words. Aside from the spelling checker flagging such words as misspelled (simply because they're not in Excel's very basic dictionary), there's the tedium of typing them over and over and dealing with the increased margin of error for typos that long or complex words present. I feel your pain.

What can you do? You can add these terms to Excel's list of AutoCorrect entries, turning them into automatic entries that you can trigger with an abbreviation. For example, if you need to type *gerrymandering* (a legal and political term), you could turn it into an AutoCorrect entry that is triggered by your typing *grym* whenever you want to insert the entire term. As soon as you type *grym*, Excel will turn it into *gerrymandering*. Need to type *pseudoephedrine*? Create an AutoCorrect entry that will turn *psud* into *pseudoephedrine* every time.

As long as the trigger (the characters you type that get changed into the term you want to appear in the worksheet) isn't a real word, which you'd want to be able to type without it turning into something else, the list of entries is as unlimited as the list of terms you're tired of typing.

How to fix it

1. In any open worksheet, click AutoCorrect Options on the Tools menu to display the AutoCorrect dialog box. ▶

2. In the Replace box, type the trigger that you want to turn into another word when you type it.

3. Press Tab to move your insertion point to the With box.

4. Type the replacement—the text that the trigger should turn into.

5. Click the Add button.

6. Repeat steps 2 through 5 for as many entries as you want to create.

7. Click OK to close the dialog box.

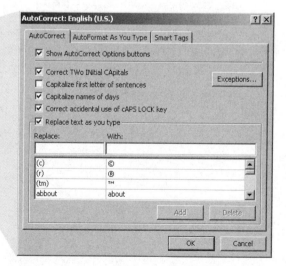

Pulling the trigger

AutoCorrect entries can outlive their usefulness. If a term, name, or phrase becomes unnecessary, you can get rid of it. When you want to remove an AutoCorrect entry you created, simply click AutoCorrect on the Tools menu and type the trigger in the Replace box. The entry appears in the With box. Click the Delete button in the dialog box, and the entry is deleted. Repeat these steps for any other entries you want to get rid of and then click OK to exit AutoCorrect.

If you make a mistake when creating an AutoCorrect entry, you can edit entries instead of deleting them. Click AutoCorrect on the Tools menu to open the AutoCorrect dialog box and type the trigger for the entry in question in the Replace box. When the With box content appears for that entry, make your edits to the trigger, the replacement text, or both. Click the Replace button to store the entry with the changes you've made and then click OK to close the AutoCorrect dialog box.

> **Tip**
>
> Another great use for AutoCorrect is for inserting names. Do you create reports that refer to various personnel within your organization? Store AutoCorrect entries for each person and have their initials turn into their name when inserted in a cell. For example, if you need to type *Alexander Nicodopolous* every week, store AJN (if his middle name is John), or AxN (if you don't know his middle name or he doesn't have one) as an AutoCorrect entry. Storing AN would be a bad idea, as it's a real word.

> **Tip**
>
> When you create Auto-Correct entries, the entries are available and functional in all the applications that support AutoCorrect. So, if you create an entry in Excel, you'll be able to use it in Word as well. This doubles the usefulness of your entries.

I hit the darn Caps Lock key again

If you've ever pressed the Caps Lock key by mistake, only to look up and see that what you've typed looks like a ransom note (with uppercase and lowercase text all jumbled up), you're not alone. I always hit Caps Lock when I'm reaching for the A key with my little finger. But I never end up with that ransom note look. Why? Because AutoCorrect fixes it.

Among other things, AutoCorrect fixes accidental Caps Lock use by changing all uppercase to lowercase (and vice versa) as soon as you type a word with a lowercase first letter and caps for the rest of the word. On the Tools menu, click AutoCorrect, and in the AutoCorrect dialog box, select the Correct Accidental Use Of Caps Lock Key check box, and then click OK.

AutoCorrect's fixes can save you from looking like you were typing with mittens on. For example, it can capitalize the names of days of the week and the first letters of sentences. It can also fix the kind of typo that occurs when you hold down the Shift key too long and end up with two initial capitals.

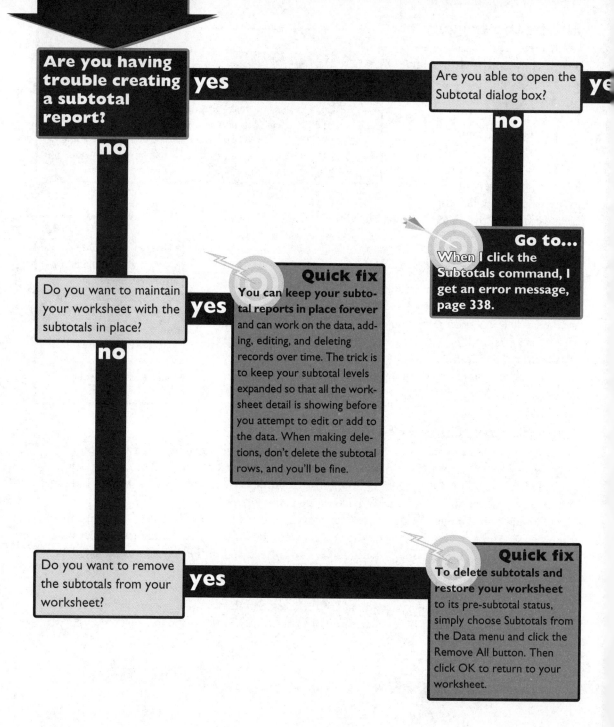

Are you having trouble creating a subtotal report?

yes → **Are you able to open the Subtotal dialog box?** → **ye**[s]

no

no

Do you want to maintain your worksheet with the subtotals in place?

yes →

Quick fix

You can keep your subtotal reports in place forever and can work on the data, adding, editing, and deleting records over time. The trick is to keep your subtotal levels expanded so that all the worksheet detail is showing before you attempt to edit or add to the data. When making deletions, don't delete the subtotal rows, and you'll be fine.

Go to...

When I click the Subtotals command, I get an error message, page 338.

no

Do you want to remove the subtotals from your worksheet?

yes →

Quick fix

To delete subtotals and restore your worksheet to its pre-subtotal status, simply choose Subtotals from the Data menu and click the Remove All button. Then click OK to return to your worksheet.

Subtotal reports

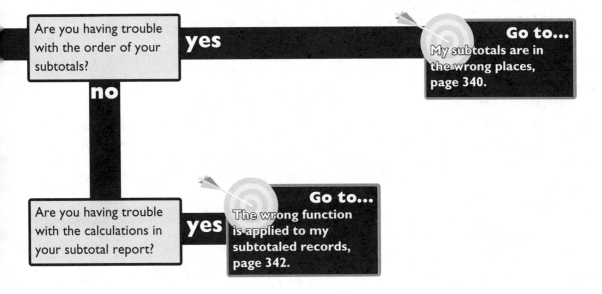

Are you having trouble with the order of your subtotals?

yes → **Go to...** My subtotals are in the wrong places, page 340.

no

Are you having trouble with the calculations in your subtotal report?

yes → **Go to...** The wrong function is applied to my subtotaled records, page 342.

If your solution isn't here, check these related chapters:

- Entering data, page 108
- Functions, page 192
- Sorting data, page 310

Or see the general trouble-shooting tips on page xv.

When I click the Subtotals command, I get an error message

Source of the problem

In order to use Microsoft Excel's Subtotals feature, you need a list of records called a *database*. If you have such a database, you need to select a single cell within it, not a range of cells, when you click Subtotals on the Data menu. If the selected cell isn't in your database, or if you have a range of cells or a series of rows or columns within the database selected at the time you click the command, you'll receive one of three error messages:

- If you have a range (as few as two cells) selected, Excel tells you that it can't detect which row in your database contains column labels.

- If you have a series of rows (not including row 1) selected, Excel tells you that it found a row of cells above the selection and asks you to verify that they're your column labels. ▶

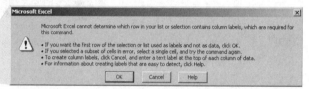

- If you're in a cell outside of the database, Excel tells you that no database was found. This error also appears if your worksheet contains no database at all.

So the cause of your error message is either that no database exists (because you don't have a database of identically structured rows in your worksheet) or that you had a range of cells or rows selected before you issued the Subtotals command. The solution? Make sure your worksheet contains the right kind of database to be subtotaled and that only a single cell within that data is active when you click Subtotals on the Data menu.

How to fix it

To make sure your worksheet has the kind of content that lends itself to the process of creating a subtotal report, keep in mind this list of requirements:

- Your database should contain at least three rows—one that contains your column labels and at least two rows of data.

- Your database shouldn't contain blank rows, either between the column labels and the data or between rows of data.

● Your database shouldn't contain blank columns between the first column in the database and the last. For example, if your database uses columns A through H, columns B, C, D, E, F, G, and H must contain labels. There can be blank cells in the columns in each of your rows, but the columns must have labels. ▶

That's a rather short list. And it's the same list of requirements that a database must meet in order to be sorted or filtered using either the AutoFilter or the Advanced Filter feature. (You access both features by pointing to Filter on the Data menu.) If you adhere to these requirements, you should have no problem creating a subtotal report for your database.

	Last Name	First Name	Department	Date Hired	Current Salary	Bonus %	Insurance Y/N	Insurance Carrier
	Employee Data							
	Chambers	Rosemary	Accounting	11/15/1996	$ 65,500.00	5.7%	Y	HMO
	Patrick	Kaitlin	Accounting	9/23/1995	$ 62,500.00	5.8%	N	None
	Freifeld	Iris	Accounting	8/3/1993	$ 78,500.00	6.2%	Y	HMO
	Balsamo	Anthony	Administration	2/27/1997	$ 74,325.00	6.7%	N	None
	Geiger	Mary	Administration	4/30/1992	$ 63,250.00	6.5%	Y	HMO
	Lambert	Harry	Administration	2/15/1998	$ 62,500.00	7.0%	Y	BCBS
	Elmaleh	Miriam	Human Resources	8/24/1995	$ 72,250.00	5.0%	N	None
	Ulrich	Lillie	Human Resources	12/15/1992	$ 73,000.00	5.5%	Y	HMO
	Zerbe	Robert	Human Resources	11/27/1993	$ 75,650.00	6.3%	Y	BCBS
	Fox	Seymour	Marketing	7/15/1993	$ 65,500.00	6.0%	Y	BCBS
	Kline	Desiree	Marketing	3/15/1997	$ 68,500.00	7.2%	Y	BCBS
	Miller	David	Marketing	9/24/1995	$ 62,500.00	5.0%	N	None
	Talbot	Ann	Marketing	6/7/1997	$ 65,000.00	5.0%	Y	BCBS
	Balinski	Joseph	Sales	9/2/1989	$ 68,500.00	6.8%	Y	HMO
	Frankenfield	Daniel	Sales	5/25/1992	$ 78,500.00	6.8%	Y	HMO
	Fuller	Robert	Sales	11/18/1995	$ 78,500.00	6.0%	Y	HMO
	Maurone	Richard	Sales	6/13/1999	$ 76,000.00	6.5%	Y	BCBS
	Mermelstein	David	Sales	10/4/1993	$ 76,500.00	6.2%	Y	BCBS
	Pederzani	Bruce	Sales	1/3/1995	$ 75,000.00	6.2%	Y	BCBS
	Shuster	Merrick	Sales	4/30/1995	$ 75,500.00	6.5%	N	None

Be a data pack rat

Your database's power is in the data you choose to store in it. The more information you store, the more data you can use, and the more uses you'll have for your data.

Now that's not saying sumthing

In order for a subtotal report to have some value, some numerical data must be included—preferably data that can be summed or averaged to derive some useful information. Otherwise, all you can do is perform a count of items in subtotaled groups, and although that can be useful, it's just the tip of the iceberg in terms of what subtotal reports can tell you about your data.

This is certainly true when it comes to using the Subtotals feature—the more data you maintain in your database, the more sorting options you have for placing the database in ordered groups, and the more analysis you can do with subtotals.

For example, if you're keeping an employee database, don't just keep names and social security numbers—keep track of which department employees are in, when they were hired, how many vacation days they have. You'll have that much more information to sort by and subtotal to show how many people are in each department, which departments keep employees the longest, and, if you're keeping salary information, what the cost of running each department is.

My subtotals are in the wrong places

Source of the problem

When you create a subtotal report, you can choose where the subtotals will appear by choosing which fields to subtotal. Typically, these are points in the worksheet where groups have been created by sorting data by fields that contain a lot of common content, such as a list of employees sorted by their departments. The sorting you do prior to creating the subtotals (or having Excel create them for you) controls the effective placement of your subtotals, and that can make or break your subtotal report's usefulness. If you're finding that the subtotals in your report aren't where you want them, the problem lies with the setup procedure you used.

In this example, a subtotal report is applied to the Department field but it should have been applied to the Current Salary field for a more useful report.

To solve the problem, simply remove the subtotals and start again, paying close attention to the fields you choose to subtotal. Do you have to remove the current subtotals? Well, strictly speaking, no, but if the ones that are there are in the

	Last Name	First Name	Department	Date Hired	Current Salary	Bonus %	Insurance Y/N	Insurance Carrier
1	Employee Data							
3	Last Name	First Name	Department	Date Hired	Current Salary	Bonus %	Insurance Y/N	Insurance Carrier
4	Chambers	Rosemary	Accounting	11/15/1996	$ 65,500.00	5.7%	Y	HMO
5	Patrick	Kaitlin	Accounting	9/23/1995	$ 62,500.00	5.8%	N	None
6	Freifeld	Iris	Accounting	8/3/1993	$ 78,500.00	6.2%	Y	HMO
7			Accounting Total		0			
8	Balsamo	Anthony	Administration	2/27/1997	$ 74,325.00	6.7%	N	None
9	Geiger	Mary	Administration	4/30/1992	$ 63,250.00	6.5%	Y	HMO
10	Lambert	Harry	Administration	2/15/1998	$ 62,500.00	7.0%	Y	BCBS
11			Administration Total		0			
12	Elmaleh	Miriam	Human Resources	8/24/1995	$ 72,250.00	5.0%	N	None
13	Ulrich	Lillie	Human Resources	12/15/1992	$ 73,000.00	5.5%	Y	HMO
14	Zerbe	Robert	Human Resources	11/27/1993	$ 75,650.00	6.3%	Y	BCBS
15			Human Resources Total		0			
16	Fox	Seymour	Marketing	7/15/1993	$ 65,500.00	6.0%	Y	BCBS
17	Kline	Desiree	Marketing	3/15/1997	$ 68,500.00	7.2%	Y	BCBS
18	Miller	David	Marketing	9/24/1995	$ 62,500.00	5.0%	N	None
19	Talbot	Ann	Marketing	6/7/1997	$ 65,000.00	5.0%	Y	BCBS
20			Marketing Total		0			
21	Balinski	Joseph	Sales	9/2/1989	$ 68,500.00	6.8%	Y	HMO
22	Frankenfield	Daniel	Sales	5/25/1992	$ 78,500.00	6.8%	Y	HMO
23	Fuller	Robert	Sales	11/18/1995	$ 78,500.00	6.0%	Y	HMO
24	Maurone	Richard	Sales	6/13/1999	$ 76,000.00	6.5%	Y	BCBS
25	Mermelstein	David	Sales	10/4/1993	$ 76,500.00	6.2%	Y	BCBS
26	Pederzani	Bruce	Sales	1/3/1995	$ 75,000.00	6.2%	Y	BCBS
27	Shuster	Merrick	Sales	4/30/1995	$ 75,500.00	6.5%	N	None
28			Sales Total		0			

wrong place, adding more subtotals won't solve that problem. Better to wipe the slate clean and start over.

How to fix it

1. Click any cell in the data and then click Subtotals on the Data menu.

2. In the Subtotal dialog box, make sure the Replace Current Subtotals check box is selected.

3. Verify the field selected in the At Each Change In list. This should show the field (the column label) that your database was sorted by prior to creating the subtotal report.

4. Click a function in the Use Function list that will be appropriate for the fields you intend to subtotal. If, for example, you're subtotaling a field containing dollar amounts, SUM is a good choice. If you're subtotaling the number of people belonging to a particular organization or the number of products in a particular warehouse, use COUNT.

5. Scroll through the Add Subtotal To list, selecting the check boxes for the fields you want to subtotal and clearing the check boxes for the fields you don't want to subtotal. ▶

6. Click OK to create the subtotal report.

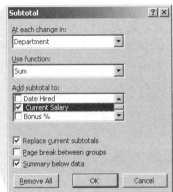

Now what do I do with it?

When the subtotal report appears, you'll notice small buttons numbered 1, 2, and 3 on the left side of the worksheet to the left of your row numbers. As you click these small buttons, you'll discover that:

● Clicking 1 reduces your database to the grand totals for the field or fields you chose to subtotal. All detail for each sorted group disappears.

● Clicking 2 reduces your database to just the subtotals, followed by a grand total. ▶

● Clicking 3 displays the entire database, showing all detail lines from each subtotaled group of rows.

F29			*fx* =SUBTOTAL(9,F4:F27)					
1 2 3	A	B	C	D	E	F	G	H	I
1		Employee Data						
2								
3		Last Name	First Name	Department	Date Hired	Current Salary	Bonus %	Insurance Y/N	Insurance Carrier
7				Accounting Total		$ 206,500.00			
11				Administration Total		$ 200,075.00			
15				Human Resources Total		$ 220,900.00			
20				Marketing Total		$ 261,500.00			
28				Sales Total		$ 528,500.00			
29				Grand Total		$1,417,475.00			
30									
31									

You'll also notice that as soon as a section of the worksheet is collapsed (hidden), a plus sign appears to the left of the worksheet. You can click any plus sign to expand particular subtotals, displaying their details.

What else can you do with a subtotal report? You can print it. You can copy the subtotals to other worksheets and workbooks. (But you have to keep your subtotal report in force in the active sheet. Otherwise, the other worksheet or workbook that uses the subtotals will no longer work properly.) You can also refer to the subtotals in other reports, such as departmental budgets, referencing the subtotals through formulas.

The wrong function is applied to my subtotaled records

Source of the problem

Excel is an intuitive product, but not intuitive enough to know which function you want applied to your subtotals. Rather than guess, it relies upon you to choose a function. If you're subtotaling a numerical field (a column containing numbers), you might want to total all the numbers in the field using the SUM function or you might want to average them. If you're subtotaling a text field (a column containing letters as well as numbers), you probably want to count the items in the field using the COUNT function.

These are just assumptions, however. The choice of which function to apply to your subtotals is yours. One thing to remember: you can choose only one function per subtotal operation, so if you're subtotaling an assortment of both text and numerical fields all at once, chances are one of the subtotals will be less than useful. That's because the same function probably won't be appropriate for all of your subtotaled fields. In this example, the COUNT function works well for the Department field, but it isn't very useful for the Current Salary field.

To solve this problem, remove the existing subtotals and then apply the subtotals again, being careful to choose the appropriate function and *only* the fields for which that function would make sense. You can then perform multiple subtotals on the same database of information, selecting a different function and different fields for each successive use of the Subtotals command.

	Last Name	First Name	Department	Date Hired	Current Salary	Bonus %	Insurance Y/N	Insurance Carrier
4	Chambers	Rosemary	Accounting	11/15/1996	$ 65,500.00	5.7%	Y	HMO
5	Patrick	Kaitlin	Accounting	9/23/1995	$ 62,500.00	5.8%	N	None
6	Freifeld	Iris	Accounting	8/3/1993	$ 78,500.00	6.2%	Y	HMO
7			Accounting Count		3			
8	Balsamo	Anthony	Administration	2/27/1997	$ 74,325.00	6.7%	N	None
9	Geiger	Mary	Administration	4/30/1992	$ 63,250.00	6.5%	Y	HMO
10	Lambert	Harry	Administration	2/15/1998	$ 62,500.00	7.0%	Y	BCBS
11			Administration Count		3			
12	Elmaleh	Miriam	Human Resources	8/24/1995	$ 72,250.00	5.0%	N	None
13	Ulrich	Lillie	Human Resources	12/15/1992	$ 73,000.00	5.5%	Y	HMO
14	Zerbe	Robert	Human Resources	11/27/1993	$ 75,650.00	6.3%	Y	BCBS
15			Human Resources Count		3			
16	Fox	Seymour	Marketing	7/15/1993	$ 65,500.00	6.0%	Y	BCBS
17	Kline	Desiree	Marketing	3/15/1997	$ 68,500.00	7.2%	Y	BCBS
18	Miller	David	Marketing	9/24/1995	$ 62,500.00	5.0%	N	None
19	Talbot	Ann	Marketing	6/7/1997	$ 65,000.00	5.0%	Y	BCBS
20			Marketing Count		4			
21	Balinski	Joseph	Sales	9/2/1989	$ 68,500.00	6.8%	Y	HMO
22	Frankenfield	Daniel	Sales	5/25/1992	$ 78,500.00	6.8%	Y	HMO
23	Fuller	Robert	Sales	11/18/1995	$ 78,500.00	6.0%	Y	HMO
24	Maurone	Richard	Sales	6/13/1999	$ 76,000.00	6.5%	Y	BCBS
25	Mermelstein	David	Sales	10/4/1993	$ 76,500.00	6.2%	Y	BCBS
26	Pederzani	Bruce	Sales	1/3/1995	$ 75,000.00	6.2%	Y	BCBS
27	Shuster	Merrick	Sales	4/30/1995	$ 75,500.00	6.5%	N	None
28			Sales Count		7			
29			Grand Count		20			

F7 =SUBTOTAL(3,F4:F6)

How to fix it

1. Click any cell in the report and then click Subtotals on the Data menu.

2. In the Subtotal dialog box, click Remove All to return your database to a nonsubtotaled state.

3. Review your fields and choose the ones you want to subtotal. Thinking of each one and the type of data it contains, decide which function will be most appropriate for each field. (It's best to make these decisions while you're examining your database, rather than when you're working in the Subtotal dialog box.)

4. On the Data menu, click Subtotals to reopen the Subtotal dialog box.

5. Click a field name (a column label) in the At Each Change In list. The field name you click in this list should be the field by which you sorted or organized the entire database. If you sorted the database by more than one field (by clicking Sort on the Data menu to access the Sort dialog box—see "Sorting data" on page 310), this is normally the first field by which you sorted.

6. Scroll through the Use Function list and click the function you want to use for the fields you intend to subtotal. Remember that you can use only one function per subtotal operation, so the one you choose has to be appropriate for all of the fields you want to subtotal.

7. In the Add Subtotal To list, select the check boxes for the fields you want to subtotal and clear any check boxes for fields you don't want to subtotal or that won't work with the chosen function.

8. Click OK to create the subtotal report.

9. Leaving the first subtotal process intact, repeat steps 4 through 8 for each successive subtotal operation. Select a different function for each one and select only the fields that will make sense with that function. ▶

Total number of people working in Accounting

Sum of salaries for people in Accounting

Tip

It's a good idea to duplicate your database and subtotal just one or two fields on each copy rather than have too many fields subtotaled on any one version of your database. If too many fields are subtotaled, you create visual chaos and limit the report's effectiveness.

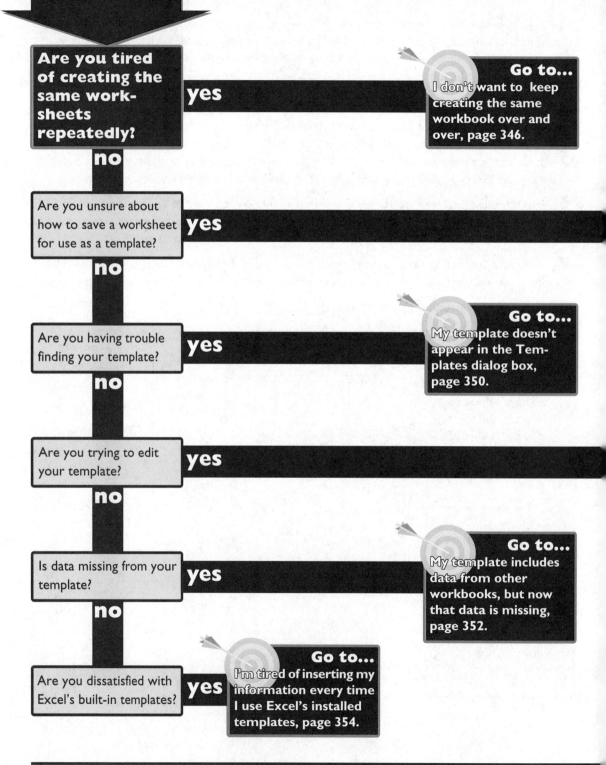

Are you tired of creating the same work-sheets repeatedly?

yes → **Go to...** I don't want to keep creating the same workbook over and over, page 346.

no

Are you unsure about how to save a worksheet for use as a template?

yes →

no

Are you having trouble finding your template?

yes → **Go to...** My template doesn't appear in the Templates dialog box, page 350.

no

Are you trying to edit your template?

yes →

no

Is data missing from your template?

yes → **Go to...** My template includes data from other workbooks, but now that data is missing, page 352.

no

Are you dissatisfied with Excel's built-in templates?

yes → **Go to...** I'm tired of inserting my information every time I use Excel's installed templates, page 354.

Templates

Quick fix

To make sure your templates appear in the Templates dialog box, you need to save them to the Templates folder. When you're in the Save As dialog box, preparing to save a workbook as a template, click the Save As Type drop list, and from that list, choose Template (.xlt). This automatically moves you to the Templates folder (see the Save In drop list). Don't change the location for this new file, other than to add a subfolder to the Templates folder and save the file to that new folder.

Quick fix

If you need to edit a template, open it from its source. Go to C:\Documents and Settings\Default\Application Data\Microsoft\Templates. You should find your template in that folder, or one of its subfolders, if you created any to categorize your templates.

If your solution isn't here, check these related chapters:

- Formatting worksheets, page 168
- Saving, page 278

Or see the general troubleshooting tips on page xv.

I don't want to keep creating the same workbook over and over

Source of the problem

Every day, every week, every month, or at some other all-too-frequent interval, you create a workbook. Its design is the same as the one before it—what changes is the data specific to that particular workbook. The title is the same, the layout is the same, the column and row labels are the same, and the sheets within the workbook are named and ordered in the same manner. The formulas are the same, even the text and border formatting is the same. Yet you're recreating the darn thing every time.

This has caused you problems beyond simply wasting your time and contributing to your carpal tunnel syndrome—each version of the workbook is a little different than the previous one. Some of the formatting is lost; column labels are slightly reworded. Once you even forgot an important column, and when you put it back in later, you had to redo a bunch of formulas to include the missing data. You tried opening an old workbook and editing it to reflect new data, but then you accidentally saved the file, overwriting the older workbook, and now that's lost. You can't risk that happening again, but you need each new workbook to be the same as the old ones.

What can you do? Isn't there a way to create the same workbook over and over again, with the same content and formatting, whenever you need it? Why, yes there is! You can turn a workbook into a template and use it over and over again to create similar workbooks, with no risk to the original workbook. The content, formatting, layout, names, and order of individual worksheets within the workbook will be the same every time you use the workbook template as the basis of a new file. ▶

How to fix it

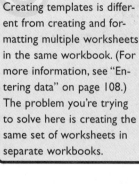

Tip

Creating templates is different from creating and formatting multiple worksheets in the same workbook. (For more information, see "Entering data" on page 108.) The problem you're trying to solve here is creating the same set of worksheets in separate workbooks.

To turn an existing workbook into a template, follow these steps:

1. Open the existing workbook that you want to use as your template.

2. Delete any specific data that you don't want in every new workbook that's created from this template. (You can keep formulas, labels, titles, and formatting; just be sure to delete any data that was specific to this existing workbook.)

3. Make any formatting or content changes you want reflected in the new workbooks created from this template. Check your spelling and your formulas and clean up inconsistencies in formatting. Also make sure the individual worksheets in the workbook are named and ordered the way you want them to be.

4. When the file is cleaned up and ready, click Save As on the File menu. Be very careful not to click Save, because doing so will overwrite the existing file, and you'll lose the original.

5. Click the Save As Type drop-down list and select Template (*.xlt) from the list. This ensures that the file is saved as a template in the correct folder.

6. Type a file name for the template. (Don't type any extension; let Microsoft Excel add the .xlt extension that designates the file as a template.) ▶

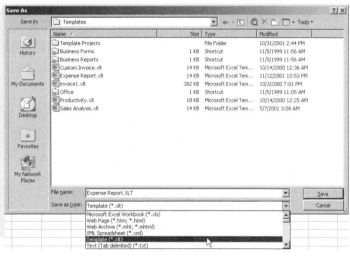

7. Click Save to create the template. Excel closes the workbook that you used as a basis for the template, preserving it in its original state.

8. Close the template.

I don't want to keep creating the same workbook over and over

(continued from page 347)

To use the template, follow these steps:

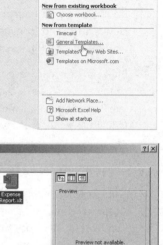

1. On the File menu, click New. The New Workbook Task Pane appears, displaying several text links for you to follow in selecting a template for your new workbook. ▶

2. Click the General Templates link, which opens the Templates dialog box. The dialog box contains two tabs—General and Spreadsheet Solutions. Click the General tab and double-click the icon for the template you want to use for your new workbook. ▶

3. Enter the data that's specific to this new workbook and click the Save button. In the Save As dialog box, note that you can save the new workbook with the standard workbook (.xls) format in My Documents or any other folder, just as you would any new workbook. (The template itself is used only as the basis of this new workbook.) Give the workbook a unique name, make sure that Microsoft Excel Workbook (.xls) appears in the Save As Type box, and then click Save.

Cookie cutter ideas

Templates give you the ability to create instant expense reports, invoices, sales reports, and payroll workbooks—anything you create repeatedly that varies only in terms of the situational content. Each time you use the template, you start out with a new workbook containing only the basic stuff that was part of the template at the time you created it. Think about any workbooks you create more than once or twice a year and consider creating templates for them. Templates also make it easy to have standardized forms and reports throughout an office or company. Share your templates with coworkers so everyone can have quick and easy consistency in their workbooks.

Warning

Don't confuse the templates you create with the Balance Sheet, Expense Statement, Loan Amortization, Sales Invoice, and Timecard templates that come with Excel. Those templates are automated and filled with features you must edit or tweak for your own needs (and some of the features can't be altered). The templates you create yourself can be molded over time as your needs change. The only thing these two types of templates have in common is the way you access them. To access these templates, click New on the File menu. Templates that you create will be on the General tab; the templates that come with Excel will be on the Spreadsheet Solutions tab. Click the tab that houses the template you want, and then double-click the name of the template. If you double-clicked any of the built-in templates, click Enable Macros to open a workbook based on whichever one you chose.

My template doesn't appear in the Templates dialog box

Source of the problem

You created a template, and now you're ready to use it. You click New on the File menu, and you've clicked the General Templates link in the New Workbook Task Pane. But in the resulting Templates dialog box, you don't see a template with the name you gave it. What gives?

The fact that your template doesn't appear in the Templates dialog box (on the General tab) is because it's not stored in the Templates folder or in a direct subfolder of that folder. That one step in the template-creation process is key to the accessibility of templates, yet it's the one that people ignore most often.

Excel tries to make it easy to do it right by switching to the Templates folder as soon as you choose Template (.xlt) for your file type when you save the template in the first place. People feel compelled, however, to change folders and to save the template with other workbook files. An understandable mistake, but a mistake just the same, because saving templates to anywhere other than the prescribed Templates folder (or one of its subfolders) will make your new template inaccessible.

To solve the problem, you have to find the file and then move it to the Templates folder.

How to fix it

To find your file, follow these steps:

1. On the File menu, click Open.

2. In the Open dialog box, click the Tools button and then click Search on the drop-down menu to open the Search dialog box.

3. The Search dialog box defaults to searching for Excel files in your My Documents folder and anywhere else on your local C drive. In addition, it's set to search only for Excel files. These defaults may not suit the search for your template file, so you may need to adjust them. ▶

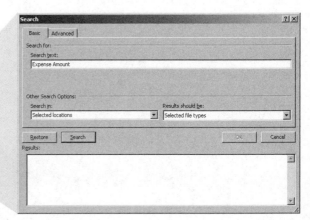

4. Using the Search In drop-down list, click the plus sign next to My Computer to reveal that My Documents and your local C drive are selected as sites to search. Adjust this as needed by placing a check mark in the check boxes next to any folders or subfolders you wish to search for your template.

5. In the Results Should Be drop-down list, choose the file type(s) to search for (in this case, Excel Files) by leaving the check mark next to that file type intact. If any other types are selected (due to previous searches), remove those check marks.

6. In the Search Text dialog box, type some text that's exclusive to the template you seek—a department name, a person's last name, the number of a product you sell, or something else that's unique to the template and few, if any, other files.

7. Click Search. The word "Searching..." appears in the Results box and remains there until the file you seek is found or no file matching your search criteria is located.

Assuming the file is located (it will appear by name in the Results box), you're ready to move the template file to the correct folder so that it will be available through the Templates dialog box. Follow these steps:

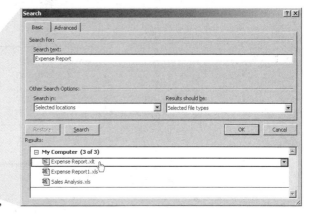

1. Click once on the file name as it appears in the Results box in the Search dialog box. ▶

2. Click OK to select the file and the path to it and return to the Open dialog box, where that path and file name now appear in the File Name box.

3. Click Open. The file opens in the Excel application window.

4. Choose Save As from the File menu and use the Save As Type drop-down list to choose Template (.xlt). This changes the Save In location to the Templates folder, from which you will not deviate this time!

5. As needed, rename the file and then click Save to place the file in the Templates folder.

Now that the file is in the Templates folder, when next you choose File, New and use the General Templates link on the New Workbook Task Pane, your template will appear on the General tab of the Templates dialog box.

Tip

You can always go back and delete the duplicate file in whichever folder you originally saved it, using the Windows Explorer, My Computer, or even Excel's Open dialog box.

My template includes data from other workbooks, but now that data is missing

Source of the problem

This is a very frustrating problem, especially if the workbooks from which your template draws data aren't entirely under your control. If your template worked the last time you used it, and if you've done nothing to edit it in any way since then, the reason that some of the external data is missing (particularly in a formula with links to another workbook) can only be that the source of that data—the other workbook—has been moved or deleted, or its contents have been edited so that the data you're looking for isn't where it was when you set up your template. If others can edit and delete data within the source workbook or move or delete the workbook files that contain the data, your template isn't safe. ▶

What can you do? That depends. If you have no control over access to the other workbook, you're stuck dealing with your template's vulnerability, unless you can make and maintain a copy of the other workbook and make that the source of your template's external data. If that's not feasible (perhaps the other workbook requires ongoing updates by another person in order to remain useful), you might have to live with the fact that your template relies on data that's not under your careful control.

F5	▼	f_x =SUM('[Expense data.xls]January 2002'!$C$2:$C$25)

Tip

Depending on your work environment, you can try asking the person or persons responsible for maintaining your template's external source to be more aware of your dependency on their workbook. If they're willing, you can apply protection and passwords so that only a select few careful users have access to the file on which your template depends. See "People keep changing my text formatting, and I don't want them to" on page 166 for more about protecting your files from unwanted changes.

The solution then becomes fixing your template by relocating the source of the external data and updating the references to those external cells. This requires verifying the location of the other workbook and checking to see what happened to the cells that your template refers to. To verify the location of your template's external data, you use the Trace Precedents command. Once you've verified the location, you can update your template so that it finds the data it needs. (See "When I edit the cells referenced in my formula, the result doesn't change" on page 186 for more about the Trace Precedents tool.)

How to fix it

1. If you haven't done so already, create a new document based on the template from which data is missing. You'll use this new document to find the source of your template's external data.

2. Click once on the cell that should contain data from another workbook. The cell you click can contain a formula or simply display the content of a cell in the other workbook.

3. On the Tools menu, point to Formula Auditing and then click Trace Precedents. Precedent arrows appear, and one should point from a workbook icon. ▶

4. Point to the external precedent reference (the icon) and double-click. The Go To dialog box opens, and the external reference is displayed. Click the external reference in the Go To list and then click OK. The source workbook, if it's still where it was when you created the template, opens with the cell referenced in your template displayed.

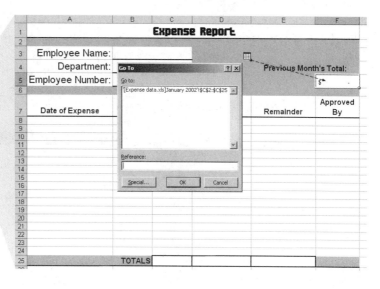

If the workbook is where it was when you set up your template's reference to it, all you have to do is reenter the data that's missing or edit the data so that it works with your template. For example, if a formula in your template references this cell, and now the cell contains text or something that won't work in the formula, edit the cell to contain what it should. After this adjustment, the template should work, because it will find what it needs where it expects to find it.

If the workbook is missing, you have to find out where it is or if it's been deleted. The fastest way to do that is probably to ask the person who works with it. If that's not possible, find the missing workbook by using the Find feature, which is described in "My template doesn't appear in the Templates dialog box" on page 350. If the file is missing (perhaps it's been deleted or has a new file name), you might have to redesign your template to find the needed data elsewhere or to use data from within itself.

I'm tired of inserting my information every time I use Excel's installed templates

Source of the problem

Excel's installed templates for spreadsheets such as timecards, loan amortizations, balance sheets, sales invoices, and expense statements are handy if you don't have any of these worksheets of your own or if you don't use a separate accounting application that provides such forms for you. The templates are functionally (if not visually) well designed, and many users swear by them. They contain generic information and placeholders for things specific to your organization, such as your company logo, your company name and address, the date, and—in the case of the Sales Invoice template—a unique invoice number and a space for payment terms. So, they're quite customizable.

Suppose you think it's important that your logo be on these forms, but you're tired of inserting it every time you use one of the templates. Your problem with the logo is common. It comes from not fully understanding how the templates work. The solution requires you to do some customization, after which the template will offer a completely customized version of itself each time you base a new workbook on it.

To customize the template, you don't need to open it, but rather simply to open a new workbook based on it. Then use the built-in customization options to make it look the way you want it to. You have to do this only once. (The Sales Invoice template is used as the example in this section; you can apply the steps to the other templates in Excel as you want.)

How to fix it

1. On the File menu, click New.

2. In the New Workbook task pane, click the General Templates link, and in the resulting Templates dialog box, double-click one of the template icons, such as that for the Sales Invoice template. A new workbook appears, based on the template.

3. Where desired (and in the case of the Sales Invoice template, where it says Insert Company Information Here) type your information—your company name, address, web address, phone number—whatever you want at the top of every invoice you send. ▶

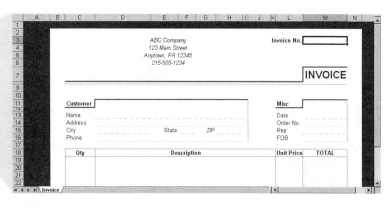

4. You'll notice that you can't change the fonts or text sizes or apply any color formatting to cell content or the cells themselves. This is because the templates are meant to be entirely generic, and any formatting is disabled. You can't even open the Format dialog box, and most of the Formatting toolbar's tools are dimmed. Restrict your changes to content such as new text, and then only in the cells where you can click to activate the cell—these are the only cells that can be altered.

5. Once your changes and additions (within the limits described above) are made, you can save the file as a new template with a new name. Pass the mouse pointer over one of the blocks to read the instructions. ▶

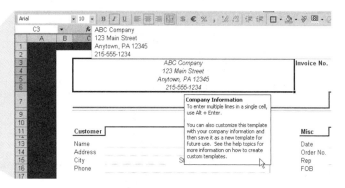

6. Choose Save As from the File menu and, using the Save As Type drop-down list, choose Template (.xlt). The Save In selection is changed to the Templates folder.

7. Give your new template a unique name, or keep the Sales Invoice 1 (or 2, or some other chronologically applied number) that's applied when you use the template to start a new file.

8. Click Save to save the template with an .xlt extension. The template appears on the General tab of the Templates dialog box the next time you go to start a new worksheet.

I'm tired of inserting my information every time I use Excel's installed templates

(continued from page 355)

But what about pictures? Shading? Other cool stuff?

If you want to set up a template for invoicing or any of the other types of worksheets that are represented on the Spreadsheet Solutions tab, learn from the installed templates and then go create your own. The ability to do anything more than type your company name and address, terms, and some sort of "thank you" sign-off is seriously limited when you use the installed templates, even if you attempt to reformat or add anything other than text to a worksheet created with the templates.

Better to create a template of your own from scratch (based on the Blank Workbook template, so no controls are in place from the start) and use the installed templates if you're not sure how the worksheets should operate—which formulas to use and where, and so on. If we look again at the Sales Invoice template, you can see that any invoice needs a place to put the quantity of

items ordered, when they were ordered, a description of the products, and pricing per item so that charges can be calculated and taxed, and any shipping charges added. You can structure your invoice template very similarly, but you can be much more creative and use graphics and color to snazzy things up.

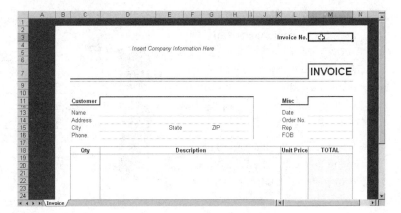

Templates

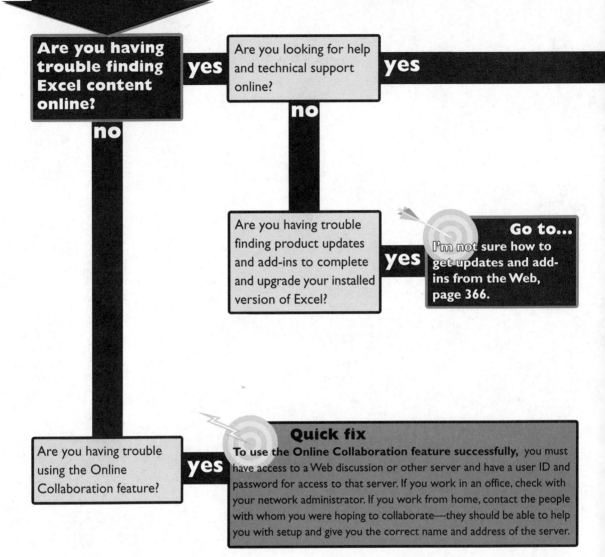

Are you having trouble finding Excel content online?

yes → Are you looking for help and technical support online?

yes →

no

no

Are you having trouble finding product updates and add-ins to complete and upgrade your installed version of Excel?

yes →

Go to...
I'm not sure how to get updates and add-ins from the Web, page 366.

Are you having trouble using the Online Collaboration feature?

yes →

Quick fix
To use the Online Collaboration feature successfully, you must have access to a Web discussion or other server and have a user ID and password for access to that server. If you work in an office, check with your network administrator. If you work from home, contact the people with whom you were hoping to collaborate—they should be able to help you with setup and give you the correct name and address of the server.

Web tools

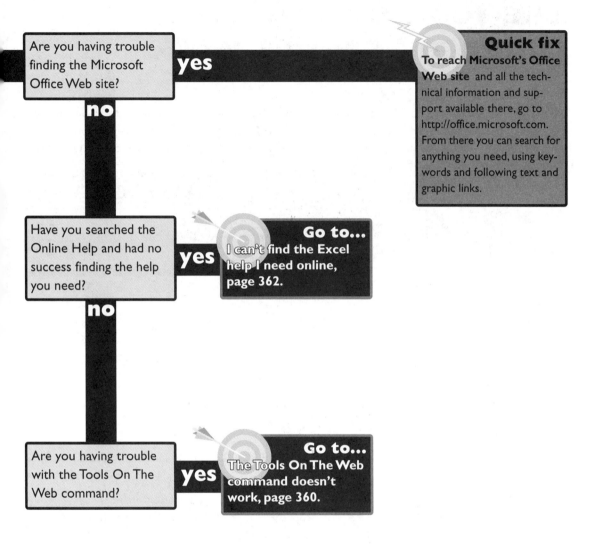

Are you having trouble finding the Microsoft Office Web site?

yes

no

Quick fix
To reach Microsoft's Office Web site and all the technical information and support available there, go to http://office.microsoft.com. From there you can search for anything you need, using keywords and following text and graphic links.

Have you searched the Online Help and had no success finding the help you need?

yes

Go to...
I can't find the Excel help I need online, page 362.

no

Are you having trouble with the Tools On The Web command?

yes

Go to...
The Tools On The Web command doesn't work, page 360.

If your solution isn't here, check these related chapters:

- Hyperlinks, page 214
- Web tools, page 358
- Workspace customization, page 368

Or see the general troubleshooting tips on page xv.

The Tools On The Web command doesn't work

Source of the problem

Microsoft Excel 2002's Tools On The Web command should take you directly to the Tools on the Web site, which is maintained by Microsoft for Microsoft Office users. From that page, you select your location by clicking a map to indicate where you are in the world, and you're off to the Tools on the Web home page. It offers an entire screen full of links to tips, tricks, and help for users of any application within the Office XP suite. ▶

So what could go wrong? If you click the Tools On The Web command (found in the Tools menu) and get an error message, chances are you're not online. If you believe you're online, check to make sure by checking your dial-up status or try opening your browser and visiting another Web site. If you can reach that site, you're online. If you can't, you need to connect to the Internet and then retry the Tools On The Web command.

How to fix it

To make sure you're online, you'll need access to the My Computer icon, which is found on your Windows Desktop. From there, follow these steps:

1. Double-click the My Computer icon. The My Computer window opens, displaying a series of icons.

2. If you're using Windows 98 or Windows Me (Millennium),

No thanks, just browsing

Another potential problem—your default browser isn't installed properly or it's malfunctioning. In order to take you to the Tools on the Web site, Excel will open a browser window, choosing the browser software you have set as your default. Whether that's Microsoft Internet Explorer (which comes with Microsoft Windows), Netscape Navigator, or some other browser, a browser window opens, and the Tools on the Web site will be accessed. If that doesn't happen—if no browser window opens or if you receive an error message indicating that the software can't be found or is "not responding," you need to reinstall the browser software or get new browser software and install it properly. This is probably the least likely source of your problem, however, so first check your online status.

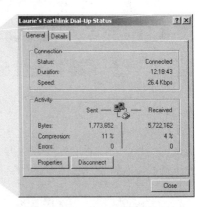

double-click the Dial-Up Networking icon. If you're using Windows 2000, click the Network And Dial-Up Connections link and then double-click your Dial-Up Networking icon, found in a new window.

3. This displays your current dial-up status. ▶

4. If you find that you aren't connected, a dialog box may appear, offering you the opportunity to connect to the Internet through an available feature (probably a Dial-Up icon that mentions your Internet service provider [ISP]). ▶

But I'm already connected, thank you!

And what if you're already online? Then what? Well, if you can't access the Tools on the Web page through Excel, try opening your browser and going directly to this address: *http://office.microsoft.com/*

This should take you to the Tools on the Web page, from which you can search for help and poke around at will for tips, tricks, and any other information that strikes your fancy. Note that you may have to select your geographic location using a page that appears before you're taken to the Tools on the Web page. Once you're on that page, though, you can go directly to Office XP topics by clicking the Get Help Using Office Products link. ▶

You can also get to that page by clicking the Assistance Center link on the left side of the page. Then click the Excel text link. From the resulting page, you can choose from a variety of topic categories—everything from Analyzing Data to Upgrade/Setup issues. Each category spawns a

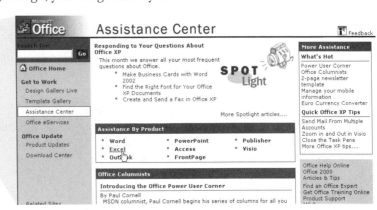

new list of subtopics, and you can keep clicking text links until you find a topic that sounds like what you're looking for.

To go directly to the Assistance Center page for Excel, type this address into your browser's Address or Location bar: *http://search.office.microsoft.com/assistance/producttask.aspx?p=Excel.*

I can't find the Excel help I need online

Source of the problem

When you use Excel's regular Help (by means of the Help menu or the F1 key), you may find that none of the assistance offered pertains to your problem. Maybe the keyword you typed into the index isn't found or the question you presented to the Answer Wizard doesn't get you the answer you were looking for. Maybe using the Contents tab has failed you because you can't find the help category you need. If this happens, online help is just a click away—you'll see a button in the lower-right corner of the Help window that says Search On Web. ▶

If you click the Search On Web button, the Help window changes to display a set of search tools that will search the Microsoft Office Web site. To use this handy-dandy search feature, type your question—or one or more keywords—into the provided text box and then click Send And Go To The Web. ▶

A Web page will appear behind the Help window (click the new window to put it on top of the Help window), asking you to specify your location among options such as Canada, the United States, Europe, or Hong Kong (pick the one closest to where you are). Once you click your spot on the map, you will be taken to a list of help articles pertaining to the question or keywords you typed in the Search pane in the Help window.

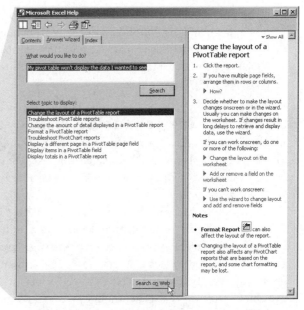

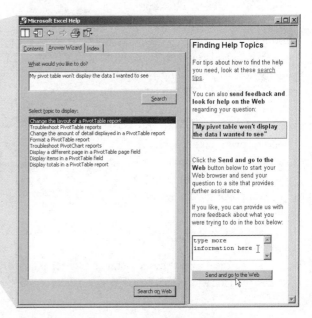

Now, this sounds foolproof, doesn't it? Sounds like you'd get the help you need, served up quickly and easily, right? Well, usually. But sometimes it's anything but quick and easy, and you may encounter the same wall you ran into when searching your local Help files. What to do? If you

encounter a message saying that "Your Search Returned 0 Results" or an "Answers to Your Questions About Excel 2000" text link, you've hit a wall, but not an impenetrable one. Just use the Refine Your Search tools to switch to Office XP's Help and then pose a new question using the Search tool to the left. ▶

Search text box **Version drop-down list**

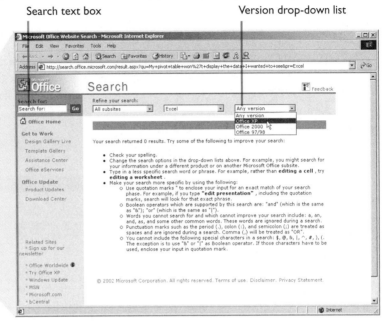

How to fix it

To refine your search to Office XP and repose your question, follow these steps:

1. Click the Version drop-down list. You can choose Any Version, Office 97/98, 2000, or XP. Choose XP, of course!

2. Look to the left, where you will see a Search For text box accompanied by a Go button. Type your question or keywords in the text box, keeping the entry simple and to the point. Click the Go button to present your question to the Web site's search engine.

Keep it simple

When working with your local Help files or the online Help, keep the wording of your questions and your list of keywords simple. For example, if you want help on using a PivotTable, don't type "I can't get the PivotTable to display my 2001 data the right way." That's more information than the search tools need, and many of those words will either confuse the search engine or be ignored. Instead, try "PivotTable display" or "PivotTable data." If you want to state your criteria in the form of a question, avoid extra words. "Why can't I see my PivotTable data?" is better than "Where is my 2001 accounting data that I put into a PivotTable?"

I can't find the Excel help I need online

(continued from page 363)

3. View the search results, which should be a list of articles that pertain to the question or keywords you typed. ▶

Yeah, that's nice, but...

And what if you *still* can't find the help you need? Consider the Office e-Services link, found in the left side of the Search window. This link takes you to several training and reference alternatives that you can explore. After you click the Office e-Services link, click the Training and Reference link on the resulting page. A new page appears that offers Online Training, Locate an Expert, Reference Desk, and Directory Services. The one you might want to explore first is Locate an Expert. You can try the service once for free, and then, after that, it's fee-based—but you get to present your questions to a bona fide Office XP guru and get the answers you need. ▶

I'm not sure how to get updates and add-ins from the Web

Source of the problem

You have some friends who use Excel all the time, and they always seem to have the latest and greatest gadgets that make Excel do more than your right-out-of-the-box copy can. Well, catch up to them! You can download tons of new Excel tools from the Downloads page at *http://office.microsoft.com.* ▶

Of course, in order to download these features, you must be online so you can get to the downloads page. You also have to have Office XP installed on your computer and have your program CD ready in case you need it (some downloads require you to put the CD in and may require you to have the CD key that came with the software). Other than that, you're good to go!

Downloads for Excel 2002/XP   Downloads from Other Providers

Title	Date ▾	Type
Office XP Euro Currency Converter Smart Tag Download Now! 232kb / 2 mins The Microsoft Office XP Euro Currency Converter Smart Tag converts 12 currencies to euro and vice versa.	27-Nov-2001	Converter
Office XP/2000 Add-in: Office Sounds Download Now! 472kb / 3 mins Install these sounds to have fun audio cues play as you work with Microsoft Office XP or 2000 programs.	18-Sep-2001	Add-in
Excel 2002 Update: October 4, 2001 Download Now! 8570kb / 52 mins The Excel 2002 Update: October 4, 2001 addresses a vulnerability that could allow a macro to open without warning, which then could run malicious code on your computer.	17-Sept-2001	Update
Excel 2002 Add-in: OLAP CubeCellValue Download Now! 1024kb / 7 mins The CubeCellValue add-in for Microsoft Excel contains the CubeCellValue function which allows you to retrieve a single value from an Online Analytical Processing (OLAP) data provider and enter it into a single cell on your spreadsheet.	15-Aug-2001	Add-in
Office XP Tool: Web Components Download Now! 8802kb / 53 mins Microsoft Office Web Components are a collection of Component Object Model (COM) controls for publishing spreadsheets, charts, and databases to the Web, and for viewing the published components on the Web.	13-Aug-2001	Add-in

How to fix it

To access the downloads page, follow these steps:

1. Choose Tools, Tools On The Web. This should take you to the Tools on the Web page at *http://office.microsoft.com.*

2. On the left side of the page, click the Download Center text link.

3. On the Download Center page, choose the Product (Excel) and Version (2002/XP) and choose the types of downloads you want to see—Updates, Add-ins, or Converters. If you want to see them all, check all three boxes. ▶

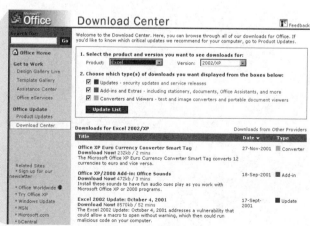

4. Click the Update List button to get the list of the downloads that meet your criteria.

5. On the resulting list, click the bold blue text for any download you want to look at—the name of the download is the link to a page that describes the item in detail, including the size of the file and how long it will take to download. ▶

6. On the page for the individual download item, click the Download Now button if you're ready to download the Update, Add-In, or Converter. If you don't want it, click the Back button in your browser window to go back to the full list of downloadable items.

7. After you opt to download an item, a dialog box appears, asking how you want to go about downloading the file—running it from the site where it's currently stored (not recommended for security reasons) or saving it to your local drive for installation later. To be safe, choose Save This Program To Disk and click OK.

8. Next, you need to choose where to save the file you're about to download. I usually choose Desktop (from the Save In drop-down list), because I can get to the downloaded file easily to install it later. Make your own selection and click Save.

9. A progress bar and download statistics appear next. When the download is complete, you'll see the file appear in the place you designated for it to be saved. ▶

To install the downloaded item, double-click the icon for the file you downloaded—an installation program starts, and it takes you step-by-step through the installation process.

Download Center

Excel 2002 Add-in: Report Manager

You can combine Microsoft Excel 2002 worksheets, views, and scenarios into reports that can be printed by using the Report Manager add-in program. Once you add a report, it is saved with the workbook so that you can print the report later.

Note Although it was not necessary to download this add-in with previous versions of Excel (it was shipped with the product), you must download it here in order to use it with Excel 2002.

Total Download Size = 165 kb
Total Download Time = 1 minute @28.8

Download Now

To install this download:

1. You may want to print this page to use as a reference when you are offline.
2. Quit Excel if it's running.
3. Download the file from the Microsoft Office Tools on the Web site by clicking the **Download Now** button (above) and following the instructions in the dialog boxes.
4. Double-click the **rptmgr.exe** program file on your hard disk to start the setup program.
5. Follow the instructions on the screen to complete the installation.
6. Start Excel.
7. On the **Tools** menu, click **Add-ins**.
8. Select the **Report Manager** check box.

Instructions for use:

Need help with Office XP?
Talk Live to Office Experts on Keen
Securely store and share files online!

Download details:
Works with Excel 2002
Filename rptmgr.exe
Last Updated 05-01-2001
Languages Supported US English

Tip

You should close all Office XP applications before downloading and installing any upgrades. When you go to install the add-ins and upgrades, you should be prompted to close any open Office applications. In case the one you're downloading doesn't prompt you, it's a good idea to close the applications even before you get started.

Tip

The Download Center Web page will remain open during and after the download—you can go back to it and download other items from the list, one at a time, until you've gathered all the cool Excel stuff you need.

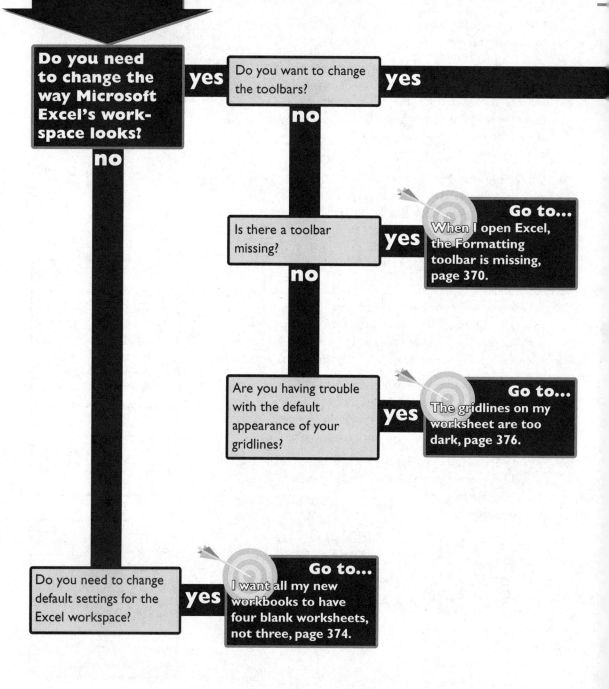

Do you need to change the way Microsoft Excel's workspace looks?

yes Do you want to change the toolbars? **yes**

no

no

Is there a toolbar missing?

yes Go to... When I open Excel, the Formatting toolbar is missing, page 370.

no

Are you having trouble with the default appearance of your gridlines?

yes Go to... The gridlines on my worksheet are too dark, page 376.

Do you need to change default settings for the Excel workspace?

yes Go to... I want all my new workbooks to have four blank worksheets, not three, page 374.

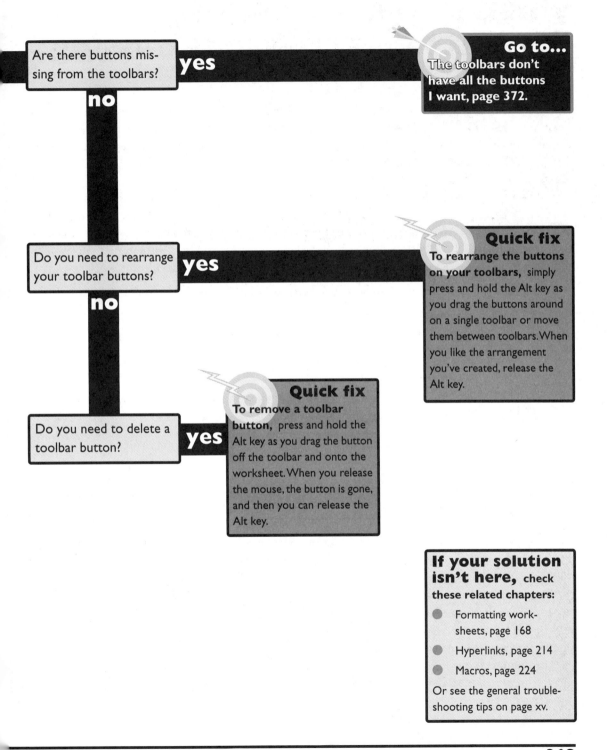

Are there buttons missing from the toolbars?

yes

no

Go to...
The toolbars don't have all the buttons I want, page 372.

Do you need to rearrange your toolbar buttons?

yes

no

Quick fix
To rearrange the buttons on your toolbars, simply press and hold the Alt key as you drag the buttons around on a single toolbar or move them between toolbars. When you like the arrangement you've created, release the Alt key.

Do you need to delete a toolbar button?

yes

Quick fix
To remove a toolbar button, press and hold the Alt key as you drag the button off the toolbar and onto the worksheet. When you release the mouse, the button is gone, and then you can release the Alt key.

If your solution isn't here, check these related chapters:

- Formatting worksheets, page 168
- Hyperlinks, page 214
- Macros, page 224

Or see the general troubleshooting tips on page xv.

When I open Excel, the Formatting toolbar is missing

Source of the problem

Don't you just hate that? Your Microsoft Excel workspace should look the same every time you open the application, with all the tools you know and love right where you left them. It can be aggravating and, for many users, disorienting, not to find a toolbar where you expect to see it. You can't blame this one on the gremlins that haunt your office, despite the fact that people like to blame them for everything.

Excel's toolbars were designed to put the most commonly used features within easy reach of your mouse pointer, but the placement of toolbars and toolbar buttons isn't carved in stone. You can turn off toolbars quite easily, and you can even move and remove toolbar buttons (see "The toolbars don't have all the buttons I want" on page 372). Nope, a missing Formatting toolbar or toolbar button wasn't caused by gremlins. The problem was created in one of three ways:

- You accidentally turned off the Formatting toolbar during the current session or the last time you used Excel.

- Someone else who uses your computer turned off the toolbar.

- You have the Standard and Formatting toolbars set to share one row (a Microsoft Office XP feature), and the Formatting toolbar is getting the short end of the stick in terms of toolbar buttons that appear on the visible portion of the row.

If either of the first two reasons causes your problem, it's easy to fix. Simply redisplay the toolbar and make sure it's there when you exit Excel. Unless someone else uses your computer and turns off the Formatting toolbar, it will be there the next time you start the software.

If your problem is the result of the toolbars sharing one row, that feature can be turned off. In fact, I recommend turning off this feature the minute Office XP is installed!

> **Tip**
>
> What if the toolbar you want to display is already selected in the Toolbars list (indicating that it's already displayed), but you just can't see it? Perhaps the toolbar you're looking for is displayed as a floating toolbar and has been positioned so far to one side of the workspace that you can't see it. Or perhaps it's already docked down a side of the workspace where you wouldn't normally expect to see it, and you've simply overlooked it.

How to fix it

To display a missing toolbar, follow these steps:

1. Right-click any toolbar or the menu bar to display a list of toolbars.

2. Click the name of the toolbar you want to display.

3. If the toolbar appears as a floating toolbar (like this Formatting toolbar), drag it to the top of the workspace to dock it there. ▶

To make the Standard and Formatting toolbars appear on two separate rows (with all of their respective buttons showing) rather than share one row, follow these steps:

1. On the Tools menu, click Customize to display the Customize dialog box.

2. Click the Options tab and make sure the Show Standard And Formatting Toolbars On Two Rows option is selected. ▶

3. Click Close to put the toolbars on separate rows.

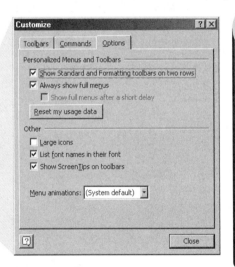

Tip

If you'd like to see a menu in its entirety as soon as you select it, you can check the Always Show Full Menus check box on the Options tab of the Customize dialog box. With this option turned on, your menus are fully displayed right away, and none of the menu commands appear on the menus with a lighter background, no matter when they were last used.

Float like a toolbar, sting like a bee

If you prefer to use floating toolbars, you can drag the docked toolbars away from the edges of the workspace. Simply point to a toolbar's handle (the vertical bar on the far left end of the toolbar), and when (and only when) your mouse pointer turns into a four-headed arrow, drag the toolbar away from the workspace edge. When you release the mouse button, your toolbar will be converted to a floating toolbar that you can drag around while you work. To dock a floating toolbar, grab it by its title bar and drag it back to any edge of the workspace. When the title bar disappears, the toolbar is docked.

The toolbars don't have all the buttons I want

Source of the problem

When they selected the commands to go on the toolbars, Microsoft's software engineers and designers did their best to choose the commands that are used most often by most users. Of course, they didn't call you, so the ones you want aren't there. Isn't that always the way? Don't feel bad, though. They didn't call me, either!

The solution to this problem is to stock the toolbars with the buttons you want to see—the ones that represent the commands you use often enough to warrant taking up valuable toolbar real estate.

How to fix it

1. Right-click any of the displayed toolbars and click Customize at the bottom of the list of toolbars. You can also choose Customize from the Tools menu.

2. In the Customize dialog box, click the Commands tab.

3. In the Categories list, click the name of the menu that contains the command you want to add to the toolbar.

4. In the corresponding Commands list (on the right side of the dialog box), locate the command you want to add. (You might need to scroll to find it.)

5. Drag the command to the toolbar, releasing the mouse button when the I-beam pointer is where you want to place the button. ▶

The I-beam and plus sign indicate a button is being added here.

Drag the command from the dialog box.

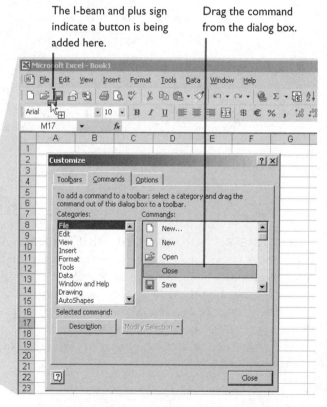

6. If the button appears as text (not a picture) and you want a picture, click the Modify Selection button in the Customize dialog box and then click Text Only (In Menus) on the drop-down menu.

7. Click Modify Selection again and then click Change Button Image. A palette of button images appears.

8. Click the button image you want for your new button.

9. Repeat steps 3 through 8 for as many buttons as you want to add. Some of them will have their own default pictures; in that case, you can skip steps 6 through 8.

10. Click Close when you have finished adding and modifying all the buttons you want.

Tip

If you regret the way you positioned your new button, hold down the Alt key, drag the new button to a new position on the toolbar, and then release the mouse button. You can move all the buttons, not just your new one, and you can move them between toolbars. Be careful, though, because you will remove a button if you drag it off the toolbar entirely.

Gimme a shiny new toolbar

If you have a batch of toolbar buttons that you want to see on the screen together and you don't want to clutter up your existing toolbars with them, you can create a brand new toolbar. On the Toolbars tab of the Customize dialog box, click New. In the Toolbar Name box of the New Toolbar dialog box, type a name for the new toolbar and then click OK. An empty floating toolbar appears. To add buttons to it, click the Commands tab and then drag the commands that you want to add from the Commands list to the new toolbar. ▶

Continue dragging commands onto the new toolbar until you've created the quintessential toolbar for your needs. Click Close to close the Customize dialog box. You can leave your new toolbar in a floating state or

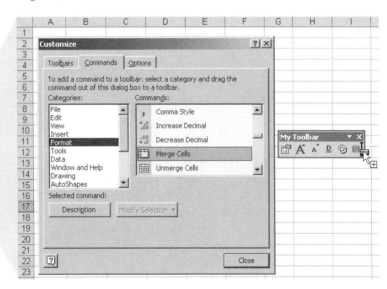

you can dock it along an edge of the workspace. You close it and then reopen it by right-clicking any displayed toolbar and clicking the new toolbar's name on the Toolbar list.

I want all my new workbooks to have four blank worksheets, not three

Source of the problem

It doesn't sound like a big problem when you read it here, does it? Certainly adding an extra sheet to the default three that appear when you start a new, blank workbook isn't a lot of work, but if you want four sheets (or five, or six, or twenty-three) in every new workbook, by golly, you should have 'em. The fact that the default is based on the needs of the average user—many of whom started using spreadsheet programs when there was only one worksheet per file, and who still don't need more than one for their typical workbook—makes three seems like a bonanza.

As more people become more adept in the use of Excel, however, the more complex and the larger the "average" user's workbooks become. Perhaps future versions of the software will have a greater number of sheets as the default for new workbooks. For now, however, the blank workbook template for the latest and greatest version of Excel still coughs up just three worksheets.

While we wait for this change to be added to a future version of Excel, you can adjust the default so that all of your workbooks (based on the blank workbook template) open with as many worksheets as you want. The process is incredibly simple, which may be why the software engineers haven't increased the default number of sheets. If you want more, it's easy to have more.

How to fix it

1. On the Tools menu, click Options to display the Options dialog box.

2. Click the General tab to view the main settings for the way all workbooks (not just the one that's open now) will work. ▶

3. In the Settings section of the dialog box, increase or decrease the number of sheets to appear in a new workbook by clicking the up or down arrows on the Sheets In New Workbook box. (The default is 3; you can display as few as 1 or as many as 255 sheets in a new workbook.)

4. Click OK to save this setting and close the dialog box.

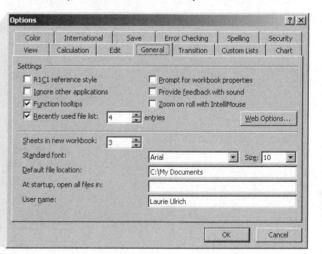

ce customization

The defaults, they are a-changin'

Excel gives you the ability to change 12 different defaults on the Options dialog box's General tab alone. Here are a few you might be interested in changing:

- **R1C1 Reference Style.** Clear by default, this check box, when selected, numbers the columns instead of labeling them alphabetically. For example, cell B2 now would be called R2C2 (row two, column two) under the R1C1 style. If you have trouble remembering that column G is the seventh column (in cases where that's an important perspective), you might like R1C1 Reference Style.

- **Recently Used File List.** If you would like quick access to more than the four files that you've opened in your most recent Excel sessions, increase the setting from the default of 4 to as many as 9. Conversely, if you don't like people who share your computer to see which files you've had open, you might want to reduce the default to 1 or 0. The latter will result in the removal of the check mark from the option and no recently used files will appear on the File menu.

- **Standard Font.** Arial is a highly legible, visually clean font. If, however, you would prefer another font for your default in all worksheets, change this setting. You can also change the size for whichever font you choose by clicking a size in the Size list. (The default size is 10 points.)

- **User Name.** This default is set by the information provided when Excel (or Office XP) was installed. If you're not the person listed in this field or if your name has changed (or if you don't want your name to appear at all), edit the box accordingly.

Tip

If you type a number instead of using the up and down arrows to change the Sheets In New Workbook setting, you can type any number you want. However, if the number you type is zero, if it isn't a whole number (e.g., 3.5), or if it is greater than 255, an error prompt will appear when you click OK.

Tip

Whenever you change default settings, make sure they'll be the best settings for the vast majority of your workbooks, not just for the one you're working on at the time or for a small number of your files.

Tip

The General tab's Default File Location option is covered thoroughly in "Saving" on page 278.

The gridlines on my worksheet are too dark

Source of the problem

By default, the color of your gridlines is set to Automatic. What color is that, you might ask? Even if you had the 64-color box of crayons as a kid, you probably don't have a clue what color "Automatic" is. This "color" comes from the Display properties for your computer and, specifically, from the Window text color you chose there. If, for example, your Window text were set to a shade of blue, that same shade would be the color of your gridlines. For most people—those who have kept the default Windows Standard scheme—the color of the gridlines is gray. ▶

If you want your gridlines setting to follow something other than the Window text color, you can change their color for the active worksheet in your current workbook or for all workbooks in Excel.

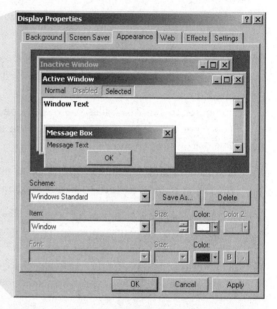

- If you want to change the color of gridlines for all workbooks in Excel, you must change the Window text color on the Appearance tab of the Display Properties dialog box and leave the gridline color set to Automatic.

- If you want to change the color of gridlines for the active worksheet, you need to make some adjustments on the View tab of the Options dialog box.

How to fix it

To change the color of gridlines for an active worksheet, follow these steps:

1. Make sure the worksheet in which you want to change the gridlines' color is visible (or that the group of sheets you want to change are grouped) and then click Options on the Tools menu.

See what you want to see

If you want to change the window text color, thus changing the Automatic color applied to gridlines, right-click an empty spot on your Windows desktop and click Properties on the short-cut menu. Click the Appearance tab in the Display Properties dialog box and click Window in the Item list. Click a color in the Color palette and then click OK to apply the change and close the dialog box. As long as the gridline color in Excel is set to Automatic, the gridlines in all your workbooks will follow this new window text color setting.

2. Click the View tab.

3. Make sure the Gridlines check box is selected and then click a color on the Color palette. ▶

4. Click OK to close the dialog box and apply the change to your gridlines.

A worksheet with a view

You can change a lot of things about your Excel workspace, but do so with care. The View tab has many options that are turned on by default, meaning that to change them, you'd turn them off. On the other hand, two options are turned off by default:

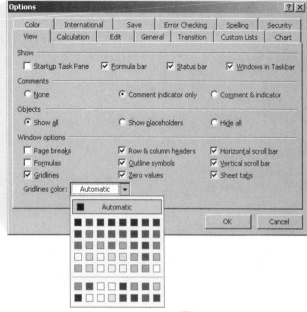

- **Page Breaks.** By default, you can see your page breaks only in Page Break preview. If you select this check box, they'll be shown as dashed lines in normal view. (To insert a page break, click Page Break on the Insert menu.)

- **Formulas.** To see your formulas rather than their results in your worksheet cells, select this check box. This is a helpful feature if you're doing an overhaul or review of your formulas.

Tip
If you insert a page break while the check box for Page Breaks is cleared on the View tab of the Options dialog box, the feature is activated, but only for the active workbook.

Squinting gives you wrinkles

If you find your worksheet gridlines too dark (or too light, or too bright, or too dim), you might also want to change the size of your toolbar icons—either making them smaller or making them larger, depending on your preference and eyesight. To change the size of your toolbar icons, click Customize on the Tools menu and then click the Options tab. Select the Large Icons check box and then click Close to magnify the toolbar icons to a larger size.

The Task pain... er, I mean pane
This new feature in Excel 2002 is very handy. When you want it to appear, that is. If it's still coming up automatically, terminate this with the Options dialog box. On the View tab, remove the check mark next to Startup Task Pane. This will prevent the pane from appearing as soon as you open Excel. The pane will appear when it's needed or when a command you give requires use of the pane. When you're finished using it, you can close it by clicking the X (Close) button in its upper-right corner.

Glossary

3-D reference The data included in a cell or range of cells on more than one worksheet. If, for example, you want to add the values in cell C6 from the first three worksheets of your workbook, you would point Microsoft Excel to this data with the 3-D reference *=SUM(Sheet1:Sheet3!C6)*.

absolute cell reference A specific —and fixed—address of a cell. An absolute cell reference (for example, $C$2) is used in a formula when you want to be able to refer to a particular cell even if you copy the formula to a different location. To turn a cell address into an absolute reference, press the F4 key while your cursor is on that address within the formula.

active cell The cell that is currently selected, the one in which data would appear if you were to begin typing. You can identify the active cell by the heavy border that surrounds it as well as by looking in the Name box, which is to the far left immediately above the worksheet.

arguments Values such as text and cell references that are used to perform calculations. In the function =COUNTIF(C6:C27,20), the range of C6:C27 is an argument, and 20, the criteria for the function, is also an argument. Arguments are typically separated by commas.

auditing Examining a worksheet or workbook to ensure accuracy.

AutoComplete The Excel feature that allows you to automatically fill in non-numerical data in a cell based on similar data that you've already entered in other cells in the same column. For example, if you've entered *hedgehogs* in a cell, the next time you type *h* in a cell in that column, Excel will offer to complete the entry with the word *hedgehogs*. AutoComplete does not apply to cells containing purely numerical content— if you typed 10,502 in a cell earlier in the column, typing 1 in the current cell will not trigger AutoComplete to insert 10,502.

AutoFill The Excel feature that allows you to enter a series of values based on the value of a single cell or a range of cells. Using AutoFill, Excel recognizes a series (for example, it recognizes *Monday* as the first in the series of the days of the week) and fills in the cells you indicate with as many of the remaining values of that series as you want. You can also create patterns with AutoFill by entering, for example, 10, 20, and 30 into a series of three contiguous cells. By dragging the AutoFill handle through adjacent cells, you can continue a pattern of numbers, each increasing by 10.

AutoFilter   The Excel tool that helps you construct filters, which are used to selectively view rows in a worksheet.

AutoFormat   The command that allows you to apply a collection of predefined formats to a range of cells. You'll find AutoFormat in the Format menu.

AVERAGE function   The Excel function that calculates the arithmetical mean of a selection of values.

callouts   Labels (boxes, circles, and the like) that you can add to worksheets, charts, or drawn objects to explain or identify data.

cell   The box that is the point of intersection of a column and a row. For example, cell B5 is the intersection of column B and row 5. The cell is the basic unit of an Excel worksheet.

cell range   Any group of cells. The range can be contiguous, or it can include stray cells that were added to the range by clicking on them while holding down the Ctrl key.

cell reference   The name of a cell, arrived at by combining the row and column intersection. For example, the cell reference for the point at which column H and row 17 intersect is H17.

chart   Sometimes called a graph, a chart is a visual depiction or summary of data. Charts allow you to create pictures or illustrations using your data, and they are a useful way to present information for comparison and analysis.

chart area   A chart and its contents.

chart sheet   A worksheet that contains only a chart.

column   A vertical line of cells in a worksheet. Each column in an Excel worksheet has 65,536 cells.

conditional formats   Formats that Excel applies only to those cells that meet a specified set of criteria, which you set.

database   In Excel, a list of data represented as a series of rows in a worksheet. Information arranged in a database can be filtered and sorted in a number of useful ways. For example, a database of customers can be sorted by name (in alphabetical order, say), or by ZIP code. An Excel database can be sorted by up to three criteria at a time. Microsoft Access, a database application that is much more powerful than Excel, can manipulate information stored in a database in many more ways. Excel databases can easily be imported into Access.

data label   A label on a chart that provides additional information about a data marker. *See also* data marker.

data marker   A symbol in a chart that represents a single data point or value. A worksheet cell is the source for this value.

data point   Another term, possibly more common than *data marker*, for a single cell's data as it is plotted on a chart or graph.

data series   A group of related data points or values.

dependents   Formulas that refer to a specific cell or cells in order to perform their calculations.

Glossary

embedded chart   A chart that is included in a worksheet rather than created as a separate chart sheet. The advantage of using an embedded chart is that it allows you to view and print the chart or PivotChart report with its source data.

emoticon   A combination of characters that roughly depicts a facial expression, used to convey an emotion in e-mail or on the Internet. For example, :-), the "smiley" emoticon, is used to convey happiness.

field   In an Excel data list, a column is a field. In a record (row) within that list, individual cells are also known as fields.

fill handle   The small black square in the lower-right corner of a selected cell. If you point to a fill handle, the pointer changes to a black cross. With the black fill handle cross displayed, you can drag through contiguous cells to perpetuate a pattern or repeat the content of the selected cell or cells.

fill series   The feature in Excel that allows you to insert a series of values by indicating a starting value for the series and the increment of the values.

filter   A rule or a set of rules used to selectively display data. For example, you can filter a list of data so that only the five greatest numbers in a column are shown or so that only records with a particular entry in a particular field are displayed.

formula   A mathematical expression that is used to calculate a value. In Excel, a formula must always begin with the equal sign (=). For example, =10*3+8 is a formula that multiplies 10 by 3 and then adds the result (30) to 8.

freeze titles   Especially handy when you're working with a long database list because you can keep your column headings (field names) visible as you continue to scroll by freezing the row that contains the headings. A solid line appears underneath the frozen row to indicate where the freezing begins and ends. Select the row beneath the one you want to freeze, and choose Window, Freeze Panes.

Goal Seek   The Excel tool that works backward from the result of a calculation to give you the value a selected cell would need to contain for the result of the calculation to be true.

graph   Also called a chart, a graph is a visual depiction or summary of data.

HTML (Hypertext Markup Language)   A formatting system for documents published on the Web. HTML uses a system of tags that dictate how browser software should display the contents of a Web document. *See also* tag.

hyperlink   A link that connects one file to another on the Web or on an intranet. Text hyperlinks are indicated by color and are usually underlined. A graphic can also serve as a hyperlink. When you point to a hyperlink with your mouse, the pointer changes from an arrow to a pointing hand.

Hypertext Markup Language
See HTML.

labels   The names that you assign to cells based on their location, content, and purpose within a worksheet.

locked cells   Cells that can't be altered unless the user knows the appropriate password, which has been assigned by the worksheet creator.

macro   A series of commands or actions that have been recorded and that can be called upon to run whenever you need them. This is a useful shortcut for automating tasks that you perform often. Macros are created using a programming language called Visual Basic for Applications (VBA), but you don't need to know VBA in order to record and run a macro.

name   In Excel, a word or set of characters assigned to a cell, range of cells, formula, or constant value.

named range   A group of cells defined by a single name.

ODBC (Open Database Connectivity)   An interface that allows the transfer of data between databases and other programs.

operator   A symbol or character that indicates an action to be performed on an element. For example, the arithmetical operator for multiplication is the asterisk (*), and in the formula =C5*D8, the operator is causing the numbers in cells C5 and D8 to be multiplied.

order of operations   The use of parentheses to control the default order in which mathematical operations are performed in a formula. By default, the order is parentheses, multiplication, division, addition, subtraction. By using parentheses around portions of the formula that should be performed out of this default order, you

are controlling the order of operations. For example, =(C5-D8)*2 would cause the subtraction of D8 from C5 to be performed first. Without the parentheses, D8 would be multiplied by 2, and then the subtraction from C5 would occur.

outline   An arrangement of data in a worksheet into levels of hierarchical or topical content. Worksheets that contain lists that are sorted by one or more columns with many duplicate entries are the best candidates for outlining because the groups formed by sorting will create the levels within the outline.

PivotChart   A chart that provides a graphical view of the PivotTable to which it is linked. PivotCharts can be used to highlight different aspects of the same data by changing their layout and organization.

PivotTable   An interactive table that combines and compares large amounts of data. By rotating the table's rows and columns, you can see different summaries of the source data.

precedents   Cells that are referred to in a formula.

printer driver   A file designed to create compatibility between printers and other software by telling your computer and the software on it how to "talk" to a printer and what the printer is capable of—how fast it prints, whether it prints in color, how much memory it has, which fonts it supports, and so on.

query   In Excel, Access, and other database software, a statement that locates records in a database. Queries present criteria to a database and "ask" that all records meeting that criteria be displayed. You can, for example, query a name and address database for all people in a certain city or an inventory database for all the products that cost more than a certain amount (assuming City and Cost are fields in the databases).

range   A group of cells.

records   In a database, where each row is a record, records are a collection of rows within that database.

report   A document generated by establishing links to data in a worksheet or worksheets. Reports are used to summarize or compare data, as well as to display it in an easily read format.

row   A horizontal line of cells in a worksheet. Each row in an Excel worksheet has 256 cells in it.

scenarios   Sets of values that you can name, save, and use to substitute for other values in your worksheet. Scenarios are used to see the impact that changes in your data will have on your worksheet. *See also* what-if analysis.

sheet   *See* worksheet.

shortcut menu   A menu, displayed by right-clicking an item or pressing Shift+F10, that reveals a list of commands.

Smart Tags   In Excel, the feature that allows you to connect the contents of your worksheets to related information on the Web. All of the applications in the Microsoft Office XP suite include Smart Tags.

sort   To organize data in an order based on a set of criteria. For example, you can sort the contents of a column alphabetically or numerically, in ascending (A-Z, 1-9) or descending order (Z-A, 9-1).

split bar   When you choose Window, Split, a moveable bar appears on the screen at the point where your active cell was when the command was issued. The split bar breaks the window into two parts, enabling you to scroll through different parts of the same worksheet.

table   A structure made up of cells arranged in columns and rows. Within the Office XP suite, Word is used to create tables for storing and organizing text, and those tables can be pasted into an Excel worksheet. When this is done, each table cell translates to a worksheet cell, and the table contents become part of the worksheet. In databases and in an application such as Access, you'll see lists of data also referred to as tables.

tag   In markup languages such as HTML and XML, a code that identifies an element in a document for the purposes of formatting, indexing, and linking that element. For example, in an HTML document the tag <p> separates paragraphs and <h1> formats text as a first-level heading. Many tags come in pairs, with an opening tag (<body>) and a closing tag (</body>) surrounding the content to which they apply.

template   A workbook or worksheet that is used as the basis for other workbooks and worksheets. Excel templates are identified by the file extension .xlt.

trendline On a chart or graph, a line that follows a series of data points, showing the path that the data took over a period of time. For example, charts that show rising and falling sales figures over the course of a year or years often use trendlines to make the fluctuating sales figures easily viewed and understood.

validation rules A set of rules that you create to ensure that only entries that conform to a specific format or range of values can be entered into a cell or range of cells. For example, if your company's products are identified by six numbers followed by a letter (568970C), you can construct a validation rule that makes it impossible for anyone to enter anything other than six numbers followed by a letter into cells in a specified region of your worksheet.

Visual Basic for Applications (VBA) A version of Microsoft Visual Basic that uses a macro language to customize and add functionality to Excel and other Windows-based applications.

what-if analysis A type of spreadsheet analysis that allows you to see the effect that changes in your values will have on your data. For example, you might perform a what-if analysis to see what the impact would be on your overall budget if you raised or lowered certain costs.

workbook An Excel file, made up of one or more worksheets.

worksheet The equivalent of a page in an Excel document. Each Excel workbook opens with 3 worksheets, and each worksheet contains 256 columns and 65,536 rows (16,777,216 cells).

worksheet tab The identifying protrusion at the bottom of a worksheet. The worksheet tab contains the worksheet name, which is Sheet1 (or Sheet2 or Sheet3) or a name you enter by double-clicking the tab and typing a name that's more indicative of the worksheet's contents or role within the workbook.

workspace file A file (recognizable by the extension .xlw) that saves information about how you want particular workbooks to be displayed when you open them. If you save a workbook in a workspace, every time you open that workbook it will appear with the same print areas, window sizes, and the like.

Quick fix index

Index

bar charts, 12
blank data, PivotTables, 260–61
blank fields, filtering records, 137
blank workbook, hyperlinks creating, 222–23
blinking insertion points, 111
blue drop-down arrows, filters, 138–39
blue triangle
    indicating edited cells, 41
    indicating Track-Change comments, 36, 38
    turning on/off, 37
bold format, row height and, 26
Break Link button, 132
browsing
    default browser, 360
    hyperlinks and, 219, 221

calculator, discrepancy with formulas, 184–85
callouts
    comments vs., 102
    fraction formatting and, 153
    not pointing to correct items, 102–03
Caps Lock, accidental use of, 335
Case Sensitive check box, Sort dialog box, 313
cell names, 234–43
    column and row labels, converting into names, 240–41
    flowchart, 234–35
    locating cells and, 236
    in multiple worksheets, 242–43
    naming ranges of cells, 238–39
    renaming/deleting old names, 237
    rules for, 241
    steps in, 237
cell ranges
    content, entering into, 109
    naming, 238–39
    PivotTable reports, 258
    referencing, 5
    selecting noncontiguous, 46
Cell Reference box, 217
Cell Value Is, 47–48
cells
    active, selecting, 110–11
    comment symbols in, 36
    conditional formatting and, 50, 51
    content, cutting/copying, 22–23

content, entering into range of cells, 109
    content, moving, 125
    content, risk of replacing during moves, 29
    formats of, 84
    moving cell without moving formatting, 170–71
    referencing, 181
    referencing functions in, 200–201
    referencing ranges in, 5
    selecting active, 110–11
    shading, 169
    when cell reference changes but formula
        results don't, 186–88
Change Button Image, toolbar buttons, 373
chart objects, resizing, 8–9
Chart Wizard, 5
charts
    columns, selecting noncontiguous, 5
    exporting into Word, 130–33
    flowchart, 2–3
    printing, 10–11
    protecting, 7
    resizing, 8–9
    types, 2, 3, 12–13
    unwanted data, 4–5
    updating, 6–7, 131
circular references, formulas, 181
clip art
    installing, 208–09
    organizing, 212–13
    sources of, 208
Clip Gallery, 206–07
Clip Organizer
    accessing, 212
    clip art, organizing, 212–13
    collection categories, 213
    searching for graphics, 206–07
clipboard
    cutting/copying content, 22–23
    flowchart, 14–15
    interactive buttons on, 16–17
    links, creating/severing, 18–19
    memory capacity and, 22
    pasting content from, 20–21
    removing items from, 22
    text, moving between diagrams, 95
    Web content, saving to, 288
clipboard task pane, 21
colon (:), formulas and, 181
color
    of diagrams, 92–93
    of gridlines, 376
    Line Color button, 103
    of text, 376

callouts, not pointing to correct items, 102–03
flowchart, 96–97
grouping objects and, 98–99
objects, techniques for moving, 100–101
Drawing toolbar
Arrow Style, 103
displaying, 97
Group, 99
inserting text boxes, 63
Line Color button, 103
Line or Arrow tools, 13
multiple objects, selecting and grouping, 98–99
Text Box, 163
drivers, reinstalling, 210–11
drop-down arrows, blue, 138–39

Edit Comment command, 38
Edit Hyperlink command, 220, 222
Edit menu
Find, 293–94
Links, 132
Undo, 296
e-mail, regional settings, 65
encryption, 281. *See also* cryptography
Enter (keyboard shortcut), moving
between cells, 111
environmental noise, speech recognition
and, 322
equal to (=) operator, 46, 299
Error Alert tab, data validation, 143
errors
Advanced Filter feature, 144–45
Auto Outline, 248–49
conditional formatting, 51
data table setup, 68
dictation, 324–25
Find command, 294–95
formulas, 180–82
functions, 198–99
imported objects, editing, 120
macros, 228, 230–31
sorting data, 311, 318
spelling, 330–31
subtotal reports, 338–39
euro currency, 60–61
Euro Currency Tools add-in, 60
exclamation point (!), referencing cell
ranges and, 5

export/import, 120–35
Access tables, exporting Excel data into, 134–35
flowchart, 120–21
object types supported, 122–23
Word documents, exporting charts into, 130–33
Word tables, exporting Excel cells into, 126–28
Word tables, importing into Excel, 124–25

field names, sorting data and, 317
File menu
Close, 277
Open, 276
Print Preview, 271
Save As, 286–87
File Properties dialog box
keyword searches, 307
name, changing/removing, 306–07
files
finding, 350–51
naming, 281, 286–87
protecting, 280–81, 303
read-only option, 281
Recently Used File List, 283, 375
saving as templates (.xlt files), 351
saving to new locations, 286–87
searching for, 284–85
filters, 136–45
Advanced Filter feature, 144–45
AutoFilter, missing criteria, 140–41
data inconsistencies and, 142–43
Data menu, 33
flowchart, 136–37
tips for applying, 139
when all records disappear, 138–39
Find and Replace (Ctrl+H), 142
Find and Replace feature, Word, 128
Find command/Find dialog box
database records, 141, 292–93
error messages, 294–95
Match Case and Find Entire Cell Only, 293
options of, 295
workbooks/files, 284–85
worksheets, searching all, 291
Find (Ctrl+F), 141, 293–94
Fit To option, Page Setup dialog box, 270–71
floating toolbars, 371
folders
creating, 282
organizing, 282–83
Program Files folder, 122

About the author

Laurie Ulrich has been using computers and helping others to use them for nearly 20 years. After working on the management side of the computer training industry for a while, she decided prosperity (in the financial, personal, and spiritual senses of the word) was more likely to be found on the freelance side of things. She began teaching people through corporate training centers and at Temple University in the early 1990s.

Soon after, Laurie formed her own company, Limehat & Company, Inc., and began providing comprehensive computer services to growing companies and non-profit organizations. In recent years, Laurie's organization has expanded to offer Web site design, hosting, and webmaster services, and she continues to support clients in the Delaware, New Jersey, New York, and Pennsylvania areas. Since 1997, Laurie has authored, coauthored, and contributed to more than 20 nationally published books about computers and software.

For more information, including a complete bibliography, résumé, and links to a variety of interesting Web sites, visit Laurie's personal Web site at *http://www.planetlaurie.com*. To find out more about her company and its offerings, visit *http://www.limehat.com*. Laurie can be reached at *laurie@planetlaurie.com*, and she is happy to answer reader inquiries.

The manuscript for this book was prepared and galleyed using Microsoft Word 2000 and Microsoft Word 2002. Pages were composed using Adobe PageMaker 6.52 for Windows, with text in ACaslon Regular and display type in Gill Sans. Composed pages were delivered to the printer as electronic prepress files.

Cover designer

Landor Associates

Interior graphic designer

James D. Kramer

Production services

nSight, Inc.

Project manager

Tempe Goodhue

Technical editor

Christopher M. Russo

Copy editor

Joe Gustaitis

Principal compositor

Patty Fagan

Editorial Assistants

Rebecca Merz, Rob Saley

Proofreaders

Janice O'Leary, Dan Shaw

Indexer

Jack Lewis

Target your problem and
fix it yourself—
fast!

When you're stuck with a computer problem, you need answers right now. *Troubleshooting* books can help. They'll guide you to the source of the problem and show you how to solve it right away. Get ready solutions with clear, step-by-step instructions. Go to quick-access charts with *Top 20 Problems* and *Prevention Tips*. Find even more solutions with *Quick Fixes* and handy *Tips*. Walk through the remedy with plenty of screen shots. Find what you need with the extensive, easy-reference index. Get the answers you need to get back to business fast with *Troubleshooting* books.

roubleshooting Microsoft® Office XP
BN 0-7356-1491-1

oubleshooting Microsoft® Access Databases
overs Access 97 and Access 2000)
BN 0-7356-1160-2

oubleshooting Microsoft® Access 2002
BN 0-7356-1488-1

oubleshooting Microsoft Excel Spreadsheets
overs Excel 97 and Excel 2000)
BN 0-7356-1161-0

oubleshooting Microsoft Excel 2002
BN 0-7356-1493-8

Troubleshooting Microsoft® Outlook®
(Covers Microsoft Outlook 2000 and Outlook Express)
ISBN 0-7356-1162-9

Troubleshooting Microsoft Outlook 2002
(Covers Microsoft Outlook 2002 and Outlook Express)
ISBN 0-7356-1487-3

Troubleshooting Your Web Page
(Covers Microsoft FrontPage® 2000)
ISBN 0-7356-1164-5

Troubleshooting Microsoft FrontPage 2002
ISBN 0-7356-1489-X

Troubleshooting Microsoft Windows®
(Covers Windows Me, Windows 98, and Windows 95)
ISBN 0-7356-1166-1

Troubleshooting Microsoft Windows 2000 Professional
ISBN 0-7356-1165-3

Troubleshooting Microsoft Windows XP
ISBN 0-7356-1492-X

Troubleshooting Your PC
ISBN 0-7356-1163-7

crosoft Press® products are available worldwide wherever quality computer books are
ld. For more information, contact your book or computer retailer, software reseller, or
:al Microsoft Sales Office, or visit our Web site at microsoft.com/mspress. To locate
ur nearest source for Microsoft Press products, or to order directly, call 1-800-
SPRESS in the U.S. (in Canada, call 1-800-268-2222).

ces and availability dates are subject to change.

Microsoft
microsoft.com/mspress

Take creative control *of the*

built-in programming language
in Microsoft Excel 2002
and Access 2002

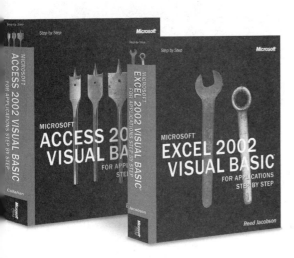

Teach yourself how to use Microsoft Visual Basic for Applications (VBA) to take command of Microsoft Excel 2002 and Access 2002. Choose your own best starting point in these self-paced guides to learn how to automate spreadsheets and databases, write your own functions and procedures, customize menus and toolbars, connect applications to the Web, and more. Easy-to-follow lessons with real-world scenarios and examples show you exactly how to maximize the built-in programming power of the popular desktop applications. Numerous screenshots and a CD-ROM full of practice files in each guide help you master step-by-step programming procedures. Find out how to create custom solutions—and then keep the guides nearby as ongoing desktop references to VBA functions and features.

**Microsoft® Excel Version 2002
Visual Basic® for Applications
Step by Step**

ISBN: 0-7356-1359-1

**Microsoft Access 2002
Visual Basic for Applications
Step by Step**

ISBN: 0-7356-1358-3

Microsoft Press® products are available worldwide wherever quality computer books are sold. For more information, contact your book or computer retailer, software reseller, or local Microsoft® Sales Office, or visit our Web site at microsoft.com/mspress. To locate your nearest source for Microsoft Press products, or to order directly, call 1-800-MSPRESS in the United States (in Canada, call 1-800-268-2222).

Prices and availability dates are subject to change.

Microsoft®
microsoft.com/mspress

Work smarter—
conquer your
software *from the inside out!*

ey, you know your way around a desktop. Now dig into Office XP applications and the Windows XP
perating system and *really* put your PC to work! These supremely organized software reference titles pack
undreds of timesaving solutions, troubleshooting tips and tricks, and handy workarounds in a concise,
ast-answer format. They're all muscle and no fluff. All this comprehensive information goes deep into the
ooks and crannies of each Office application and Windows XP feature. And every *Inside Out* includes a
D-ROM full of handy tools and utilities, sample files, links to related sites, and other help. Discover the
est and fastest ways to perform everyday tasks, and challenge yourself to new levels of software mastery!

MICROSOFT WINDOWS® XP INSIDE OUT
ISBN 0-7356-1382-6

MICROSOFT® OFFICE XP INSIDE OUT
ISBN 0-7356-1277-3

MICROSOFT WORD VERSION 2002 INSIDE OUT
ISBN 0-7356-1278-1

MICROSOFT EXCEL VERSION 2002 INSIDE OUT
ISBN 0-7356-1281-1

MICROSOFT OUTLOOK® VERSION 2002 INSIDE OUT
ISBN 0-7356-1282-X

MICROSOFT ACCESS VERSION 2002 INSIDE OUT
ISBN 0-7356-1283-8

MICROSOFT FRONTPAGE® VERSION 2002 INSIDE OUT
ISBN 0-7356-1284-6

MICROSOFT VISIO® VERSION 2002 INSIDE OUT
ISBN 0-7356-1285-4

crosoft Press® products are available worldwide wherever quality
mputer books are sold. For more information, contact your book or
mputer retailer, software reseller, or local Microsoft® Sales Office, or visit
r Web site at microsoft.com/mspress. To locate your nearest source for
crosoft Press products, or to order directly, call 1-800-MSPRESS in the
ited States (in Canada, call 1-800-268-2222).

ces and availability dates are subject to change.

Microsoft
microsoft.com/mspress

Work smarter,
add value,
and get results!

U.S.A. **$39.99**
Canada $57.99
ISBN: 0-7356-1434-2

For every business professional swamped with e-mail, drowning in paper, and wading through data, here are real-world solutions for turning all that information into business results! TAMING THE INFORMATION TSUNAMI demonstrates simple ways to change how you think about and use everyday technologies such as Microsoft® Office and Microsoft Internet Explorer—helping you match the right tool to the task, the right solution for your situation. Apply the skills, principles, and habits that empower you to work smarter and faster—and get out from under the deluge of too much work, too little time! Learn best practices for turning information into knowledge. Use Microsoft Office XP and other software to take control of your worklife. Work even smarter using the tools and eBook included on the CD-ROM!

rosoft Press® products are available worldwide wherever quality
nputer books are sold. For more information, contact your book or
nputer retailer, software reseller, or local Microsoft® Sales Office, or visit
Web site at microsoft.com/mspress. To locate your nearest source for
rosoft Press products, or to order directly, call 1-800-MSPRESS in the
ted States (in Canada, call 1-800-268-2222).

es and availability dates are subject to change.

microsoft.com/mspress

Work anywhere, anytime
with the Microsoft guide to
mobile technology

MOBILIZE YOURSELF!
The Microsoft Guide to Mobile Technology

Rob L. Bogue

| U.S.A. | $29.99 |
| Canada | $43.99 |

ISBN: 0-7356-1502-0

Okay. You're at the airport but your flight has been delayed. For four hours. No worries—you've got your laptop so you're ready to work. Or are you? Can you connect to the Internet? What about reliable battery power? Here's the answer: MOBILIZE YOURSELF! THE MICROSOFT GUIDE TO MOBILE TECHNOLOGY. This comprehensive guide explains how to maximize the mobility of the technology you have today. And it provides smart answers about the mobile technologies and services you might be considering. From PDAs to the wireless Web, this book packs the insights and solutions that keep you—and your technology—up and running when you're out and about.

rosoft Press® products are available worldwide wherever quality nputer books are sold. For more information, contact your book or nputer retailer, software reseller, or local Microsoft® Sales Office, or visit Web site at microsoft.com/mspress. To locate your nearest source for rosoft Press products, or to order directly, call 1-800-MSPRESS in the ted States (in Canada, call 1-800-268-2222).

es and availability dates are subject to change.

microsoft.com/mspress

Self-paced
training that works
as hard as you do!

Information-packed STEP BY STEP courses are the most effective way to teach yourself how to complete tasks with the Microsoft® Windows® XP operating system and Microsoft® Office XP applications. Numbered steps and scenario-based lessons with practice files on CD-ROM make it easy to find your way while learning tasks and procedures. Work through every lesson or choose your own starting point—with STEP BY STEP'S modular design and straightforward writing style, *you* drive the instruction. And the books are constructed with lay-flat binding so you can follow the text with both hands at the keyboard. Select STEP BY STEP titles also provide complete, cost-effective preparation for the Microsoft Office User Specialist (MOUS) credential. It's an excellent way for you or your organization to take a giant step toward workplace productivity.

- **Microsoft Windows XP Step by Step**
  ISBN 0-7356-1383-4

- **Microsoft Office XP Step by Step**
  ISBN 0-7356-1294-3

- **Microsoft Word Version 2002 Step by Step**
  ISBN 0-7356-1295-1

- **Microsoft Excel Version 2002 Step by Step**
  ISBN 0-7356-1296-X

- **Microsoft PowerPoint® Version 2002 Step by Step**
  ISBN 0-7356-1297-8

- **Microsoft Outlook® Version 2002 Step by Step**
  ISBN 0-7356-1298-6

- **Microsoft FrontPage® Version 2002 Step by Step**
  ISBN 0-7356-1300-1

- **Microsoft Access Version 2002 Step by Step**
  ISBN 0-7356-1299-4

- **Microsoft Visio® Version 2002 Step by Step**
  ISBN 0-7356-1302-8

Microsoft Press® products are available worldwide wherever quality computer books are sold. For more information, contact your book or computer retailer, software reseller, or local Microsoft Sales Office, or visit our Web site at microsoft.com/mspress. To locate your nearest source for Microsoft Press products, or to order directly, call 1-800-MSPRESS in the United States. (in Canada, call 1-800-268-2222).

Prices and availability dates are subject to change.

microsoft.com/mspress

Get a **Free**
e-mail newsletter, updates,
special offers, links to related books,
and more when you
register on line!

Register your Microsoft Press® title on our Web site and you'll get a FREE subscription to our e-mail newsletter, *Microsoft Press Book Connections*. You'll find out about newly released and upcoming books and learning tools, online events, software downloads, special offers and coupons for Microsoft Press customers, and information about major Microsoft® product releases. You can also read useful additional information about all the titles we publish, such as detailed book descriptions, tables of contents and indexes, sample chapters, links to related books and book series, author biographies, and reviews by other customers.

Registration is easy. Just visit this Web page and fill in your information:

http://www.microsoft.com/mspress/register

Microsoft

Proof of Purchase

Use this page as proof of purchase if participating in a promotion or rebate offer on this title. Proof of purchase must be used in conjunction with other proof(s) of payment such as your dated sales receipt—see offer details.

Troubleshooting Microsoft® Excel 2002
0-7356-1493-8

CUSTOMER NAME

Microsoft Press, PO Box 97017, Redmond, WA 98073-9830